Test Policy and the Politics of Opportunity Allocation: The Workplace and the Law

Evaluation in Education and Human Services

Editors:

George F. Madaus, Boston College, Chestnut
    Hill, MA, U.S.A.
Daniel L. Stufflebeam, Western Michigan
    University, Kalamazoo, MI, U.S.A.

***National Commission on Testing
and Public Policy***

Gifford, B.; *Test Policy and the Politics of
    Opportunity Allocation: The Workplace and
    the Law*

Gifford, B.; *Test Policy and Test Performance:
    Education, Language, and Culture*

Test Policy and the Politics of Opportunity Allocation: The Workplace and the Law

edited by

Bernard R. Gifford

Graduate School of Education
University of California, Berkeley

Kluwer Academic Publishers
Boston   Dordrecht   London

Distributors for North America:
Kluwer Academic Publishers
101 Philip Drive
Assinippi Park
Norwell, Massachusetts 02061 USA

Distributors for all other countries:
Kluwer Academic Publishers Group
Distribution Centre
Post Office Box 322
3300 AH Dordrecht, THE NETHERLANDS

Library of Congress Cataloging-in-Publication Data

Test policy and the politics of allocation : the workplace and the law
  / [edited] by Bernard R. Gifford.
      p.   cm. — (Evaluation in education and human services)
    "Proceedings prepared under the aegis of the National Commission
on Testing and Public Policy"—Introd.
    Includes index.
    ISBN 0-7923-9015-6 (v. 1)
    1. Employment tests—Law and legislation—United States—
Congresses.   2. Educational tests and measurements—Law and
legislation—United States—Congresses.   3. Employment tests—United
States—Congresses.   4. Educational tests and measurements—United
States—Congresses.   I. Gifford, Bernard R.   II. National
Commission on Testing and Public Policy (U.S.)   III. Series
KF3457.3.A75T47   1989
344.73'012596—dc19
[347.30412596]   89-2381
                                                                     CIP

Contents

Contributing Authors

Robert F. Adams, Professor, Board of Studies in Economics, Crown College, University of California, Santa Cruz

John Sibley Butler, Associate Professor, Department of Sociology, University of Texas, Austin

Norman J. Chachkin, Assistant Counsel, NAACP Legal Defense and Educational Fund, Inc., New York

Raymond C. Fisher, Member and Past President, Los Angeles Civil Service Commission; Attorney at Law, Heller Ehrman, Los Angeles, California

John J. Fremer, Senior Development Leader, Educational Testing Service, Princeton, New Jersey

Robert Gelerter, Chief, Special Studies and ADP Section, Office of Federal Contract Compliance Programs, U.S. Department of Labor, Washington, D.C.

Bernard R. Gifford, Dean and Chancellor's Professor of Education, Graduate School of Education, University of California, Berkeley

Henry M. Levin, Director, Center for Educational Research at Stanford; Professor of Education and Economics, Graduate School of Education, Stanford University, Stanford, California

William D. Love, Assistant Vice-President, Agent Selection Services, Life Insurance Marketing and Research Association, Hartford, Connecticut

Andrew G. Neiner, Director, Special Services, Human Resources Division, Life Office Management Association, Atlanta, Georgia

Patrick O. Patterson, Co-Director, Western Regional Office, NAACP Legal Defense and Educational Fund, Inc., Los Angeles, California

Michael A. Rebell, Attorney at Law, Rebell and Katzive, New York

Donald J. Schwartz, Staff Psychologist, Research and Analytic Services, Equal Employment Opportunity Commission, Washington, D.C.

Carolyn Webber, Research Associate, Institute of Urban and Regional Development, University of California, Berkeley

Introduction

Bernard R. Gifford

In the United States, the standardized test has become one of the major sources of information for reducing uncertainty in the determination of individual merit and in the allocation of merit-based educational, training, and employment opportunities. Most major institutions of higher education require applicants to supplement their records of academic achievements with scores on standardized tests. Similarly, in the workplace, as a condition of employment or assignment to training programs, more and more employers are requiring prospective employees to sit for standardized tests. In short, with increasing frequency and intensity, individual members of the political economy are required to transmit to the opportunity marketplace scores on standardized examinations that purport to be objective measures of their abilities, talents, and potential. In many instances, these test scores are the only signals about their skills that job applicants are permitted to send to prospective employers.

THE NATIONAL COMMISSION ON TESTING AND PUBLIC POLICY

In view of the importance of these issues to our current national agenda, it was proposed that the Human Rights and Governance and the Education and Culture Programs of the Ford Foundation support the establishment of a "blue ribbon" National Commission on Testing and Public Policy to investigate some of the major problems as well as the untapped opportunities created by recent trends in the use of standardized tests, particularly in the workplace and in schools. The commission's charter is to conduct a systematic, *policy-oriented analysis* of these issues, particularly the role that standardized tests—as measures of individual merit and as predictors of future classroom and workplace performance—play in the allocation of educational, training, and employment opportunities.

The three primary objectives of the National Commission on Testing and Public Policy are:

1. To conduct a comprehensive survey of the array of policy-relevant issues and problems resulting from the growing use of standardized paper-and-pencil tests in the allocation of educational, training, and employment opportunities in the United States today, identifying and explicating a critical subset of these issues that can reasonably be expected to yield to a thorough, interdisciplinary policy analysis;

2. To commission and coordinate the work of experts from a variety of disciplines in the analysis of select issues isolated in the first phase, particularly

those that promise to yield suggestions for eliminating some of the more problematic aspects of testing; and to issue policy-sensitive recommendations that might inform and influence future directions in testing research, practice, and policy; and

3. To prepare and disseminate materials resulting from the first and second phases, designing them for and directing them to audiences with a strong interest in the proper use of tests to allocate educational, training, and employment opportunities. This dissemination objective is particularly important because to make changes in current test policies and practices requires effective communication and collaboration within and between different groups of discipline-based testing experts; non-expert test users; policymakers in education, training, and employment; and representatives of interest groups that have traditionally been excluded from technical and policy debates about the uses and consequences of testing.

In accomplishing these three objectives, the commission will focus on a set of five main issue areas chosen because they call for consideration both of the functional role of testing within employment, training, and educational institutions, and of the social consequences of testing in the society as a whole.

1. The political, social, and economic logics of testing in opportunity allocation: What kinds of political, social, and economic assumptions, objectives, and constraints influence test makers and test users in the construction and administration of tests and in the interpretation and use of test scores?

2. The role of law and regulation in resolving testing conflicts: What are the possibilities and limitations of preventing and/or ameliorating testing conflicts through regulation and litigation?

3. Language, culture, and standardized tests: What is the current state of testing research and development with respect to a) the improved design of tests administered to individuals from language minority backgrounds; b) more informed interpretation of the scores of examinees from language minority backgrounds on existing standardized tests; and c) increasing understanding of the differential performance of majority and minority populations on standardized tests?

4. General versus specific functions and methods of testing and assessment: What are the problems and opportunities associated with the use of general ability tests, compared to the advantages and disadvantages of assessing specific skills in specific contexts using devices such as subject matter achievement tests, essays, biodata questionnaires, assessment centers, work samples, and the like?

5. Future directions in testing and assessment: How will factors such as recent advances in cognitive science, technological developments, and the growing linguistic and cultural diversity of the population affect the instruments and the methods by which educators and employers identify

talent and find the best fit between students and educational opportunities, and between workers and training and job opportunities?

CONTENTS OF THIS VOLUME

This is the first volume in a two-volume set that is the first in a series of works to appear under the aegis of the National Commission on Testing and Public Policy. The papers were prepared for presentation at a conference to plan the commission, which took place at the University of California at Berkeley on December 11–13, 1986. Experts in a number of fields relevant to testing policy contributed significantly to the shaping of the commission's aims. Each section is composed of papers focusing on a particular area of interest; in addition to the formal papers, several sections contain written versions of informal remarks presented at the conference.

What do we know about the way people use tests in the real world? Before we can address unsolved problems, we must review the givens of testing use and policy. The papers in this volume were commissioned with that purpose in mind. Each paper provides a background to a set of issues central to the making of policy regarding standardized test use. Here I will briefly review the issues and dimensions that emerge in each section, issues and dimensions that will lay part of the groundwork for the findings and recommendations of the National Commission on Testing and Public Policy. Taken together, the papers in this volume point to the view that standardized testing and the interpretation of its results are inextricably linked to political factors.

The first section, "Grounding Testing Policy: Three Perspectives," presents three papers which examine some of the basic notions that underlie current testing policy. Each paper takes a different perspective: a policy analyst, a historian, and a member of the testing industry highlight what they consider to be the key beliefs, understandings, and institutional factors that drive testing policy in the real world.

The second and third sections consider testing policy and its relationship to regulation and law. "Testing and the Law: Title VII and the Federal Guidelines" focuses mainly on the way that federal regulations regarding testing for employee selection have developed out of the purpose and language of the Civil Rights Act of 1964, as interpreted by various administrations, the judiciary, and the testing profession. These papers chronicle the development of federal guidelines as testing policy and practice shaped and changed them. They also describe how government regulation has shaped and changed testing policy and practice.

The papers in the third section, "Testing and the Law: The Role of the Courts," examine the role played by the courts in the testing arena. The positive and negative contributions of the courts in several educational cases are reviewed, with careful consideration both of the strengths and the pitfalls of judicial intervention in testing policy in the schools.

The fourth and final section, "Testing in the Workplace: Theoretical and Practical Perspectives," raises a number of central issues involved in making employment-related testing policy decisions. The perspectives range from those of economists, who examine labor market factors that must be considered when assessing the value of testing for personnel selection, to those of members of the public and private sectors who are immersed in making daily hiring and promotion decisions under complex circumstances. From these papers emerges a picture of the complexity of practical, psychometric, economic, and social issues that constitute the problem domain.

ACKNOWLEDGMENTS

There are a number of people who contributed to the efforts that culminated in this volume. Lynn Walker, Deputy Director of the Human Rights and Governance Program of the Ford Foundation, committed the funds for the planning and execution of the conference on which this volume is based. Linda C. Wing organized the conference program and played a major role in coordinating the editing and production of this volume. Catherine O'Connor assisted in the review and substantive editing of the papers. Suzanne Chun and Mary Lou Sumberg served as able copy editors. Word processing and technical assistance were efficiently provided by Mandy Rasmussen, Alissa Shethar, Nancy Vasquez, and Darren Wong.

I

GROUNDING TESTING POLICY:
THREE PERSPECTIVES

The Allocation of Opportunities and the Politics of Testing: A Policy Analytic Perspective

Bernard R. Gifford

The use of standardized tests as a means to allocate significant opportunities to individuals is an increasingly ubiquitous feature of American life. Tests determine who is designated as gifted or talented, who competes for admission to prestigious colleges and universities, who enters the bidding for highly desired and economically rewarding employment slots, who wins places in job training or apprenticeship programs, and who will practice particular crafts or professions. While the nation's opportunity allocation process is not yet a "testology," as some predicted it would become, it is definitely moving in the direction of becoming a "testocracy." Given the current widespread acceptance and use of tests in nearly every sector of American life—as measures of individual aptitude, achievement, potential, worth, and merit—it would seem that the role that standardized tests play in the opportunity allocation process is a settled issue, and that the level of acrimony over the value of testing programs would be on the decline. But the debate over mass, standardized testing programs continues and the level of acrimony has not subsided. If anything, these debates are growing increasingly rancorous and bitter. To some, this outcome is counter-intuitive. If standardized testing programs are becoming more accepted, why are tests increasingly coming under attack? Why are test advocates doing so much better and feeling so much worse?

The answer is simple: problems are the raw materials of any political economy. The means and ends used to allocate opportunities form the core problem of a democratic political economy. Therefore, in a democracy, debates about the means and ends used to direct the flow of opportunities cannot be anything but acrimonious (unless, of course, that democracy is characterized by unbounded wealth). Stripped of its sophisticated philosophical rationale, democracy is a system of governance designed to solve one major political problem: How can a polity organize its political economy to enable its members to: (1) enter the opportunity marketplace, free of any impediments except their own willingness to display, barter, and exchange their skills, talents, and expertise for desired opportunities; (2) gain the rewards and benefits commensurate with the potential "price" that this type of opportunity-seeking behavior imposes on the individual; (3) freely and independently calculate the price of thwarted opportunities; and (4) be judged strictly on their demonstrated ability to make good on the promises they make in the course of being involved in the opportunity marketplace?

Adam Smith, writing in *The Wealth of Nations*, addressed the core problem of democracy more than two hundred years ago. His solution was an opportunity market based upon the principle of individual exchange, in which the price of opportunities would ultimately be set and borne by the individuals operating in the market:

> The value of any commodity, therefore, to the person who possesses it and means not to use or consume it himself, but to exchange it for other commodities, is equal to the quantity of labour which it enables him to purchase or command. Labour, therefore, is the real measure of the exchangeable value of all commodities.

> The real price of every thing—what every thing costs to the man who wants to acquire it—is the toil and trouble of acquiring it. What every thing is really worth to the man who has acquired it, and who wants to dispose of it or exchange it for something else, is the toil and trouble which it can save to himself and which it can impose upon other people (Smith 1948, 346).

In this opportunity marketplace, one of the basic appeals of standardized testing programs is their purported contribution to market efficiency, through the provision both to opportunity seekers and opportunity providers of "objective" information thought to be useful in predicting the success or failure of the bargaining between them. In theory, armed with test-score comparisons and other information, opportunity seekers limit their search for opportunity to markets suitable to their level of achievement and ability. Armed with similar information, opportunity providers restrict their search for ability to those candidates with the right psychometric profile. This combination of more informed searches and better selection decisions, it is said, leads to a more efficient method for allocating opportunities. Clearly, at one level, the debate between testing advocates and testing skeptics is a debate over the added efficiency claims of testing advocates. The claim of increased efficiency is indeed a persuasive one, as is the counterclaim that it makes little sense to reject individuals "out of hand because they do not conform to criteria established by statistical technicians" (Hoffmann 1964, 217). Nevertheless, even if the efficiency claims of test advocates were accepted at face value (Jensen 1981), the growing use of tests as an allocative device would still pose problems.

This paper is about one of those problems—the conflict between our traditional theories of how the opportunity allocation process should work in a democracy, influenced and guided by the views of Adam Smith, and the increasing use of test scores as "objective" measures of individually demonstrated talent, skill, and expertise in an opportunity allocation marketplace that is fair as well as efficient. Unlike many other analysts of the role standardized tests play in the opportunity allocation process, and the auditing measures used to determine whether or not particular test score-driven formulae for allocating opportunities are fair (or unfair), we will say relatively little about the techniques and technology of testing. Were we to characterize these issues of applied psychology and mathematics, they might be said to focus almost exclusively on questions of test application and test applicability, the "how" and "when" of standardized testing.

These issues deserve careful scrutiny. We will argue here, however, that before any of these psychometric issues about test application and test applicability can be productively examined, it is essential to conduct first a more theoretical and philosophical examination of the role that standardized tests play in the allocative process—especially the role that standardized testing programs play in societies that are pluralistic and committed to democratic politics, allocative fairness, and the market economy. In short, instead of the "how" and "when," we want to focus on the issue of "why." Or more specifically: "Why testing programs in a democracy?" Because we are interested in the proper role of testing programs in a democracy, we will make a conscious attempt to anchor our inquiry to the same philosophical framework used to rationalize, justify, and defend democracy. We will pay special attention to the logical underpinnings of the arguments put forth by proponents of standardized testing programs and to those put forth by proponents of political democracy, locating, examining, and elaborating upon the points at which these systems of logic conflict. The conduct of such a linked examination is a major objective of this essay.

We believe that debate over the use of standardized tests to allocate opportunity is a good sign: It reflects the vigorous good health of our democratic political economy. We will also pay special attention to the potential "harm" that ill-conceived and improperly deployed testing programs can inflict on politically weak and/or economically impoverished subpopulation groups in a democracy. Here again, however, we will restrict our analysis to those instances where the harm done is due to the logic of testing, or to the logic of democracy.

This essay is divided into three major sections. In section one, we present a brief review of the logic of democracy. In section two, we examine the roles played within this logic by the use of standardized tests. In section three, we present some case studies of the use of standardized tests as a means to allocate important opportunities, attempting, wherever possible, to draw lessons from and connections to the more theoretical discussions of sections one and two.

I. THE LOGIC OF DEMOCRACY

In his classic little book, *Politics: Who Gets What, When, How,* Harold Lasswell (1972), the great political scientist and one of the creators of the craft of policy analysis, reminds us that "who gets what?" and "what means are utilized to determine who gets what?" are the two questions members of a polity most frequently ask—regardless of the nature of the political economy in which the polity functions. The reason these questions are frequently asked is easy to understand. In attempting to predict whether or not a particular political economy will remain cohesive or factionated, harmonious or contentious, democratic or autocratic, we must first know what rationale that political economy invents to explain and justify its allocative mechanisms, as well as how it responds to the disappointments and failures of individual members of the polity. Where a consensus exists that questions about allocation—which are really questions about how a political economy allocates its educational and employment opportunities, its rewards and benefits (including favors, honors, and prestige)—are answered in a fair, credible, and comprehensive manner, the polity is much more likely to remain cohesive, harmonious, and democratic. And where no consensus is possible, where no sense of fairness exists, the polity will have a hard time keeping itself together.

Clearly, a polity's confidence in the fairness of its allocative mechanisms is essential to its smooth functioning. This is the case for any political economy, but it is even more important in market-oriented, democratic political economies.[1]

Democracy and Fairness

The theory of political democracy assumes that every citizen's political preferences should be equal in power and influence to the political preferences of every other citizen. Exceptions are those circumstances when some individuals are provisionally granted, usually through an open election, the authority to speak and act on behalf of a group of like-minded individuals. It is argued by democratists that it is the free play of these personal political preferences, the uninhibited clash of interest groups in the political marketplace, that generates and ensures the optimum degree of political freedom for both the individual and the polity.

While democratic politics is thought to optimize political freedom for the larger polity, it does not follow that democratic politics maximizes freedom for every individual member of the polity. Such an outcome is impossible as long as any individual disagrees about solutions for particular political

---

[1] As the reader will soon discover, I have deliberately avoided defining the concept "fairness," leaving the reader to infer my definition from my usage. For a rigorous and analytical definition of fairness, see Baumol (1986).

problems. All that democratic politics can promise individuals and interests is a mechanism by which differing interests are conciliated, as well as influence over the conciliation process itself. In keeping with the nature of democracy, we can expect that competing individuals and interests will be able to influence the conciliation process roughly in proportion to their influence over, and importance to, the larger polity.

Similarly, the goal of allocative fairness—with respect to, say, the allocation of educational, employment, and training programs—is built on the premise that the opportunities generated in a democracy should be available equally to all individuals who seek them. More specifically, allocative fairness in a democracy requires that the opportunity allocation process be governed exclusively by the free interaction of a quartet of forces: (1) the level of skills, expertise, and motivation of particular individuals in the market; (2) the particular preferences of these individuals for selected opportunities; (3) the total market supply of individuals with particular skills and expertise; and (4) the total market demand for individuals with particular skills and expertise. Again, as in the case of democratic politics, the play of these four market forces is unlikely to result in across-the-board maximum individual satisfaction. Such an outcome is impossible as long as any mismatch exists between the opportunity preferences of any single individual and the availability of the opportunity in question. All that allocative fairness can guarantee the individual is that the possession of valued skills and expertise and the proper deployment of these resources will play the determinative role in the opportunity allocation process.

Putting it simply, both democratic politics and allocative fairness depend upon the operations of the market, guided and governed by contractual arrangements between individuals who freely offer to exchange their skills and expertise in the market, with the expectation that such an exchange will maximize their aggregate satisfaction (see, for example, Dahl 1956, Macpherson 1973, and Sartori 1987). What is fair and moral in regard to the allocation of opportunities to individual members of the polity is determined by the *sum total* of the *individual behavior* of every member of the polity, comporting themselves in accordance with their *individual preferences* and their *individual assessments* of the costs and consequences of their *individual actions* in pursuing desired opportunities.

Again, what distinguishes a market democracy from all other systems of political economies is the role the individual plays in influencing the opportunity allocation market. In a market democracy, there is no centralized bureaucracy authorized to allocate workers to particular jobs, without the permission and compliance of the individual worker, just as there is no authoritative, centralized method for allocating workers and students to particular training and educational programs. Without a belief in the capacity of this system, based on the principle that there exists no higher intelligence than the collective intelligence of the polity, to reward individuals fairly for their efforts, in pursuing valued political objectives and personal value-enhancing opportunities, the idea of a market-oriented democracy cannot survive.

Thus, to describe the relationship between political democracy and allocative fairness, a democratist would write: "The idea of political democracy and the goal of allocative fairness are inseparable and interdependent." This is the central dogma of a democratic political economy. Belief by the polity in the essential fairness of market procedures for allocating society's opportunities, rewards, and benefits is the crucial factor in the maintenance of the polity's faith in the fairness of the democratic system of governance. The polity's faith and confidence in democracy's central dogma must be strong enough to withstand the skepticism and counter-pressure of those members of the polity who are dissatisfied with their share of the opportunities, rewards, and benefits of the political economy. Unless convinced otherwise, these disappointed individuals might attribute their lack of opportunities and individual failures to fundamental flaws and deeply rooted injustices in the very workings of the democratic political economy.

In the United States, the idea of fairness in the allocative process has always played a central role in political discourse. At no time, however, has this debate been more vigorous than in the last two decades. Catalyzed by the civil-rights movement of the 1960s and the women's liberation movement of the 1970s, debates about "Who gets what, when, how, and why?" dominate the nation's politics. No other group in America has been asked this question more frequently and more forcefully than the nation's educational leaders and employers, in both the public and private sectors. The "how" and "why" parts of the question have been the focus of particularly intense scrutiny, as groups representing racial, ethnic, and linguistic minorities, as well as women and other easily distinguishable subpopulations, have raised pointed questions about, and sometimes, extremely strong objections to, some of the traditional methods educational institutions and employers have used to allocate educational, training, and employment opportunities.

While much of the impetus responsible for pushing the issue of allocative fairness to the forefront of the national political agenda has come from groups whose experiences make them especially sensitive to the possibility that unfairness might exist in the allocative process—it would be an error to think that the pursuit of fairness as a dominant political theme is exclusively due to the concerns of select special interest groups. Additional impetus has also come from a second group, that of elected leaders, governmental officials, industrialists, and other political and economic elites. These groups argue that the decline in the nation's relative economic standing, vis-à-vis other industrial democracies in the world, stems from the nation's failure to allocate efficiently its investments in education and training. As a result of this inefficient ("unfair") development of human capital resources, they argue that the nation's workers are less productive than workers in other nations, and less prepared to meet the challenges of rapid technological changes.

A third interest group that has pushed the issue of allocative fairness to the forefront of national politics consists of those in the professional social work and welfare community. Representatives of this group argue that unfair allocative policies in education, training, and employment eventually manifest themselves in unwarranted ("unfair") differences in economic well-being for victimized subpopulation groups. These differences, contend representatives of the social work establishment, are not only troublesome from a moral and humanistic perspective, but they are also costly to ameliorate, and even more costly to eliminate, once they have emerged and have been rationalized as a natural outcome of the workings of the nation's political economy.

There is yet a fourth group interested in the issue of allocative fairness. Due to the heterogeneity of its "members," this group is not as easily categorized as our first three groups. Among its "members" are self-identified, "issue-oriented" elected officials, public-minded business leaders, foundation executives, academics, intellectuals, journalists, writers, clergy, and serious students of politics and public policy. This group's interest in the issue of allocative fairness is cast in broad philosophical terms, and is often formulated in language designed to inform and influence the public policy formulation process.

It is possible to identify even more groups who are keenly interested in the issue of allocative fairness, and who can be counted upon to act on these interests in the political arena. The objective here, however, is not to list all of these groups, or to examine their motives, or even to predict their behavior. The point that we want to make is that the pursuit of allocative fairness is a fundamental political constant in a market democracy. In the last thirty years of American political life, this constant has been elevated to a preoccupation. This transformation has largely been accomplished by the political struggles and the policy-making efforts of the fairness-seeking groups we have identified.[2]

Democracy and Failure

The pursuit of maximum aggregate satisfaction is accompanied by a fair amount of individual, or disaggregated, failure. Fortunately, in our hypothetical opportunity market in which aggregate satisfaction is maximized, the resulting level of disaggregated failure is minimized. Although minimized, failure is

---

[2] These struggles for allocative fairness have had their greatest impact on the views and opinions of the U.S. Supreme Court on the responsibility of the State to promote and protect allocative fairness, and to root out allocative unfairness. For more on this point, see Pole (1978). For an excellent case study of the pursuit of allocative fairness in the area of municipal services, see Harr and Fessler (1986).

nevertheless prevalent. Failure (and the resulting individual frustration) is the natural by-product of reliance on market mechanisms to generate consensus-based solutions to unresolved political problems. It is theoretically possible, in those rare instances where the polity is homogeneous and perfect harmonization of political interests is achieved, that a given political solution will completely resolve the political dispute at issue and, in the process, eliminate all feelings of personal political failure. Using a similar line of argument, it is easy to understand how failure, in the form of thwarted opportunity preferences, is the natural by-product of an opportunity allocation system governed by market forces. Again, failure can only be eliminated when all opportunity seekers and all opportunity providers are perfectly paired, achieving not only maximum aggregate satisfaction, but also maximum disaggregated (individual) satisfaction.

The reliance on market mechanisms to resolve conflicting political and opportunity demands has a number of important implications. In a truly democratic society, individuals must not only be given the opportunity to fail, but must be provided multiple opportunities to fail. A highly motivated individual in a market-oriented political economy will do just that: fail and fail and fail until success is achieved, or until a new opportunity looks more attractive than the thwarted opportunity. The importance of the individual's right to act freely upon personal preferences for particular opportunities and to pursue persistently these preferences in the opportunity marketplace, is one of the central themes of American democracy.

This emphasis on the right of the individual to exercise individual choice and individual freedom, and to fail, is so dominant in our political culture that an entire mythology has grown up around the trials and tribulations of individuals who, while in intense pursuit of preferred opportunities, have experienced repeated failure prior to achieving success. In fact, we save our loudest public applause for those individuals, who, at great personal sacrifice (usually measured in foregone alternative opportunities and damaged personal reputations), have managed to achieve success when the odds were overwhelmingly unfavorable. A few examples from the real world might make these abstractions about the relationships among market behavior and individual failure more concrete.

In baseball, America's favorite pastime, competition for "Comeback Player of the Year" (awarded to the player who has returned from the brink of professional extinction to the ranks of the player elite), is likely to be as hotly contested as competition for "Most Valuable Player in the League." Regularly, *The Wall Street Journal* features personal profiles of businesspersons, who, against all odds, and in spite of previous business setbacks, have reversed the fortunes of the failing corporations they lead. In novels and plays, few characters generate as little sympathy as the one portrayed as experiencing early and uncomplicated success. When we run across such a character, we can almost bet that failure and a long, complicated recovery is in the works. And how our character responds to this decline and rise determines whether or not he or she ends up an empty has-been, or a worthy hero, full of the force of real life. And what American aphorism is cited more frequently to American school-age children than Benjamin Franklin's advice: "It is better to try and fail, than to fail to try." If the story of success and achievement, hard on the heels of failure, is as "American as apple pie," then it can be argued that success and failure are also as American as apple pie.

In a democracy, the interrelationship between dependency on market forces as a means for allocating opportunities and the toleration of individual failure is not as strange as it might first appear. The allocation of opportunities, especially those as essential to the individual as educational and employment opportunities, entails great individual disappointment, and in some instances, even profound personal despair. Thwarted opportunity seekers could not feel otherwise, the more motivated opportunity seekers, even more so. The one belief, however, that prevents the individual experiencing disappointment and despair from transforming these feelings of personal failure into outrage directed against the larger polity, is the belief that the allocation of all opportunities in a democratic political economy is guided by impersonal, impervious, and invisible market forces. Absent such a belief, what is to prevent an individual from concluding that his or her failure is nothing more than the result of an opportunity allocation system that is biased and corrupt?

In short, democracy can potentially be blamed for all personal failures. And if democracy is to blame, then, in essence, no one is to blame. For what are democratically determined allocation opportunities but the sum of millions of little decisions made by individuals pursuing their personal preferences? When summed up, these little decisions ultimately determine who gets what, how, when, and at what cost.

Individual failure can be seen as democracy's means for protecting itself from the disintegrating force of cumulative individual failures, but it can also be viewed as some sort of message, or signal, from the market to the individual. If an individual concludes that the cost of pursuing a particular opportunity, in terms of expended energy and foregone opportunities, is too high, then that individual can decide to pursue another course of action.

We have already argued that if multiple failures by opportunity-seeking individuals are permissible, then the individual must be given multiple opportunities to fail. But multiple opportunities, by themselves, are an insufficient condition for true democracy. If multiple opportunities are to be the norm, then the price of failure cannot be so costly as to make it prohibitively expensive to individuals who want to persist in their opportunity-seeking behavior, despite repeated failure. Putting this theme more formally, we can argue that American democracy is constructed on a variant of the ideology of consumer sovereignty, in which opportunity generating agencies (for example, industrial firms and educational institutions) are required to respond fairly to the preferences of persistent opportunity seekers.

Democracy and Merit

Just as democratic politics cannot survive without a polity committed to the democratic dogma, the idea of democratic fairness cannot survive, absent some agreed-upon method of determining individual merit. In short, the issue of allocative fairness is inseparable from the issue of individual merit. Where these two concepts are perceived to be harmonious and complementary, there is less chance that allocative decisions will be challenged by those who lose out in the competition for scarce opportunities.

As our democratic political economy has grown more pluralistic and more complex, interest in the issue of allocative fairness has increased. More intense scrutiny has been focused on the methods used by institutions to identify, evaluate, and compare the relative merits of individuals competing for scarce, high-reward educational, training, and employment opportunities. Accordingly, in the last two decades, the role of standardized testing in allocating these important opportunities has become the subject of growing conflict.

Democracy, Skepticism, and Dogma

In a market democracy, politics is about conflict and conflict resolution. The core purpose of politics is to enable individuals, working alone or with others with similar interests, to agree and to disagree, to create conflicts and to resolve conflicts, in a word, to "politic." Politicking is a process of never-ending competition among disputatious interest groups attempting to persuade a majority of the larger polity to accept as "truth" their views and judgments about how a particular disagreement should be resolved.[3] It is a system where both *skepticism* and *dogma* are essential to the stability and cohesiveness of

---

[3] More than 150 years ago, Alexis de Tocqueville (cited in Meyer 1966, 177) observed the following about the origin of politics in America:

> In the United States a politician first tries to see what his own interest is and who has analogous interests which can be grouped around his own; he is next concerned to discover whether by chance there may not be somewhere in the world a doctrine or a principle that could conveniently be placed at the head of the new association to give it the right to put itself forward and circulate freely. It is like the royal imprimatur which our ancestors printed on the first page of their works and incorporated into the book even though it was not part of it.

This done, a new power is introduced into the political world.

the polity and to the capacity of the polity to tolerate dissent and guarantee minority political rights in a majoritarian political culture.[4]

Skepticism is essential, for without it there would be no challenges to the status quo by interest groups representing minority viewpoints. In a market democracy, interest groups are free to express their skepticism about the accuracy of views held by the political majority and the soundness of the underlying values that justify these views. In societies where it is not possible for political minorities to question authoritative viewpoints and the dogmas that majorities claim provide legitimacy for their authority over the political process, democracy quickly gives way to authoritarianism.

On the other hand, in a political system where there is too much skepticism, the danger to democracy is also great, not from authoritarianism, but from factionalism and anarchy. If all of the dogmas that a political system lives by are challenged all of the time, the system will soon fragment. Instead of experiencing the exhilarating impact produced by vigorous debates about ends and means, the polity that is always fighting over its fundamental values ends up fighting with itself, all of the time, instead of working to build a consensus and to promote conciliation. The only politics left is the politics of atomized interest groups, locked in battle to the bitter end. And in its extreme formulation, this battle can quickly degenerate into a battle of all against all, the state of nature that Thomas Hobbes, the most formidable of the seventeenth-century English political theorists, characterized in his classic studies of political philosophy.[5]

In order to carry out its essential function, which is to enable disagreeing interests to compromise, a polity must restrain extreme skepticism, or at least find some way to minimize its impact on the polity. The challenge for a political system pledged to optimizing individual freedom is to balance actions that encourage interest groups to voice their skepticism and actions that protect prevailing fundamental dogmas against assault from the skeptics.

How can this delicate balance between skepticism and dogma be struck? The best means would be through a tacit agreement between skeptics and dogmatists to exercise self-restraint by not fighting every battle to the bitter end. In operational terms, this requires skeptics and dogmatists to agree to restrict debates over disagreements by limiting debates over fundamental values. The best way to achieve this objective is by ruling some issues off-limits

---

[4] My discussion of the relationship among dogmatism, skepticism, and democratic politics owes much to Aaron B. Wildavsky's seminal discussion of policy analysis, *Speaking Truth to Power: The Art and Craft of Policy Analysis* (1979, 205–211). However, the connections I draw among these three variables are my own; therefore, any shortcomings in my analysis should not be attributed to Wildavsky, but to me.

[5] For an excellent study of Hobbes's political philosophy, which also illuminates many of the issues that will be discussed in this paper, see Macpherson (1962).

to politics.[6] If some of the dogmas that undergird a political system are subject to vigorous challenge, then other dogmas must remain relatively protected. Absent an agreement among the members of the polity that some dogmas must be held inviolate, it is nearly impossible for a political system to evolve mechanisms for resolving political conflicts without resorting to measures that would excessively restrict the freedom of skeptics to express themselves. It can be argued, then, that the essential ingredient for successful politics is that some "truths," or political dogmas, be held by most of the polity nearly all of the time.

II. THE LOGIC OF STANDARDIZED TESTS

Because questions of allocative fairness are at the core of political interactions, they are also at the source of most political conflicts, the focus of both skepticism and dogma. Where the question of fair opportunity allocation is not at issue, there is little need for politics, and there is little or no need for individuals to come together in a voluntary association to form a polity, except to pursue eleemosynary objectives.

Conflicts about standardized testing, then, are part of the politics of a market democracy. In the most fundamental sense, conflicts about standardized testing programs are conflicts about allocative fairness. The degree to which hard questions are asked about standardized tests says a great deal about the viability and health of the political economy; if serious debate flourishes on the *means* of opportunity allocation, this is a sign that the skeptics and dogmatists are maintaining the delicate balance that signals a healthy democratic political economy.

Given the logic of an ideal democratic political economy described above, where do the promises and the problems of standardized testing come

---

[6] In essence, this was the approach taken by the framers of the U.S. Constitution, when they found themselves attempting to forge a compromise that would bind thirteen disparate colonies together in a new nation. They evaded the issue of slavery's incompatibility with individual liberty by defining slaves as less than human—three-fifths, to be exact—thereby aggrandizing the slaveholders among the Constitution makers. They gave the abolitionists among the framers something to look forward to by incorporating into the Constitution a prohibition against the importation of new slaves after 1808. They finessed the divisive issue of one-man, one-vote by agreeing that the House should reflect individual state population totals, while the Senate should be composed of two representatives from each state, thereby giving states with low populations equal influence with states with high populations. Finally, the makers of the first "new nation," in that it "was the first major colony successfully to break away from colonial rule through revolution," decided to limit the possibility of fractious debates over individual religious beliefs, and the dogmas that make each religion unique, by prohibiting the establishment of a national religion. See, for example, Lipset (1979).

in? First let us consider the role of those who wish to make the institution of standardized testing one of the inviolable dogmas undergirding our system's way of allocating opportunity.

Dogmatism and Testing

The advocates of standardized testing programs argue that the use of tests to allocate opportunities, especially in education and in the workplace, represents the triumph of logic and science over speculation and prejudice. Those who hold these views contend that there are no other methods a pluralistic, democratic society can use to make relevant and justifiable distinctions among competitors in fairly allocating the limited supply of high-prestige educational and high-reward training and employment opportunities. They argue that in a society committed to the ideals of individual merit and to the primacy of the marketplace in determining allocative decisions, equality of opportunity, and allocative fairness, standardized tests are essential tools.

Given this view of the way the world works, testing is more than a means for instituting a fair opportunity allocation process. It is a strong and indispensable ally of democracy, saving the polity from itself by minimizing the likelihood that debates about the tragic consequences of the disappointing distribution of opportunity outcomes will grow into debates about the legitimacy of democratic politics itself. This way, when tragic consequences ensue for those individuals who fall short of their educational and employment aspirations, disappointment is more likely to be personal and transmuted into more realistic life-course goals, rather than externalized, publicly expressed anger and confrontational politics.

In short, when properly designed and used to exclude the consideration of extraneous factors in the assessment of individual achievement and potential, standardized tests are the best means to assure fairness in the allocation of employment and educational opportunities. And in so doing, in a democratic society, tests can play a major role in reducing the political conflict that inevitably accompanies the distribution and redistribution of society's rewards and opportunities from one individual to another.

Skepticism and Testing

Now let us review the beliefs of skeptics. In the last two decades, many of those who have reviewed the role that standardized tests play in our political economy have concluded that, in many instances, standardized tests are deployed in a manner that inhibits the achievement of allocative fairness, largely because these tests do not perform the tasks that educators, employers, politicians, industrial psychologists, psychometricians, and the major standardized test manufacturers claim for them.[7] Some of these reviewers have even questioned the very notion (read "dogma") that the scientific basis of standardized testing is sufficiently well-developed to warrant the faith that has been placed in tests by the groups that now rely upon them to allocate sought-after opportunities.[8] Even among reviewers who have not critiqued the underlying scientific dogma of standardized testing, many have raised pointed questions about the ways in which tests are currently misused and overused to allocate employment, training, and educational opportunities. The misequation of test scores with comprehensive measures of individual merit, the misinterpretation of test scores as highly predictive of future classroom and workplace success and failure, and the over-reliance on test scores in determining whether or not an individual will even be permitted to enter the opportunity marketplace of important educational and training opportunities, have come under the sharpest questioning of all.

Why, in spite of what testing advocates count as repeated demonstrations that many tests are valid for their stated purposes (for example, as predictors of later success), are there still those who insist that standardized tests should be limited or abolished? For some, the precise, scientific character of standardized testing is a compelling reason to ensconce standardized tests as one of the principal tools of allocation within a democracy. Why do some others reject this dogma?

Viewed in terms of the logic which underlies an ideal democracy, we can posit several reasons for skepticism about the "scientific" results of testing. One of the most important of these involves the delicate balance between (a) the individual opportunity seeker's sense of control over the exercise of preferences on his career path, and (b) that individual's beliefs about the fairness of the market's tools for allocation. Specifically, the opportunity seeker must believe that standardized tests are a mechanism which will allow him and others like him the appropriate amount of freedom to try, and of course, to fail.

If opportunity seekers perceive that their failure in the marketplace is due to their performance on a test, then maintenance of belief in the blind impartiality of the market mechanism *demands* that they see the test as a

---

[7] Although somewhat dated, one of the most incisive reviews of the misuse of tests by professional psychologists can be found in the often cited article by David C. McClelland (1973), "Testing for Competence Rather Than for 'Intelligence.'" Milder critiques of psychological testing for purposes of identifying ability and merit may be found in Howard Gardner, *Frames of Mind: The Theory of Multiple Intelligences* (1983); Robert J. Sternberg, *Beyond IQ: A Triarchic Theory of Human Intelligence* (1985); and Robert J. Sternberg and Richard K. Wagner (Editors), *Practical Intelligence: Nature and Origins of Competence in the Everyday World* (1987).

[8] For an excellent, and very critical account of the origins of testing for intelligence and ability, see Gould (1981). For a critique of the acceptance of test expertise by the courts, see Coleman (1984).

device of this fair and impartial market. Yet a test is not straightforwardly such a mechanism. It is a personal, individually experienced phenomenon, with a clear and keenly felt relationship between the personal effort of the opportunity seeker and the outcome of the test. It makes each failure in the opportunity marketplace a personal failure. If the failure is attributed ultimately to the fair, blind allocation procedures of the market, then the individual's belief in the fairness of the democracy's allocation mechanisms must be transferred to the test, as its extension.

However, as we will see below, such faith is not always warranted. In fact, essentially every test produces false negatives and false positives.[9] Even technically naive test-takers know this informally. Those who make policy, and set the level of acceptable costs for false negatives and false positives, do not experience the individual disappointment of those who feel that their low test result is really a false negative.

As described above, one of the central characteristics of a democratic political economy is an individual's right to pursue opportunity freely. When a person does poorly on a test, and is consequently barred from an educational or job opportunity, that person's right to pursue opportunity freely, according to individual preference and desire, is short-circuited. The right to try and to fail has been preempted by a supposedly scientific measure of the individual. Now, some might argue that the seeker has indeed been given the right to fail; instead of failing on the job at great expense to his employer, and possibly also to himself, he has simply failed before entry into the job. However, we must ask whether for all opportunity seekers the personal experience of failing the crucial test leads to this view. For at least some individuals it does not.

Consider, for example, members of those groups whose group performance on standardized tests is consistently lower than the average. If an individual from such a group receives a score on a test that predicts that he will fail to perform up to par on the job, he may still maintain that other factors are relevant to his future job performance, and that he deserves a chance to try to overcome whatever factors may have resulted in a poor test score. The purported scientific character of the test represents to such a person a barrier to the perceived "right" to exercise individual choice and to fail *on the job*. In such a person's mind, instead of tests being "an indispensable ally of democracy," transmuting disappointment into more realistic life goals, the institution of testing itself becomes the target of externalized anger.

Thus, a policy-oriented analysis of testing as an object of contention shows that a political, nonscientific variable—how individuals perceive the

---

[9] False-negative test errors result when tests purporting to measure performance or predict future performance underestimate the test taker's actual characteristics. Conversely, false-positive errors occur when test results overestimate the test-taker's characteristics.

fairness of tests as an allocation mechanism—may determine the success of testing policy for opportunity allocation.

III. THE POLITICS OF TESTING IN THE REAL WORLD

Now that we have reached a point in our discussion where we have some understanding of allocative fairness as a central tenet in a market democracy, it is useful to move from the abstract to the concrete. We will do this by discussing in detail two examples of test use in "the real world." In these discussions, we will utilize our theoretical perspective to exemplify and analyze some of the conflicts and controversies that inherently plague the use of testing in pursuit of allocative fairness in a market democracy.

Testing in the Real World: Case Study One

The following story appeared in the sports section of the February 2, 1987, edition of *The New York Times*:

> When Great Isn't Good Enough
>
> Suppose a country weak in basketball—England, perhaps— decided to launch a national program to upgrade the sport. Suppose Julius Erving took up residence in London and offered his help as coach. "Hold on, Julius," the English say. "You can't coach here if you don't have one of our coaching licenses." So they give him a series of exams on basketball theory and practice, devised and marked by a group of obscure English coaches. And they fail him.
>
> Something similar occurred not long ago. For England, read United States; for basketball, read soccer; and for Julius Erving, read Teófilo Cubillas, the Peruvian star who played in three World Cups and, with 10 goals, ranks fourth, right behind Pelé, among the leading scorers in World Cup history. Like Erving, he's widely respected as a player, as a gentleman and as a tutor who has a magic touch with youths.
>
> Cubillas came to the United States in 1979 to play for the Fort Lauderdale Strikers. He now lives in Florida, where he runs a string of soccer camps, and last year he expressed interest in joining the coaching staff of the various American national teams. He needed certification from the United States Soccer Federation, and so last month in Tampa, he took one of the federation's periodic tests for a "B" license. Forty of the 47 other applicants who tested with him passed; Cubillas failed, given unsatisfactory grades in 3 of 14 areas—anatomy and physiology,

practical coaching of seniors, and laws of the game—by a panel of American college coaches.

The federation says Cubillas flunked largely because he lacks command of English. Whatever the reason, the implication that he had little to offer a national program that has yet to produce even one world class player—and that has failed nine straight times since 1950 to qualify for the World Cup—struck some observers as odd. Not the least of them was Cubillas himself, who cried, "They failed me, yet passed people who don't even know how to kick a ball!"

Eric Eichmann of Clemson, a starting forward for the national team, said: "He's been a tremendous influence on my game, and an inspiration. He gave me a goal, to be like him. It wasn't so much what he said but what he could show." Added Brian Benedict of national champion Duke, a midfielder widely regarded as one of the country's most promising players: "He coached me in Florida for a year, and I learned more from watching him than from anything else. I'd have him as my coach any day."

Art Walls, chairman of the federation's coaching committee, seems to agree. "Cubillas is a special case," he said. "When I first met him, I immediately saw his potential as a specialist to the program." Walls has now sent a memo to the coaches involved in the "B" license course recommending that Cubillas be invited to re–sit for the exams.

While at first glance this article appears to be a typical sports color story, a second reading and further reflection upon the events described in *The New York Times* generates a number of impressions about the use of tests to credential soccer coaches. If one starts with the proposition that a coach is effective if he can organize and explain what he knows to novice learners, and better yet, use this knowledge to promote skilled and purposeful physical activity among his students, it would appear that Cubillas is indeed a qualified coach, even if he is unable to convince the user of the coaching test, the soccer coaching establishment, or the manufacturer of the coaching test that he possesses the knowledge to become an effective coach.

As every sports fan knows, the bottom line in evaluating coaching performance is that coaching competence, in soccer or in any other sport, must be demonstrated on the playing field. To put it bluntly, the test of coaching competence is reflected in the record of wins and losses. It is difficult to imagine any major college athletic director or owner of a professional sports franchise awarding a prized coaching assignment to a candidate solely on the basis of scores on a standardized test. It would seem that a test that takes out of context the formal knowledge that coaches must have to be successful, or discriminates against candidates whose formal academic knowledge in fields not directly related to the job of coaching may be weak, will produce little useful information about the potential coaching performance of aspiring coaches.

The above impressions are of course just that, impressionistic. However, given the gist of the *Times* story, it is likely that conveying these impressions is just what the author had in mind when filing the story. It might be instructive to look yet again at the *Times* story, this time from the perspective of the political theorist and policy analyst interested in the costs and benefits, the claims and counterclaims, of test use in the pursuit of allocative fairness. From the story we can draw at least four interconnected and indisputably policy-relevant facts:

1. A former world-class soccer player, widely acknowledged to be a gifted soccer coach as well as being the founder and owner of a chain of highly successful soccer camps, is refused a soccer coach's license because he cannot pass a standardized, multiple-choice, pencil-and-paper test.

2. This individual's failure on the soccer coaching test is not considered by any knowledgeable "expert" to be an accurate predictor of his coaching skills, nor an accurate reflection of his potential contributions as a "fully certified" soccer coach. To the contrary, even in the face of information about this individual's inability to pass the coaching test, both fully certified "expert" soccer coaches and unusually gifted soccer players continue to attest to the noncredentialed coach's professionalism, technical skills, personal virtues, and unique talents as a soccer coach.

3. The conflict between fact one and fact two is fully recognized and acknowledged by the elected head of the official body authorized to establish, monitor, evaluate, and modify the methods used to issue coaching credentials to aspiring soccer coaches.

4. As proposed by the head of the official soccer coaching standards body, the solution to the conflict is to permit the uncredentialed, but obviously talented soccer coach, to take the standardized, multiple-choice, pencil-and-paper soccer coach test again.

In sum, *The New York Times* story about the trials and tribulations of Teófilo Cubillas makes the following point quite clear: the role of tests in the allocation of opportunities—in this case employment opportunities—is politically determined.

The case of Cubillas versus the United States Soccer Federation is political because it starts with a political problem: What means and measures should be used to identify and assess individual aptitudes, skills, talents, and achievements, and how do we use these measures in allocating opportunities? The Cubillas case is fundamentally political because the answers to these questions must be politically derived. The United States Soccer Federation made a political decision when it established its policy of testing aspiring coaches for certification; it made a political decision when it decided how the test was to be validated and what criterion to use in the test validation process; and it made a political decision when it set its standards for passing the test.[10]

In making these political decisions, the United States Soccer Federation more than likely called upon psychometricians to provide advice and information. However, scientific knowledge about the relationship between testing success and successful on-the-job performance is limited and incomplete. There is no absolute certainty about what we are really measuring when we administer standardized tests, despite their express purpose, in the Cubillas case, to measure soccer coaching aptitude, skills, knowledge, talents, and achievements.[11] Furthermore, at the center of the Cubillas controversy is a measurement error. That is, the soccer coaching test produced a false-negative test score for Cubillas. Yet based on his test score, the United States Soccer Federation denied Cubillas a soccer coaching license. Apparently, the Federation determined that the costs and adverse consequences of refusing Cubillas a license, of engaging in ostensibly unfair allocative policies, were less than the costs and benefits of setting aside the false-negative score in favor of human judgments about Cubillas's record of performance or of supplementing Cubillas's score with additional assessment information, such as the results of a specially devised and administered simulated coaching exercise. In all, the case of Cubillas versus the United States Soccer Federation is an extra-scientific, political controversy. The tone and content of the article are a testament to the widespread perception that tests are flawed devices with

---

[10] Indeed, the American Psychological Association's professional standards for educational and psychological testing are products of a political process. During the development of the present standards, association members, as individuals and as coalitions, lobbied for changes and revisions from various special interest perspectives. The standards committee used the democratic process to reach consensus on the final set of standards to be issued.

[11] As Philip J. Davis and Reuben Hersh note in their book, *Descartes' Dream* (1986, 85-86), a mathematician (read "psychometrician") will say to a potential user of applied mathematics (read "user of tests"): "'If you tell me what to maximize, I will try to tell you how to do it.' This is what he says, and he means it. The onus of determining what ought to be maximized is on others." Davis and Hersh also state that testing, as one form of applied mathematics, "requires a criterion to work. The criterion must be extra-mathematical, extra-scientific."

which to allocate opportunity. That the test was blind to the obvious brilliance of Cubillas, and was not waived even in his case, only serves to confirm the perception that every instance of a failing test score may be a false negative. When the right to pursue opportunity according to one's own preferences is central to a democratic political economy, the perception that an illegitimate obstacle blocks that right will be very hard to extinguish.

As long as there is the possibility of generating false-negative or false-positive test results, and as long as there is no agreement on the methods that should be used to compute the costs of these two possible outcomes, testing will be enmeshed in politics. What is more, the intensity and pitch of the political conflict surrounding testing will be especially high and sharp when tests are used as the principal means for allocating desired employment opportunities, as in the case of Cubillas.

For many test-dependent opportunities, the political problems brought on by false-negative results are temporary, generating short-term displeasure but producing little damage that is likely to be permanent. Cubillas being denied a job as a fully credentialed soccer coach may be profoundly disappointing to the avid soccer fan, but few would argue that his absence from the ranks of the fully certified soccer coaches fraternity constitutes a major American political tragedy. Nor would many be surprised if the problems Cubillas has had with standardized tests fail to make it off of the sports pages and onto the front pages, where the political tragedies of the world are reviewed in all of their serious splendor.

Testing in the Real World: Case Study Two

Now, suppose that instead of Teófilo Cubillas, the competent but uncertifiable soccer coach, we were discussing the plight of three hundred thousand young men and women, many of them racial, ethnic, and linguistic minority group members. Also, suppose that instead of examining the politics and problems of using tests to allocate opportunities to individuals pursuing coaching careers, we were looking into the politics and problems of using tests to allocate enlistment and training opportunities. Finally, suppose that these test-use policies had the potential to weaken the nation's capacity to maintain a strong national defense by denying enlistment in the armed forces to potential recruits who score low on standardized tests, but who nevertheless are capable of successful on-the-job performances. Were this last supposition accurate, not only would such a test-driven allocative policy deny employment and training opportunities to many deserving young adults, it would also artificially inflate military personnel costs by forcing the military to compete more directly with the civilian sector for that portion of the young adult population capable of scoring high marks on service qualifying tests. As we shall discover, our three suppositions reflect fairly accurately a real dilemma in American life.

Every year the active military services select about three hundred thousand recruits from among a large pool of applicants. In addition, following enlistment, military manpower experts decide to which training programs these recruits should be directed. In carrying out these tasks, officials balance the desires of individual recruits, the needs of the military, and factors related to cost-effectiveness and efficiency. Since only a handful of each year's crop of new recruits have extensive civilian work experience, the services are forced to rely heavily, if not exclusively, on the results of standardized pencil-and-paper tests to select their recruits.

The principal selection and classification tool the services use to select recruits and to allocate training opportunity is the Armed Services Vocational Aptitude Battery (ASVAB). It consists of several subtests, four of which are combined to yield a measure of general aptitude and trainability—the Armed Forces Qualifications Test (AFQT). The potential recruit's AFQT score and educational attainment level determine enlistment eligibility. The cut-off score for potential enlistees without high-school diplomas is much higher than it is for those with high-school diplomas. Scores on individual subcomponents of the ASVAB are used to qualify recruits for specific training program opportunities.

When Norms Go Astray

In 1980, it was discovered that there was a problem with the norming of the ASVAB, and that, as a result, between 1976 and 1980, all the services were accepting a much higher proportion of low-scoring enlistees than had previously been believed. Many of these enlistees would have been rejected outright had their test scores not been inflated by the misnormed ASVAB. Over the entire period, nearly three hundred sixty thousand male recruits, or nearly one of every four recruits, would have been disqualified for enlistment if the test had been properly normed. More than two hundred thousand, or nearly one in three male army recruits, were erroneously admitted.

And of those recruits who were enlisted between 1976 and 1980 based on wrongly inflated test scores, many more would have been enrolled in training programs for enlistees with low ASVAB scores, instead of being enrolled in training programs requiring high test scores.

The numbers behind the misnorming imbroglio are startling. In fiscal year 1979–80, while only 5 percent of the total number of the new recruits had been reported as having scored between the 10th and 30th percentiles on the ASVAB (the ASVAB was then normed against the recruit population mobilized during World War II), the correct figure was 30 percent from this lowest allowable category (Category IV). Among new army recruits, only 9 percent had been reported as coming from Category IV; but the true total was 46 percent. Subcomponent ASVAB scores, used in allocating training opportunities, were also miscalibrated. As a result, of the enlistees who entered the infantry specialty in fiscal years 1977 through 1980, 42 percent scored below the intended minimum cut-off score for the assignment on the ASVAB sub-components for combat arms specialists.

What is of special relevance and significance, in light of its public policy implications, is that the on-the-job "failure rate" of enlistees whose low test scores should have kept them out of the military, was not much higher than the failure rate for enlistees who scored above the minimum ASVAB cut-off score! (Here failure rate represents a composite indicator, combining attrition, successful completion of training programs, promotions, and supervisory ratings.) According to one study:

> Higher-aptitude enlistees—as measured by either AFQT or the aptitude area composite used to qualify enlistees for the particular job—exhibited essentially the same attrition behavior as those with lower test scores. This held even for the advanced training period, when we might expect to see low-scoring recruits leaving because they were unable to complete the course. (Fernandez 1985, 10–11).

A new, correctly normed ASVAB was introduced in October 1980. This led immediately to a reduction in Category IV recruits and an increase in the proportion of enlistees scoring in the upper 35 percent on the ASVAB (Categories I and II). In the army, between 1980 and 1981 Category IV enlistees fell from 46 to 30 percent, while Category I and II enlistees increased from 15 to 23 percent.

Invalid Tests or Invalid Assumptions about Tests

The discovery of the ASVAB miscalibration has raised a number of important questions about the use of standardized pencil-and-paper tests as the major mechanism for allocating enlistment and training opportunities in the military. We will mention only a few here, emphasizing broad policy observations that are more generally applicable to the issue of how tests are used in the allocation of opportunities, rather then delving into issues requiring specialized knowledge about psychometrics. These issues are: (1) the validity of the ASVAB as a predictor of on-the-job performance; (2) the impact of changes in military instructional programs on enlistee on-the-job performance; (3) the possibility of efficiency changes in manpower planning and placement procedures; (4) changing performance standards; and (5) the efforts of the nation's military leadership to improve race relations in the military.

ASVAB Validity

Many of the enlistees who were incorrectly enrolled in training programs requiring higher aptitude test scores than they had actually obtained were successful in these training programs as well as successful on the job. One possible explanation is to conclude that the validity of the ASVAB had always been overestimated. The individual characteristics that determine test-score success and failure, and classroom success and failure, may differ sharply from those determining individual success in particular job settings, where the incentives, sanctions, motivations, and pressures associated with on-the-job performance are likely to be very different.

This would seem to be especially true in the military, where on-the-job performance failure may mean loss of life—a strong incentive for high performance, indeed. Also, in the military, most tasks are carried out in small group settings, which places a premium on cooperative and collaborative skills, whereas test performance is an individual action, requiring almost no competence in social skills except being able to decipher and interpret test items under pressure.

If this view about the dependency of on-the-job performance on particular social or contextual situations is accepted, then it is not difficult to conclude that, because ASVAB fails to take into account the differential on-the-job performance of enlistees with identical ASVAB test scores working in small-group situations under different conditions, ASVAB's invalidity is structural and endemic. Obviously, one holding this view would find it easy to conclude that the use of the ASVAB had always resulted in the false labeling as unqualified of many qualified potential enlistees (false negatives). Such an explanation would account for the inexplicable number of successful enlistees—at least in terms of ASVAB-based predictions about training program and on-the-job performance ratings—who should have never been permitted to enlist in the services in the first place, or after enlistment, should have never been permitted to enroll in certain highly technical training programs.

Instructional Improvements

A second explanation for the ASVAB test score–job performance disparity is possible, one that does not require such harsh retroactive conclusions to be drawn about the validity, or the invalidity, of the ASVAB. The services, in response to the influx of low-scoring enlistees, could have changed instructional methods in their training programs in such a way as to weaken the long-standing relationship among an individual's ASVAB test score, his success in specialized training programs, and his subsequent on-the-job performance. Such a change in instructional methods would account for the transformation of ostensibly unqualified enlistees into acceptable on-the-job performers. The U.S. Department of Defense has invested heavily in instructional improvement efforts in the last two decades, and such a change in teaching methods is not so far-fetched. Clearly, if such a transformation did take place (changing true-negatives into false-negatives), it would have profound implications not only for the military, but for the nation's entire educational enterprise.

Efficiency Improvements

A third possibility is that the services have learned to better and more efficiently match ASVAB test-score predictions and enlistee training preferences with appropriate training programs, and that this new proficiency in combining these three important factors accounts for the unpredicted on-the-job success of ostensibly unqualified enlistees. Also, it might be argued that greater efficiency in the services' manpower placement and training efforts was the inevitable consequence of an all-volunteer military. In both cases the contention is that volunteer enlistees who are well matched to training programs are more likely to work up to their capacity then ill-matched enlistees and resentful draftees.

Changing Performance Standards

A fourth explanation for the higher than expected on-the-job success rate for unqualified and underqualified enlistees, at least according to ASVAB-based conventional wisdom about what constitutes appropriate qualifications, is to assume that the military adjusted to the sudden influx of low-aptitude recruits by lowering its training program and on-the-job performance standards. This view of what might have happened is consistent with the belief that the services have always designed their jobs so as to make them "do-able" by the most poorly trained enlistees.

The lower standards explanation has received support from military officials, members of congressional oversight committees, and researchers and analysts working on military manpower issues. Given recent technological developments in military weapons systems, they are concerned that such a lowering of standards has placed the nation's defense in grave danger. (Some have even suggested today's weapons systems are so technologically complex that even the restoration of pre-1976 ASVAB test standards would not solve the problems caused by the rapid increase in the technological sophistication. Those holding these views argue that a totally voluntary military no longer makes sense, because of the growing need for high ASVAB-scoring recruits and the continued shrinking of the youth population [Binkin 1986].)

Improved Race Relations

The fifth factor that could account for the higher than expected on-the-job performance of enlistees was a change in the military's attitude about the importance of promoting harmonious race relations among service personnel. Beginning in the early 1970s, the nation's military leadership increased its efforts to combat racism and discrimination in the services. This interest in racial harmony was not entirely altruistic. As Charles C. Moskos, one of the nation's leading military sociologists, points out, the Vietnam war years:

were marked by well-publicized breakdowns of discipline among Black servicemen and, more broadly, an atmosphere of racial hostility in the ranks. Racial clashes occurred in Vietnam, on military bases around the world, and on ships at sea (Moskos 1986, 64-72).

In response to this troubling situation, the nation's military leadership introduced highly specific, and apparently very effective antidiscrimination initiatives.

For example, in the early 1970s a new category appeared in the efficiency reports for all enlisted personnel: race-relations skills. Filling out this section was mandatory, and the requirement was vigorously enforced. One result of this change was that more minorities than ever before, particularly blacks, were promoted. By 1975 all of the services had set up race-relations units to combat racial antagonism among enlisted personnel.

Although almost impossible to quantify, there is some evidence that these attempts to improve race relations in the military did have an impact on the motivation of minority military personnel. As Moskos reports:

> Since 1978 about one white member of the Army in three has been prematurely discharged for reasons of undisciplined behavior, lack of aptitude, psychological problems or the like. The figure for [B]lack male soldiers is one in four. Even among soldiers of similar educational background, Blacks are more likely than [W]hites to complete their enlistments (Moskos 1986, 68).

Given the tradition of the military mirroring racial attitudes in the larger American society, where sub-par performance by blacks is the norm, these are very significant racial differences. They are even more significant, in terms of their potential impact on overall military performance, when the racial composition of the services is taken into account. For more than a decade the percentage of blacks and Hispanics in the service has hovered between 20 and 25 percent (Binkin and Eitelberg 1982). In the army, the largest branch of the military, blacks currently account for more than one-third of all enlisted personnel. Clearly, any steps that improve the motivation and performance among such a major component of the military population will show up in improvements in measures used to evaluate military manpower performance, including the relationship between ASVAB test scores and on-the-job performance.

Policy Reviews

Their experiences with the misnormed ASVAB have raised a host of policy questions within the military about the role of tests in the allocation of enlistment and training opportunities. Researchers at the RAND Corporation, one of the nation's leading think tanks, are addressing some of these important questions (Fernandez 1985; Armor et al. 1982):

1) Can low-scoring recruits perform most military jobs, or did their influx seriously degrade military job performance?

2) Where should minimum enlistment standards be set on the correctly scored AFQT?

3) What should be done with the standards for individual jobs? Should they remain at the low levels of the miscalibrated ASVAB, raised to their former nominal levels, set somewhere in between, or pushed even higher?

4) How did the low job standards affect the abilities of the services to place recruits into the jobs for which they were best suited?

5)   Is there any objective basis for setting standards for enlistment, either into a service as a whole or into specific jobs, or for determining the "right" job for each recruit?

The efforts of RAND to develop a more comprehensive, policy-oriented understanding of test use in the military was supplemented in 1983 by the National Research Council (NRC), which set up a special task force, the Committee on the Performance of Military Personnel, whose objective:

> is to produce empirical evidence about the performance of current personnel in entry-level enlisted jobs that will be useful to policy makers who set mental standards (i.e., cut-scores on selection tests) for entry into those jobs. For this purpose it is important to know that individual X, who performs better than individual Y on the selection test, also performs better than Y on the job. But we believe that the decision maker also needs to know how much of the total job individuals X and Y can perform proficiently in order to make fully informed judgements about force quality requirements. This assessment of absolute proficiency we have designated as the assessment of overall competence or job mastery (Wigdor and Green 1986, 2).

That the military is willing to look at its testing practices and policies is encouraging. Clearly, there are very important issues to be resolved. On the other hand, that the need persists for such fundamental policy and research review efforts on the use of tests to allocate enlistment and training opportunities is astounding. Stripped of its niceties and complexities, the military is admitting that it does not know if its test policies make a difference.

The military is the largest consumer of standardized tests in the nation; each year it administers tests to millions of potential recruits and enlisted personnel. Additionally, the military has set the pace for standardized testing among all institutions in the United States ever since World War I, when it developed the first massive testing program in this country. That after seventy years of testing millions of recruits and service personnel, military manpower experts are still asking fundamental questions about testing, provides incontrovertible evidence of our real lack of knowledge and understanding about the testing enterprise. This in turn supports the analysis that the widespread contention between skeptics and dogmatists is over the issue of legitimacy: Are standardized tests in themselves appropriate tools with which to control and mediate the free exercise of personal preferences in pursuit of opportunity?

III. CONCLUSION

We have sought a deeper understanding of the sources of contention over standardized tests as tools to allocate opportunities. This brief exposition has centered on the articulation between the logic of the democratic political economy and the polity's reaction to the use of standardized tests as a means for allocating opportunity. At the level of the group and the individual test-taker, there are nonscientific, political motivations for skepticism and dispute.

The ends and means used to allocate opportunities form the core problem of any democratic political economy. It is predictable that in this highly pluralistic nation, where opportunity does not visit all groups equally, underrepresented groups perceive that allocation patterns are unfair. Thus, they may also perceive that the *methods* of allocation are unfair. A group does not need to have a scientific understanding of the causes of differential performance means on standardized tests to react nevertheless against the use of such tests as tools of allocational policy.

At the level of individual experience, a somewhat different factor emerges. As discussed above, the basis for allocative fairness in an ideal market democracy is the free interaction in the opportunity marketplace of (a) the skills and motivation of individual opportunity seekers; (b) the preferences of those individuals for selected opportunities; (c) the total market supply of individuals with a and b; and (d) the market demand for individuals with a and b. Given the widespread perception that standardized tests are not perfect as a means for determining those skills and motivations, then any test-mediated failure by an individual may potentially be perceived as an abridgement of the right to try and to fail in the opportunity marketplace.

We can see this skepticism about the means used to direct the flow of opportunities as a sign of health for two reasons. First, the dynamic balance between skeptics and dogmatists, the sign of a robust democracy, is evident. Second, the contention is focused on the *means* of allocation, not the underlying framework of the democratic opportunity market. Finally, however, the significance of these observations to policy interests is that the scientific merit of tests as predictive devices is not the only factor in their success as tools of policy. The *beliefs* and *perceptions* of individuals, about the way that standardized tests support or infringe on their rights as members of a democratic political economy, are as important to consider as issues of psychometric validity.

In this paper we have presented the beginnings of a policy-oriented perspective on opportunity allocation and the politics of testing. The approach outlined here suggests a number of questions. How should a political economy committed to the pursuit of allocative fairness, the ideals of individual merit, and the virtues of the free and uninhibited marketplace allocate scarce educational, training, and employment opportunities? More specifically, what methods of individual differentiation should the polity of a democratic political economy sanction to make distinctions among individual competitors for the limited supply of high-reward training and employment opportunities and high-prestige educational opportunities? When sanctioned, how should these methods of differentiation and distinction be rationalized, justified, and evaluated? What regulations and penalties should be put into place to protect and insure individuals against the dissemination to the marketplace of inaccurate assessments of their abilities, talents, and potential, especially to school and college admissions officers, training counselors, and employment managers? What regulations and penalties should be instituted to ensure that assessment activities are conducted fairly and objectively, and that prospective users of assessment instruments and techniques are provided with useful critiques of the shortcomings and limitations of their assessment methods and technology? Finally, what guarantees and rights should a polity put into place to protect individuals from having their opportunities diminished by the dissemination of inaccurate information about their abilities, talents, and potential?

Clearly, all of these are fundamental questions, revolving around the critical issues of how a political economy recognizes and sanctions individual differences that are truly relevant in terms of the operation of the marketplace, how it allocates its rewards and benefits to meritorious individuals, and how it protects individuals against the transmittal to the marketplace of false information about their individual abilities, talents, and potential. Unfortunately, as important and fundamental as all of these questions are, it may not be possible to pair these questions with permanent, correct answers. This is because the answers are dependent on a host of complex, political factors. In this paper, we have only begun to chart a course toward a more complete explication of the relationship between the use of standardized tests and the formulation and execution of allocative policy.

REFERENCES

Armor, David J., Richard L. Fernandez, Kathy Bers, Donna Schwarzbach (with the assistance of S. Craig Moore and Leola Cutler). September 1982. *Recruit Aptitudes and Army Job Performance: Setting Enlistment Standards for Infantrymen*, RAND Report R-2874-MRAL. Prepared for the Office of the Assistant Secretary of Defense/Manpower, Reserve Affairs and Logistics. Santa Monica, CA: The RAND Corporation.

Baumol, William J. 1986. *Superfairness: Applications and Theories.* Cambridge, Massachusetts: MIT Press.

Binkin, Martin and Mark J. Eitelberg (with the assistance of Alvin J. Schexnider and Marvin M. Smith). 1982. *Blacks and the Military.* Washington, DC: The Brookings Institution.

Binkin, Martin. 1986. *Military Technology and Defense Manpower.* Washington, DC: The Brookings Institution.

Coleman, Lee. 1984. *The Reign of Error: Psychiatry, Authority, and Law.* Boston: Beacon Press.

Dahl, Robert H. 1956. *A Preface to Democratic Theory.* Chicago: University of Chicago Press.

Davis, Philip J. and Reuben Hersh. 1986. *Descartes' Dream.* New York: Harcourt Brace Jovanovich.

Fernandez, Richard L. (with Jeffrey B. Garfinkle). January 1985. *Setting Enlistment Standards and Matching Recruits to Jobs Using Job Performance Criteria*, RAND Report R-3067-MIL. Prepared for the Office of the Assistant Secretary of Defense/Manpower, Installations and Logistics. Santa Monica, CA: The RAND Corporation.

Gardner, Howard. 1983. *Frames of Mind: The Theory of Multiple Intelligences.* New York: Basic Books.

Gould, Steven Jay. 1981. *The Mismeasure of Man.* New York: W. W. Norton.

Harr, Charles M. and Daniel W. Fessler. 1986. *Fairness and Justice: Law in the Service of Equality.* New York: Simon and Schuster.

Hoffmann, Banesh. 1964. *The Tyranny of Testing.* New York: Collier Books.

Jensen, Arthur R. 1981. *Straight Talk About Mental Tests.* New York: The Free Press.

Lasswell, Harold. 1972. *Politics: Who Gets What, When, How.* New York: World Publishing Co. (originally published by McGraw-Hill in 1936).

Lipset, Seymour Martin. 1979. *The First New Nation: The United States in Historical & Comparative Perspective.* New York: W.W. Norton.

Macpherson, C. B. 1962. *The Political Theory of Possessive Individualism: From Hobbes to Locke.* New York: Oxford University Press.

Macpherson, C. B. 1973. *Democratic Theory: Essays in Retrieval.* Oxford, Great Britain: Oxford University Press.

McClelland, David C. 1973. "Testing for Competence Rather Than for 'Intelligence.'" *American Psychologist*, 28(1): 1-14.

Meyer, J. P., ed. 1966. *Democracy in America*. New York: Anchor Books.

Moskos, Charles C. May 1986. "Success Story: Blacks in the Army." *The Atlantic Monthly*, 257(5): 64-72.

Pole, J. R. 1978. *The Pursuit of Equality in American History*. Berkeley and Los Angeles, CA: University of California Press.

Sartori, Giovanni. 1987. *The Theory of Democracy Revisited, Part One (The Contemporary Debate) and Part Two (The Classical Issues)*. Chatham, NJ: Chatham House Publishers.

Smith, Adam. 1948. *Adam Smith's Moral and Political Philosophy*, edited by Herbert W. Schneider. New York: Harper & Row.

Sternberg, Robert J. 1985. *Beyond IQ: A Triarchic Theory of Human Intelligence*. New York: Cambridge University Press.

Sternberg, Robert J. and Richard K. Wagner, eds. 1987. *Practical Intelligence: Nature and Origins of Competence in the Everyday World*. New York: Cambridge University Press.

Wigdor, Alexandra K. and Bert F. Green, Jr., eds. 1986. *Assessing the Performance of Enlisted Personnel: Evaluation of a Joint-Service Research Project*. Washington, DC: National Academy Press.

Wildavsky, Aaron B. 1979. *Speaking Truth to Power: The Art and Craft of Policy Analysis*. Boston: Little, Brown and Company.

The Mandarin Mentality: Civil Service and University Admissions Testing in Europe and Asia

Carolyn Webber

In the United States we have always been uncomfortable with formal systems dividing people into ranks. A basic premise of the French Enlightenment—that all men are created equal—underlies the enabling documents on which our nation was built. From the beginning, widespread belief in equality has governed individual behavior and public action in this country. Immigrants from class-based societies in Europe and Asia may have endured hardship as they made their places in the new nation, but here they found no barriers to opportunity such as had existed in the Old World. Given the will and good luck, one person's chance to improve his or her circumstances was as good as the next.

Perhaps that is why we are uneasy about the gatekeeping role tests fill in modern America. In effect, vocational and college admissions tests are ranking devices. Universities and employers use them to select from a large pool of applicants those judged most likely to benefit from higher education or to perform well on the job. The professionals who make and give these tests maintain that their scales are simply technical instruments for objectively sorting people. Yet these tests do seem to impinge on norms of open access. Long before the National Commission on Testing and Public Policy was created, critics questioned whether the current vocational and college admissions scales really are value-free, and if these tests select the best candidates.

Screening college applicants with tests administered by third parties goes back to 1916 in the U.S., when the College Entrance Examinations Board was created, but until after World War II, grades counted more for university admissions than test scores. Requiring applicants for government jobs to pass tests goes back further; Congress passed the Pendleton Act in 1883. By providing a merit-based mechanism for selecting civil servants, Congress aimed to limit the cronyism for which it had been so widely criticized.

As the nation industrialized during the late nineteenth century, Progressive reformers succeeded in enacting legislation designed to regulate industry. The federal work force in Washington and elsewhere slowly expanded and became subject to civil service rules, which, increasingly after the turn of the century, became formalized in the technocratic mode then being adopted by private industry. Although government workers were not subjected to time-and-motion studies, governments at all levels did introduce elements of emerging management technology—job classification, written examinations, and performance measurement on the job. Still, the tests given to select low- and mid-level government workers focused on determining only *minimum* standards. Then, as now, most high-level government jobs in Washington (and in state capitals as well) were filled by political appointment (Heclo 1984, 8–34). There is not now, nor has there ever been in the U.S., an elite, merit-based, permanent higher civil service comparable to those in Europe and Japan. Its absence is an element of American exceptionalism.

Compared to the U.S., other nations have had extensive experience ranking people with tests. Some European nations have been doing it for two centuries. In China civil service testing goes back two millennia. An exercise in historical reconstruction, this essay surveys civil service and university entrance testing at other places and times.

The Mandarin Mentality

Traditional societies of the pre-modern world justified privilege as intrinsic to the natural, God-given order. Although ancient governments relied on highborn administrators, the pyramidal social structure of such societies of fixed rank established absolute limits to the number of persons who could be chosen. Forced to expand the circle beyond those they knew, ancient rulers in many places adopted similar recruitment strategies. They used members of religious orders or the army as administrators. They mobilized conquered peoples who had useful skills. They sold administrative offices for revenue. They contracted for administrative services. They used slaves.

Only China institutionalized procedures for selecting candidates for office by merit criteria. The Imperial Civil Service Examinations held there from the second century B.C. on emerged from Confucian ethical norms then spreading through Chinese society. Writing after an era of continuous warfare among feudal states, Confucius suggested that the government could be managed better by scholars than by warriors. Accordingly, selection criteria for administrators of the Han and later dynasties encompassed activities pursued by highborn people with leisure: the study of classics—China's history and accepted schools of philosophy—and the arts of painting, calligraphy, and poetry.

The civil service examinations held in China from the beginning of the Han dynasty (about 200 B.C.) until 1905 provided competitive selection procedures for officials at all levels of its government. At least in theory, scholars from all walks of life and from anywhere in the vast empire were eligible to compete. (In practice, the population's limited literacy restricted applicants to gentry and aristocracy.) Successful candidates in local examinations advanced to another round of tests in the provincial capital, and candidates passing the provincial examinations were eligible to travel to Peking, where at three-year intervals, scholars from throughout the empire competed for the highest posts. The tests were highly selective; only 325 or 350 of the approximately 11,000 competitors in provincial examinations could advance to the next level, and only 350 out of 6,000 final candidates could hope to qualify for imperial office (Guy 1963, 744–754). With their knowledge of literature, philosophy, and the arts, the mandarins, as China's scholar-administrators were known, were cultivated generalists. Because he presumably attained office through personal merit, the mandarin commanded respect throughout China's imperial history.

Under imperial China's inheritance laws, family assets were divided equally among heirs. As equal inheritance led to land fragmentation, productivity and land income declined. Therefore, a family's continuity as gentry or aristocracy was not certain and downward mobility was common. Appointment of a family member to a civil service post was one way to sustain social rank and wealth. A close relative in the imperial service was so important, for both status and income, that families or clans would subsidize study for a promising son or nephew, sometimes for years. Schools in every village and town specialized in preparing young men for the tests. If a candidate failed the first time, a family would most likely support further study so he could try again, and again. Eventually, if he qualified, the candidate would either accept a low-ranking position or, at age fifty, would stop attending school and retire from competition, exhausted and dishonored (Ho 1962, 175, 259).

No counterpart exists in ancient western history for this merit-based procedure to determine competence for high office. Ancient governments in the West often used family background as a surrogate for literacy and numeracy, choosing officeholders from the priesthood, for example, or from other educated groups.[1]

Yet somehow the mandarin *concept* proliferated. In European governments today, an elite corps of permanent civil servants provides

---

[1] Educated prisoners of war were sometimes brought back as slaves to serve as administrators; a slave-bureaucrat's descendants might inherit his status and occupation. When the early Roman emperors wished to create a dependable corps of administrators, they appointed freedmen, former slaves who were given manumission explicitly to serve in the imperial administration. After the anarchy of the late Roman republic, the emperors sought loyal administrators; they must have believed their freedmen recruits would serve with devotion. Once attained, social status in the classical world was not easily changed. Descendants of the imperial freedmen served the empire until its western administration fell apart in the fourth century a.d. And when Charlemagne, in the ninth century, tried to restore Rome's lost legacy of centralization, the *ministeriales* who served as his administrators were also slaves.

organizational-management and policy advice for successive leaders from different political parties. Membership in the higher civil service is not open to anyone; as in imperial China, applicants must meet rigorous intellectual criteria—first for selection, and then for advancement. Whether they are educated as generalists (as in England, where higher civil servants often hold degrees in classics or humanities) or as technical specialists (as in France and Germany), aspiring civil servants must demonstrate extraordinary competence in high school and college, on civil service entrance tests, and throughout their careers. The very way Europeans talk about their higher civil servants connotes distinction: they are not, as in the U.S., pejoratively labeled bureaucrats (whose job is to push paper), but mandarins.

How, then, did this intellectual transfer of the mandarin concept from China to Europe come about? When did the tests given to select candidates for the civil service and for entrance into universities become an index of merit?

Medieval Examinations

In the universities of Paris and Bologna in the late twelfth century, we find the first examinations in Europe. I do not know the source of these tests, but suspect that the testing concept returned with merchants who were trading in western China. In any event, students aiming for certification as *magister* had to appear before their teachers for an oral inquisition on a body of knowledge. As with all examinations, these tests had a moral dimension, carrying threat of failure and public humiliation, but if the student met an examiner's expectations, his success in life was assured. The expanding feudal monarchies needed literate officials and clerks to keep order and manage government business; French kings in the late twelfth century had on their staffs "at least a dozen" *magistri*, and there were twenty-two professional graduates serving in England's court in 1302 (Hoskin and Macve 1986, 111–112).

Like the Chinese civil service examinations, medieval oral examinations had a binary outcome: students either passed or failed. Teachers in the Jesuit colleges in Europe during the sixteenth century maintained rudimentary records of student behavior and academic performance, aiming to allocate rewards and punishments commensurate with the society's hierarchical norms. The Christian brothers used a similar system during the seventeenth century. Lists of student performance, of good and bad behavior, facilitated management of a rowdy student body of reluctant aristocratic learners, but these lists were not examinations.

Testing in the modern world involves at least these three elements: (1) competition; (2) ranking of performance, based either on personal evaluation of individual test results; or, (3) increasingly since the nineteenth century, evaluation with quantified scales clothed with the authority of science. Modern tests are screening devices to determine eligibility for access, whether to education or to jobs.

Examinations in Europe

Testing for admission to universities and for employment in government, most historians agree, did not begin in Europe until the eighteenth century. In aristocratic society of the ancien régime, inherited status outweighed competence in determining qualifications for office. If the right person could be found, kings during the early modern era (fifteenth to eighteenth centuries) preferred advisors who were either nobility or high-level churchmen, individuals known to share their world view. As governments expanded during the sixteenth and seventeenth centuries and the number of high-level jobs exceeded the supply of eligible nobility, governments recruited administrators from strata lower in the social hierarchy. Priests had worked as government administrators since the Middle Ages. The rule of primogeniture in feudal society specified that family assets should be transferred intact to the oldest son. With no hope of inheritance, second and later sons from noble families often entered the church. If they became government administrators, these aristocratic clerics could be counted on to promote the king's interests.

From the sixteenth century on, developments in science and philosophy were creating an elite level in the social hierarchy based more on intellectual achievement than on wealth or birth. Kings and their counselors learned that experts trained in science and mathematics could contribute to national dominance with such innovations as improved arms and fortifications, durable roads and bridges, and high-quality manufactured goods. The scientific societies springing up in the national capitals during the seventeenth century were at first open to any interested person—in England, young Samuel Pepys, a low-ranking clerk in the Admiralty, belonged to the Royal Society. In France, Louis XIV and his minister Colbert formalized merit criteria for membership in the Acadèmie Française, chartered in 1666 with royal support and sponsorship. The academy supported the most illustrious minds in France, appointed by the crown after members' recommendations (Hahn 1971, 287–308). In exchange for a lifetime pension from the crown and generous fringe benefits, its members were obligated to turn their minds to problems with solutions that might conceivably enhance state power (Hahn 1971, 60–61; King 1949, 287-308).

France Creates a Mandarin Class

Recruitment and training of an intellectual elite devoted to state service has been the primary focus of higher education in France ever since the time of Louis XIV. Rigorous tests of competence in specialized fields qualified students for entry into the earliest state-supported military training schools in the late seventeenth century and into the *grandes écoles*, elite training schools for technocrats in civil government and the military first established in the late eighteenth century. After the sixteenth century, Jesuit scholars who had traveled to China wrote about the merit system implicit in its civil service examinations; Voltaire and other Enlightenment thinkers viewed civil service examinations as a solution to administrative problems in France and in the other European states whose rulers were trying to discard the medieval legacy of decentralized government and an officialdom selected either by sale of office or through favoritism (Guy 1963, 749).

Seventeenth- and eighteenth-century social thought in France manifests a tension among several elements. Overall, French Enlightenment thinkers had faith in the power of intelligence to create progress. In the medieval world view, the good life was delayed until the next life. Enlightenment theorists thought an approximation of paradise could be enjoyed in the present because man's ability to reason, to invent, and to organize could improve his condition. As the dominant social influence, government should actively support merit by seeking out creative minds to develop new learning, not only in science and technology, but also in pedagogy, administrative organization, or any other field of specialized knowledge that the government might need to draw upon. The potential payoff from resources invested in support of merit would be far greater than amounts spent.

Another strand in eighteenth-century French social thought centered on man's innate equality. Ideas about equality are the most important intellectual legacy of the French Enlightenment. Enlightenment theorists maintained that before God, each individual is one among equals, no matter what his background or social class. If, as seemed to be true in class-ranked European society, custom inhibited natural man's potential for creative self-expression, government should actively intervene to create appropriate conditions. Rousseau and Condillac, whose ideas were important sources of doctrines of equality, believed that resources invested in universal public education would foster progress.

The interplay between these two seminal ideas—of equality, and of progress through seeking out and then fostering merit—has pervaded public debate and influenced public policy in Western society ever since. Nineteenth-century liberal theorists in England, for example, Jeremy Bentham, James Mill and his son John Stuart Mill, found a concrete focus for the abstractions of the French Enlightenment thinkers; they favored universal publicly supported education through primary school. As the franchise expanded, they maintained that a literate public, one competent to read and understand issues, was imperative if citizens were to make informed electoral choices. And public education would help to identify talent.

By the late eighteenth century in France, proponents of both merit and equality favored an activist government directing resources into education. However state-supported education was not for everyone. Egalitarianism in education lasted for only a few years, during the radical phase of the French Revolution, when zealots abolished the venerable Academy of Science and sent some of its aristocratic members to the guillotine. The merit focus in French values was revived in 1794, when the revolutionary government converted the state-operated Ecole des Ponts et Chausses, founded under the monarchy, into a school of public works, and the following year, into a technological institute—the first of the elite grandes écoles created to educate and acculturate military leaders and civil officials. These meritocratic institutions embodied one of the central ideas of the French Enlightenment: that government support of scientific intelligence would lead to progress.

Under Napoleon the elite focus in French higher education was reaffirmed. The Academy of Science was reestablished. A new, centrally directed, centrally funded school (the Ecole Normale et Superieure) was founded in 1808 to train secondary school teachers. With the exception of a few religious training institutions, higher education in France has been centrally funded and controlled ever since. A late nineteenth-century minister of education is alleged to have reported with pride that if he went into a classroom of a given subject at the same level anywhere in the nation, all students would be turning the same page in the same book at the same time.

Throughout the nineteenth century, rigorous competitive examinations selected candidates for the grandes écoles. To sit for the examinations (concours), candidates must have completed the baccalaureate, the French secondary school certificate. Successful candidates generally studied at a few elite secondary schools in Paris with academic focus (lycées), and because a student's future rested on his performance, just as in imperial China, families were willing to invest in training for the exams. A student admitted to one of the grandes écoles received public support during three years of study; with a degree from one of the grandes écoles, his future was assured.

Candidates from provincial cities were sent to Paris lycées, viewed as better than local schools, then after graduation, to an early version of the Stanley Kaplan Educational Centers—cram schools run by Jesuit priests—in which aspiring candidates were tutored for the concours.[2] It is difficult to find out just what these exams involved; perhaps the first entry requirements for the Ecole Polytechnique provide a clue: potential students should manifest "a good behavior, attachment to republican principles" and knowledge of mathematics (Vaughan 1969, 86). Whatever their content, the exams were rigorous; during the mid-nineteenth century, it is estimated, three out of five

---

[2] Cram schools have often appeared where tests are the selection mechanism for elite institutions of higher education. Whenever and wherever they are found, these schools have manifested common characteristics: a student culture of hazing of young students by older ones; punitive discipline by strict teachers; and in the residential cram schools of past ages, a locker-room ambience.

students taking the baccalaureate exam failed (Ringer 1979, 132). Like China's literati scholars and *ronin* in Japan today, aspirants for places in France's elite schools needed supplemental training before ever trying for the grandes écoles. This is still true.

Once admitted, polytechnic students focused in depth on mathematics and physical science, along with a foreign language. Since the late nineteenth century, the curriculum has included "an initiation into other subjects relevant to understanding the modern world" (Vaughn 1969, 91).

The selection system for the grandes écoles maximized competition. Not only was rank within each class based on scores in the entry exams, but throughout the term of study, class ranking rested on performance in written course exams given every six months.[3] When they finished school, the best students got jobs with potential for interesting work and rapid advancement (Suleiman 1984, 115). Not surprisingly, nineteenth-century students in these prestigious schools were sons of aristocrats, high-status professionals, government servants, and a sprinkling of aspiring bourgeoisie (Ringer 1979, 157–172). Even with expanded scholarship aid during the late nineteenth century, three-quarters of the French population, Fritz Ringer estimates, "had almost no chance of sending their sons to any of the distinguished grandes écoles" (Ringer 1979, 179). In fact, universal state-supported secondary education did not appear in France until 1936.

The baccalaureate from a lycée was a terminal degree in France until after World War II. Nearly 4 percent of seventeen year olds held the baccalaureate in 1936, and 4.4 percent ten years later. Perhaps because of curriculum modernization during the 1930s and public support of secondary education, the proportion of seventeen year olds passing the baccalaureate exam began to go up (it reached 11.2 percent of the age cohort in 1961) (Ringer 1979, 148). Earlier generations had to pass exams in all subjects, now students can specialize. University enrollments reflect the threefold expansion in qualified candidates: in 1931, 2.9 percent of youth between ages nineteen and twenty-two were enrolled in universities; in 1961, 9.6 percent were enrolled (if the grandes écoles are included, between 11 and 12 percent) (Ringer 1979, 151–152). With universal state support of higher education since 1968, enrollments have continued to rise. By the early 1980s, about 25 percent of the age cohort between eighteen and twenty-two were enrolled in some higher educational

---

[3] Use of regular testing to determine success or failure and rank within a class spread from the Ecole Polytechnique to other educational institutions. In 1817, for example, Sylvanus Thayer, known as the "Father of West Point," borrowed from the Ecole Polytechnique its syllabus, textbooks, a teacher, and its grading system. Thayer modified Ecole grading by introducing demerits as well as positive scores. In 1821 students responded to increased discipline by setting the mess hall on fire, then pointed a cannon at Thayer's house. But apparently instruction in gunnery was not the academy's strong point; students could not make the cannon fire (Hoskin and Macve 1986, 131).

institution (Cherych 1981). Ringer and other commentators on French higher education see this expansion as a social revolution.

Yet such a two-level system, which *insures* rewards for an elite minority and offers all the others nothing but a chance to compete for jobs, creates potential for explosions such as occurred in 1968 and 1986. And some critics, for example, Joseph Ben-David, think that the selection system for elite educational institutions in France inhibits creativity. "Students receive an education that is, to a large extent, cramming. They are taught by good crammers who prepare them well to pass examinations" (Ben-David 1977, 41–42).

Genesis of the German Mandarin

Admission to higher education and to the civil service in Germany, initially elitist as in France, manifested somewhat greater equality during the eighteenth century, as increasing need for clerks led to rapid expansion of the civil service. University and civil service entry have been linked in German states since the late seventeenth century, when admission to Prussia's civil service depended on an aspirant's performance in a series of examinations. The first step, prerequisite for graduation from *gymnasium* (the academic secondary school), was an examination leading to the *abitur* certificate. Beginning in the early eighteenth century, an abitur demonstrated competence to enter Prussia's university training programs in jurisprudence and cameralistics (administration and economic management); the programs were designed to train high-level administrators.

After he completed his university studies, the aspiring bureaucrat took another set of examinations for admission to the civil service. Because placement in a post depended on available funding, qualified persons often had to wait for appointment. Meanwhile, if he could afford to, an applicant could work without salary for experience, hoping that when a post was vacated he would be appointed permanently. Or more likely, if his family's means were limited, he would take a paid job at a low level. By accumulating in-service training, he could become eligible to take an examination for a higher-level post, but for this too, he had to wait until someone died or retired.

Some historians think that the eighteenth century in Prussia was "a golden age for select men of common origin" (Fischer and Lundgren 1975, 518). During peacetime, enlisted men in the Prussian army could apply for low-level civil service jobs. If they stayed long enough they might climb a few rungs on the administrative ladder. An applicant had to be literate and know how to keep accounts. During the nineteenth century any noncommissioned officer who had served nine years (changed to twelve in 1874) had the right to claim preference for civil service clerical and accounting jobs; no doubt this was a means of social mobility (Fischer and Lundgren 1975, 521).

Beginning in the early nineteenth century, and following centralizing educational reforms in France under Napoleon, the Prussian educational system also became subject to central government control. After 1812, requirements for the secondary school-leaving examination, previously established by each school, were specified by the government, with greatest weight placed on ability to read and write Greek and Latin. Passing the exams permitted a student to enter the university, to become a mid-level civil servant, or to take exams permitting civil service entry at a higher level. For a while universities resisted centralization of secondary education standards; if students could pass a relatively easy exam set by each university faculty, universities continued to accept students without the abitur. (Private tutors had prepared aristocratic students for the exams during the eighteenth century, and the practice continued until 1834, when the abitur from the gymnasium became the only means of entry into universities) (Ringer 1979, 36). Other German states followed the Prussian model.

In the early nineteenth century, the government began to administer examinations, not only to recruit civil servants, but also to establish standards for private sector employment in such fields as pharmacy, construction, chemistry, and engineering. In fact, says Ringer (1979, 36), "there was hardly a discipline in which one or more state, or diploma examinations were not eventually established." During the nineteenth century the government opened numerous technical institutes to prepare students for these certification exams. In West Germany today, technical high schools still grant trade certificates.

Until 1906, university entrance, as well as some higher civil service exams in Germany, reflected the professoriate's conservatism. The exams stressed knowledge of high culture, especially Latin and Greek.

University professors in the German states were paid by cultural ministries throughout the nineteenth century; together with the ministerial civil servants they had trained, professors developed questions and established standards for the civil service examinations. There was only a small group of students whose families could afford to send them to a gymnasium, and among these, high rates of attrition from the impractical classical curriculum limited the number of graduates. In 1885 in Prussia, for example, 30 out of every 10,000 students went to a gymnasium, and of these, only 1.5 graduated with the abitur (Ringer 1969, 39). Thus, while entrance into the civil service at low or middle levels provided opportunities for mobility, high-level civil servants and the university professors who shaped their world view came disproportionately from the highest social class. In 1820, 42 percent of higher civil servants in Germany came from the aristocracy; in 1911, 37 percent were of aristocratic background, nearly half of them sons of officials or military officers (Mayntz 1984, 180). Privileged and generally well paid, the nineteenth-century professoriate and higher civil servants in Germany have been characterized as mandarins. The higher civil service became less attractive to educated people after 1900 when, as Germany industrialized, good jobs opened up in industry, providing an alternative career choice for university graduates.

The higher civil service in Germany is no longer the powerful force for social conservatism that it once was, but its membership, largely from middle- and upper-middle-class professional families, reflects the still-limited access to higher education in Germany. As of 1960, notes Ringer (1979, 68), "little more than 15 percent of German children reached secondary schools, about a third of those eventually earned the abitur, and 5 percent entered university level institutions." Many more West German students make it into universities now. In 1977, according to the European Cultural Foundation's Institute of Education, 19.4 percent of twenty to twenty-two year olds were being *admitted* to universities, and by 1980 about 21.4 percent of that age cohort were still *enrolled* (Cherych 1981). According to Gade (pers. com. 1986), university admissions have risen further since then; by 1987 about 30 percent of twenty to twenty-two year olds were entering universities.

Testing in England: A Departure from the Continental Model

In England, unlike France and Germany, there has not been a direct link between access to higher education and entry into the civil service. Until the Victorian era there was no civil service; ministers who were political appointees personally conducted much of the work of government, and, in general, favoritism or nepotism determined who would serve as subordinates. As King George III is alleged to have put it: "Anyone was fit to occupy any place he could manage to get" (Roach 1971, 4).

Nor did public examinations exist in Britain until the beginning of the nineteenth century. Like medieval universities on the Continent, from the twelfth century on, Oxford and Cambridge faculties conducted oral examinations of students to grant degrees of bachelor and master; the degrees certified competence to teach or work in civil administration. The universities and their colleges were relatively independent of civil government until the sixteenth century, when religious conflict in England led King James I to limit degree holders to members of the Church of England (Montgomery 1965, 5).

After the civil war, university standards declined until, by mid-eighteenth century, the average student who went up to Oxford "passed the time in the study of a novel or other entertaining work"(Montgomery 1965, 7). If the aristocracy sent its sons to the universities, it was to fill a few years with camaraderie and to inculcate conformity to class values. Instruction focused mainly on "building character" and fostering "civility" (Rothblatt 1982, 5). The venality characteristic of England's politics during the eighteenth century permeated its universities as well. Private examiners with no special qualifications conducted degree examinations, and sometimes degree requirements were measured in pounds sterling (Montgomery 1965, 6).

Merit in the Universities

Student performance standards at Cambridge never fell so low as they did at Oxford. Between 1747 and 1750 Cambridge began to publish a list of student performance on its Mathematical Tripos, with students ranked by merit. The Tripos was an oral exam, presumably named for the three-legged stool students sat on during this test. Earlier tests at Oxford and Cambridge had involved theological disputation in Latin. The Tripos, which was more a test of logical thinking than mathematical knowledge, was conducted in English (Roach 1971, 13). Within ten years, Cambridge examiners were requiring degree candidates to sit for written exams in classics as well as mathematics and theology. In 1779 its examiners enhanced meritocracy by dividing the ranked Tripos list into classes. (By then it had been awarding medals for achievement in classics for nearly thirty years.)

A shift to merit criteria in awarding Oxford degrees was recommended in the last quarter of the eighteenth century; the university implemented reforms in 1800. Aiming to judge student performance by a common standard, the university appointed public examiners for bachelor's degree candidates, and it began to publish a list of the twelve best candidates. This procedure anticipated the present honors degree system (Montgomery 1965, 6–7).

The examination system at both Cambridge and Oxford was refined during the first half of the nineteenth century; by mid-century it had largely attained its present form. Students had only one chance at degree examinations. The rank awarded a candidate by his examiners—first- or second-class honors, or ordinary (poll) degrees—followed a graduate for life. Cambridge and Oxford exams were widely recognized as tests of merit in which the country's best minds met in competition (Montgomery 1965, 8). Attending a university was no longer simply a pleasant sojourn among friends. Students wrote home about pressure, of hours spent studying, of anxiety, and even illness brought on by worry over impending exams. Among the upper-class students who attended these universities, poor performance on exams did not necessarily restrict life opportunities, but because of the honor (or stigma) associated with degree rank, the prospect of sitting for exams was intimidating. Gradually an emphasis on competitive sports helped to mitigate concern over academic competition. Some Oxford students (including Charles Darwin) dropped out. The majority who stayed took ordinary degrees. Yet with all its pressure, the system produced eminence in scholarship and in public life (Rothblatt 1982). This focus on excellence, I should note, related to *getting out* of Oxford and Cambridge. Anyone who could pay could get in. Fees ran to about 1,000 pounds a year (equivalent to 10,000 to 15,000 pounds now).

Civil Service Examinations in England

The Oxbridge examinations' merit emphasis reached beyond the universities and into public life, where it merged with intellectual currents from the Anglo-Scottish Enlightenment. During the eighteenth century the great universities at Glasgow and Edinburgh (unlike Cambridge and Oxford) were vital centers wherein scholars formulated and explored novel ideas about social organization.

Edinburgh professor of moral philosophy Adam Ferguson and his pupil Adam Smith differed from Continental thinkers who believed government should direct modernization. These scholars were convinced that mercantilist policies had negative effects on Britain's social and economic life, hence they proposed to abandon central direction. Instead of active intervention, they thought government should do the minimum. It should establish loose guidelines for action, but social forces—individual self-interest interacting with an unregulated market—should determine outcomes.

The value of individual merit was an unstated, but implicit premise of this argument. In a society organized along competitive principles, it was in the individual's interest to do as well as, or better than, his peers.

Free-market ideas became fashionable among intellectuals and merchants in England during the first quarter of the nineteenth century, popularized in good measure by Jeremy Bentham. Several of the institutions delineating the relationship between individuals and modern democratic government emerged from the fertile mind of this remarkable man: the public commission of experts, mental hospitals, humane prisons. Bentham believed that every individual is the best judge of his personal interests, whether in seeking public appointment or in any other activity, and that the collective interest is best served by allowing each person free occupational choice.

In 1827 Bentham proposed a market-oriented scheme for selecting civil servants. His method differed from procedures in France and Germany. While he thought central government was best equipped to organize and direct the examinations, Bentham's civil service tests were to be conducted in public and would be open to anyone. Questions on each subject would be published so applicants could study beforehand. To discourage fraud in administering the test, questions were to be chosen by lottery by a very young child. Here Bentham departs from merit principles governing selection of civil servants on the Continent. Each candidate who passed the test (graded by an "Examination Judiciary") had to submit a sealed bid specifying the salary he would accept; the lowest bidder in this silent auction would get the job (Montgomery 1965, 9).

Bentham's ideas appealed to a group of young intellectuals trained at Oxbridge who gained influence in the Liberal party when it split off from the Tory party in the late 1830s. The Liberals were committed to free-market principles when they gained control of Parliament in 1842; and, although they

46 Carolyn Webber

did not favor central direction, they did support civil service reform. Industrialization and growth of empire placed demands on government that the old-style political appointee was not equipped to satisfy. Following the example of the Oxbridge degree examinations, during the 1840s, a few government departments (Treasury, Privy Council) started to screen prospective appointees to high-level positions with an examination. After 1849, before anyone could buy a commission in the army or navy, he was required to demonstrate competence in English, history, geography, arithmetic, algebra, fortification, and a language (Roach 1971, 22). The exams established minimum standards for venal candidates for military office. When William Ewart Gladstone (who held a double-first honors degree from Oxford) became Chancellor of the Exchequer in 1852, he began to speak out for "competition" in government service, "as against restriction and private favour." Aiming to "apply a like principle to the Civil Service and the great government departments," Gladstone appointed Charles Trevelyan and Sir Stafford Northcote (both eminent public figures) co-chairmen of a commission to study implementation of civil service reform, especially at the highest level.

The Northcote-Trevelyan Report

The Northcote-Trevelyan report, submitted in 1854, recommended that the government aim to attract into its service "the most promising young men available by a competing examination on a level with the highest description of education in this country" (Roach 1971, 25). The report suggested different tests for clerical and high-level appointments. Good penmanship was the principal requirement for clerks, "handwriting (which is) rapid, neat, and of that even stroke which requires legible copies to be taken by pressing" (Montgomery 1965, 26). A general education in a wide range of subjects should qualify young men to apply for high-level positions. Civil service entry examinations, to be administered by an appointed board of civil service examiners, would measure competence in classics, mathematics, history, jurisprudence, political economy, modern languages, political and physical geography, and other matters. Such diverse competence, the report maintained, would insure that "the greatest and most varied amount of talent would be secured"(Roach 1971, 26). Candidates from all over the country would sit for exams in regional centers; their papers, submitted to a central office, would be sorted, then sent out to readers for grading before final assessment. The applicants finally selected should be "employed from the first upon work suited to their capacities and their education, and should be made constantly to feel that their promotion and future prospects depend entirely on the industry and ability with which they discharge their duties" (Montgomery 1965, 131).

England's disastrous military performance in the Crimea stimulated public interest in reform of civil and military administration, but opinion was far from unanimous. Some commentators dismissed the whole proposal as nothing but a schoolmaster's scheme. Others, including the Queen and opposition leader Benjamin Disraeli, believed that appointment to a high-level position required more than demonstrated merit; it entailed refined social perception—in short, aristocratic values (Roach 1971, 30).[4] Nevertheless, in 1853 Parliament did agree to implement procedures for testing candidates for the Indian Civil Service.

In 1855, Palmerston, the prime minister, established a Civil Service Commission by executive order. It administered tests for the Indian Civil Service, but it had limited authority over domestic appointments until after 1870. After 1871, when purchase of army commissions was abolished, boys wanting military careers had to pass exams to get into army and navy training schools. Britain's civil service reform had been completed by the turn of the twentieth century; all candidates for offices in the army, navy, colonial service, and domestic civil service sat for civil service examinations.

Since the tests covered more than the traditional classical curriculum, secondary schools began to teach modern subjects and some schools specialized in preparing students for specific tests. After secondary school, weak students might attend one of the "crammers" springing up to supply supplemental tutoring. Winston Churchill took the Sandhurst (Britain's equivalent of West Point) admissions exam three times before he passed. Perhaps the cram school he attended helped. In its advertisements the school claimed to have made "a scientific study of the mentality of the Civil Service Commissioners" (Montgomery 1965, 30). Overall, the best performers, who were appointed to positions with potential for greatest advancement, held honors degrees from Cambridge and Oxford. Until World War I, most high achievers in Britain's higher civil service had studied classics, and once again,

---

[4] The tension between merit and class loyalty criteria in selection of civil servants has been expressed repeatedly over the centuries. In China during the Tang dynasty (a.d. 600–900), for example, selection of high officials bypassed the civil service examinations to appoint sons of high-level mandarins. Such favoritism was justified, according to a contemporary commentator, because "from their childhood they have been accustomed to this type of function, because their eyes are used to the affairs of the court, and because the rules of palace etiquette are known to them without having to be taught, whereas a man of common birth, even if he is gifted with exceptional talent, will not necessarily be able to get used to it" (Webber and Wildavsky 1986, 61). Responding to proposed reforms in civil service recruitment procedures, a Prussian nobleman wrote in 1807: "Middle class people know only how to work, not how to govern. It is not unusual, therefore, to appoint bourgeois councilors with the prudent intent to make work easier for the noble councilors so that the latter will have time for more important matters" (Rosenberg 1958, 181).

having come from professional or aristocratic backgrounds, they were characterized as mandarins.

Secondary School Reform

During the second quarter of the nineteenth century, academic standards at Oxbridge were affecting Britain's secondary schools. By the early 1830s, schoolmasters in public schools were beginning to adapt curricula to the great universities' rising demands. The public schools taught Greek and Latin, prominent in the Oxbridge curriculum, and a secondary school's reputation came to be related to the number of its students awarded university scholarships (Wilkenson 1964, 10–11). (Colleges in the universities had independent resources for funding scholarships; most assistance went to clergymen's sons.) During the 1860s, following a report by a national government commission, the public schools started to offer modern languages and toward the end of the century, science.

The universities aimed to establish minimum standards for entering students. An Oxford entrance examination was proposed in 1837 and again in 1852. While the elite public schools did try to prepare their aristocratic students for the universities, secondary schools for middle-class youth generally had lower standards than the public schools and different curricula.

Beginning in the 1830s, measures for improving middle-class secondary education occasionally appeared. After the mid-1840s the proposals contained recommendations for screening secondary students before graduation. The method, all commentators agreed, should be an examination covering the secondary curriculum. The question was, who should administer this test?

Opinion during the 1850s did not favor government action. The great universities did have experience administering degree examinations, and reformers looked toward these wealthy institutions for help. Besides raising standards in secondary schools, examinations were needed, they argued, to identify talented sons of farmers and the middle class.

More was involved in the secondary school testing proposal, however, than raising university admission standards. The Liberal party was committed to expanding the electorate by abolishing property qualifications for voting. John Stuart Mill, who became the party's chief theorist and counselor, believed that education was the key to making disenfranchised subjects into citizens competent to make electoral choices. Government's role in improving education, he wrote, should be to enforce standards. Like modern supply-siders, Mill (1984, 210) favored payment of schools according to results:

> The true principle for the remuneration of schoolmasters of all classes and grades, wherever it is possible to apply it, is payment for results. The results of their teaching can in general, only be tested by examinations conducted by independent public

examiners; and if this examination were partly of a competitive character, extending to the pupils of all endowed middle-class schools, somewhat after the model of the Oxford and Cambridge local examinations, it might be made a basis for proportioning the remuneration of schoolmasters to the success which their pupils obtained in the examinations.

The Oxford University Locals, approved by the university's council in 1857 and introduced in 1858, were England's first public secondary school examinations (Montgomery 1965, 48). The tests covered English, history, mathematics, physical science, religious studies, and "other studies forming part of the liberal education of youth" (Montgomery 1965, 48) Cambridge University began to administer secondary school exams during the same year. As with the university degree examinations, the Cambridge and Oxford locals were highly competitive: examiners divided passing students into ordinary and ranked honors passes. Scholarship support for prospective university students rested on performance in these examinations.

The tests, weighted heavily toward religion and classics, screened out so many applicants that they provoked criticism. The Oxford local for high school seniors contained four sections—English, languages, mathematics, and physics. Students took exams in two of these subjects, plus either art or music. The English exam covered:

> English history from Bosworth Field to the Restoration and the outlines of the history of English literature during the same period; Shakespeare's *Lear* and Bacon's *Essays*, the outlines of political economy and English law (the syllabus being defined by the first book of *The Wealth of Nations* and the first volume of Blackstone's *Commentaries*) and physical, political and commercial geography. In order to pass, it was necessary for a candidate to show a fair knowledge of one of these divisions (Roach 1971, 93).

As for languages, students could be tested in either Latin, Greek, French, or German. For mathematics they had to know algebra to quadratic equations and the first four books of Euclid. In physics the test covered natural philosophy, chemistry, and vegetable and animal physiology. Students had to answer one of these sections, demonstrating "a practical acquaintance with the subject matter" (Roach 1971, 93).

Each university, not only Oxford and Cambridge, but also the new provincial universities established at Liverpool, Manchester, and Leeds, and The University of London (founded in 1836 on Benthamite principles) administered its own entrance exam. Late nineteenth-century educational reformers periodically decried the fragmented testing, but in spite of recommendations in 1868 by a national commission that central government oversee university admissions testing, each university continued to go its own way.

There was, however, agreement that the competitive ranking of the first Oxford and Cambridge locals was too much pressure for fifteen and sixteen year olds. Some educators argued that the exams fostered inequality. Since public knowledge of the number of Oxbridge admissions from a school was good publicity for that school, the schools would neglect boys with ordinary ability and push bright students who stood a good chance of passing. Others thought the high standard set by bright boys would raise performance levels throughout a school. Educators also worried that the best, and also the richest, students would prepare for the exams with tutors (Roach 1971, 98).

Public Debate over Educational Policy

The competitive merit focus in secondary and higher education did not suit everyone, even during the nineteenth century when selection procedures were most intense. In 1888, for example, several hundred professors, teachers, and citizens signed a document claiming that exams had no educational purpose. While they did not claim that cramming for exams inhibited creativity, they did think that coaching children to pass exams interfered with good teaching. Encouraging competition for scholarships, they maintained, was to train children like racehorses. Winning scholarships and high honors is *not* the chief aim of education, they said. In 1889 a German visitor commented on the competitive ethos in Britain: in examinations and in sport, he said, the English do everything by way of racing (Montgomery 1965, 256).

Anticompetitive arguments persisted, becoming stronger and more focused after 1900, as the number of students eligible for higher education increased. Teachers found it difficult to prepare students for so many different university entrance exams. And, because increasing numbers of students aimed for low- and mid-level jobs in the civil service, secondary schools had continuously to discourage good students from dropping out to study in a civil service cram school (Montgomery 1965, 65).

After passage of the Education Act of 1902, some public funding became available to secondary schools; these "direct grant" schools retained their independence as long as they reserved at least a quarter of their entrance slots for scholarship students selected by merit in public examinations. The act empowered a preexisting body, the national Board of Education, to oversee the direct grant schools, and its existence suggested a way to coordinate university entrance testing.

In 1911, a board report proposed standardized examinations for schools receiving the direct grants and for any other schools signing up for the tests. One set of exams, to be given to sixteen year olds and graded either "pass" or "credit," might permit universities to select entering students. Another series on specialized subjects given to eighteen year olds, would encourage students to expand what they knew. These recommendations, modified several times before World War I, sound like the present O and A levels, but the war inhibited change (Montgomery 1965, 69–71).

The Secondary School Examinations Council, established in 1917 to advise the Board of Education on university admissions testing, represented all the contending interests: the university examining committees, local education authorities and teachers. By 1920 the council was negotiating with university admissions officers over their entry requirements, and a few years later professional schools and the Civil Service Commission accepted the council's secondary school certificates as qualification for entry (Montgomery 1965, 71–72). Unlike university admissions procedures in France and Germany, the state was not directly involved. But by providing a forum in which all the contending interests could negotiate their concerns, just as Bentham and Mill had suggested, the government had, in effect, established minimum standards.

Public debate over educational equality in Britain since World War I has not focused on university admissions testing, but on selection of secondary school scholarship recipients. Between the wars, some local education authorities adapted the new technology of intelligence and ability testing to this task. Yet compared with the U.S., such "objective" measures of merit were slow to catch on. In the Eleven-Plus tests given to screen children for academically oriented secondary schools, as with O and A levels for school leavers and university entrants, testing authorities continued to use essay questions graded subjectively by external examiners (Sutherland 1984, chap. 9).

Not until the Education Act of 1944 was universal free public primary and secondary education offered in England. Access to universities came initially through admission to the academic secondary grammar schools at age eleven, and subsequently by passing a new set of examinations approved in 1950 to replace the preexisting tests for secondary school certificates. These G.C.E. (for General Certificate of Education) exams nationalized criteria for selection and admission to higher education, for the tests are administered by the Ministry of Education (Montgomery 1965, 148).

The tests, given at three levels—ordinary (O level) at sixteen years, advanced (A level) at eighteen, and advanced with scholarship if students stayed on a year longer—covered forty-three subjects, far more than the English, foreign languages, and mathematics tested for previously. Now a student had to pass tests granting certificates in five or six subjects, at least two at the advanced level (Ringer 1969, 218–219; Montgomery 1965, 143). These were the minimum requirements. In practice, especially as secondary and then university enrollments went up during the 1950s and 1960s, universities demanded greater specialization and higher A-level scores. Cambridge and Oxford accepted only the best applicants, those who had attained honors passes on A levels.

During the late 1950s social critics pointed to the antiegalitarian outcome of government higher education policies; they condemned as invidious the direction of public resources to the children of middle- and upper-class families who were receiving government stipends to attend universities. In 1958 Michael Young published his educational dystopia; it caricatured the socially divisive outcome of merit selection procedures for access to higher education (Young 1958). A survey published in 1957 had provided the substantiating evidence. Children of manual workers were more likely to leave secondary school at the minimum school-leaving age, it claimed, than middle-class children (Floud, Halsey and Martin 1957). These books provoked debate about national secondary-school education policy. As a consequence, the secondary-school entrance exam at age eleven was eventually abolished. Local educational authorities established comprehensive secondary schools open to all achievement levels as an alternative to the grammar schools.

As for university admissions policies, nothing much has changed. University students no longer receive public grants, but they still sit for A levels, and there is no talk of changing this mode of access to higher education. Like the nineteenth-century German quoted earlier, some commentators even claim that merit and competition are ingrained in the British national character. Perhaps because of elitism, reports Gade (pers. com. 1986), university attendance in Great Britain is lower than in France and Germany; in the early 1980s, about 13 percent of eighteen and nineteen year olds were enrolled in universities.

Elitism and Meritocracy in Japan

Testing is a national obsession in modern Japan; in no other country are college admissions tests covered on TV. The cultural stereotype of the Japanese "examination momma" is widely known in the West, and literature on Japanese testing reports student suicide as if it were, if not the normal response to failure, at least a common response. So to explore university admissions testing in modern Japan, we must first ask how these tests originated, and, next, how Japan's testing methods compare with those used to screen university applicants in France, Germany, and England.

Between the late sixteenth and mid-nineteenth centuries, government in Japan combined institutional vestiges of feudalism with centralization. The *shoguns* who gained power early in the seventeenth century curbed the warfare among local feudal notables that had been continuous during the two preceding centuries. The shoguns' centralization strategies eliminated feudal magnates' (*daimyos'*) capacity to make war by taxing away their resources, and by requiring each daimyo, accompanied by a large retinue, to live in Edo (Tokyo) for six months each year. Heavy ceremonial obligations associated with court attendance drained away whatever surplus a daimyo managed to retain after paying taxes. He could no longer afford to go to war.

Before long, deprived of their role as warriors, the *samurai*, as feudal elites were known, began to take up peaceful occupations. Confucian ethics embodying reverence for scholarship, always strong in Japan, justified action. By the mid-seventeenth century, the samurai's metamorphosis from illiterate jock to cultivated gentleman scholar was well under way.

Each daimyo established a school for samurai in the territory he governed. These schools must have been well attended, for by late seventeenth century, instead of fighting skills, knowledge of art and literature conferred status among samurai. Illiteracy connoted social stigma no matter how much land and how many retainers a samurai controlled.

Literature and the arts flourished throughout the eighteenth century. As in China, samurai fluent in Confucian classics could find administrative roles in the expanding central government. A late seventeenth-century shogun had established a school for samurai in Edo, open to any medium-rank (or higher-rank) samurai who could pay its fee (Dore 1965). A late eighteenth-century shogun increased the school's endowment, broadened its curriculum and instituted regular examinations (Dore 1965, 26). The exams followed the Chinese system. Every three years students took written tests requiring ability to interpret texts of Confucian classics and history and to compose prose in acceptable style. The local schools founded by daimyo soon copied the *bakufu* (shogunal) school exams. Yet there was a problem with exams in Japan that did not appear elsewhere. Since rank was a powerful determinant of status, it would not be proper if a low-ranking samurai were to do better on his exams than a higher-ranking classmate. My sources do not say how the schools dealt with this problem. Perhaps, since the exams were given to instill discipline, poor performance did not really matter. Although assessment of merit was not originally intended, school authorities did want to provide some incentive for students to study for these exams. By the mid-nineteenth century, in all schools, performance on end-of-year examinations determined promotion or failure. In one prefecture, a special remedial school tutored students failing secondary-school entrance exams. But standards varied among prefectures, and, in general, status still outweighed merit in determining students' rank in school (Dore 1965, 84–89). Since a samurai's education was designed to build character, performance on tests was less important to school authorities than qualities such as loyalty and respect (Dore 1965, 180).

Yet merit standards implicit in testing must have impinged on status to some extent. Toward the end of the Tokugawa era, in the mid-nineteenth century, classical knowledge was deemed inadequate to manage government, especially its finances. During the 1850s and 1860s, schools in some prefectures began to teach modern subjects in Japanese, not Chinese, and to select candidates for responsible administrative posts from among the fastest learners. Some fiefdoms provided scholarships for the best students to study at better schools in Tokyo or abroad (Dore 1965, 112, 207–209). During the 1860s (the Tokugawa regime ended in 1868) some schools accepted commoners, though not on equal terms with samurai (Dore 1965, 210–211).

The Meiji Restoration (the name given to Japan's modernizing revolution) in 1868 permitted rapid change and there were immediate efforts to impose western educational practices. In 1871 reformers created a national Ministry of Education. Echoing egalitarian ideals of the French Enlightenment and educational theories of Bentham and Mill, the ministry was to administer a national educational system open to everyone, irrespective of rank. The centralized Ministry of Education in France was the model, though as before, prefectoral governments were to provide school funding (Passin 1965, 69). Educational consultants from Europe, and especially from the U.S., introduced western pedagogical methods into newly established schools. They opened coeducational elementary schools throughout the country, and even brought in childrens' desks from Boston. The new schools used direct translations into Japanese of French, English, and U.S. textbooks; their content must have been remote from a Japanese student's experience (Passin 1965, 71). Master teachers from schools in the West came to teach these unfamiliar materials, and some normal schools were established to train native teachers.

The reformers aimed to establish eight national universities; Tokyo University was the first one opened. By 1879 it commanded nearly a third of the national budget for education and by 1881, 43 percent (Passin 1965, 73–74).

During the 1880s, conservative reaction against such rapid change inhibited further innovation. Japan was left with a mixed educational system incorporating egalitarian influences from the U.S. at the primary level and centralized and elitist European elements in its selection methods for secondary schools and universities. Elitism was consistent with admission practices in daimyo schools during the Tokugawa era.

As in Europe, the first selection came after elementary school, when students entered either vocational schools or middle schools with an academic curriculum oriented toward university entrance (Passin 1965, 103–104). The middle schools served mainly sons of former samurai. As in Europe, students had to pass examinations to get in and to pay fees. (Public education served only primary students.)

Capacity to pass secondary-school entrance exams has been construed as a measure of ability in Japan ever since. During the nineteenth century, when 80 percent of middle-school students did not attend universities, employers selected graduates from middle schools with the most difficult entrance examinations (Rohlen 1983, 58–59).

Entrance into any of the five "higher" middle schools created during the 1870s directed select (male) students into the elite national universities. [Here the model is the German abitur from a gymnasium (Rohlen 1983, 57–58)]. From the outset, competition for places in these elite schools was fierce. During the late nineteenth century, only one out of twenty-five applicants passed higher middle-school entrance exams (compared to one out of thirteen admitted to ordinary middle schools). Later (in 1929) there were seven applicants for each slot in the thirty-three elite university preparatory schools (Passin 1965, 104). By 1935, public and private universities had places for a third of middle school graduates. Less than one out of six applicants to higher middle schools passed entrance tests that year, and the imperial universities admitted only one out of two applicants. As in Germany, the more secondary education a student obtained and the better the school he attended, the greater was the competition he faced getting into the best universities. Overall, higher education served a tiny elite; less than 3 percent of elementary school graduates attended a university (Rohlen 1983, 60).

It was not so much what a student learned in these elite institutions that mattered, but the fact that he got in. Once a student entered a university, pressure relaxed; even those who did poorly seldom dropped out (Passin 1965, 107). A powerful "old boy" network emerged from the higher middle schools and the imperial universities. Japanese business and the higher civil service selected personnel exclusively from Tokyo Imperial University (*Tokaido*) during the Meiji Restoration, and although graduates of other institutions now compete with Tokaido alumni, admission to Tokaido guarantees a successful career.

Immediately following the Meiji Restoration, Japan's modernizers created a national civil service; applicants for higher civil service positions must have graduated from a university curriculum in law and administration. Selection for the civil service rested on the candidate's performance in written and oral tests.

During the late nineteenth century, law professors from Tokaido and Kyoto Imperial University made up the written civil service tests and heard the oral exams as well; often the applicant found the same questions on the civil service written exam that he had answered in university exams a few weeks before. It is not surprising, therefore, that most of those who were finally selected came from the law curricula of these two universities (Pempel 1984, 89–90).

Nevertheless, once a student had graduated from these prestigious universities, merit, rather than status criteria determined whether he entered the civil service and how rapidly he advanced. Well before World War II, nearly three-quarters of Japan's higher civil servants came from non-noble families. If anything, entry into the higher civil service has become more competitive since the war, as the number of well-qualified applicants has increased. In 1970, for example, there were 20,000 applicants for about 1,300 higher civil-service posts; by 1979, the number had increased to 60,000 applicants (Pempel 1984, 91). Senior civil servants themselves view the selection process as open and meritocratic. Although they may not come from high-status families, higher civil servants in Japan do constitute an intellectual elite. Like mandarins in Europe, they view their role as support of an abstract conception of public interest (Pempel 1984, 92).

The most significant educational change in Japan during the Meiji era, Thomas Rohlen believes, was formalization of merit criteria for admission to middle and higher middle schools and to the national universities. Talent (as measured by capacity to pass entrance exams) gained a qualified applicant admission to these institutions irrespective of social origin. Pressure on these elite institutions intensified as Japan's population expanded (Rohlen 1983, 61).

If anything, the egalitarian educational reforms introduced during the occupation of Japan after World War II have exacerbated pressure. MacArthur's educational planners abolished the higher middle schools, introduced coeducation at all educational levels, made state-supported education through secondary school compulsory, and established post-secondary institutions similar to junior colleges in the U.S.

The relatively flat income structure in prosperous modern Japan has produced a growing middle class with high aspirations. As in the U.S., Japanese parents view higher education as a child's passport into an adulthood characterized by stable income and enhanced social status. With Japan's early retirement age, low retirement salaries and minimal social security, a child's potential earning capacity is important to parents. Until very recently, parents typically moved in with the oldest son when the father retired.

Apart from career prospects generated by admission to the national universities, Japanese parents hope to benefit from public subsidies. There is no tuition at the national universities; parents pay only for living expenses, books, and supplies. In fact, there is a pluralistic system of higher education in modern Japan, with public and private institutions matching a wide spectrum of student interests and abilities. As in the U.S., each institution establishes its own admissions criteria. High school teachers typically advise students to apply to colleges whose entrance exams they are likely to pass. In the early 1980s, about 30.7 percent of eighteen and nineteen year olds were enrolled in a college or university (Cherych 1981).

Why, then, the intense, obsessive preoccupation with secondary school and college entrance exams? As outlined above, for both parents and offspring, a lot rests on admission to the best public universities.

But is failure so disgraceful that it justifies suicide? When student suicides occur, they are likely to be precipitated by repeated failure. As with civil service candidates in imperial China, a student who fails to get into his first-choice institution will study another year and try again, and perhaps again. In modern Japan these repeat candidates for admission to the public universities are called *ronin*, after low-status samurai of earlier eras. Having neither land, retainers, nor, as a consequence, a daimyo who would accept his allegiance, the ronin (like the six warriors in Kurasawa's film *The Seven Samurai*) wandered from prefecture to prefecture. Up to a third of each year's candidates for admission to Japan's elite universities are repeat performers, probably also patrons of Japan's extensive network of cram schools. Japan's rate of adolescent suicide was highest in the world during the 1950s; now it is much lower. Perhaps there are more students attending their second- or third-choice universities.

What do outsiders make of such a system? After looking at four modern Japanese high schools, including an elite boys' prep school reminiscent of the outlawed higher middle schools, Thomas Rohlen concludes that for bright students with professional parents and family support, the intellectual discipline involved in preparation for admissions tests generates behavior likely to ensure success in work-oriented modern Japan. Yet he sees in such students, successful by adult standards, an inner life distorted by the need to conform to group values. Cramming for tests leaves little time for fantasy and it inhibits creativity (Rohlen 1983, 109–110). Ronald Dore, who has written on all aspects of Japanese life, speaks of "the devastating effects" on high school curricula of the need to prepare students for college entrance tests. Yet, he reports, Japan's educators maintain that there may be some relation between Japan's recent economic success and its selection mechanism for higher education (Dore 1976, 49–50).

Conclusion

The "objective" tests given to assess student competence in the U.S. derive more from a technocratic tradition than from cultural elitism. We like to think that our way of admitting students to universities selects only for merit; objective college admissions tests presumably identify the best and the brightest students irrespective of social background.

Although the tests given to entering students in other nations also aim to assess merit, both in the past and at present, the screening methods used in France, Germany, and England have consistently selected young people, if not solely from the aristocracy, at least from professional family backgrounds. Over time, the intense focus on merit, subjectively determined by central state examiners in France, Germany, and England, has created and then perpetuated a new, occupation-based elite. Compared to the past and present university admissions testing systems I have surveyed, the SAT does not seem all that bad.

REFERENCES

Ben-David, Joseph. 1977. *Centers of Learning: Britain, France, Germany, United States.* New York: McGraw Hill.

Cherych, Ladislaw. September 1981. *Student Flows and Expenditure in Higher Education 1965–1979.* Oxford: Institute of Education, European Cultural Foundation.

Dore, Ronald P. 1965. *Education in Tokugawa Japan.* Berkeley and Los Angeles: University of California Press.

———. 1976. *The Diploma Disease, Education, Qualification and Development.* Berkeley and Los Angeles: University of California Press.

Fischer, Wolfran and Peter Lundgren. 1975. "The Recruitment of Administrative Personnel." In *The Formation of National States in Western Europe,* edited by C. Tilly, 456–561. Princeton: Princeton University Press.

Floud, Jean E., A. Halsey and J. F. M. Martin. 1957. *Social Class and Educational Opportunity,* London: William Heinemann.

Gade, Marian. 1986. Personal communication. Berkeley Center for the Study of Higher Education, University of California.

Guy, Basil. 1963. "The Chinese Examination System and France, 1569–1847." In Vol. 25 of *Studies on Voltaire and the Eighteenth Century,* edited by Theodore Besterman, 741–778. Geneva: Institut et Musée Voltaire.

Hahn, Roger. 1971. *Anatomy of a Scientific Institution, The Paris Academy of Sciences 1666–1803.* Berkeley and Los Angeles: University of California Press.

Heclo, Hugh. 1984. "In Search of a Role, America's Higher Civil Service." In *Bureaucrats and Policy Making, A Comparative Overview,* edited by Ezra N. Suleiman, 8–34. London: Holmes and Meier.

Ho, Ping Ti. 1962. *The Ladder of Success in Imperial China, Aspects of Social Mobility, 1368–1911.* New York: Columbia University Press.

Hoskin, Keith W. and Richard H. Macve. 1986. "Accounting and the Examination: A Genealogy of Disciplinary Power." *Accounting, Organizations and Society* 11(2):105–136.

King, James E. 1949. *Science and Rationalism in the Government of Louis XIV 1661–1683.* Baltimore: Johns Hopkins University Press.

Mayntz, Renate. 1984. "German Federal Bureaucrats and Administration." In *Bureaucracy and Policymaking, A Comparative Overview,* edited by Ezra N. Suleiman, 174–205. London: Holmes and Meier.

Mill, John Stuart. 1984. "Educational Endowments." In *Essays on Equality, Law and Education, Collected Works of J. S. Mill,* Vol. 21, Toronto and Buffalo: University of Toronto Press.

Montgomery, R. J. 1965. *Examinations, An Account of Their Evolution as Administrative Devices in England.* London: Longmans Green.

Passin, Herbert. 1965. *Society and Education in Japan*. New York: Teacher's College Press and East Asian Institute, Columbia University.

Pempel, T. J. 1984. "The Higher Civil Service in Japan." In *Bureaucrats and Policymaking, A Comparative Overview*, edited by Ezra N. Suleiman, 72–106. London: Holmes and Meier.

Ringer, Fritz. 1969. *The Decline of the German Mandarins*. Cambridge, MA: Harvard University Press.

———. 1979. *Education and Society in Modern Europe*, Bloomington: Indiana University Press.

Roach, John. 1971. *Public Examinations in England 1850–1900*. Cambridge: Cambridge University Press.

Rohlen, Thomas P. 1983. *Japan's High Schools*. Berkeley and Los Angeles: University of California Press.

Rosenberg, Hans. 1958. *Bureaucracy, Aristocracy and Autocracy, The Prussian Experience 1660–1815*. Boston: Beacon Press.

Rothblatt, Sheldon. 1982. "Failure in Early Nineteenth Century Oxford and Cambridge." *History of Education* 11(1):1–21.

Suleiman, Ezra M. 1984. "Bureaucracy and Politics in France." In *Bureaucracy and Policymaking, A Comparative Overview*, edited by Ezra M. Suleiman, 107–135. London: Holmes and Meier.

Sutherland, Gillian. 1984. *Ability, Merit and Measurement, Mental Testing and English Education, 1880–1940*. Oxford: Clarendon Press.

Vaughan, Michalina. 1969. "The Grandes Ecoles." In *Governing Elites, Studies in Training and Selection*, edited by Rupert Wilkenson, 74–107. New York: Oxford University Press.

Webber, Carolyn and Aaron Wildavsky. 1986. *A History of Taxation and Expenditure in the Western World*. New York: Simon and Schuster.

Wilkenson, Rupert. 1964. *Gentlemanly Power: British Leadership and the Public School Tradition*. London and New York: Oxford University Press.

Young, Michael. 1958. *The Rise of the Meritocracy 1870–2033*. London: Thames and Hudson.

Testing Companies, Trends, and Policy Issues: A Current View from the Testing Industry

John J. Fremer[1]

This chapter starts with a description of the major testing companies. Based on my observations about the nature of these companies and the people who work in testing, I then speculate on the possibilities for bringing about change in the industry. Finally, I outline trends in educational and employment testing. Included throughout the chapter are comments on policy-relevant issues that the National Commission on Testing and Public Policy might address. The chapter is divided into four main parts:

    I. Overview of the Testing Industry
    II. General Trends in Testing
    III. Trends in Educational Testing
    IV. Trends in Employment Testing

I. OVERVIEW OF THE TESTING INDUSTRY

What is the testing industry? One useful resource on this point is a Russell Sage Foundation book *Educational and Psychological Testing: A Study of the Industry and Its Practices* (Holmen and Docter 1972). Holmen and Docter divide the industry into four categories: commercial publishers (large, medium, and small); state educational testing programs; governmental testing, including civil service and military; and contract and proprietary programs.

However, there have been many changes in testing since the Holmen and Docter volume was written. For example, the book makes no mention of teacher testing, an area of much current interest. Holmen and Docter's analysis, however, can be used to make some comparisons between 1972 and 1986.

---

[1] At the time of the Planning Conference for the Commission on Testing and Public Policy, John J. Fremer was an employee of The Psychological Corporation, Harcourt Brace Jovanovich, Publishers. The author is now a Senior Development Leader in the College Board Programs Division of the Educational Testing Service. Address/telephone: ETS, Mailstop 06-E, Princeton, NJ 08541, (609) 734-5610.

The focus of this chapter is on the first two categories from Holmen and Docter's list, publishers and state programs. However, I define publishers to include not just the commercial (for profit) concerns, but also the two major nonprofit companies (the American College Testing Program and the Educational Testing Service). I do not address the important areas of civil service and military testing. Even so, this description covers a significant portion of the industry. The tests developed by the organizations discussed herein affect virtually every person attending school in our country, as well as many individuals seeking licensing or certification.[2] The companies reviewed in this chapter provide a useful context for thinking about the important testing issues that are raised in this volume.

Key Facts about Testing Industry Leaders

The following table provides a few key facts about six leaders in the testing industry. The points of information shown are rank (total testing revenues), time of entry into field, corporate status, and major testing areas. My sources are Holmen and Docter for the 1972 data, and my own armchair analysis, supplemented by interviews, for the 1986 information.

Revenues

The major testing companies have enjoyed dramatic growth in the last five years, stimulated in good part by the educational reform movement. Looking at the rank of the companies by revenue, note the following:

Rank 1:   Educational Testing Service (ETS) retains its top-ranking position over the fourteen-year span.
ETS is much larger than any of the other companies that derive their revenue primarily from managing test programs and from test sales, that is, all the large companies except National Computer Systems.

Rank 2:   Test-related work is only a part of the business activity of National Computer Systems (NCS), but I have ranked it as the second largest testing company because of its dominant role in test scoring. NCS also provides services to state testing programs

---

[2] It should be recognized, though, that a large amount of testing takes place outside the realm of the large testing companies reviewed. The GED Testing Service and the Medical College Admission Test are two major testing activities in education that are not covered. In addition, the military services test millions of men and women for selection, classification or placement, and promotional purposes. Millions more are tested in connection with licensing, certification, selection, and promotion programs directed by state and other governmental agencies and by professional associations.

and has a unit that publishes psychological/individual tests, notably the Minnesota Multiphasic Personality Inventory (MMPI). Although it has large testing revenues, the test-publishing component of NCS is significantly smaller than that of CTB/McGraw Hill, The Psychological Corporation, or The Riverside Publishing Company.

Rank 3.5: CTB/McGraw Hill and The Psychological Corporation both reported that they were the largest commercial test publisher as of December 1986. CTB/McGraw Hill has enjoyed dramatic growth since 1972 and has moved far ahead of Science Research Associates. (Science Research Associates has not kept up with the other companies.)

Rank 3.5: The Psychological Corporation was very close to CTB/McGraw Hill in total revenues as of December 1986 and may have larger test publishing revenues as of 1988. The Psychological Corporation had the most active program of acquisitions and new development of any of the major test publishing companies during the 1982–1986 period.

Rank 5: The American College Testing Program (ACT) is the fifth largest testing company and the youngest company on this list, after NCS.

Rank 6: The Riverside Publishing Company combines both book and test publishing, but the test-publishing component is large enough to rank Riverside sixth among test companies.

Other Features

Looking at other features of these six companies, note that:
•ETS and ACT are nonprofit.
•CTB/McGraw Hill, The Psychological Corporation, and Riverside are subsidiaries of large publishing companies.
•NCS is an independent, publicly held company.
•The major test revenue for all the companies comes from education.
•Two of the companies deal primarily with higher education: ETS (College Board programs as well as other higher education testing and financial aid programs), and ACT (high school to college transition and college level programs).
•Four of the companies are devoted primarily to elementary and secondary education: CTB/McGraw Hill, The Psychological Corporation, The Riverside Publishing Company, and NCS.

TABLE 1

Key Facts About Testing Industry Leaders

Rank by Testing Revenue 1972 (Holmen and Docter)	1986 (Fremer)	Company	Entry into Field	Corporate Status	Major Testing Areas
1	1	Educational Testing Service (ETS)	Founded 1947, College Board one of creators of ETS, founded 1900	Independent, Nonprofit	• College Board Programs • Graduate & Professional Admissions • Credentialing Programs • Research
Unranked	2	National Computer Systems (includes former Measurement Research Center)	NCS chartered 1968	Independent, 1962; Public Company	• Test Scoring/Machine Sales • State Testing Contracts • Psychological/Individual Tests
4	3.5	CTB/McGraw Hill	Founded 1926	Subsidiary of McGraw Hill, Public Company	• Elementary/Secondary Group Tests • Credentialing Programs
2	3.5	The Psychological Corporation (TPC)	World Book, one of companies subsumed within TPC, founded 1905; TPC founded 1921	Subsidiary of Harcourt Brace Jovanovich Publishers, Public Company	• Elementary/Secondary Group Tests • Psychological/Individual Tests • Speech/Language Tests • Business Tests • Admission Tests
Unranked	5	American College Testing Program (ACT)	Founded 1959	Independent, Nonprofit	• High School to College Transition, College Level • Credentialing Programs
5	6	The Riverside Publishing Company	Entered testing 1916	Subsidiary of Houghton Mifflin, Public Company	• Elementary/Secondary Group Tests • Psychological/Individual Tests

ETS and The Psychological Corporation

Although I present some information about all six of the companies listed, I have worked for only two of them—ETS and The Psychological Corporation. I will provide additional detail on these two companies.

Educational Testing Service

ETS is a broadly diversified testing company but does not play a significant role in elementary and secondary level testing, except for high school to college transition testing. Moreover, ETS is not a major test *publisher* at any educational level. The main business of ETS is the management of testing and financial aid programs.

Although ETS is extraordinarily open and professional in its testing, research, and service activities, it serves as a "magnet" or "lightning rod" for all criticism of testing. The document, ETS *Standards for Quality and Fairness* (available from ETS), sets forth the policies the company has adopted to ensure adherence to high standards in its testing and other activities.

ETS is an excellent source of ideas and materials for individuals interested in measurement—see, for example, *Redesign of Testing*, the report of the 1985 ETS Invitational Conference (ETS 1986). ETS is also a major center for psychometric research and applications of technology to testing.

The Psychological Corporation

The Psychological Corporation is the most diversified test publisher and was the fastest growing in the period 1982–1986, when it doubled in size. Among its well-known products are the Stanford and Metropolitan Achievement Tests, the Differential Aptitude Tests, The Wechsler Intelligence Scales, and the Miller Analogies Test.

The Psychological Corporation had fifty new and revised tests under development in December 1986, the time of the Planning Conference for the National Commission on Testing and Public Policy.

Smaller Companies

In their 1972 book, Holmen and Docter list twenty-two companies with sales from $25,000 to $1,000,000. I estimate that there are now at least thirty-five testing companies with revenues of over $1 million a year, counting test publishers (such as American Guidance Service, American Testronics, Communication Skill Builders, Consulting Psychologists Press, DLM/Teaching Resources, Institute for Personality and Ability Testing, Jastak, London House, Pro-Ed, Science Research Associates, and Western Psychological Services), firms that develop custom tests on a contract basis (such as Advanced Systems in Measurement in Evaluation, Instructional Objectives Exchange, National

Evaluation Systems, and Scholastic Testing Service), and firms that both develop tests and provide ongoing test program management services (such as Assessment Systems, Inc., and Professional Examination Services).

While some of the smaller companies, including ones listed above, have long and distinguished reputations earned by consistently excellent work, other small companies do not. The companies that do shabby work will be exposed in the long run, and will have difficulty selling products or winning new development contracts from former clients. However, competitive bidding laws and the tremendous demand for testing help to keep some companies with poor performance records in business.

Changing the Testing Industry

Although some critics of testing see so little merit in existing standardized tests that they want only to eliminate them, other critics believe the tests can be improved. What factors about the testing industry are significant in trying to effect change?

Looking first at the structure of the field, it is an industry with dominant leaders in some segments but not in others. College level testing, for example, is the province of The College Board/Educational Testing Service and of the American College Testing Program. Washington is the only state where these two companies do not handle the testing component of the high school to college transition process. (Washington conducts its own state-level, pre-college testing program.) A similar situation exists in the elementary and secondary-school testing market with respect to group administered and nationally normed ability and achievement tests. The overwhelming majority of such tests are purchased from CTB/McGraw Hill, The Psychological Corporation, or The Riverside Publishing Company.

A different situation exists, however, with employment tests. Among the large companies, The Psychological Corporation is the one with the greatest number of business testing products, but it does not dominate the field. The tests used in business settings come from a wide variety of sources and include many instruments developed by associations within a field, such as the Life Office Management Association or by industrial/organizational consulting firms who incorporate tests into their services to organizations. One testing company in the business domain, London House, is publicly owned, and its annual report for 1987 shows $7 million of revenues.

Competition is very strong throughout the testing industry. In some market segments the competition is among a small group of dominant leaders, in others, among many different potential suppliers. This atmosphere of competition provides a continuing pressure for change in order to be responsive to the needs of test users. Given this constant push to be responsive to the needs of consumers, why do critics find such a great need for change?

I believe that a partial answer lies in differences in those people who work in the testing business and those who criticize it—for example, in the different experiences with testing of these two groups of people. I will use my own experience with standardized tests as an example:

1. In grade five, I was tested in school with an individually administered IQ test and "skipped" to grade six.

2. In grade nine, I was placed in my high school's honors program on the basis of standardized ability and achievement tests.

3. In grade twelve, I won a test-based scholarship to a technical school.

4. After I had dropped out of college for a year, I received a test-based scholarship (NY State Regents) as an alternate and was encouraged to return to college (even though the award amount was only $150).

5. As a night college student applying to graduate school, I won a fellowship to attend graduate school full-time at Columbia University, Teachers College based on my undergraduate grades and my scores on the Miller Analogies Test and Graduate Record Examination (GRE).

In my own life and in the experience of nearly all the people I have worked with in the development and publishing component of the testing business, tests have opened doors, not served as barriers to important life objectives. I have had much less ongoing contact with the critics of testing than I have had with professional measurement people, but I have been struck by the number of times I have read and heard about the critics' negative personal experiences with testing. In *Citizen Nader* (McCarry 1972), for example, we read of consumer advocate Ralph Nader's bad experience with the Law School Admission Test. At conferences and hearings on testing, I have heard many accounts, often by articulate and thoughtful critics, of ways that they felt their life chances were diminished as a result of their test performance. Clearly, the makers and critics of tests bring to discussions of testing issues very different attitudes and feelings, as well as different areas of training and professional perspectives.

As I see it, there is also a poor match between many of the demands of critics and what those who use tests actually want. The standardized ability and achievement tests that are widely used in the schools are the winners of competitive battles fought over more than fifty years. While critics are correct in stating that these tests measure only a narrow range of skills, these skills are the ones that schools want measured. Moreover, in contrast to critics, most schools want tests that are intact collections of test questions, not test-item banks from which they can choose the questions for their tests.

Evaluating fairness is the area where those who make and use tests and those who criticize them disagree the most. Although there are competing definitions of fairness within the measurement community, none of the typically accepted definitions would lead to fairness as defined by many critics. A fair test, to a measurement person, is one that meets recognized professional standards in development and is administered and used appropriately. A fair test accurately describes the level of skill and knowledge that a person has developed, and measures appropriate attributes for decisions that will be based, at least in part, on the test results. Thus, where you have two groups that differ with respect to their level of skill and knowledge in a domain, the results of a fair test will reflect that difference.

Whereas my measurement analysis focuses on qualities of the test and testing process, many critics of testing focus instead on outcomes and consequences. Any *difference* in performance between two groups may be viewed as evidence that the test is unfair to the lower scoring group. One important example of score differences between groups is discussed by Michael Rebell (see Rebell, this volume)—the outcome of lower test performance by black teacher preparation candidates and the projected consequence of fewer black teachers in our schools. This outcome is often viewed as unacceptable and also as "unfair." Critics view any attempt to defend this outcome as fair, in a psychometric sense, as naive or irresponsible, or shortsighted or racist, or in a variety of other ways, but none of them positive. Of course, testers may hold similar views of the arguments forwarded by critics, regardless of the merits—psychometric or otherwise—of the arguments made about test unfairness.

If the commission could help establish better communication between testers and critics of testing, across the barriers of different experiences and different definitions of issues such as fairness, this would be a major contribution.

II. GENERAL TRENDS IN TESTING

Major Increase in Testing

All of the large companies and many of the smaller testing companies have experienced substantial increases in revenues from testing in the last five years. Consider, for example, the following revenue figures (in millions of dollars) from two of the largest educational testmakers:

	1982	1986
Educational Testing Service	$123	$190
The Psychological Corporation	25 (est.)	50 (est.)

It should be noted that The Psychological Corporation does not report financial information independent of its parent company, Harcourt Brace Jovanovich, Publishers. These figures are based on public statements rather than company reports.

In recent years, there has also been a return to testing for employment-related decisions. Not only have sales increased for a wide variety of business tests, but businesses are now asking to use tests that were dropped from test publishers' catalogues some time ago. It is clear that personnel departments and the outside consultants who work with personnel departments are reinstating testing programs for use in selection and personnel management.

Expanded Role for State-Level Agencies

The role of state agencies in educational testing has increased significantly in recent years. The states are now the most important market for group achievement and ability tests. State agencies exert an influence that goes beyond the revenue from the state testing contract. Often school districts will choose for their local test the same test adopted by the state. In this way students and teachers in a local district deal with the same standardized test at all grade levels tested.

Higher education appears to offer the same potential for an expansion of state influence in testing. The commission should study the role of state educational agencies in testing and assessment. Among the questions that might be explored: How are measurement and evaluation decisions made? How could we raise standards of practice?

Broadening of Measurement

Critics of standardized testing have frequently voiced concerns about the restricted coverage of widely used tests and about the inherent limitations of the multiple-choice format. One response to this concern has been the increased use of direct measures of writing ability. State testing programs, achievement tests developed by publishers, and major admissions testing programs have added essay tests of writing skills despite the substantial increases in scoring costs associated with this type of testing.

Other instances of broadening of test coverage include the addition of tests of critical thinking and of computer skills. The addition of an Analytical Score to the GRE General Test is another example of expanding the scope of measurement in a major program.

Interest in Professional Standards

Among the recent publications on professional testing standards are the *Standards for Educational and Psychological Testing,* published in 1985 by the American Educational Research Association (AERA), the American Psychological Association (APA), and the National Council on Measurement in Education (NCME), and the third edition of *Principles for the Validation and Use of Personnel Selection Procedures,* published by the Society for Industrial and Organizational Psychology (Division 14 of APA) in the fall of 1986.

AERA, APA, and NCME also initiated a Joint Committee on Testing Practices which is developing a Code of Fair Testing Practices in Education. The code spells out the obligations of test developers and test users to protect the rights of test takers. The American Association for Counseling and Development/Association for Measurement and Evaluation in Guidance and the American Speech-Language-Hearing Association have joined as sponsors of the joint committee. The code covers the areas of developing/selecting appropriate tests, interpreting scores, striving for fairness, and informing test takers.

The Joint Committee on Testing Practices will seek endorsement of the Code of Fair Testing from a wide variety of professional organizations and testing groups.

The *Uniform Guidelines on Employee Selection Procedures* were issued by the federal government in 1978. These guidelines and the preceding Equal Employment Opportunity Commission (EEOC) guidelines raised the level of professional practice in personnel selection and classification, a moribund area in industrial/organizational psychology until the early seventies. The *Uniform Guidelines* are being reviewed with the goal of revision, as case law has invalidated some sections, and as they do not reflect recent revisions in professional standards.

Policy Developers' Knowledge of Measurement

Whenever tests have been used in situations where important decisions are made (at least to some degree) on the basis of test scores, individuals outside the field of testing typically play dominant roles. Thus legislators, educational administrators, and judges often make decisions about test quality, test use, and test interpretation. Rarely do these individuals have training in measurement or practical experience in selecting, developing, administering, or scoring tests, or interpreting test scores.

The commission could contribute substantially to improving policy uses of tests by examining what individuals in different policy development or implementation roles need to know about testing. This is not a job that measurement experts are likely to do well on their own. As with any specialty, measurement-trained people may set unrealistically ambitious knowledge and experience goals for users and interpreters of test results. A combination of measurement-oriented and policy-oriented people who would work closely enough together to gain mutual respect and understanding could make real progress in specifying both what knowledge is needed and how it might be acquired.

Another Round of Test Criticism

Increased use of tests (especially for teacher evaluation but also for district-level and state-level comparisons) has brought another round of criticism of testing. Although much of this criticism is poorly informed and adversarial in nature, some critics have raised important questions about the nature and consequences of testing.

One of the criticisms that has received widespread press coverage is that standardized school achievement tests give a misleading and overly optimistic view of student performance. Cannell (1987) argues that an implausible proportion of school districts and students are being described as "above average" in test performance; for example, all the states with statewide testing programs report that they are higher than the national average. Cannell argues that more realistic assessments of student performance would serve as a needed impetus for improved education.

Some of the current criticism of testing is presented within the legal or adversarial model of discourse. To someone trained in the research-oriented, scholarly approach to determining the "truth" of an issue, the adversarial model is both foreign and fundamentally offensive. In the scholarly model, I must help those who disagree with me so that, working together, we can see whose hypothesis or theory best accounts for the available evidence. I have a responsibility to report my misgivings about my approach as well as any data that do not fit my theory. Those who disagree with me will do the same. Otherwise they are not researchers or scholars. The legal or adversarial model presents evidence selectively, citing only those points that support an argument, and ignoring, or even misrepresenting, data that do not support the advocate's position.

Since I believe that the legal and the measurement professions are equally interested in fairness and quality in testing, perhaps the commission could help build bridges between the scholarly and adversarial approaches to testing, as both affect policy development. I have surely overstated the case for the scholarly approach. Nevertheless, I feel that a difference in approach does exist and presents serious communication problems. The commission might investigate what methods exist for bringing more of the openness of the ideal scholar to legal analyses of testing. Similarly, how can informed advocacy working within the operational world of testing contribute to the improvement of testing? Are there additional ways for advocates to work directly with those who select, develop, publish, and use tests to achieve improvement of tests and testing practices?

III. TRENDS IN EDUCATIONAL TESTING

Expansion of Basic Testing Programs

As might be inferred from my earlier statements about increased revenues for the major testing companies and about growth in state-level testing programs, the basic school testing program employing a publisher's standardized achievement test battery is a feature of every school district in the U.S. Some districts use specially developed objectives-referenced tests, but the nationally normed test continues to be dominant and its use has grown in recent years. School districts have added additional grade levels to their existing programs. Whereas state programs employ achievement tests, particularly in reading, mathematics, and writing, local district programs frequently incorporate science or social studies testing and a group ability test.

The use of individually administered tests for students experiencing academic problems continues to be the established practice of school districts. In California, however, there has been a controversial ruling on test use. In *Larry P. v. Riles* , a September 25, 1986 Order Modifying Judgment (No. C-71-2270 RFP) prohibits the use of IQ tests with black students in California schools. School districts cannot use intelligence tests in the assessment of black pupils referred for special education services. This disturbing development shows the inability of test-making and test-using professionals to communicate effectively about the value of test-based information.

As California school district professionals develop various ways of adapting to the *Larry P. v. Riles* case, the commission might look at methods to improve the communication between advocates and the educational professionals who select, develop, and use tests.

Teacher Competency Testing

The expansion of teacher testing has been a dramatic national trend. The testing of preservice teachers appears to be widely accepted, but the testing of inservice teachers remains controversial.

Three aspects of the public discussion about teacher testing seem noteworthy to me. First there is a clear tendency to look at teacher competency broadly, so that assessment is only one element along with the recruitment, training, and ongoing professional development of teachers. Secondly, the discussion of alternatives to existing teacher tests seems extremely broad in scope. There is substantial willingness to increase both testing time and expense, if doing so will significantly affect the quality of testing. States appear quite willing, for example, to accept the use of combination approaches that employ knowledge and skill testing supplemented by classroom observations. Finally, as mentioned earlier, profound issues of social and educational values are at stake in the discussions of the consequences of balancing a variety of different excellence and equity issues. We want to support appropriate standards of professional competence, but we also want to attract and retain good teachers from each of the subpopulations that make up the school population.

National Indicators Movement

The national indicators movement is an effort to employ a broad set of educational indicators, not limited to standardized tests, to discover which educational practices, staffing patterns, etc., are effective. Where problem areas are identified, steps would then be taken to remedy these problems. One feature of the movement is its strong emphasis on relating student achievement to what actually occurs within the school program. Significant attention is being given to ways that the National Assessment of Educational Progress could play an expanded role in evaluating the effectiveness of elementary and secondary education in the U.S.

The broad support the national indicators movement has received at the state level is striking. In August 1986, the National Governors' Association released a report called *Time for Results: The Governors' 1991 Report for Education*. Here are two quotes from *Education Week*'s coverage of the Governors' report. The first deals with why governors are so interested now in education:

> Most governors here gave two reasons for their collective interest in schooling. First, education accounts for a rising proportion of most state budgets. Second, the public is making the connection between better schools and the ability of their state and the nation to compete economically.

The second quote concerns the public commitments made by the governors:

> To keep in focus on education, the governors' association has committed itself to work with the E.C.S. (Education Commission of the States) and the Council of Chief State School Officers for the next five years to produce an annual progress report on what each state is doing to carry out the recommendations in its 1991 report.

The national indicators movement could be an opportunity for close cooperation among local, state, and federal education agencies to minimize the amount of testing required and to maximize the information available to each educational level. It could also be the arena for territorial battles and faultfinding that undermine the attempt to collect reliable and consistent data across states and over time. Perhaps the commission could use the activities of this movement and its actual progress to help to understand the forces that shape testing in the service of public policy objectives.

Direct Measurement of Writing

I noted earlier the introduction of essay tests of writing ability as a general example of broadening the measurement of skills in testing programs. I want to note here the extraordinary extent of this interest in essay testing. Within national testing programs I can point to the following examples:

•The College Board reintroduced an essay into the English Composition Test.

•The Law School Admission Test added a writing sample to be graded by law schools.

•The National Teacher Examinations added a writing test.

•The Medical College Admission Test has included an essay test, on a trial basis, in the battery.

•The Test of English as a Foreign Language carried out experimental work on the possible use of a writing test.

In addition, both state assessment programs and commercially developed achievement batteries have added essay tests of writing ability. This major development clearly demonstrates that testing procedures can and will change when those who select and purchase tests make their needs clear. Little is accomplished, however, when test publishers prepare products that schools ought to want but do not.

Subject Matter Testing

Recent years have seen a dramatic increase in the use of the subject matter tests in the College Board's Advanced Placement Program. This development appears to be related both to a general growth in high school subject matter testing—evidenced by state-mandated subject matter testing, as in California—and to a desire to set challenging standards for high school students.

As is frequently the case in this field, the impact of a nationally available testing program, Advanced Placement, is matched by development work at commercial test publishers. Both CTB/McGraw Hill and The Riverside Publishing Company offer subject matter tests. The commercial publishers' tests, however, are not major sellers, perhaps because of content coverage variation in high school courses.

Increased Interpretation by Test Program Developers

Test developers and test program administrators are taking on a greater role in the interpretation of test information for their users. The National Assessment of Educational Progress has been a leader in this area, employing interpretive press conferences, extended commentaries on test results, and the use of proficiency scales to add meaning to test results.

State assessment staff and test publishers have introduced narrative reports in a related effort to add meaning to test results. People like test reports that are in everyday language rather than in tables of numbers. Also, narrative reporting can influence what stands out in test data. States and school districts have found that they must provide a context for test results or else reporters will draw their own inferences, possibly quite inaccurate ones. If you do not provide a context when you report test information, you cannot really complain about the inferences that are drawn.

One element of increased interpretation of results can be closer linking of testing and instruction. To accomplish this goal, information about educational programs must be collected in a way that can be related to student performance data.

Increase in Test Preparation Material

The last few years have seen substantial growth in test preparation materials and services. The companies that develop tests, both the nonprofit and the commercial publishers, have expanded their publications about tests. Moreover, test disclosure legislation has led to the availability of a large number of previously administered test forms for tests such as the Scholastic Aptitude Test (SAT).

Test-coaching schools for national admissions tests, both those affiliated with national companies and those offered only in local communities, have also grown. Even though such coaching is likely to have little effect on student test scores, it is clear that the courses have very strong appeal to students and their families. We have also seen strong positive reaction to the initial versions of computerized test preparation materials. Harcourt Brace Jovanovich's Computer SAT, for example, was a bestseller in the educational software domain.

What are the benefits and disadvantages of this emphasis on test preparation? Who does and who does not have access to test preparation of various types? Is the motivational effect of preparing for a specific test and paying for the privilege leading to significant learning? How is the regular school program being affected? How much coaching is enough? Perhaps the commission could help formulate the questions that should be asked about test preparation activities and then could propose answers to these questions.

Computer Applications to Educational Testing

The last few years have seen computer usage extend beyond the psychometric domain to the realm of test content, test administration, local scoring, and test interpretation. Word processing, production, and data analysis capacities are now widely available within testing companies. Even quite sophisticated applications of computer adaptive testing are readily obtainable, permitting the development of computer-delivered tests tailored to each test taker. Very precise results are available immediately upon completion of a test; it takes only about half the time a paper-and-pencil test takes and requires no separate scoring. Computerized adaptive testing must be the wave of the future, right? Yes, but the key word here is *future*. At this time, computer tests are not widespread. Perhaps this is because student time is not highly valued. Perhaps it is because it is so handy to test students in groups with paper-and-pencil tests. Whatever the reason, I do not expect paper-and-pencil tests to disappear soon. As far as I know, there is no bestselling computer test yet, and until there is one, I do not anticipate a shift in usage or development across many educational tests.

One development to watch, however, may be the growth in student learning about computers and, as a consequence, of test making in this area. I have noted the following:

•The 1986 National Assessment of Educational Progress included computer competence among the areas tested.

•The Northwest Regional Education Laboratory distributed a pool of computer-literacy items.

•The Psychological Corporation has published the *Computer Competence Tests*.

Perhaps increased student knowledge about computers will lead to the increased use of computers to test other aspects of student knowledge and skill.

Possible New Generation of Tests

Although the trends in educational testing that I have reviewed are important to test publishers, I do not see them as having as much relevance for policy as another development, one about which I am very optimistic. This is the possibility of starting over in the area of ability and aptitude testing. By this I mean building a new generation of tests founded on the theory that student skills and abilities can be learned and developed. This shift in orientation could help us break away from the aptitude/achievement distinction. Instead, as we look at human ability, we need to describe, measure, and report results in a way that encourages test takers and test users to continue to develop skills. We need to de-emphasize classification testing, deciding who is a snail and who is a bluebird, and to emphasize testing for the purpose of developing each person's abilities.

IV. TRENDS IN EMPLOYMENT TESTING[3]

Substantial Attention to Job Success Criteria

Job performance is multidimensional. There is no "ultimate criterion." Performance can be divided into several aspects, such as "can do" (job proficiency), "will do," and "does do" (motivational and attitudinal aspects such as tenure and attendance). More attention is being paid to methods and findings of job analysis to identify important characteristics of jobs for the development of criterion measures for selection and training. More attention is being paid to the methods and content of performance assessment. Examples are job knowledge tests, work samples, ratings of all kinds (task performance, job performance, work habits, and attitudes) by various groups of people (supervisors, peers, subordinates, clients), and archival records.

Impact of Validity Generalization

The validity generalization movement has substantially increased opportunities for test publishers in employment testing. There have been meta-analyses of hundreds, if not thousands, of criterion-related validity studies. Validity (correlation) coefficients have been corrected for sampling error, range restriction, criterion unreliability, and have been cumulated across studies. The overwhelming conclusion is that for normal populations, cognitive ability tests predict job proficiency criteria reasonably well in most jobs. Cognitive tests appear to be more valid for jobs that are more cognitively demanding.

The limitation is that unexplained criterion variance remains. Also, other aspects of job performance, such as attrition and turnover, are not well predicted by cognitive tests.

Use of Tests of Typical Performance

Tests of typical performance look at what people are likely to do rather than what they are capable of doing. These instruments include measures of vocational interests, biographical information or biodata, and personality tests.

---

[3] Dr. Hilda Wing was a major contributor to this section. She was an employee of The Psychological Corporation, San Diego, California, at the time that she provided assistance.

They are used to predict the noncognitive aspects of job performance such as longevity, satisfaction, and other motivational outcomes. The premise of these measures is that the best predictor of future performance is past performance.

There is potential controversy with such measures. The questions included in them must be job-related to avoid being too intrusive. They need to be focused on normal populations, not pathological ones. Two current and controversial applications are these:

1. Some clinical personality tests, such as the Minnesota Multiphasic Personality Inventory, are being used in selection for high-stress occupations such as nuclear power plant operator, air-traffic controller, and police work. Such tests may have an unacceptably high rate of "false positives," that is, indicating that a problem may exist when there is none.

2. Many companies are using "honesty testing" to predict employee theft and pilferage. The measures look like biodata or personality tests. This area is very problematical, as the criterion is difficult to evaluate in a psychometrically acceptable manner. A frequent criterion in such research has been a polygraph test, which itself has significant problems. While polygraphs may have some utility in detecting prior commission of crime, they have much less utility, if any at all, in predicting who will commit a crime.

Use of Computers

Two aspects of computer use are important in employment testing. The first is the sheer operational advantage of quick, efficient assessment and scoring of evaluations of people, for selection, classification, diagnosis, training, and so on. One future prospect is the embedding of personal assessment into computerized human resource management systems. Such systems will improve current practice for many companies, and enable acceptable practice by other companies that currently do not have the resources to adhere to the best professional practices.

The second important aspect is the improvement in the scientific technology behind test computerization, specifically, item response theory and certain areas of cognitive psychology. Computers will continue to expand and improve assessment in ways we can barely envision.

Utility Analysis

There has been increased concern with estimating the dollar value of improved productivity on the job as a result of particular personnel practices, especially selection methods that rely on testing. A variety of different approaches are being investigated and explored. The procedures date back to a classic work by Cronbach and Gleser of the 1960s; the past five years or so have seen increased attention to this area.

Concerns about Fairness

Because of the increasing emphasis on productivity in the last five years, issues of fairness and equity in employment testing have received less attention. However, these issues remain vital areas in research and practice. Two active concerns are gender and racial bias in prediction, as well as the issue of comparable worth.

There is also concern with making sure that the test serves the test taker as well as other parties involved in test use. Concern about test misuse remains. Fair tests and responsible test use represent the best personnel practices, as they will help to match job applicants to the jobs for which they are best suited.

V. CLOSING STATEMENTS

In this chapter, I have described the major testing companies, their governance, and their major areas of activity. I have pointed out that testing is a field with growing and successful companies. I have also described trends in testing and have indicated those that seem to me to have significant policy implications. This is an excellent time to provide guidance to those of us who work in testing. Our field is doing very well, and, even though we have critics, we have more supporters than we have had in years. We do not want to see our products misused, and we are open to ideas to help avoid misuse.

REFERENCES

Cannell, John J. 1987. *Nationally normed elementary achievement testing in America's public schools: how all fifty states are above the national average.* Beckley, WV: Friends for Education.

Committee to Develop Standards for Educational and Psychological Testing of the American Educational Research Association, The American Psychological Association, and The National Council on Measurement in Education. 1985. *Standards for educational and psychological testing.* Washington, DC: American Psychological Association. (Known as APA *Standards*).

Educational Testing Service. 1986. *The redesign of testing for the 21st century.* Princeton, NJ: Educational Testing Service.

Equal Employment Opportunity Commission, Civil Service Commission, Department of Labor, Department of Justice. 1978. Uniform guidelines on employee selection procedures. *Federal Register* 43 (166) 38290-38315.

Holmen, Milton G. and Richard F. Docter. 1972. *Educational and psychological testing: A study of the industry and its practices.* New York: Russell Sage Foundation.

McCarry, Charles. 1972. *Citizen Nader.* New York: Saturday Review Press.

Society for Industrial and Organizational Psychology, Inc. 1987. *Principles for the validation and use of personnel selection procedures.* 3d. ed. College Park, MD: Author.

II

TESTING AND THE LAW:
TITLE VII AND THE FEDERAL GUIDELINES

Employment Testing and Title VII of the Civil Rights Act of 1964

Patrick O. Patterson[1]

I. INTRODUCTION

Long before employment testing became a matter of concern to civil rights law and lawyers, psychologists and social scientists knew that certain kinds of tests disproportionately screened out minorities and women. The standard texts on psychological testing have recognized for many years that as groups, blacks, Hispanics, and other minorities generally do not perform as well as Anglos on standardized tests and other selection criteria that emphasize verbal skills and mastery of the dominant culture.[2] They have also recognized that women, as a group, generally do not perform as well as men on tests that emphasize certain mechanical and physical skills.[3]

While questions of causation and remediation continue to be contested, there is no longer any serious doubt as to the existence of these longstanding patterns of differential test performance.[4] As stated in the report on testing issued in 1982 by the National Research Council and the National Academy of Sciences:

> The salient social fact today about the use of ability tests is that blacks, Hispanics, and native Americans do not, as groups, score as well as do white applicants as a group. When candidates are ranked according to test score and when test results are a

---

[1] The author presented this paper in December 1986, on behalf of the Lawyers' Committee for Civil Rights Under Law and the NAACP Legal Defense and Educational Fund, Inc., to the Planning Conference for the National Commission on Testing and Public Policy. Subsequent developments in the law are noted at the conclusion of the paper. The author wishes to acknowledge the valuable advice and assistance of Richard T. Seymour of the Lawyers' Committee and Barry L. Goldstein of the NAACP Legal Defense Fund.

[2] See A. Anastasi, *Psychological Testing* 343-45 (5th ed. 1982); L. Cronbach, *Essentials of Psychological Testing* 383 (4th ed. 1984).

[3] *Id.*

[4] See, for example, Haney, "Employment Tests and Employment Discrimination: A Dissenting Psychological Opinion," 5 *Indus. Rel. L.J.* 1, 26-27 and n.131 (1982); Hunter and Schmidt, "Ability Tests: Economic Benefits Versus the Issue of Fairness," 21 *Indus. Rel.* 293, 294 (1982); Lerner, "Employment Discrimination: Adverse Impact, Validity, and Equality," 1979 *Sup. Ct. Rev.* 17, 41-42.

determinant in the employment decision, a comparatively large
fraction of blacks and Hispanics are screened out. . . .

So long as the[se] groups . . . continue to have a relatively high
proportion of less educated and more disadvantaged members
than the general population, those social facts are likely to be
reflected in test scores. That is, even highly valid tests will have
adverse impact.[5]

With the enactment of Title VII of the Civil Rights Act of 1964,[6] the law
and lawyers began to recognize this serious social problem as a civil rights
problem, and they began to develop legal strategies and principles to solve it.[7]
This paper traces the development of the law of employment testing under
Title VII, and it outlines some of the important legal issues that remain
undecided.

II. THE DEVELOPMENT OF TITLE VII TESTING LAW

Title VII of the Civil Rights Act of 1964, as amended, prohibits discrimination in
public and private employment on the basis of race, color, religion, sex, and
national origin.[8] In the more than twenty years that have passed since the
enactment of Title VII, courts and enforcement agencies have resolved
thousands of claims asserting that the use of tests or other employee selection
procedures has resulted in unlawful discrimination. In the process of resolving
these claims, the courts and agencies have developed—and are continuing to
develop—legal principles under Title VII governing the use of tests and other
selection procedures for hiring, promotion, and other employment decisions. A
complete discussion of the historical development of those principles is

---

[5]   Committee on Ability Testing, National Academy of Sciences/National Research
Council, *Ability Testing: Uses, Consequences, and Controversies* 143, 146 (1982)
("NAS/NRC Report on Ability Testing"). *Cf. Brunet v. City of Columbus*, 41 E.P.D. para.
36,498 (S.D. Ohio 1986) (physical test and mechanical reasoning test administered to
firefighter applicants had an adverse impact on women); *Burney v. City of Pawtucket*,
559 F. Supp. 1089 (D. R.I. 1983) (physical agility requirements and police academy
physical training program had an adverse impact on female police officer applicants);
Berkman v. City of New York, 536 F. Supp. 177 (E.D. N.Y. 1982), *aff'd*, 705 F.2d 584 (2d Cir.
1983) (physical test administered to firefighter applicants had an adverse impact on
women).

[6]   42 U.S.C §§2000e *et seq.*

[7]   See Cooper and Sobol, "Seniority and Testing Under Fair Employment Laws: A
General Approach to Objective Criteria of Hiring and Promotion," 82 *Harv. L. Rev.* 1598,
1638-41 (1969); Note, "Legal Implications of the Use of Standardized Ability Tests in
Employment and Education," 68 *Colum. L. Rev.* 691, 692-95 (1968).

[8]   42 U. S. C. §§2000e-2(a)-(d)

beyond the scope of this paper.[9] However, some knowledge of how Title VII testing law has developed will be helpful in understanding what it has become.

Statutory Language and Legislative History

The doctrinal development of Title VII testing law has focused on two subsections of the statute: §703(a), which prohibits "discrimination;"[10] and §703(h), which provides an exception for "professionally developed ability tests" that are not "designed, intended, or used to discriminate."[11]

The language of §703(a) originated as an amendment by the House Judiciary Committee to H.R. 7152,[12] the Kennedy Administration's omnibus 1963 civil rights bill.[13] The language of this section today is essentially the same[14] as the language reported by the House Judiciary Committee in 1963[15]

---

[9]   For other discussions of the development of legal principles governing employment testing under Title VII, see Gold, "Griggs' Folly: An Essay on the Theory, Problems, and Origin of the Adverse Impact Definition of Employment Discrimination and a Recommendation for Reform," 7 *Indus. Rel. L.J.* 429 (1985); Haney, "Employment Tests and Employment Discrimination: A Dissenting Psychological Opinion," 5 *Indus. Rel. L.J.* 1 (1982); Booth and Mackay, "Legal Constraints on Employment Testing," 29 *Emory L.J.* 121 (1980); Note, "*The Uniform Guidelines on Employee Selection Procedures:* Compromises and Controversies," 28 *Cath. U. L. Rev.* 605 (1979). See also B. Schlei and P. Grossman, *Employment Discrimination Law* 80-205 (1983).

[10]   Section 703(a)(1) states it is unlawful for an employer "to fail or refuse to hire. . . any individual, or otherwise to discriminate against any individual with respect to his compensation, terms, conditions, or privileges of employment, because of such individual's race, color, religion, sex, or national origin." 42 U.S.C. §2000e-2(a)(1). Section 703(a)(2) states that it is unlawful for an employer "to limit, segregate, or classify his employees or applicants for employment in any way which would deprive or tend to deprive any individual of employment opportunities or otherwise adversely affect his status as an employee, because of such individual's race, color, religion, sex, or national origin." 42 U.S.C. §2000e-2(a)(2). Other provisions of Title VII use similar language to describe unlawful practices of labor organizations and employment agencies. See 42 U.S.C. §§2000e-2(b), 2(c), and 2(d).

[11]   Section 703(h) states that, "[n]otwithstanding any other provision of this [title], it shall not be an unlawful employment practice for an employer . . . to give and to act upon the results of any professionally developed ability test provided that such test, its administration or action upon the results is not designed, intended, or used to discriminate because of race, color, religion, sex, or national origin." 42 U.S.C. §2000e-2(h).

[12]   See H.R. Rep. No. 570, 88th Cong., 1st Sess. (1963).

[13]   See Vaas, "Title VII: Legislative History," 7 *B.C. Indus. and Com. L. Rev.* 431, 433 (1966).

[14]   The language prohibiting "discrimination" was amended on the House floor by the addition of "sex" as a protected class. 110 Cong. Rec. 2577-84, 2718, 2720-21 (1964). See Vaas, "Title VII: Legislative History," 7 *B.C. Indus. and Com. L. Rev.* 431, 439-42 (1966). Section 703(a) was later amended by the Equal Employment Opportunity Act of 1972,

and passed by the House in 1964.[16] The House bill, however, did not contain §703(h) or any other provision that specifically addressed testing. That provision was added by the "Tower Amendment" in the Senate.[17]

In the first years after enactment of Title VII in 1964, the congressional purpose underlying these sections became a subject of debate in the courts and law journals. Everyone agreed that the statute prohibited the intentionally discriminatory use of employment tests, but most courts[18] and writers[19] rejected the view that Title VII imposed any requirement that tests be related to the jobs for which they were used. Some courts[20] and writers,[21] on the other hand, had begun to recognize that many tests had an adverse impact on blacks and other minorities, and they argued that Title VII prohibited the use of tests that were not sufficiently job related. Bits and pieces of evidence bearing on the elusive question of legislative purpose were marshalled on both sides of this debate. Although there was some evidence that Congress had meant to

---

Pub. L. No. 92-261, expressly to prohibit discrimination against "applicants for employment" as well as discrimination against "employees." See H.R. Rep. No. 92-238, 92d Cong., 1st Sess. 30 (1971); S. Rep. No. 92-415, 92d Cong., 1st Sess. 43 (1971). Congress regarded this amendment as "declaratory of existing law." Id. at 43. See also Subcommittee on Labor, House Committee on Labor and Public Welfare, Legislative History of the Equal Employment Opportunity Act of 1972 1849 (1972) (section-by-section analysis of H.R. 1746 as reported by the Conference Committee citing, inter alia, Phillips v. Martin-Marietta Corp., 400 U.S. 542 [1971]). The language of §703(a) otherwise remains the same today as when it was first enacted in 1964.

[15] See H.R. Rep. No. 914, 88th Cong., 1st Sess. 10 (1963).

[16] See 110 Cong. Rec. 2804 (1964).

[17] 110 Cong. Rec. 13492-505, 13274 (1964). See Vaas, supra note 14, at 449.

[18] See, for example, Griggs v. Duke Power Co., 292 F. Supp. 243, 250 (M.D. N.C. 1968), aff'd in part and rev'd in part, 420 F.2d 1225 (4th Cir. 1970), rev'd, 401 U.S. 424 (1971).

[19] See, for example, M. Sovern, Legal Restraints on Racial Discrimination in Employment 73 (1966); Rachlin, "Title VII: Limitations and Qualifications," 7 B.C. Indus. and Com. L. Rev. 473, 486-90 (1966).

[20] See United States v. H.K. Porter Co., 296 F. Supp. 40, 78 (N.D. Ala. 1968); Dobbins v. Electrical Workers Local 212, 292 F. Supp. 413, 433-34, 439 (S.D. Ohio 1968).

[21] See, for example, Cooper and Sobol, "Seniority and Testing Under Fair Employment Laws: A General Approach to Objective Criteria of Hiring and Promotion," 82 Harv. L. Rev. 1598, 1649-54 (1969); Note, "Legal Implications of the Use of Standardized Ability Tests in Employment and Education," 68 Colum. L. Rev. 691, 706-11 (1968).

enact a job-relatedness standard,[22] many statements in the legislative record seemed to suggest the opposite conclusion.[23]

1966 EEOC *Guidelines*

In 1966, the Equal Employment Opportunity Commission (EEOC)—the agency created by Congress to enforce Title VII[24]—reviewed the legislative history and decided to adopt the job-relatedness standard in its first *"Guidelines on Employment Testing Procedures."*[25] These *Guidelines* stated in part that

> [t]he Commission . . . interprets "professionally developed ability test" to mean a test which fairly measures the knowledge or skills required by the particular job or class of jobs which the applicant seeks, or which fairly affords the employer a chance to measure the applicants' ability to perform a particular job or class of jobs. The fact that a test was prepared by an individual or organization claiming expertise in test preparation does not, without more, justify its use within the meaning of Title VII.[26]

The 1966 EEOC *Guidelines*, like the early court decisions suggesting a job-relatedness standard, did not distinguish between those tests that did and those that did not have an adverse impact on minorities. Through its experience in investigating and attempting to conciliate complaints of employment discrimination, the EEOC "began to notice a pattern of test useage [sic] which was excluding minorities without serving any job related purpose or

---

[22]   See *supra* note 21.

[23]   See Gold, "Griggs' Folly: An Essay on the Theory, Problems, and Origin of the Adverse Impact Definition of Employment Discrimination and a Recommendation for Reform," 7 *Indus. Rel. L.J.* 429, 489-578 (1985).

[24]   See 42 U.S.C. §2000e-4 and 5.

[25]   EEOC *Guidelines on Employment Testing Procedures*, reprinted in CCH Empl. Prac. Guide para. 16,904 (1967).

[26]   *Id.*

business need. . . ."[27] When the EEOC responded by adopting the 1966 *Guidelines*, it focused not on the question of whether a particular test had an adverse impact, but rather "on the employer's actual job needs and the reasonableness of the test in measuring those needs."[28] Instead of treating adverse impact as a preliminary inquiry that must be made with respect to a particular test before the question of job-relatedness would arise, the 1966 *Guidelines* appeared to regard *every* test as suspect under Title VII and to require that *all* tests be job related.[29]

The 1966 EEOC *Guidelines*, based on the recommendations of "a panel of outstanding psychologists"[30] whose report was issued along with the *Guidelines*, endorsed the *Standards for Educational and Psychological Tests and Manuals* (APA *Standards*), which had been adopted earlier in 1966 by the

---

[27] Robertson, *A Staff Analysis of History of EEOC Guidelines on Employee Selection Procedures* 15 (1976) (unpublished report submitted to the General Accounting Office by Peter C. Robertson, Director, Federal Liaison, Equal Employment Opportunity Commission, August 1976) (on file with the author). This report further states that:

> Very early in its operations EEOC discovered that employers were utilizing discriminatory employment testing which had proved to be a major barrier to minority advancement. Written findings of probable cause that these tests were discriminatory formed the basis of early conciliation attempts, but employers who disagreed with EEOC's perception of discrimination refused to conciliate. An *ad hoc* approach left the impression that individual conciliators were taking a personal position that . . . the tests were discriminatory and had to be eliminated. This was replaced with a formal institutionalized position in which the policymakers defined agency policy through Commission Guidelines. . . .

> When EEOC began to notice a pattern of test useage [sic] which was excluding minorities without serving any job related purpose or business need[,] it consulted with experts in the design and study of mechanisms to identify employee capability. Specifically, EEOC asked a panel of psychologists to advise it with respect to issues relating to the development, introduction and administration of test of aptitude and/or ability in industrial settings as related to problems of employment discrimination. . . .

Id. at 14-15 (footnotes omitted). See also Blumrosen, "Strangers in Paradise: *Griggs v. Duke Power Co.* and the Concept of Employment Discrimination," 71 *Mich. L. Rev.* 59, 59-60 (1972) (EEOC officials "knew that many companies had introduced tests in the 1950s and early 1960s when they could no longer legally restrict opportunities of blacks and other minority workers and that the tests had proved to be major barriers to minority advancement").

[28] Cooper and Sobol, *supra* note 22, at 1654.

[29] *Id.* But *cf.* Cooper and Sobol *supra* note 22 at 1664-65.

[30] *Id.*

American Psychological Association and other professional organizations concerned with testing standards and practices.[31] The EEOC offered not only its *Guidelines* but also the APA *Standards* to employers as "a scientifically sound, industrially-proven, and equitable basis for matching manpower requirements with human aptitudes and abilities."[32] Over the next twenty years, the professional standards of psychologists—including subsequent versions of the APA *Standards*[33] as well as the *Principles for the Validation and Use of Personnel Selection Procedures* ("Division 14 Principles") adopted by the APA's Division of Industrial-Organizational Psychology (Division 14)[34]—have remained influential in shaping Title VII testing law and agency guidelines.

1970 EEOC *Guidelines*

In 1970, the EEOC issued new guidelines that were described by one of their drafters as "a more detailed version of the [1966] guidelines. . . ."[35] In fact, the 1970 *Guidelines*[36] departed from the 1966 *Guidelines* in a number of significant respects, including the adoption of far more specific and technically complex validation standards.[37] The most fundamental change in the 1970 *Guidelines*, however, was the EEOC's explicit adoption of the concept of adverse impact as part of the inquiry to be made in determining compliance with Title VII.

---

[31]   American Psychological Association, American Educational Research Association, and National Council on Measurement in Education, *Standards for Educational and Psychological Tests and Manuals* (1966).

[32]   1966 *Guidelines*. In 1968 and 1969, respectively, the Department of Labor's Office of Federal Contract Compliance, see 33 Fed. Reg. 11392 (1968), and the Civil Service Commission, see FPB Supp. 335.1 (1969), issued their own testing guidelines.

[33]   American Psychological Association, American Educational Research Association, National Council on Measurement in Education, *Standards for Educational and Psychological Tests* (1974); American Educational Research Association, American Psychological Association, National Council on Measurement in Education, *Standards for Educational and Psychological Testing* (1985). (Known as APA *Standards.)*

[34]   Division of Industrial-Organizational Psychology, American Psychological Association, *Principles for the Validation and Use of Personnel Selection Procedures* (1975); Division of Industrial-Organizational Psychology, American Psychological Association, *Principles for the Validation and Use of Personnel Selection Procedures: Second Edition* (1980) ("Division 14 Principles").

[35]   Blumrosen, *supra* note 27, at 60 n.5.

[36]   EEOC *Guidelines on Employee Selection Procedures*, 35 Fed. Reg. 12333 (1970), codified at 29 C.F.R. §§1607.1 *et seq.* (1970).

[37]   *Id.*, §§1607.4-1607.8. The 1970 *Guidelines* continued to rely on the APA *Standards*. *Id.*, §1607.5.

According to the 1970 *Guidelines*, the Commission had detected a
decided increase in total test usage and a marked increase in
doubtful testing practices which, based on our experience, tend to
have discriminatory effects. In many cases, persons have come to
rely almost exclusively on tests as the basis for making the
decision to hire, transfer, [or] promote . . . , with the result that
candidates are selected or rejected on the basis of a single test
score. Where tests are so used, minority candidates frequently
experience disproportionately high rates of rejection by failing to
attain score levels that have been established as minimum
standards for qualification.

It has also become clear that in many instances persons are using
tests as the basis for employment decisions without evidence that
they are valid predictors of employee job performance. . . . A test
lacking demonstrated validity (i.e., having no known significant
relationship to job behavior) and yielding lower scores for classes
protected by Title VII may result in the rejection of many who
have necessary qualifications for successful work performance. [38]

In keeping with these findings, the 1970 *Guidelines* adopted an
expansive definition of the term "test,"[39] and they defined "discrimination" as

[t]he use of any test which *adversely affects* hiring, promotion,
transfer or any other employment or membership opportunity of
classes protected by Title VII . . . unless: (a) the test has been
validated and evidences a high degree of utility . . . , and (b) the
person giving or acting upon the results of the particular test can
demonstrate that alternative suitable hiring, transfer or
promotion procedures are unavailable for his use.[40]

The 1970 EEOC *Guidelines* thus abandoned the apparent view of the 1966
Guidelines that Title VII required every test to be job related; they provided

---

[38] *Id.*, §1607.1(b)

[39] ". . . . [T]he term 'test' is defined as any paper-and-pencil or performance measure
used as a basis for any employment decision. . . . This definition includes, but is not
restricted to, measures of general intelligence, mental ability and learning ability;
specific intellectual abilities; mechanical, clerical and other aptitudes; dexterity and
coordination; knowledge and proficiency; occupational and other interests; and
attitudes, personality or temperament. The term 'test' includes all formal, scored,
quantified or standardized techniques of assessing job suitability including, in addition
to the above, specific qualifying or disqualifying personal history or background
requirements, specific educational or work history requirements, scored interviews,
biographical information blanks, interviewers' rating scales, scored application forms,
etc." *Id.*, §1607.2.

[40] *Id.* (emphasis added).

instead that, at least in the absence of intentional discrimination,[41] an inquiry into job-relatedness or validation would be appropriate only after it was determined that the use of a test had an adverse impact on a protected group.[42]

Griggs v. Duke Power Company

The 1970 EEOC *Guidelines* did not put an end to the debate over the proper application of Title VII to employment tests. In 1971, the issue found its way to the Supreme Court in the case of *Griggs v. Duke Power Co.*,[43] which became not only the most important testing case ever decided under Title VII, but "the most important court decision in employment discrimination law."[44]

The employer in *Griggs* had required applicants for all jobs in its higher paying departments (including the Coal Handling, Operations, and Maintenance Departments) to have a high school diploma and to receive satisfactory scores on two standardized aptitude tests—the Wonderlic Personnel Test and the Bennett Mechanical Comprehension Test. Although the employer had not adopted these requirements for the *purpose* of discriminating against black applicants, both requirements had the *effect* of "render[ing] ineligible a markedly disproportionate number of Negroes . . . ,"[45] and neither requirement was "shown to bear a demonstrable relationship to successful performance of the jobs for which it was used."[46] Indeed, the record showed that the requirements had been adopted "without meaningful study of their relationship to job-performance ability. Rather, a vice president of the company testified, the requirements were instituted on the company's judgment that they generally would improve the overall quality of the work force."[47]

---

[41]   See *Id.*, §1607.11 ("Disparate Treatment").

[42]   In 1971, the Office of Federal Contract Compliance adopted additional testing guidelines which endorsed an adverse impact interpretation of Executive Order 11246. See 36 Fed. Reg. 19307 (1971). In 1972, the Civil Service Commission adopted new testing guidelines which, while stating a policy of nondiscrimination, did not mention adverse impact analysis. See 37 Fed. Reg. 12984 (1972).

[43]   401 U.S. 424 (1971).

[44]   B. Schlei and P. Grossman, *supra* note 9, at 5.

[45]   401 U.S. at 429.

[46]   *Id.* at 431.

[47]   *Id.*

In a sweeping opinion authored by Chief Justice Burger,[48] the Supreme
Court unanimously endorsed the adverse impact interpretation of Title VII
that had been adopted by the EEOC:

> Congress has now provided that tests or criteria for employment
> or promotion may not provide equality of opportunity only in the
> sense of the fabled offer of milk to the stork and the fox. On the
> contrary, Congress has now required that the posture and
> condition of the job seeker be taken into account. It has—to resort
> again to the fable—provided that the vessel in which the milk is
> proffered be one all seekers can use. The Act proscribes not only
> overt discrimination but also practices that are fair in form, but
> discriminatory in operation. The touchstone is business necessity.
> If an employment practice which operates to exclude Negroes
> cannot be shown to be related to job performance, the practice is
> prohibited.[49]

* * *

> The facts of this case demonstrate the inadequacy of broad and
> general testing devices as well as the infirmity of using diplomas
> or degrees as fixed measures of capability. History is filled with
> examples of men and women who rendered highly effective
> performance without the conventional badges of accomplish-
> ment in terms of certificates, diplomas, or degrees. Diplomas and
> tests are useful servants, but Congress has mandated the
> common-sense proposition that they are not to become the
> masters of reality.[50]

The Court in *Griggs* found that the 1966 EEOC *Guidelines*—a s
"elaborated" in the 1970 *Guidelines*[51]—were "entitled to great deference" by
the courts: "Since the Act and its legislative history support the Commission's
construction, this affords good reason to treat the *Guidelines* as expressing the
will of Congress."[52] Thus, the Court joined the EEOC in holding that, under Title
VII, an employer may not use a test that has an adverse impact on a protected
group unless the employer can prove that the test "bear[s] a demonstrable
relationship to successful performance of the jobs for which it [is] used."[53]

---

[48]   See B. Woodward and S. Armstrong, *The Brethren* 122-23 (1979).

[49]   401 U.S. at 431.

[50]   *Id.* at 433.

[51]   *Id.* at 434 n.9.

[52]   *Id.* at 434.

[53]   *Id.* at 431.

Echoing the principles underlying the *Guidelines*, the *Griggs* opinion repeatedly emphasized that Title VII, in seeking "to achieve equality of employment opportunities and remove barriers that have operated in the past to favor an identifiable group of white employees over other employees,"[54] was not limited to a prohibition of intentional discrimination:[55]

> [G]ood intent or absence of discriminatory intent does not redeem employment procedures or testing mechanisms that operate as "built-in headwinds" for minority groups and are unrelated to measuring job capability. . . .

> Congress directed the thrust of the Act to the *consequences* of employment practices, not simply the motivation. More than that, Congress placed on the employer the burden of showing that any given requirement must have a manifest relationship to the employment in question.[56]

The Equal Employment Opportunity Act of 1972

Some have argued that the *Griggs* decision misread the language and purpose of Title VII; the legislative history available to the Court at the time of the *Griggs* decision, according to this argument, showed that Congress meant to prohibit only intentional discrimination, not to regulate tests or other practices that had an adverse but unintended impact on minorities or women.[57] As noted above, the legislative evidence as to what Congress intended in 1964 was at best inconclusive.[58] Soon after the Court decided *Griggs*, however, Congress disposed of any lingering doubts by enacting the Equal Employment Opportunity Act of 1972.[59]

The 1972 Act amended Title VII in a number of respects and extended its coverage to federal, state, and local government employment. The House and Senate committee reports on this legislation expressly recognized and approved the interpretation of Title VII that had been developed by the EEOC

---

[54]   *Id.* at 429-30.

[55]   The Supreme Court has suggested, but has never decided, that the adverse impact standard of *Griggs* might be limited to claims under §703(a)(2), and that §703(a)(1) might prohibit only intentional discrimination. See *General Electric Co. v. Gilbert*, 429 U.S. 125, 137 and n.13 (1979).

[56]   *Id.* at 432 (emphasis in original).

[57]   See Gold, *supra* note 23, at 489-578; Lyons, "An Agency with a Mind of Its Own: The EEOC's Guidelines on Employment Testing," 17 *New Perspectives* 20 (1985).

[58]   See *supra* notes 18-23.

[59]   Pub. L. No. 92-261, 86 Stat. 103 (1972).

in its guidelines and had been endorsed by the Supreme Court in *Griggs*. The report of the House Committee on Education and Labor stated in part:

> Employment discrimination, as we know today, is a far more complex and pervasive phenomenon [than previously believed]. Experts familiar with the subject generally describe the problem in terms of "systems" and "effects" rather than simply intentional wrongs. The literature on the subject is replete with discussions of the mechanics of seniority and lines of progression, perpetuation of the present effects of earlier discriminatory practices through various institutional devices, and testing and validation requirements. . . . A recent striking example was provided by the U.S. Supreme Court in its decision in *Griggs v. Duke Power Co*. . . . where the Court held that the use of employment tests as determinants of an applicant's job qualification, even when nondiscriminatory and applied in good faith by the employer, was in violation of Title VII if such tests work a discriminatory effect in hiring patterns and there is no showing of an overriding business necessity for the use of such criteria.[60]

The report of the Senate Committee on Labor and Public Welfare included similar language,[61] and additionally directed the federal Civil Service Commission

> to develop more expertise in recognizing and isolating the various forms of discrimination which exist in the system it administers. . . The Commission should not assume that employment discrimination in the Federal Government is solely a matter of malicious intent on the part of individuals. It apparently has not fully recognized that the general rules and procedures that it has promulgated may in themselves constitute systemic barriers to minorities and women. Civil Service selection and promotion techniques and requirements are replete with artificial requirements that place a premium on "paper" credentials. Similar requirements in the private sectors of business have often proven of questionable value in predicting job performance and have often resulted in perpetuating existing patterns of discrimination (see e.g. *Griggs v. Duke Power Co.*). The inevitable consequence of this kind of a technique in Federal employment, as it has been in the private sector, is that classes of persons who are socio-economically or educationally disadvantaged suffer a heavy burden in trying to meet such artificial qualifications.

---

[60] H.R. Rep. No. 92-238, 92d Cong., 1st Sess. 8 (1971) (footnote and citations omitted).

[61] See S. Rep. No. 92-415, 92d Cong., 1st Sess. 5 (1971).

It is in these and other areas where discrimination is institutional, rather than merely a matter of bad faith, that corrective measures appear to be urgently required. For example, the Committee expects the Civil Service Commission to undertake a thorough re-examination of its entire testing and qualification program to ensure that the standards enunciated in the *Griggs* case are fully met.[62]

Thus, in enacting the Equal Employment Opportunity Act of 1972, Congress unequivocally ratified the interpretation of Title VII that had been adopted by the EEOC in its guidelines and by the Supreme Court in *Griggs*.

Albemarle Paper Company v. Moody

The early guidelines, the *Griggs* opinion, and the 1972 statutory amendment sketched in the broad outlines of Title VII testing law. The Supreme Court's 1975 decision in *Albemarle Paper Co. v. Moody*[63] provided some of the finer details.

The Court in *Albemarle* began by reaffirming its holding in *Griggs*: "Title VII forbids the use of employment tests that are discriminatory in effect unless the employer meets 'the burden of showing that any given requirement [has] . . . a manifest relation to the employment in question.'"[64] The Court noted that the employer's burden of justification arises only after the complaining party "has shown that the tests in question select applicants for hire or promotion in a racial pattern significantly different from that of the pool of applicants."[65] The opinion went on to state that, even if the employer meets its burden of showing that its tests are job related, the complaining party may still prove a violation of Title VII by showing "that other tests or selection devices, without a similarly undesirable racial effect, would also serve the employer's legitimate interest in 'efficient and trustworthy workmanship.'"[66]

Like the employer in *Griggs*, the employer in *Albemarle* required applicants for jobs in higher paying lines of progression in an industrial plant to obtain minimum scores on two standardized "general ability tests"[67]—the Beta Examination and the Wonderlic Test. There was little or no dispute that

---

[62] *Id.* at 14-15.

[63] 422 U.S. 405 (1975).

[64] *Id.* at 425, quoting *Griggs v. Duke Power Co.*, 401 U.S. 424, 432 (1971).

[65] *Id.*

[66] *Id.*, quoting *McDonnell Douglas Corp. v. Green*, 411 U.S. 792, 801 (1973).

[67] *Id.* at 427.

the use of these tests had an adverse impact on blacks.[68] The Court's opinion therefore focused primarily on the issue of job-relatedness. Restating the view expressed in Griggs that the EEOC *Guidelines* were entitled to great deference, the Court in *Albemarle* concluded that

> [t]he message of these [1970] *Guidelines* is the same as that of the *Griggs* case—that discriminatory tests are impermissible unless shown, by professionally acceptable methods, to be "predictive of or significantly correlated with important elements of work behavior which comprise or are relevant to the job or jobs for which candidates are being evaluated."[69]

Drawing upon those *Guidelines* and the 1966 and 1974 APA *Standards*, and expressing its skepticism about a validation study conducted by a party to litigation on the eve of trial,[70] the Court in *Albemarle* set forth a relatively detailed and technical critique of several aspects of the employer's validation evidence.[71]

First, the Court criticized the "odd patchwork of results" demonstrated by the employer's concurrent criterion-related validity study. The study found significant correlations between test scores and job performance for some jobs but not for others; since there was no analysis of the jobs involved, the Court found "no basis for concluding that 'no significant differences' exist among the lines of progression, or among distinct job groupings within the studied lines of progression. Indeed, the study's checkered results appear to compel the

---

[68]   Until 1964, the company had a formal policy of racially segregating the lines of progression. By 1971, a study of 105 incumbent employees in relatively high ranking jobs included 101 whites and 4 blacks. 422 U.S. at 429 n.25.

[69]   422 U.S. at 431, quoting 1970 EEOC *Guidelines*, 29 C.F.R. §1607.4(c).

[70]   "It cannot escape notice that Albemarle's study was conducted by plant officials, without neutral, on-the-scene oversight, at a time when this litigation was about to come to trial. Studies so closely controlled by an interested party in litigation must be examined with great care." 422 U.S. at 433 n.32.

[71]   Chief Justice Burger dissented from this part of the Court's opinion on the ground that the majority's analysis was "based upon a wooden application of the EEOC *Guidelines*." 422 U.S. at 451. The Chief Justice complained that, unlike the 1966 EEOC *Guidelines* approved in *Griggs*, the 1970 *Guidelines* "relate[d] to methods for *proving* job relatedness; they interpret no section of Title VII and are nowhere referred to in its legislative history. Moreover, they are not federal regulations which have been submitted to public comment and scrutiny as required by the Admininstrative Procedure Act. Thus, slavish adherence to the EEOC *Guidelines* regarding test validation should not be required." *Id.* at 452 (emphasis in original; footnote omitted).

opposite conclusion."[72] Second, noting the possibility of bias,[73] the Court disapproved the study's use of vague and subjective supervisory ratings as performance measures.[74] Third, the Court found fault with the study's focus on job groups near the top of the lines of progression, rather than on the entry level jobs. The Court endorsed the view of the 1970 EEOC *Guidelines* that performance measures should be based on higher level jobs only where the employer can show that "new employees will probably, within a reasonable period of time and in a great majority of cases, progress to a higher level."[75] Finally, the Court noted that the study "dealt only with job-experienced, white workers; but the tests themselves are given to new job applicants, who are younger, largely inexperienced, and in many instances nonwhite."[76] Relying on both the APA *Standards* and the EEOC *Guidelines*, the Court indicated that validation studies should focus on persons similar to those with whom the tests are used, and that differential validity studies should be done on minority and nonminority groups wherever technically feasible.[77]

Although the Supreme Court has reaffirmed and applied the basic principles of *Griggs* and *Albemarle* in a number of subsequent cases,[78] the opinion in *Albemarle* remains the Court's most detailed discussion to date of Title VII's job-relatedness requirement.

Uniform Guidelines on Employee Selection Procedures

By the time Congress amended Title VII in 1972, the EEOC, the Civil Service Commission, and the Department of Labor each had its own separate set of employment testing guidelines.[79] The existence of potentially conflicting guidelines had by then become a matter of concern to enforcement agencies, employers, unions, civil rights groups, and others. In response to such

---

[72] 422 U.S. at 432, quoting 1970 EEOC *Guidelines*, 29 C.F.R. §1607.4(c)(2).

[73] *Id.* at 432-33 and n.30, quoting 1970 EEOC *Guidelines*, 29 C.F.R. §§1607.5(b)(3) and (4).

[74] Supervisors were told to "determine which ones [employees] they felt irrespective of the job that they were actually doing, but in their respective jobs, did a better job than the person they were rating against." 422 U.S. at 433.

[75] *Id.* at 434, quoting 1970 EEOC *Guidelines*, 29 C.F.R. §1607.4(c)(1).

[76] *Id.* at 435.

[77] *Id.* at 435, quoting 1966 APA *Standards*, para. C5.4, and 1970 EEOC *Guidelines*, 29 C.F.R. §1607.5(b).

[78] See *International Brotherhood of Teamsters v. United States*, 431 U.S. 324 (1977); *Dothard v. Rawlinson*, 433 U.S. 321 (1977); *New York City Transit Authority v. Beazer*, 440 U.S. 568 (1979); *Connecticut v. Teal*, 457 U.S. 440 (1982).

[79] See *supra* notes 32 and 42.

concerns, in 1972 Congress established the Equal Employment Opportunity Coordinating Council and charged it with responsibility for developing and implementing uniform enforcement policies.[80] The agencies thereafter intensified efforts they had previously undertaken to develop a single set of uniform guidelines on employee selection procedures, but they were unable to accomplish this goal. In 1976, after several years of unsuccessful efforts, three of these agencies—the Department of Justice, the Department of Labor, and the Civil Service Commission—reached agreement and issued the Federal Executive Agency Guidelines on Employee Selection Procedures ("FEA Guidelines").[81] The EEOC, disagreeing with some provisions of the "FEA Guidelines," then reissued its own 1970 *Guidelines*.[82]

Despite substantial discord among the agencies on a number of issues during this period, there was complete agreement as to the correctness and applicability of the basic principles enunciated by all the agencies in their previous guidelines, approved by the Supreme Court in *Griggs* and *Albemarle*, and reaffirmed by Congress in the Equal Employment Opportunity Act of 1972. The agencies agreed that Title VII prohibits selection procedures that have an adverse impact unless those procedures are shown to be job related; they agreed that statistical evidence should be maintained by employers and should be used to determine adverse impact; and they agreed that job-relatedness should be shown by professionally acceptable methods. The disagreements among the agencies did not concern these fundamental principles, but centered instead on the details of their implementation—that is, the types of statistical analyses that should be used in assessing adverse impact, and the technical details of the validity studies necessary to demonstrate job-relatedness.[83]

More than a year later, after further debate and negotiation, all the agencies finally reached agreement and jointly published a proposed draft of the *Uniform Guidelines on Employee Selection Procedures* in December 1977.[84] The agencies also published a notice of proposed rulemaking, solicited

---

[80]   See 42 U.S.C. §2000e-14.

[81]   41 Fed. Reg. 51737 (1976).

[82]   41 Fed. Reg. 51984 (1976).

[83]   See Booth and Mackay, *supra* note 9, at 124-40; Note, *The Uniform Guidelines on Employee Selection Procedures: Compromises and Controversies*, *supra* note 9, at 607-10.

[84]   42 Fed. Reg. 65542 (1977). Before publishing this proposed draft, the enforcement agencies circulated an earlier draft and obtained comments from representatives of state and local governments, psychologists, private employers, and civil rights groups. See *"Uniform Guidelines*, Supplementary Information: Analysis of Comments," 43 Fed. Reg. 38292 (1978).

written comments, and held a public hearing and meeting at which testimony was given by representatives of private industry, state and local governments, labor organizations, civil rights groups, and psychologists.[85] After considering the written comments submitted by more than two hundred organizations and individuals, the testimony elicited at the public hearing and meeting, and the views expressed in informal consultations,[86] the EEOC, the Civil Service Commission (now the Office of Personnel Management), and the Departments of Justice, Labor, and the Treasury revised the proposed draft and adopted the *Uniform Guidelines* in September 1978.[87]

The *Uniform Guidelines* state that they "are designed to provide a framework for determining the proper use of tests and other selection procedures."[88] They are "built upon court decisions, the previously issued guidelines of the agencies, and the practical experience of the agencies, as well as the standards of the psychological profession," and they are "intended to be consistent with existing law."[89]

Section 3 of the *Uniform Guidelines* restates the *Griggs-Albemarle* interpretation of Title VII, which underlies all the remaining provisions: "The use of any selection procedure which has an adverse impact . . . will be considered to be discriminatory and inconsistent with these guidelines, unless the procedure has been validated."[90] Section 4 contains record-keeping provisions[91] and methods for determining whether a selection procedure has an adverse impact.[92] Under section 6, employers "may choose to utilize

---

[85] See "Notice of Proposed Rulemaking," 42 *Fed. Reg.* 65542 (1977); "Notice of Issues of Particular Interest for Public Hearing and Meeting," 43 *Fed. Reg.* 11812 (1978); "*Uniform Guidelines*, Supplementary Information: Analysis of Comments," 43 Fed. Reg. 38292-93 (1978).

[86] See "*Uniform Guidelines*, Supplementary Information: Analysis of Comments," 43 Fed. Reg. 38292-93 (1978).

[87] See 43 Fed. Reg. 38312 (1978) (EEOC); 43 Fed. Reg. 38310 (1978) (Civil Service Commission [Office of Personnel Management]); 43 Fed. Reg. 38311 (1978) (Department of Justice); 43 Fed. Reg. 38314 (1978) (Department of Labor); 43 Fed. Reg. 38309 (1978) (Department of the Treasury). The *Uniform Guidelines* are codified in 29 C.F.R. §1607 (EEOC); 5 C.F.R. §300.103(c) (Civil Service Commission [Office of Personnel Management]); 28 C.F.R. §50.14 (Department of Justice); 41 C.F.R. §60-3 (Department of Labor). This paper will use the EEOC codification in 29 C.F.R. §1607 for citations to the *Uniform Guidelines*.

[88] 29 C.F.R. §1607.1B.

[89] 29 C.F.R. §1607.1C.

[90] 29 C.F.R. §1607.3A.

[91] 29 C.F.R. §§1607.4A-B.

[92] 29 C.F.R. §§1607.4C-E.

alternative selection procedures in order to eliminate adverse impact."[93] Thus, when an employer finds that its selection procedures have an adverse impact, it has two options under the *Uniform Guidelines:* Either validate the procedures, or eliminate the impact.[94] An employer choosing to validate its procedures will find general standards for criterion-related, content, and construct validity studies in section 5.[95] More detailed technical standards for validity studies are set forth in section 15.[96] Additionally, under section 3B a validity study "should include . . . an investigation of suitable alternative selection procedures and suitable alternative methods of using the selection procedure which have as little adverse impact as possible."[97]

The *Uniform Guidelines* have remained in effect since their adoption in 1978.[98] Several provisions of the *Guidelines*, however, have been challenged on grounds that they are inconsistent with Title VII case law or incompatible with accepted professional standards and practices. Some of those provisions are discussed in the remainder of this paper.

III. CURRENT ISSUES IN TITLE VII TESTING LAW

The purpose of this part of the paper is to outline some of the important legal issues that are currently before courts and administrative agencies. The discussion will be suggestive, not exhaustive.

The legal principles that have developed and are developing under Title VII continue to generate a good deal of controversy, much of which in recent years has focused on the provisions of the *Uniform Guidelines*. Section 3A of those *Guidelines* states the fundamental principle, drawn from the Supreme Court's decisions in *Griggs* and *Albemarle*, that "[t]he use of any selection procedure which has an adverse impact . . . will be considered to be discriminatory . . . unless the procedure has been validated."[99] Although this

---

[93]   29 C.F.R. §1607.6A.

[94]   See *Bushey v. New York State Civil Service Commission*, 733 F.2d 220, 224-28 (2d Cir. 1984), *cert. denied*, 105 S. Ct. 803 (1985).

[95]   29 C.F.R. §1607.5.

[96]   29 C.F.R. §1607.15.

[97]   29 C.F.R. §1607.3B.

[98]   The enforcement agencies have subsequently issued "Questions and Answers to Clarify and Provide a Common Interpretation of the *Uniform Guidelines on Employee Selection Procedures.*" See 44 Fed. Reg. 11996 (March 2, 1979); 45 Fed. Reg. 29530 (May 2, 1980).

[99]   29 C.F.R. §1607.3A. This principle, in one form or another, has been incorporated in testing guidelines that have been issued at least ten times, by five different federal agencies, through two Democratic and two Republican administrations. The 1966 EEOC

principle was called into question for a time by EEOC Chairman Clarence Thomas,[100] it does not at present seem to be seriously disputed.[101] However, many other questions remain concerning the content and meaning of Title VII testing law. As discussed below, those questions often focus on claims that provisions of the *Uniform Guidelines* are inconsistent with Title VII or incompatible with accepted professional standards and practices.[102]

The Griggs Principle and Subjective Procedures

For some years after the Supreme Court approved the disparate impact interpretation of Title VII in *Griggs*, many courts took an expansive view of its application, holding that adverse impact could be shown in a variety of ways

---

Guidelines and the 1968 OFCC Guidelines—which appeared to require validation even in the absence of adverse impact—were issued during the Johnson administration. See *supra* notes 25-32. The 1970 EEOC *Guidelines* and the 1971 OFCC Guidelines were issued during the Nixon administration. See *supra* notes 35-42. The 1976 FEA Guidelines were issued by the Department of Justice, the Department of Labor, and the Civil Service Commission during the Ford administration. See *supra* note 81. The 1970 EEOC *Guidelines* were also reissued in 1976 during the Ford administration. See *supra* note 82. And the 1978 *Uniform Guidelines* were issued by the EEOC, the Civil Service Commission, and the Departments of Justice, Labor, and the Treasury during the Carter administration. See *supra* notes 84-98.

[100] Mr. Thomas argued in 1985 that the *Uniform Guidelines* reflected a "fundamentally flawed approach to enforcement of the anti-discrimination statutes," and announced that he therefore intended to propose major substantive revisions of the *Guidelines*. Office of Management and Budget, *Regulatory Program of the United States Government* at 523 (Aug. 8, 1985) (Statement of Clarence Thomas). At that time, Mr. Thomas expressed the view that the *Guidelines* were "founded on the premise that but for unlawful discrimination, there would not be variations in the rates of hire or promotion of people of different races, sexes, and national origins." *Id.* at 526. He also stated that the *Guidelines* "seem[ed] to assume some inherent inferiority of blacks, Hispanics, other minorities, and women by suggesting that they should not be held to the same standards as other people, even if those standards are race- and sex-neutral." *Id.*

[101] After the House Committee on Education and Labor held hearings on Mr. Thomas's proposals, and after the Senate Committee on Labor and Human Resources rejected the nomination of the chief architect of those proposals to the office of EEOC General Counsel, Mr. Thomas announced—during Senate consideration of his own renomination as Chairman of the EEOC—that modification of the *Uniform Guidelines* was no longer a major goal for him.

[102] See GAO Report, *Uniform Guidelines on Employee Selection Procedures Should Be Reviewed and Revised* (FPCD-82-26) (1982) ("1982 GAO Report"); Ad Hoc Group on Uniform Selection Guidelines, *A Professional and Legal Analysis of the Uniform Guidelines on Employee Selection Procedures* (1981) ("Ad Hoc Group Analysis"); Equal Employment Advisory Council, *Employee Selection: Legal and Practical Alternatives to Compliance and Litigation* (2d ed. 1986) ("EEAC Analysis").

and that disparate impact theory could be applied to a wide range of employment practices and systems. In determining adverse impact, courts variously considered—sometimes in the same case—differences in passing rates, failure rates, and selection rates, as well as statistics showing underutilization of minorities or women in comparison to the applicant pool, the general population, and differing conceptions of the relevant labor market.[103] And courts routinely applied the *Griggs* principle not only to paper-and-pencil tests and educational requirements but also to multicomponent selection systems and to subjective employment criteria.[104]

More recently, however, the Supreme Court has suggested a more restrictive approach, both to the kinds of evidence that might be required to prove adverse impact,[105] and to the kinds of employment practices that might be subject to challenge under a disparate impact theory.[106] Some lower courts have responded to these suggestions by more closely scrutinizing evidence offered to prove adverse impact, and by holding that disparate impact theory does not even apply when a multistep selection process or an individual subjective criterion has an adverse impact. According to these cases, the most prominent of which is the Fifth Circuit's decision in *Pouncy v. Prudential Life Insurance Co.*,[107] the *Griggs* disparate impact interpretation of Title VII applies only "when an employer has instituted a specific procedure, usually a selection criterion for employment, that can be shown to have a causal connection to a class-based imbalance in the work force."[108] Other kinds of selection procedures and other employment practices—even if they have substantial

---

[103] See B. Schlei and P. Grossman, *supra* note 9, at 98-100 and cases cited therein; Lerner, *supra* note 4, at 21-39; Booth and Mackay, *supra* note 8, at 142-51.

[104] See B. Schlei and P. Grossman, *supra* note 9, at 162-205 and cases cited therein.

[105] See *New York City Transit Authority v. Beazer*, 440 U.S. 568, 583-87 (1979) (statistics showing disproportionate percentage of minority employees referred for suspected use of narcotics and disproportionate percentage of minorities receiving methadone maintenance in public programs held insufficient to show that employer's policy against employment of methadone users had an adverse impact).

[106] See *Furnco Construction Corp. v. Waters*, 438 U.S. 567, 575-76 and nn.7-8 (1978) (*McDonnell Douglas* standard, rather than *Griggs-Albemarle* standard, applied where case "did not involve employment tests . . . or particularized requirements such as . . . height and weight specifications . . . , and it was not a 'pattern or practice' case").

[107] 668 F.2d 795 (5th Cir. 1982).

[108] *Id.* at 800.

adverse impact and even if they are not job related—will not violate Title VII unless they are shown to be intentionally discriminatory.[109]

The *Uniform Guidelines*, on the other hand, include subjective criteria within their broad definition of "selection procedures,"[110] and they apply disparate impact analysis to all "tests and other selection procedures which are used as a basis for any employment decision."[111] A number of courts, agreeing with the position of the *Guidelines* on this question, have rejected the restrictive approach of Pouncy and similar cases on the ground that it would encourage employers to use subjective criteria and multicomponent selection processes having an unjustified adverse impact. These courts have held that disparate impact analysis applies not only to specific, objective, facially neutral practices, but also to more diffuse selection systems having a cumulative adverse impact, as well as to subjective selection criteria.[112] The Supreme Court probably will resolve this question within the next few years.

The Duty To Investigate Alternatives

Another unresolved issue concerns the nature and extent of an employer's duty under Title VII to investigate and adopt alternative selection procedures or uses having less adverse impact. This is a matter of great practical importance for the enforcement of Title VII. Persons opposed to the imposition of such an obligation argue that it perpetuates:

---

[109] *Id.* See also *Antonio v. Wards Cove Packing Co.*, 768 F.2d 1120, 1131-33 and n.8 (9th Cir. 1985); *Spaulding v. University of Washington*, 740 F.2d 686 (9th Cir.), *cert. denied*, 105 S. Ct. 511 (1984); *Vuyanich v. Republic National Bank*, 723 F.2d 1195 (5th Cir. 1984); *Talley v. United States Postal Service*, 720 F.2d 505 (8th Cir. 1983); *EEOC v. Federal Reserve Bank*, 698 F.2d 633 (4th Cir. 1983); *Mortensen v. Callaway*, 672 F.2d 822 (10th Cir. 1982). See generally B. Schlei and P. Grossman, *supra* note 9, at 1287-90. *Cf.* Bartholet, "Application of Title VII to Jobs in High Places," 95 *Harv. L. Rev.* 947, 959-78 (1982).

[110] The *Guidelines* define "selection procedures" to include "the full range of assessment techniques from traditional paper and pencil tests, performance tests, training programs, or probationary periods and physical, educational, and work experience requirements through informal or casual interviews and unscored application forms." 29 C.F.R. §1607.16Q.

[111] 29 C.F.R. §1607.2B.

[112] See *Griffin v. Carlin*, 755 F.2d 1516, 1522-25 (11th Cir. 1985); *Lasso v. Woodmen of the World Life Insurance Co.*, 741 F.2d 1241 (10th Cir. 1984); *Segar v. Smith*, 738 F.2d 1249 (D.C. Cir. 1984); *Page v. U.S. Industries, Inc.*, 726 F.2d 1038 (5th Cir. 1984); *Wang v. Hoffman*, 694 F.2d 1146 (9th Cir. 1982); *Rowe v. Cleveland Pneumatic Co.*, 690 F.2d 88 (6th Cir. 1982); *Rowe v. General Motors Corp.*, 457 F.2d 348 (5th Cir. 1972); *Allen v. Issac*, 39 E.P.D. para. 35,989 (N.D. Ill. 1986); *Shidaker v. Bolger*, 593 F. Supp. 823 (N.D. Ill. 1984). *Cf. Soria v. Ozinga Brothers, Inc.*, 704 F.2d 990 (7th Cir. 1983) (noting but not resolving the issue). See generally Bartholet, *supra* note 109, at 978-98.

the myth of the alternative screening-method solution to the problem of adverse impact, forcing employers who use valid selection devices to spend time and money searching for other, equally valid devices with lesser adverse impact. In most cases, this is a chimera because there is no real alternative to the need for literacy, numeracy, and other job- and life-relevant skills that valid tests measure.[113]

Proponents, on the other hand, contend that the legal duty to investigate and adopt such reasonable alternatives is "vital" to achieving Title VII's goal of integrating minorities and women into the American economic mainstream.[114]

Some recent cases illustrate the importance of this issue. In a pending case against the police and fire departments of Akron, Ohio, for example, the Lawyers' Committee for Civil Rights Under Law contends that separate item analyses for blacks, Hispanics, and Anglos can identify particular test items that are not good predictors of job performance for persons of each racial or ethnic group.[115] When those items are rewritten to cover the same content in different terms, much of the test's adverse impact can be eliminated.[116]

---

[113] Lerner, *supra* note 4, at 43. See also NAS/NRC Report on Ability Testing, *supra* note 5, at 144 (finding "no evidence of alternatives to testing that are equally informative, equally adequate technically, and also economically and politically viable"). *Cf.* Hunter and Schmidt, "Ability Tests: Economic Benefits Versus the Issue of Fairness," 21 I*ndus. Rel.* 293, 299-301 (1982) (arguing that alternative uses of cognitive ability tests result in reduced productivity).

[114] Bartholet, *supra* note 109, at 1024. See *United Steelworkers v. Weber*, 443 U.S. 193, 202 (1979).

[115] An item analysis separately examines each item on a test, and compares the responses to that item with the responses to all other items on the test. If test takers who generally have made correct responses to other items are found to have made random or near-random responses to the item being examined, the test researcher concludes that the item is not useful because it does not help to distinguish between high and low scorers. This may be because the item was badly written, because the test takers were unfamiliar with the words used in the item or with culturally specific knowledge required by the item, or due to other reasons. When separate item analyses are done for different racial and ethnic groups, particular items that have an adverse impact on minorities can be identified and eliminated.

[116] This is essentially a variation of the "Golden Rule Procedure," named for a 1984 out-of-court settlement between the Educational Testing Service, the State of Illinois, and the Golden Rule Insurance Company concerning the Illinois Insurance Agent Licensing Examination. Under the settlement, ETS is required to conduct separate race-based item analyses and, within groups of equally difficult items in the same content areas, to select those items that display the least difference in correct answer rates between majority and minority test takers.

Another case, involving promotional testing in the St. Louis Fire Department,[117] was settled by eliminating the paper-and-pencil tests that had disproportionately excluded blacks from promotion and developing a new selection procedure based on "real world" problems. The city had previously followed the usual civil service practice of making promotions based on ranked scores on a multiple-choice test asking about such matters as the meaning of abstruse parts of the local fire code and the proper deployment of firefighters and equipment in described situations. Under the settlement, several experts developed real-world simulations that involved, for example, taking the candidates to a building, asking them to imagine a fire of a particular type and intensity, telling them the available equipment, and then asking them to give the kinds of orders they would actually give if they were in charge of the firefighting effort at the building. This resulted in both the virtual elimination of adverse impact on minorities and the development of a much more useful selection procedure.[118]

Another alternative to paper-and-pencil testing is the biodata approach. This approach is based on the theory that future performance on a job can be predicted more successfully by an inquiry into the applicant's past experiences than by a traditional paper-and-pencil test. Studies have shown that biodata are related to job performance, and that their use may significantly reduce the degree of adverse impact on minorities. At the request of the Justice Department, the Lawyers' Committee has agreed to participate in the development of a biodata alternative to traditional testing in a case involving police and fire department hiring in Birmingham and Jefferson County, Alabama.

What remains unclear is whether Title VII *requires* employers to investigate and implement such alternatives, and if so, to what extent. Section 3B of the *Uniform Guidelines* states in part that a validity study "should include . . . an investigation of suitable alternative selection procedures and suitable alternative methods of using the selection procedure which have as little adverse impact as possible."[119] Questions have been raised as to whether this duty to investigate alternatives is consistent with Title VII case law.

---

[117] *Firefighters Institute for Racial Equality v. City of St. Louis*, Civil Action Nos. 74-30(c)(3) and 74-200(c)(3) (E.D. Mo.). Filed in 1974, the case went to the Eighth Circuit three times. The last decision on appeal is reported at 616 F.2d 350 (8th Cir. 1980), *cert. denied*, 452 U.S. 938 (1981).

[118] The parties in *Hammon v. Barry*, Civil Action Nos. 84-0903, 85-0782, and 85-0797 (D. D.C.), in accordance with recommendations of the Lawyers' Committee and the Legal Defense Fund as *amici curiae*, have agreed to develop a similar procedure to resolve disputes over fire department promotions in the District of Columbia.

[119] 29 C.F.R. §1607.3B.

For example, in its 1982 report recommending revision of the *Uniform Guidelines*, the General Accounting Office cited a "perceived inconsistency" between this section of the *Guidelines* and the following language from the Supreme Court's opinion in *Albemarle*:

> If an employer does then meet the burden of proving that its tests are "job related," it remains open to the complaining party to show that other tests or selection devices, without a similarly undesirable racial effect, would also serve the employer's legitimate interest in "efficient and trustworthy workmanship."[120]

The Equal Employment Advisory Council (EEAC) also has taken the position that §3B of the *Guidelines* is "inconsistent with *Albemarle*" and should be "revised to conform to federal court precedent which places the burden of showing suitable alternative selection procedures on the plaintiff or the enforcement agencies."[121]

The obligation to investigate alternatives with less adverse impact is also said to be inconsistent with the Supreme Court's statement in *Furnco* that "Title VII . . . does not impose a duty to adopt a hiring procedure that maximizes hiring of minority employees."[122] According to this view, in litigating a case "an employer need do no more than show that a procedure is job-related, and it is improper to require a further showing that the use of the procedure is the use that maximizes the hiring of minorities. *Griggs* . . . requires no more than validation to dispel the implication of discrimination arising from a statistical showing of adverse impact."[123]

However, neither *Albemarle* nor *Furnco* directly addresses the question of whether Title VII imposes an affirmative duty to investigate or adopt reasonable alternatives. Instead, these cases concern the order and allocation

---

[120] 1982 GAO Report, *supra* note 102, at 8-9, quoting *Albemarle*, 422 U.S. at 425 (citations omitted).

[121] EEAC Analysis, *supra* note 102, at 33. See also Ad Hoc Group Analysis, *supra* note 102, at 41; Booth and Mackay, *supra* note 9, at 189-93; Thompson and Christiansen, "Court Acceptance of *Uniform Guidelines* Provisions: The Bottom Line and the Search for Alternatives," 8 *Empl. Rel. L.J.* 587, 598-602 (1983); Rubenfeld and Crino, "The *Uniform Guidelines*: A Personnel Decision-Making Perspective," 7 *Empl. Rel. L.J.* 105, 117 (1981).

[122] *Furnco Construction Corp. v. Waters*, 438 U.S. 567, 578 (1978).

[123] Ad Hoc Group Analysis, *supra* note 102, at 41. See also EEAC Analysis, *supra* note 102, at 34 (*Furnco* "holds that an employer is not required to use selection procedures that maximize the employment opportunities of minorities and women"); Booth and Mackay, *supra* note 9, at 191-92; Thompson and Christiansen, *supra* note 121, at 600.

of proof during litigation.[124]   As a principal critique of the *Guidelines*
acknowledges, these decisions announce "only . . . rule[s] of evidence, not . . .
rule[s] of law."[125]

A few courts appear to have accepted the argument that imposing a
duty to investigate alternatives may be inconsistent with *Albemarle* or
Furnco.[126] Other courts, however, have held that the law does impose such a
duty.[127] Even where there is some evidence of a selection procedure's validity,
some courts have ruled that failure to consider the degree of adverse impact
resulting from cutoff scores or ranking, and failure to implement reasonable
alternative uses having less adverse impact, may lead to a finding that the
employer's use of the procedure is not job related.[128] Conversely, employers
who have investigated and adopted reasonable alternative procedures or uses
that reduce or eliminate adverse impact on minorities have been protected
from liability in "reverse discrimination" suits.[129] Some courts have even
based findings of *intentional* discrimination against minorities on an

---

[124] See, for example, *Gillespie v. State of Wisconsin*, 771 F.2d 1035, 1045-46 (7th Cir.
1985), *cert. denied*, 106 S. Ct. 854 (1986) (plaintiff in litigation did not satisfy burden of
demonstrating equally valid alternative selection procedures with less adverse impact);
Clady v. County of Los Angeles, 770 F.2d 1421, 1432-33 (9th Cir. 1985) (same).

[125] Ad Hoc Group Analysis, *supra* note 102, at 41.

[126] *Cormier v. PPG Industries, Inc.*, 519 F. Supp. 211, 281 (W.D. La. 1981), *aff'd per
curiam*, 702 F.2d 567, 568 (5th Cir. 1983) (federal agencies "cannot, through the guise of
interpreting their own regulations or by issuing 'guidelines,' overrule decisions of the
Supreme Court"); *I.M.A.G.E. v. Bailar*, 518 F. Supp. 800, 811-12 (N.D. Cal. 1981)
("Whatever weight might be given the failure to follow that instruction [to investigate
alternatives] in the consideration of the value of the validity studies presented in
evidence or in consideration of suitable relief after a finding of liability, this court does
not find that this statement in the EEOC guidelines should be enforced by [preliminary]
injunction, particularly in the face of the case law distributing the burden of proof
differently").

[127] See, for example, *Allen v. City of Mobile*, 464 F. Supp. 433, 439-40 (S.D. Ala. 1978)
(citing *Uniform Guidelines* §3B with approval and holding that defendants had not
made an adequate showing of job-relatedness due in large part to failure to conduct a
reasonable search for alternatives).

[128] See *infra* Part III(E). See, for example, *Guardians Association v. Civil Service
Commission of the City of New York*, 630 F.2d 79, 100-06 (2d Cir. 1980), *cert. denied*, 452
U.S. 940 (1981); *Ensley Branch, NAACP v. Seibels*, 616 F.2d 812, 822 (5th Cir.), *cert. denied*,
449 U.S. 1061 (1980); *Louisville Black Police Officers Organization v. City of Louisville*,
511 F. Supp. 825, 838-39 (W.D. Ky. 1979).

[129] See *Bushey v. New York State Civil Service Commission*, 733 F.2d 220, 224-28 (2d
Cir. 1984), *cert. denied*, 105 S. Ct. 803 (1985); *Kirkland v. New York State Department of
Correctional Services*, 628 F.2d 796, 798-801 (2d Cir. 1980), *cert. denied*, 450 U.S. 980 (1981).

employer's failure to consider and adopt reasonable alternatives with less adverse impact.[130] The Supreme Court has yet to decide the issue.

Validation Against Training Performance

Prior to the Supreme Court's 1976 opinion in *Washington v. Davis*,[131] it seemed well settled that evidence, standing alone, of a relationship between performance on a test and performance in a training program, was not sufficient to show that a test was "job related" under the Title VII standards of *Griggs* and *Albemarle*; it was necessary for the employer to establish in addition that performance in the training program was itself manifestly related to performance on the job.[132] In *Washington v. Davis*, however, the Court— suggesting in a non-Title VII case that it might be applying "standards similar to those obtaining under Title VII"[133]—announced a new and "much more sensible construction" of the job-relatedness requirement: A "positive relationship between the test and training-course performance was sufficient to validate the [test] wholly aside from its possible relationship to actual performance as a police officer."[134] Two years later in *NEA v. South Carolina*,[135] a Title VII case, the Court summarily affirmed a three-judge district court ruling that "the decision to validate [the National Teacher Examinations] against the academic training program rather than job performance is specifically endorsed in principle in *Davis*."[136] In a dissenting opinion in *NEA*, however, Justice White appeared to disavow the implications of his own prior opinion for the majority in *Davis*:

> *Washington v. Davis* . . . was thought by the District Court [in *NEA*] to have warranted validating the test in terms of the applicant's training rather than against job requirements; but *Washington v.*

---

130 See *Easley v. Anheuser-Busch, Inc.*, 572 F. Supp. 402, 410 (E.D. Mo. 1983); *Dickerson v. United States Steel Corp.*, 472 F. Supp. 1304, 1352 (E.D. Pa. 1978).

131 426 U.S. 229 (1976).

132 See, for example, *Vulcan Society v. Civil Service Commission of the City of New York*, 490 F.2d 387, 396 and n.11 (2d Cir. 1973); *Pennsylvania v. O'Neill*, 348 F. Supp. 1084 (E.D. Pa. 1972), *aff'd in pertinent part*, 473 F.2d 1029 (3d Cir. 1973); *United States v. City of Chicago*, 385 F. Supp. 543, 556 (N.D. Ill. 1974), *aff'd in pertinent part*, 549 F.2d 415 (7th Cir.), *cert. denied*, 434 U.S. 875 (1977); *Officers for Justice v. Civil Service Commission of the City of San Francisco*, 371 F. Supp. 1328, 1337 (N.D. Cal. 1973).

133 426 U.S. at 249.

134 *Id.* at 250-51.

135 434 U.S. 1026 (1978).

136 *United States v. South Carolina*, 445 F. Supp. 1094, 1113 (D. S.C. 1977), *aff'd sub nom. National Education Association v. South Carolina*, 434 U.S. 1026 (1978).

Davis, in this respect, held only that the test there involved, which sought to ascertain whether the applicant had the minimum communication skills necessary to understand the offerings in a police training course, could be used to measure eligibility to enter that program. The case did not hold that a training course, the completion of which is required for employment, need not itself be validated in terms of job relatedness. Nor did it hold that a test that a job applicant must pass and that is designed to indicate his mastery of the materials or skills taught in the training course can be validated without reference to the job. Tests supposedly measuring an applicant's qualifications for employment, if they have differential racial impact, must bear some "manifest relationship to the employment in question," *Griggs* . . . , and it is insufficient for the employer "to demonstrate some rational basis for the challenged practices." *Washington v. Davis.*[137]

Not surprisingly, subsequent Title VII cases are divided on the question of whether a selection procedure may be validated against training performance alone. Some cases simply cite *Davis* and hold that "[i]t is sufficient that the test validly predicts performance at the police academy. It need not also bear a positive correlation to satisfactory performance as a police officer."[138]

More of the cases, however, wrestle with the confusingly contradictory Supreme Court opinions, distinguish *Davis* as a non-Title VII case, and conclude that employers must show that selection procedures are related not just to training performance but also to job performance. For example, the Ninth Circuit has reasoned that, "[i]f employers were permitted to validate selection procedures without reference to job performance, then non-job-related selection devices could always be validated through the simple expedient of employing them at both the pre-training and training stage."[139] In the Ninth Circuit's view, the Supreme Court did not consider this danger in *Davis* and NEA because the danger was minimal in those cases; however, where (unlike NEA) both the selection procedure and the training program are under the employer's control, and where (unlike *Davis*) the selection procedure is used to measure something more than minimum communication skills, the

---

[137] 434 U.S. at 1027-28 (White, J., dissenting). For differing perspectives on the significance of these opinions, compare Haney, *supra* note 4, at 16-26, with Booth and Mackay, *supra* note 9, at 128-41.

[138] *Rivera v. City of Wichita Falls*, 665 F.2d 531, 538 n.9 (5th Cir. 1982). See also *Corley v. City of Jacksonville*, 506 F. Supp. 528, 532-36 (M.D. Fla. 1981).

[139] *Blake v. City of Los Angeles*, 595 F.2d 1367, 1382 n.17 (9th Cir. 1979), *cert. denied*, 446 U.S. 928 (1980).

employer must show "that the test correlates significantly with important elements of [training] academy performance *and* that those elements are important to actual job performance."[140] The Second Circuit has similarly noted that allowing employers to validate tests against training performance alone "would undermine Title VII's goal of eliminating arbitrary barriers to the employment of minorities," and therefore has continued to require "a showing that examinations testing performance at training school are themselves job-related."[141]

Other post-*Davis* court decisions have also held that selection procedures having an adverse impact must be shown to be related not merely to training performance but also to job performance.[142] These decisions appear to be consistent with the *Uniform Guidelines*,[143] the APA *Standards*,[144] and the "Division 14 Principles."[145] Nevertheless, until the Supreme Court clarifies its position on this issue, the law will remain uncertain.

Validity Generalization

In the last few years, "validity generalization"—the theory that a finding of test validity for one job in one setting may be freely generalized or transported to other jobs in different settings—has become a focus of debate in the psychological community, and it is beginning to become a legal issue as well (see also Henry Levin, this volume). Some historical background will be helpful in understanding this subject.

---

[140] *Craig v. County of Los Angeles*, 626 F.2d 659, 663 (9th Cir. 1980), *cert. denied*, 450 U.S. 919 (1981) (emphasis in original). But see *Clady v. County of Los Angeles*, 770 F.2d 1421, 1426 (9th Cir. 1985) (accepting validation against training performance alone where "[p]laintiffs did not contest the appropriateness of the performance criteria against which the exam was correlated").

[141] *Guardians Association v. Civil Service Commission of the City of New York*, 633 F. 2d 232, 244-45 (2d Cir. 1980), *cert. denied*, 103 S. Ct. 3568 (1983).

[142] See *Harless v. Duck*, 619 F.2d 611, 616-17 (6th Cir.), *cert. denied*, 449 U.S. 872 (1980); *Ensley Branch, NAACP v. Seibels*, 616 F.2d 812, 822 n.25 (5th Cir.), *cert. denied*, 449 U.S. 1061 (1980); *Brunet v. City of Columbus*, 41 E.P.D. para. 36,498 (S.D. Ohio 1986); *Dickerson v. United States Steel Corp.*, 472 F. Supp. 1304, 1347-49 (E.D. Pa. 1978).

[143] See 29 C.F.R. §§1607.5B and 1607.14B(3).

[144] See 1985 APA *Standards, supra* note 33, at 60-62.

[145] See 1980 "Division 14 Principles," *supra* note 34, at 7, 12.

The origins of modern psychological testing[146] lie in nineteenth century theories of dispositionalism, genetic determinism, and racial inferiority.[147] Although genetic determinism and racial inferiority have been largely rejected by present-day psychologists and social scientists,[148] the dispositionalist view of human personality and behavior has to some extent remained a central assumption underlying many aspects of test theory.[149] Early theoreticians and practitioners of psychological testing believed that people possessed relatively stable and consistent traits and abilities which varied little from one situation to another, and that those traits and abilities could always be measured by appropriate tests.[150] "It is the presumed stability of these attributes that provides the rationale for their measurement; if attributes were inconsistent or unstable, there would be little value or utility in measuring them."[151]

As time went on, however, evidence and experience contradicted these basic assumptions; over and over, industrial psychologists found that, even where their studies showed that a test was valid for a particular job in a particular setting, they could not show the same test to be valid for different jobs, or even for quite similar jobs in different settings.[152] Psychologists therefore gradually moved away from the "dispositional" model of human behavior and toward a "situational" model, which views behavior as highly dependent on the immediate situation or environment in which it occurs.[153] As stated in the current edition of a leading text on psychological testing,

---

[146] Systematic employment testing is thought to have originated in China around 2200 B.C., when the emperor began examining his officials every third year to determine their fitness to continue in office. The elaborate civil service testing system that evolved in imperial China was adapted by France in the late eighteenth century and by Britain in the nineteenth century (see also Carolyn Webber, this volume). The United States picked up the movement from Britain in the late nineteenth century, and began to develop and use civil service tests in the 1880s. P. DuBois, *A History of Psychological Testing* 3-6 (1970). Professional psychologists did not become involved in employment testing until early in the twentieth century. *Id.* at 82.

[147] See Haney, *supra* note 4, at 3-13. See also S. Gould, *The Mismeasure of Man* 20-29 (1981).

[148] But see A. Jensen, *Bias in Mental Testing* (1979).

[149] Haney, *supra* note 4, at 50.

[150] See Haney, *supra* note 4, at 50. The principal trait the early testers were trying to measure was "intelligence." They turned to psychological tests for this purpose after they gave up on craniometry—the science of measuring heads. See S. Gould, *supra* note 147, at 30-107.

[151] Haney, *supra* note 4, at 50.

[152] See *id.* at 49 and nn.228-29.

[153] See *id.* at 51-55.

"[c]autious professional opinion has urged for decades that any selection plan be validated afresh in each firm."[154] Cognitive psychologists now refer (rather pejoratively) to the dispositional model as "fundamental attribution error."[155]

By the time the EEOC began formulating legal standards for employment testing in its 1966 and 1970 *Guidelines*,[156] the agency and its psychologist-advisers were well aware of the professional consensus that validity results could be safely generalized only in limited circumstances. The 1966 *Guidelines* thus defined the statutory phrase "professionally developed ability test" to mean "a test which fairly measures the knowledge or skills required by the *particular* job or class of jobs which the applicant seeks, or which fairly affords the employer a chance to measure the applicant's ability to perform a *particular* job or class of jobs."[157] The focus on the need for a match between a specific test and a specific job is also apparent in the 1970 EEOC *Guidelines* and in the language of the Supreme Court's opinions in *Griggs, Albemarle,* and subsequent cases.[158] Indeed, in *Albemarle* the Court relied on the 1970 EEOC *Guidelines* in holding that "[a] test [having an adverse impact] may be used in jobs other than those for which it has been professionally validated only if there are 'no significant differences' between the studied and unstudied jobs."[159]

This basically situationalist view was never seriously questioned even during the period of interagency conflict over different versions of the guidelines, and it was reaffirmed when the agencies adopted the *Uniform Guidelines* in 1978.[160] Although this view finds expression in many provisions of the current *Uniform Guidelines*, it is perhaps most evident in §§7 and 8, which govern the "transportability" of validity evidence. These sections permit the transportation only of criterion-related validity evidence, and they impose relatively stringent requirements on employers attempting to rely on such

[154] L. Cronbach, *supra* note 2, at 400.

[155] R. Nisbett and L. Ross, *Human Inference: Strategies and Shortcomings of Social Judgment* 31 (1980). Nisbett and Ross define "fundamental attribution error" as the "assumption that behavior is caused primarily by the enduring and consistent dispositions of the actor, as opposed to the particular characteristics of the situation to which the actor responds." *Id.* They maintain that this inferential error is so "thoroughly woven into the fabric of our culture" that "children growing up in our culture come to hold an increasingly dispositional view of the causes of behavior." *Id.*

[156] *Supra* notes 25 and 36.

[157] 1966 EEOC *Guidelines, supra* note 25 (emphasis added).

[158] See *supra* notes 43-78.

[159] *Albemarle Paper Co. v. Moody*, 422 U.S. 405, 432 (1975).

[160] See *supra* notes 84-98.

evidence.[161] The courts generally have adopted the cautious approach to transportability and validity generalization reflected in the *Guidelines*.[162]

The dispositional model, however, now appears to be making a comeback among some prominent industrial and personnel psychologists. Frank Schmidt, John Hunter, and other psychologists have published a series of recent articles in which they reexamine old validity studies and conclude that the variance in the outcomes of those studies was not caused by actual differences in validity depending on the particular situations in question, but instead was "largely an illusion created by statistical artifacts" resulting from differences between studies in test reliability, criterion reliability, range restriction, and sampling error.[163] They use this conclusion to support a broad view of "validity generalization," claiming that tests of "general cognitive ability" are valid for *all* jobs, that "massive research findings" have shown that such tests are not unfair to minority applicants, and that increased use of these tests would raise productivity in the United States by billions of dollars annually.[164] They assert that their research not only proves that "validity generalization is possible on a widespread basis," but also shows that it is finally possible to "develop the general principles and theories that are

---

[161] 29 C.F.R. §§1607.7 and 1607.8. The requirements for transportability include: (1) "clear" evidence of validity; (2) job analyses showing that incumbents in the borrowing user's jobs and incumbents in the jobs on which the study was conducted perform "substantially the same major work behaviors"; and (3) an investigation of test fairness for each race, sex, and ethnic group constituting a significant factor in the borrowing employer's relevant labor market. 29 C.F.R. §1607.7B. The *Guidelines* further restrict transportability to circumstances in which there are no "variables in the user's situation which are likely to affect validity significantly." 29 C.F.R. §1607.8B. See also 29 C.F.R. §§1607.7C and 1607.7D.

[162] See *Albemarle Paper Co. v. Moody*, 422 U.S. at 432; *Brunet v. City of Columbus*, 41 E.P.D. para. 36,498 (S.D. Ohio 1986); *Dickerson v. United States Steel Corp.*, 472 F. Supp. 1304, 1338-40 (E.D. Pa. 1978); *Vanguard Justice Society, Inc. v. Hughes*, 471 F. Supp. 670, 732-35 (D. Md. 1979); *Berkman v. City of New York*, 536 F. Supp. 177, 212-16 (E.D. N.Y. 1982), *aff'd*, 705 F.2d 584 (2d Cir. 1983). *Cf. Rivera v. City of Wichita Falls*, 665 F.2d 531, 538 n.10 (5th Cir. 1982).

[163] Pearlman, Schmidt, and Hunter, "Validity Generalization Results for Tests Used To Predict Job Proficiency and Training Success in Clerical Occupations," 65 *J. App. Psych.* 373, 374-76, 399-400 (1980). See also Schmidt and Hunter, "Employment Testing: Old Theories and New Research Findings," 36 *Am. Psych.* 1128 (1981) (brief review of recent findings); Schmidt, Hunter, and Pearlman, "Task Differences and Validity of Aptitude Tests in Selection: A Red Herring," 61 *J. App. Psych.* 166 (1981); Schmidt, Hunter, Pearlman, and Shane, "Further Tests of the Schmidt-Hunter Bayesian Validity Generalization Procedure," 32 *Pers. Psych.* 257 (1979); Schmidt and Hunter, "Development of a General Solution to the Problem of Validity Generalization," 62 *J. App. Psych.* 529 (1977).

[164] Hunter and Schmidt, *supra* note 4, at 295-98.

necessary to take the field [of personnel psychology] beyond a mere technology to the status of a science."[165]

While Schmidt and Hunter take their validity generalization theory to an extreme, it has been accepted to some extent by a few courts[166] and by many psychologists. As one standard text on psychological testing states,

> Schmidt, Hunter, and their co-workers were able to show that the validity of tests of verbal, numerical, and reasoning aptitudes can be generalized far more widely across occupations than had heretofore been recognized. . . . Evidently, the successful performance of a wide variety of occupational tasks depends to a significant degree on a common core of cognitive skills. . . . It would seem that this cluster of cognitive skills and knowledge is broadly predictive of performance in both academic and occupational activities demanded in advanced technological societies.[167]

Another standard text, however, concludes that "validities are much less generalizable than Schmidt's group suggests."[168] Both the 1980 "Division 14 Principles"[169] and the 1985 APA Standards[170] acknowledge the Schmidt-Hunter research, but they maintain a cautious approach to the subjects of transportability and validity generalization. The "Division 14 Principles" note that "[m]any questions regarding generality are still open to debate," and they hopefully predict that "[c]ontinued evidence . . . should enable further extensions of validity generalization."[171] The APA Standards restrict the use of transported validity evidence to circumstances in which "it can be demonstrated that the test has generated a significant record of validity in

---

[165] Pearlman, Schmidt, and Hunter, *supra* note 163, at 400, 374. Stephen Jay Gould might characterize these assertions as an example of "physics envy"—the yearning of some social scientists to find simplifying laws and basic particles that will reduce the outward complexity of the social world to a simpler, underlying reality. See S. Gould, *supra* note 147, at 262.

[166] See *Friend v. Leidinger*, 588 F.2d 61, 65 (4th Cir. 1978); *Pegues v. Mississippi State Employment Service*, 488 F. Supp. 239, 254 and n.1 (M.D. Miss. 1980), *aff'd on other grounds*, 699 F.2d 760 (5th Cir.), *cert. denied*, 104 S. Ct. 482 (1983).

[167] A. Anastasi, *supra* note 2, at 143-44. See also *id.* at 437-38.

[168] L. Cronbach, *supra* note 2, at 401. See also James, Demaree, and Mulaik, "A Note on Validity Generalization Procedures," 71 *J. App. Psych.* 440 (1986) (a critical review of the Schmidt-Hunter studies).

[169] 1980 "Division 14 Principles," *supra* note 34, at 15-16.

[170] 1985 APA *Standards, supra* note 33, at 12 and 59-62.

[171] 1980 "Division 14 Principles," supra note 32, at 15-16.

similar job settings for highly similar people or that it is otherwise appropriate to generalize from other applications."[172]

The cautious approach of the profession to validity generalization is also reflected in the 1982 recommendations of the National Academy of Sciences/National Research Council report on ability testing:

> Government agencies concerned with fair employment practices should accept the principle of cooperative validation research so that tests validated for a job category such as fire fighter in a number of localities can be accepted for use in other localities on the basis of the cumulated evidence. It would remain incumbent on the user of such a test to develop a persuasive showing—based on close examination of the test, the work, and the applicant pool—that it is appropriate for use in the conditions that obtain in the local situation.[173]

As noted above, the validity generalization debate within the psychological community has already begun to spill over into the courts and administrative agencies, which ultimately will have to decide how this developing concept might affect their interpretations of Title VII.

Cutoff Scores and Ranking

A final developing legal issue concerns the extent to which Title VII requires employers to justify particular methods of using otherwise valid selection procedures. Such requirements have been applied primarily to methods of use that have greater adverse impact than other methods—especially the use of cutoff scores and the practice of ranking on the basis of test scores. Many of the issues raised by such requirements have already been discussed in connection with the more general obligation to investigate and implement reasonable alternative procedures or uses with less adverse impact.[174] These issues are separately considered here for three reasons: (1) industrial and personnel psychologists generally regard cutoff scores and ranking as presenting unique problems; (2) a number of courts that have been unwilling or unable to master the complexities of many other testing and validation issues have shown that they are capable of understanding and applying the more basic, commonsense principles concerning the use of test scores; and (3) the use of cutoff scores, ranking, and related practices are ubiquitous features of civil service testing at all levels—and therefore affect the job opportunities of millions of people, including large numbers of minorities and women.

---

[172] 1985 APA *Standards, supra* note 31, at 59.

[173] NAS/NRC Report on Ability Testing, *supra* note 5, at 148.

[174] See *supra* Part III(B).

The *Uniform Guidelines* contain several provisions which, in essence, require employers to consider the degree of adverse impact and to justify the setting of particular cutoff scores[175] and the use of ranking[176] even when the employer's selection procedure is otherwise valid.[177] This approach finds some support in the 1982 study of the National Academy of Sciences/National Research Council, which urged courts and enforcement agencies to "distinguish between the technical psychometric standards that can reasonably be imposed on ability tests and the legal and social policy requirements that more properly apply to the rules for using test scores and other information in selecting employees."[178] The study also recommended that federal authorities "concentrate on providing employers with guidelines that set out the range of legally defensible decision rules to guide their use of test scores."[179]

The "Division 14 Principles", on the other hand, adopt a dramatically different approach. According to the Principles, cutoff scores may be set "as high or as low as the purposes of the organization require, if they are based on valid predictors," and "the relationship between a predictor and a criterion

---

[175] See 29 C.F.R. §1607.5H (cutoff scores "should normally be set so as to be reasonable and consistent with normal expectations of acceptable proficiency within the work force"; where ranking results in effectively higher cutoff scores, "the degree of adverse impact should be considered").

[176] See 29 C.F.R. §1607.5G ("if a user decides to use a selection procedure on a ranking basis, and that method of use has a greater adverse impact than use on an appropriate pass/fail basis . . . , the user should have sufficient evidence of validity and utility to support the use on a ranking basis").

[177] See also 29 C.F.R. §§1607.14B(6) and 1607.14C(9).

[178] NAS/NRC Report on Ability Testing, *supra* note 5, at 148.

[179] *Id.* at 148. The report also states that "[t]he goals of efficiency and representativeness are more likely to be brought into a workable balance by altering the decision rule ([e.g.,] ranking and the rule of three) that determines how test scores are used. This might be in the form of a weighting formula that recognizes high ability, ethnic diversity, and other socially valued considerations in selecting from the portion of the applicant population that has demonstrated the threshold level of ability or skill necessary to satisfactory job performance." *Id.* at 147.

may [usually] be assumed to be linear."[180]   In other words, if a test is otherwise valid, an employer may set any cutoff score it likes and may use the test as a ranking device without any further justification. This approach has been incorporated in the EEAC's proposed revisions of the *Uniform Guidelines*.[181]

In a small number of cases, the courts—usually without meaningful discussion or explanation—have upheld the use of cutoff scores and ranking solely because they found tests to be otherwise valid.[182] The great majority of courts, however, have endorsed the imposition of additional requirements. Both before[183] and since[184] the adoption of the *Uniform Guidelines*, "[c]ourts

---

[180] 1980 "Division 14 Principles", *supra* note 34, at 18. The relevant portion of the Principles states in full:

> Selection standards may be set as high or as low as the purposes of the organization require, if they are based on valid predictors. This implies that (a) the purposes of selection are clear and (b) they are acceptable in the social and legal context in which the employing organization functions. In usual circumstances, the relationship between a predictor and a criterion may be assumed to be linear. Consequently, selecting from the top scorers on down is almost always the most beneficial procedure from the standpoint of an organization if there is an appropriate amount of variance in the predictor. Selection techniques developed by content-oriented procedures and discriminating adequately within the range of interest can be assumed to have a linear relationship to job behavior. Consequently, ranking on the basis of scores on these procedures is appropriate.

[181] See EEAC Analysis, *supra* note 102, at 47-48.

[182] See *Gillespie v. State of Wisconsin*, 771 F.2d 1035, 1045 (7th Cir. 1985), *cert. denied*, 106 S. Ct. 854 (1986) (upholding cutoff scores based on "an estimate of the ability levels needed," an effort to "select . . . as many qualified minority applicants as possible," and a policy of insuring "that the interviewers would not be overwhelmed by the sheer number of candidates"); *Contreras v. City of Los Angeles*, 656 F.2d 1267, 1284 (5th Cir. 1981), *cert. denied* 455, U. S. 1021 (1982) (upholding cutoff score and ranking on the ground that "the purpose of a civil service examination" is "to rank applicants so that only the top few may be hired"); *Cuesta v. State of New York Office of Court Administration*, 571 F. Supp. 392, 395 n.3 (S.D. N.Y. 1983) (rejecting without explanation challenges to cutoff score and ranking); *Cormier v. PPG Industries, Inc.*, 519 Supp. 211264 (W.D. La. 1981), *aff'd per curiam*, 702 F.2d 567, 568 (5th Cir. 1983) (upholding cutoff scores on the basis of Dr. Schmidt's testimony that higher cutoff scores result in increased dollar savings in productivity). *Cf.* Hunter and Schmidt, *supra* note 4, at 300-01 ("[s]ince the relationship between ability and performance is linear, any departure from top down hiring will result in a loss in the mean productivity of the work force").

[183] See *Rogers v. International Paper Co.*, 510 F.2d 1340, 1351 (8th Cir. 1975); *Boston Chapter, NAACP v. Beecher*, 504 F.2d 1017, 1023 (1st Cir. 1974), *cert. denied*, 421 U.S. 910 (1975); *Walston v. County School Board*, 492 F.2d 919, 927 (4th Cir. 1974); *Kirkland v. New York State Department of Correctional Services*, 374 F. Supp. 1361, 1377 (S.D. N.Y.

have regularly rejected rank ordering as inadequately validated . . . ," and
"[c]utoff scores have similarly met with strict scrutiny by the courts."[185]

The leading case in this area is the Second Circuit's decision in
Guardians Association v. Civil Service Commission (Guardians IV).[186]
Although the court in *Guardians IV* generally criticized the *Uniform Guidelines*
and otherwise upheld the validity of an entry-level police officer examination, it
expressly endorsed the *Guidelines* with respect to cutoff scores and ranking,
and on that basis held that the employer's use of the exam was unlawful. The
court found that §14C(9) of the *Guidelines*, providing that rank ordering should
be used only if it can be shown that "a higher score . . . is likely to result in better
job performance,"[187] is

> reasonable and consistent with Title VII's provision that the
> "results" of a test may not be "used to discriminate." 42 U.S.C.
> §2000e-2(h). If test scores do not vary directly with job
> performance, ranking the candidates on the basis of their scores
> will not select better employees. . . .
>
> [C]lose scrutiny is required because rank-ordering makes such a
> refined use of the test's basic power to distinguish between those
> who are qualified to perform the job and those who are not. . . . A
> test may have enough validity for making gross distinctions
> between those qualified and unqualified for a job, yet may be
> totally inadequate to yield passing grades that show positive
> correlation with job performance. . . .

1974); *Western Addition Community Organization v. Alioto*, 360 F. Supp. 733, 738 (N.D.
Cal. 1973), *appeal dismissed*, 514 F.2d 542 (9th Cir.), *cert. denied*, 423 U.S. 1014 (1975).

[184] See *Guardians Association v. Civil Service Commission of the City of New York*,
630 F.2d 79, 100-06 (2d Cir. 1980), *cert. denied*, 452 U.S. 940 (1981); *United States v. City of
Chicago*, 631 F.2d 469, 476 (7th Cir. 1980); *Firefighters Institute for Racial Equality v. City
of St. Louis*, 616 F.2d 350, 357-60 (8th Cir. 1980), *cert. denied*, 452 U.S. 938 (1981); *Ensely
Branch, NAACP v. Seibels*, 616 F.2d 812, 822 (5th Cir.), *cert. denied*, 449 U.S. 1061 (1980);
Brunet v. City of Columbus, E.P.D. para. 36, 498 (S.D. Ohio 1986); *Walls v. Mississippi
Department of Public Welfare*, 542 F. Supp. 281, 313 (N.D. Miss. 1982), *aff'd*, 730 F.2d 306,
320 (5th Cir. 1984); *Vanguard Justice Society, Inc. v. Hughes*, 592 F. Supp. 245, 266-69 (D.
Md. 1984); *Easley v. Anheuser-Busch, Inc.*, 572 F. Supp. 402, 409 (E.D. Mo., 1983); *Burney
v. City of Pawtucket*, 559 F. Supp. 1089, 1103 (D. R. E. 1985) *Berkman v. City of New York*,
536 F. Supp. 177, 210-12 (E.D. N.Y. 1982), *aff'd*, 795 F.2d 584 (2d Cir. 1983); *Louisville Black
Police Officers Organization, Inc. v. City of Louisville*, 511 F. Supp. 825-39 (W.D. Ky.
1979); *Vanguard Justice Society, Inc., v. Hughes*, 471 F. Supp. 670, 735, 741 (D. Md. 1979);
Allen v. City of Mobile, 464 F. Supp. 433, 440-41 (S.D. Ala. 1978).

[185] B. Schlei and P. Grossman, *supra* note 9, at 155-56 (footnotes omitted).

[186] 630 F.2d 79 (2d Cir. 1980), *cert. denied*, 452 U.S. 940 (1981).

[187] 29 C.F.R. §1607.14C(9).

The frequency with which . . . one-point differentials are used for important decisions in our society, both in academic assessment and civil service employment, should not obscure their equally frequent lack of demonstrated significance. Rank-ordering satisfies a felt need for objectivity, but it does not necessarily select better job performers. In some circumstances the virtues of objectivity may justify the inherent artificiality of the substantively deficient distinctions being made. But when test scores have a disparate racial impact, an employer violates Title VII if he uses them in ways that lack significant relationship to job performance.[188]

Thus, although the court had concluded that there was sufficient evidence of validity to permit some use of the test, it held that the evidence was not adequate to satisfy the employer's "substantial task in demonstrating that rank-ordering is sufficiently justified to be used."[189]

The court in *Guardians IV* also reviewed §5H of the *Uniform Guidelines*, which provides that cutoff scores "should normally be set so as to be reasonable and consistent with normal expectations of acceptable proficiency within the work force."[190] The court found that this provision

also makes sense. No matter how valid the exam, it is the cutoff score that ultimately determines whether a person passes or fails. A cutoff score unrelated to job performance may well lead to the rejection of applicants who were fully capable of performing the job. When a cutoff score unrelated to job performance produces disparate racial results, Title VII is violated.[191]

The employer in *Guardians IV* did not select a cutoff score on the basis of any relationship with job performance. Instead, like many civil service employers, it "merely chose as many candidates as it needed, and then set the cutoff score so that the remaining candidates would fail."[192] The court held that, since the cutoff score had an adverse impact on minorities and was not adequately justified, this practice was unlawful.[193]

---

[188]   630 F.2d at 100.

[189]   630 F.2d at 103. See also *Berkman v. City of New York*, 536 F. Supp. 177, 211 (E.D. N.Y. 1982), *aff'd*, 705 F.2d 584 (2d Cir. 1983) (evidence held insufficient to support the "extraordinary pretense at precision" reflected in rank ordering).

[190]   29 C.F.R. §1607.5H.

[191]   630 F.2d at 105.

[192]   *Id.*

[193]   *Id.* at 105-06.

At present, the courts and enforcement agencies are nearly unanimous in adopting the view expressed in *Guardians IV*: Where cutoff scores or ranking cause or increase adverse impact, Title VII requires a substantial showing that their use is justified. However, the contrary position of many industrial and personnel psychologists, expressed in the Division 14 Principles, is likely to make this a disputed legal issue in the future.

IV. CONCLUSION

Psychologists and social scientists have long known that certain kinds of employment tests disproportionately screen out minorities and women. With the enactment of Title VII of the Civil Rights Act of 1964, the law and lawyers began to recognize this serious social problem as a legal problem, and they began to develop legal strategies and principles to solve it.

Through more than twenty years of interpretation and evolution, the courts and enforcement agencies have firmly established the basic principles of Title VII testing law. The most fundamental of those principles—repeatedly reaffirmed by the Supreme Court and incorporated in guidelines issued over the last two decades by all the federal enforcement agencies—is that, regardless of the presence or absence of discriminatory intent, it is unlawful to use a test or other selection procedure that has an adverse impact on minorities or women unless the selection procedure is shown to be job related.

Many legal issues, however, remain unresolved. These issues include whether the *Griggs* "disparate impact" interpretation of Title VII applies to multicomponent selection systems and to subjective employment criteria; whether Title VII imposes a duty to investigate and adopt alternative selection procedures or uses having less adverse impact; whether Title VII's job-relatedness requirement may be satisfied by showing that test performance is related to training performance alone; whether the validity generalization concept will result in easing requirements for the transportability of validity evidence, and perhaps in reducing or eliminating other validation requirements; and whether Title VII requires employers to justify the use of cutoff scores or ranking where such methods of use cause or increase the adverse impact of an otherwise valid selection procedure.[194] As the courts and enforcement agencies continue to grapple with these and other issues, Title VII testing law will continue to evolve.

---

[194] Since the writing of this chapter, the U.S. Supreme Court handed down a decision in *Watson v. Fort Worth Bank and Trust* (108 S. Ct. 2777 1988). While the full and lasting implications of the Court's decision have yet to be determined, it is clear that Title VII disparate impact analysis may now be applied to subjective employment criteria.—Ed.

Non-Discriminatory Use of Personnel Tests

CONFERENCE REMARKS

Donald J. Schwartz[1]

My remarks will cover three major areas. These are: (1) the development of government regulation of test use; (2) the influence of these regulations on testing practices; and (3) new issues in testing and how these issues may impact on the role of the government.

GOVERNMENT REGULATION OF TEST USE: DEVELOPMENT

The basic federal government policy concerning the nondiscriminatory use of tests and other selection procedures derives from Section 703(h) of Title VII of the Civil Rights Acts of 1964, as amended. This regulation provides that personnel decisions may be based on test scores, unless the test is designed, intended, or used to discriminate on the basis of race, sex, or ethnic group membership. This policy has been implemented by federal agencies in part through the issuance of a number of guidelines. The first set of testing guidelines, adopted by the Equal Employment Opportunity Commission (EEOC) in 1966, was primarily a general statement that tests which have an adverse impact are discriminatory unless they have been professionally validated. What constitutes "professional validation" was described in an attached policy statement prepared by three consultants to the EEOC, one of whom was an industrial psychologist.

The second set of guidelines, adopted by the EEOC in 1970, was somewhat more detailed and incorporated by reference the professional testing standards published by the American Psychological Association (APA). In addition to the incorporated standards, the 1970 guidelines included a strong emphasis on job analysis, the need to avoid bias in criterion measures, and the need to validate tests separately for the different race, sex, and ethnic groups. In essence, these guidelines drew from professional standards those aspects which were perceived as important in avoiding discrimination against race, sex, or ethnic groups.

---

[1] Donald J. Schwartz is a staff psychologist with the United States Equal Employment Opportunity Commission (EEOC). These remarks were contributed by the author in his private capacity. No official support or endorsement by the EEOC or any other agency of the United States government is intended or should be inferred.

The current guidelines, the *Uniform Guidelines on Employee Selection Procedures*, were adopted in 1978 by the EEOC and by the other federal agencies with enforcement responsibilities in civil rights: the Office of Personnel Management, the Department of Justice, the Department of Labor, and the Department of the Treasury. The *Uniform Guidelines* are more detailed than earlier versions. They provide a rule of thumb, commonly known as the "80%" or "four-fifths" rule, for establishing the existence of adverse impact; minimum requirements for validity studies which are intended to be consistent with professional standards; and, for the first time for the EEOC, documentation requirements describing in detail what an acceptable validation report must include.

The trend in federal guidelines over the years, then, has been a change from general guidance to more specific and detailed guidelines. At the same time, however, professional standards have been moving from specific technical requirements to more general guidance so that, at present, the *Uniform Guidelines* appear much more specific in several aspects than corresponding sections of the 1985 APA *Standards for Educational and Psychological Testing*.

The American Psychological Association, when comparing the *Uniform Guidelines* to its *Standards*, has issued some rather contradictory statements. Some official statements, on the one hand, have indicated that the *Uniform Guidelines* are consistent with existing APA *Standards*; others, on the other hand, have indicated that the *Guidelines* need to be revised to reflect changes in the *Standards*. On July 18, 1985, the Subcommittee on Employment Opportunities of the Education and Labor Committee of the U.S. House of Representatives held a hearing on possible revisions to the *Uniform Guidelines* and asked the American Psychological Association to send a representative to present its views on the subject. In fact, not one but two representatives showed up. Dr. Wayne Cascio, representing the APA, testified that the membership was divided as to whether the *Guidelines* should be revised or retained as is. Dr. Benjamin Schneider, also representing the APA, testified that there was consensus among the membership that the *Guidelines* had to be revised. The subcommittee was obviously quite puzzled at this unexpected development. The result was another hearing in October, in part to cast further light on the situation.

THE IMPACT OF REGULATION ON TESTING PRACTICES: THREE TENDENCIES

The impact of government regulation on testing practices has been in three directions. First, there is a tendency on the part of employers to avoid triggering the rule of thumb that defines adverse impact. The "80% rule" in the *Guidelines* provides that adverse impact is generally present only when the selection rate for a race, sex, or ethnic group is less than four-fifths, or 80%, of the highest selection rate. If this rule is not met, an employer does not have to provide validity evidence to an enforcement agency or a court. This might make a number of industrial psychologists less wealthy, perhaps, but it unclutters the courts to some extent.

The tendency to avoid triggering the "80% rule" has manifested itself through three strategies. First, cutoff scores on tests have been lowered in ways that still provide a pool of qualified applicants from which individuals can be selected in a nondiscriminatory manner. We know that in general, especially when cognitive ability tests are used, lowering the cutoff reduces adverse impact and that at a certain point adverse impact does in fact disappear. Second, different percentile conversions for the various race, sex, and ethnic groups have been applied to raw scores so that employees are being selected on the basis of within-group percentile scores. Although this practice is becoming identified with validity generalization, it did not originate with that concept. It was, in fact, recommended by E. F. Wonderlic in 1972 for setting different cutoffs on an aptitude test. The concept has also been used in personality testing where sex differences on various scales have been noted. Finally, alternative indicators of proficiency have been used in which, for example, the majority of applicants would be given a written test but the test score waived for those applicants who have previous experience on the job or who provide other evidence of qualifications. The response to a charge of adverse impact resulting from the test would typically be that the test is given, but there is no absolute cutoff score and no set strategy for using test scores other than to combine them with other sources of information.

The second tendency which has resulted from government regulation is an improvement in the quality of validity studies. There was a general perception in the early days of government regulations that no validity study could meet the requirements of the *Guidelines* or professional standards if it were subject to scrutiny by the courts and enforcement agencies. In other words, once there has been a determination that a test has resulted in adverse impact, the employer has lost. Recently, however, several validity studies have not only met the criteria of the *Guidelines*, but have survived challenges in court. One example is *Craig v. County of Los Angeles* (24 FEP 1106), concerning an ability test used to screen deputy sheriff applicants; another is *Cormier v. P. P. G. Industries* (26 FEP 652), concerning use of the Wonderlic Personnel Test for one specific job in the company.

Several aspects of validity studies have significantly improved in quality. First, job analysis procedures that are currently used are much better than earlier techniques. The job analysis procedures used by Albemarle Paper Company were strongly criticized by the Supreme Court in *Albemarle Paper Co. v. Moody* (10 FEP 1181). In that instance, the expert apparently spent only half a day in the plant and based his conclusions concerning the important aspects of the jobs on that visit. Since that time, a number of good, solid techniques have been developed. There are problems, of course, with some of these new techniques, but in general a large number of advances in job analysis has resulted from the work that has gone into the development of the new procedures.

Second, job-specific tests which are aimed at assessment of the necessary knowledge and skills for a specific job have been developed. There is, of course, a counter-tendency, based on the work of Dr. Frank Schmidt and Dr. John Hunter, to return to general ability tests—in some cases, to the same general ability tests which were developed in the 1930s and 1940s and which were roundly criticized in those days. It would be an interesting endeavor to go back to the *Mental Measurements Yearbooks* of those days and read the professional reviews of some of the tests now being depicted as valid.

Third, criterion measures are vastly improved. We have behaviorally anchored rating scales, where performance is compared to job-specific "anchors," and computer-measured production output (which is the subject of some employee dissatisfaction). These developments contribute to higher observed validity coefficients.

Finally, virtually every criterion-related validity study I have seen recently has at least considered the possibility of differential prediction, where scores have different meanings in terms of expected job performance for the different race, sex, and ethnic groups. Techniques based on comparing regression equations rather than just validity coefficients are now commonly used. The very existence of these data is an improvement, even though there is a feeling that differential prediction is not a real problem. At least, the data can provide evidence on that question one way or the other.

The third tendency which has resulted from government regulation has been the development of alternatives to the use of written tests. There has been increased use of assessment centers, the development of biographical inventories (bio-data), and some work in the use of self-assessments. The use of these alternatives has, of course, raised questions about their validity, and there have been at least two comparisons of the validities of the techniques. Some of these alternative methods have less adverse impact than written tests, especially cognitive ability measures, and to this extent their development may be useful.

NEW ISSUES IN TESTING

The new issues in testing encompass two major areas. First, there has been a change (or perceived change) in professional standards. The present APA *Standards* were adopted in 1985 after five years of debate within the organization. Several standards in earlier publications were removed because of professional disagreements, deriving in part from published court decisions.

New Division 14 *Principles for the Validation and Use of Personnel Selection Procedures,* which were adopted at the APA convention in August 1986, are being published in January 1987. The differences between the *Standards* and the *Principles* further illustrate continuing professional dissension on some issues.

One example of these existing professional differences concerns appropriate validity evidence. The 1974 APA *Standards* emphasized three different strategies for validation studies: content, construct, and criterion-related. The 1985 APA *Standards* dropped this concept of distinct strategies and referred to "lines of validity evidence." The appropriate validation strategy for any given situation might include a mixture of these lines of evidence. In other words, any particular study could include content, construct, and criterion-related evidence, with the appropriate mixture determined by the type of test being validated and the use to which the test is to be put. Since many employment testing experts have felt that a predictive criterion-related validity study provides the best evidence to support use of a test for selection of new employees, the 1985 APA *Standards* might be interpreted by some as preferring criterion-related evidence where feasible. The Division 14 *Principles,* on the other hand, retain the concept of validity strategies as separate entities "to avoid an abrupt departure from tradition."

Another example of differences in professional opinion concerns the test fairness issue. Despite professional concerns about differential prediction, the APA *Standards* continue to require these studies where feasible whenever there is a substantial prior probability of its occurence. The Division 14 *Principles,* on the other hand, state that there is little evidence to support its existence and imply that these studies should not be required. Recent studies indicate that there is substantially more evidence for one aspect of differential prediction (differences between intercepts of regression lines) than had been believed. These differences almost always demonstrate an overprediction of job performance for minorities. Whatever this means in practical terms, the problem must be dealt with under the APA *Standards*. The *Guidelines* require appropriate investigations of test fairness, a concept which includes other aspects as well as differential prediction. The use of models which avoid adverse impact by using separate conversions for different race, sex, and ethnic groups may be an appropriate remedy for test unfairness, even when it is not justified as a remedy for differential prediction.

The second new area in testing concerns technical advances in testing. One of the major new techniques is validity generalization (see also Henry Levin, this volume). I believe that it is important to consider the three steps in validity generalization separately, because they are all very important in establishing the usefulness of this approach. The first step is the accumulation (meta-analysis) of observed validity coefficients in the available studies. This step, when done appropriately, results in a distribution of observed validities which, for cognitive ability tests, is remarkably similar to that found by Ghiselli many years ago. That is, the average validity for these tests is around .20, few validities exceed .30, there is a high level of situational specificity, and frequently studies do not result in statistically significant validity coefficients for a specific job.

The second step is the correction of the distribution of validity coefficients for criterion unreliablity and for restriction of range. These corrections are necessary to support the conclusions that all cognitive ability tests are valid for all jobs in the U. S. economy.

The third step, advocated by Schmidt and Hunter and implemented by the U. S. Employment Service, is the use of separate percentile conversions by race. This step, which is claimed to preserve 95 percent of the utility of the test but which is also claimed to be a quota system, may exempt the validity evidence supporting the test from scrutiny under the *Uniform Guidelines*, because there is no adverse impact resulting from its use. These conversions are highly important because, without them, the use of validity generalization techniques could easily result in the exclusion of racial minorities from every job in the U. S. economy. While it is claimed that race differences in test performance reflect race differences in job performance, the degree to which this claim is supported by evidence remains doubtful.

Another new technique is computer-assisted testing, especially adaptive testing. An important issue resulting from this development is the effect, in terms of fairness, of administering different test items to different people, but placing the scores on a common scale.

The third new technique is criterion-referenced measurement, where cutoff scores on tests are set on the basis of minimum competency standards within an occupation. The *Uniform Guidelines* require that cutoff scores be set so as to be reasonably related to acceptable job performance and, to the extent that criterion-referenced methods can be used to quantify judgments of minimum competency, they can be very useful in supporting the use of specific cutoffs.

The Uniform Guidelines and Subjective Selection Criteria and Procedures

CONFERENCE REMARKS

Robert Gelerter[1]

I would like to talk about one aspect of public policy surrounding the use of testing. Before I get into it, let me just say that I am neither a lawyer nor a psychologist; I am more like a cop on the beat. I come from an agency that is responsible for measuring adverse impact, and if there is adverse impact, we then place some obligations on employers. What I would like to do is talk about our agency and how we go about doing our business, and in order to do that I want to make an appeal. As you look at the question of testing, you should broaden the concept of testing to include subjective measures such as evaluations and interviews. Robert Adams (see Adams, this volume) has discussed the need to go beyond entry level jobs, to consider adverse impact in promotions and higher level jobs; if you are going to do that, you will have to begin to talk about subjective measures like evaluations and interviews.

The Office of Federal Contract Compliance Programs, which I will refer to as OFCCP, is in the U.S. Department of Labor; and so when we are talking about the Department of Labor's application of the *Uniform Guidelines on Employee Selection Procedures*, we are talking about OFCCP's application of the guidelines. The OFCCP, among other things, administers Executive Order 11246 that prohibits government contractors and subcontractors who sell goods and services to the federal government from discriminating on the basis of race, sex, religion, or national origin. In addition, it also requires the larger of those contractors to take affirmative action and it is this latter aspect that differentiates the scope of authority of the OFCCP from that of the Equal Employment Opportunity Commission, with resepect to enforcement of Title VII of the Civil Rights Act. Also, our world is a little bit more limited, we focus on private employers who are doing business with the government; we have no authority over private employers who do not do business with the government.

---

[1] Robert Gelerter is chief of the Special Studies and ADP Section, Office of Federal Contract Compliance Programs, U.S. Department of Labor. These remarks were contributed by the author in his private capacity. No official support or endorsement by the U.S. Department of Labor or any other agency of the United States government is intended or should be inferred.

Historically, the OFCCP has scrutinized the impact of employment tests on selection rates for race, sex, or ethnic groups. The emphasis has been principally on paper-and-pencil tests and unscored objective criteria such as educational background and licensing requirements. However, OFCCP has always known that employers make subjective judgments about applicants for higher level jobs. These job selection procedures have the potential to include illegal factors causing discrimination.

What I would like to talk about today is the manner in which the courts and the government have come to grips with the concerns about employee selection procedures and the potential for these procedures to discriminate. Specifically, I hope to make the case for the need to include in the consideration of the National Commission on Testing and Public Policy, guidelines for validating these subjective procedures. Of particular concern are evaluations and interviews used for hiring and promotions and for salary advancement, and so on. I will not actually be discussing the validation procedures.

Just as Donald Schwartz has said (see Schwartz, this volume), I am not here as an official representative of the federal government, and I will make it clear that what I am presenting here are my own views. The U.S. Department of Labor and the OFCCP are not prepared at this time to take any position on the *Uniform Guidelines* themselves. I think that has to be understood up front.

I will begin my discussion with a brief examination of *Griggs v. Duke Power* because it is the classic case which set the background for the validation requirements. Then I intend to look at the economy and how the economy has shifted towards industries and occupations which traditionally have relied more on subjective types of procedures. I will then discuss the safeguards that the courts have been identifying in their decisions, which can help to insure and limit the subjective nature of the evaluations and interviews and the need, then, to evaluate those procedures. Finally I will talk about the importance of the *Uniform Guidelines* themselves to OFCCP.

The interviews and evaluations traditionally rely on the judgments of interviewers and evaluators to assess the responses, experience, and performance of applicants. With the possible exception of structured questionnaires, these devices are subjective by their very nature, since the judgments of the interviewers determine the outcomes.

The right to challenge specific selection devices which are uniformly applied, but by their operation have an adverse impact, is based on the Supreme Court's decision in *Griggs v. Duke Power*. As most of you know, this case found that Duke Power Company had discriminated against Griggs and other blacks by reason of its use of an educational attainment requirement and a test which had an adverse impact on the selection rates for minorities. Because the Duke Power Company could not show a legitimate business necessity for the use of the requirements, and even though the tests were administered in a neutral fashion, the court concluded that the tests and the educational requirements had, by their operation, a discriminatory impact. Thus, if the employer could not show that the requirements were predictors of successful performance on the job, Duke Power Company was found to be violating Title VII of the Civil Rights Act, and, by implication, Executive Order 11246. This case, and several others such as *Washington v. Davis* and *Dothard v. Rawlinson*, established that the government could substantiate race, sex, and ethnic origin discrimination based upon an adverse impact theory by showing that a facially neutral employment practice had a significant adverse impact on the selection rate for one group. Further, if this employment practice could not be shown to be justified by business neccessity, the employer would be found in violation of Title VII of the Civil Rights Act of 1964, or the Executive Order 11246. I think you need to understand the significance of these cases. They establish that an employer could be found in violation of the law not on a conscious level but by operation of a test. Employers themselves may not have made a decision to discriminate. This unintentional discrimination is, for us at OFCCP, an extremely important consideration.

Paralleling these developments in the law, the courts were struggling with judgments about subjective employee selection procedures which had an adverse impact on the selection rates of protected groups. These included evaluations and interviews used either alone or with other screening devices like a test. In cases like *Rogers v. International Paper Co.* and *Hester v. Southern Railway Co.*, the courts have found that subjective employment selection procedures are not unlawful *per se*, and that the decisions about hires and promotions of supervisors, professionals, and managers, to name a few, could not realistically be made relying solely on objective standards. As a result, the courts began to identify the circumstances under which the subjective nature of a selection procedure or criterion could be sufficiently constrained, so that adequate protections would be provided and employment opportunities would not be limited by reason of an individual's race, sex, religion, color, or national origin.

In *Rowe v. General Motors Corporation*, the court stated some clear principles which would raise the inference of discrimination due to subjectivity in making selection decisions. What was found in this case was that a single individual, a foreman, was making the selection decision. The foreman's recommendation was critical to the decision, but he had no written instructions on how to make the recommendation. Specifically, he had no instructions as to what qualifications were required for the job. The standards followed were vague and subjective, and the applicants were not notified of the qualifications. Moreover, there were no safeguards to prevent the biases of the deciding official, the foreman, from influencing the decision. And of course the courts found in Rowe's favor in that case. Based upon Rowe's concerns about the circumstances in which employers allow the prejudices of the selecting officials to influence selection decisions, the courts began to identify safeguards which provide the necessary limits to subjective employer selection procedures and protect employees from having their opportunities limited by their race, sex, religion, and so on.

In *Pounsey v. Prudential Insurance* and *Wilson v. Michigan Bell*, the courts said that employers with adequate safeguards on otherwise subjective selection procedures, like evaluations and interviews, may not be liable under the law by reason of that subjectivity. This would, of course, depend upon whether the criteria or procedures could be shown to be job related or a business necessity. The types of safeguards the courts recognized were written instructions to raters on the specific procedures and criteria to be used, the review of decisions by higher level managers, and the opportunity for employees to comment on rating results, to name a few.

The courts and federal agencies like OFCCP continue to accept as legitimate the use of subjective criteria in making employment decisions, particularly when the jobs are white-collar, like managers, professionals, supervisors, and academics. However, we expect that the subjective criteria and procedures have adequate safeguards to insure that they are fair and uniform in their application. Thus the OFCCP is beginning to treat subjective selection procedures with adequate safeguards as facially neutral, and thereupon to scrutinize them under adverse impact theories. So we are beginning to have to face the dilemma of "what do we do now?" If we have adverse impact, how do we proceed in those circumstances?

The scope of the *Uniform Guidelines* is not limited to tests alone. They apply to any selection procedure used as a basis for employment decisions. As I said earlier, the fundamental principle of the guidelines is that any employment practice or policy which has an adverse impact on the opportunities of any race, sex, or ethnic group are illegal under Title VII and the Executive Order 11426 unless justified by business necessity. The employer's intent is not relevant; it is the operation of the device which is relevant. If the operation of the procedure or practice created the adverse impact, it must be justified by business necessity. To justify a selection device which screened out a higher proportion of minorities and women, the employer would have to show that the device was fair and predicted performance on the job. To do so, the device would have to be validated by establishing its relationship to successful performance in major aspects of the job. Interviews and evaluations generally have not been subject to this type of analysis because, among other things, their subjective nature allowed the government enforcement agencies to challenge them on the basis of differential treatment. In other words, employers were said to be treating people differently, based on their race and sex. Under the direction now being taken by the courts, subjective procedures with safeguards would be able to mitigate the discriminatory effects of the subjective character of these selection devices.

Over the past ten to fifteen years our economy has been changing. We have seen a shift in the industrial mix of the economy from basic manufacturing industries like steel and other primary industries, like the automobile industry, towards service and financial industries. With these changes we are seeing a shift in the demand for workers in the labor market from blue-collar workers towards more professionals, managers, administrators, and service workers. From 1970 to 1980, the experienced civilian labor force grew by 25%. During the same period, however, employment in financial and insurance industries grew by 43%, and in the service industries by 50%. At the same time, employment in the basic manufacturing industries increased by only 5% (that's hardly keeping pace with the changes in other industries). It is these industries, the finance and service industries, which tend to rely to a higher degree on interviews and evaluations, either by themselves or with tests, to make their selection decisions. During this same period, employment in white-collar positions such as managers, professionals, technicians, sales, and administrative categories grew by 30%. However, employment in blue-collar positions increased by only 15% to 20%. Based upon this information, and upon all the predictions for the economy, the growth and demand for managers, professionals, technicians, sales, and service workers in service and finance industries will continue to outstrip that of other industries into the next century.

Based upon OFCCP's experience, we see that the employment selection procedures for white-collar jobs in the finance and service industries rely more heavily on subjective employment procedures such as evaluations and interviews, either alone or with tests. Employment selection procedures for blue-collar jobs tend to rely more on the pencil-and-paper tests and on unscored objective criteria. The enforcement agencies like OFCCP have increasingly been faced with having to make decisions about the legality of evaluations and interviews with adverse impact. The type of subjective procedures that the courts and OFCCP have been accepting as legitimate are generally interviews in which the judgments have been limited to behaviors or competencies which are necessary for successful job performance, as determined by a professional job analysis. Questions about, for example, attendance, mathematical skills, ability to write, and so forth, are usually accepted; those about attitudes may not be. Specific guidelines for evaluators, such as asking the same questions of each person, keeping notes on responses and conclusions (and mind you, these are things that the courts are saying should happen, but they are things that OFCCP tends to find does not happen), rating observable behavior rather than attitudes, permitting employees to review and comment on, for example, evaluations, using evaluation devices with fixed content, developing composite judgments by more than one rater, the existence of an appeal procedure, and so on, are the kinds of safeguards the courts want to see.

Let me talk about the importance of the *Uniform Guidelines* to OFCCP. The importance of the guidelines to OFCCP and its need for guidance on the validation of evaluations and interviews can be better seen through an understanding of the manner in which OFCCP conducts its business. OFCCP fulfills its mandate under the executive order by conducting compliance reviews and complaint investigations. Compliance reviews are designed to determine whether a covered government contractor or subcontractor has in place an affirmative action plan and is meeting its obligations under that plan. We are also asked to make decisions about all the employment decisions that the employer has made over the course of time, and to verify, after we finish that review, that the employer has made all of its employment decisions without regard to race, sex, religion, or national origin, among other things (we also administer handicapped provisions and veterans' provisions). The complaint procedures that we follow are essentially the same as those under Title VII so I will not discuss them here.

OFCCP's universe is rather large. We cover sixteen thousand major corporations employing twenty-three million workers, which is about 20% of the total U.S. work force, and we review about five thousand of these corporations on an annual basis. Because of the size of the world that we look at, and because of the need for us to say something about all employment decisions that an employer has made, we use what we call sweeping statistical scans. We look at an employer's work force composition using an adverse impact model, and by doing that we tend to come up with a lot of adverse impact. Now, granted, the data we are looking at are incumbent data, not selection rate data, but we get into the issue of beginning to look at interviews and evaluations on a rather heavy basis. At this time we have not had to face the issue of validating subjective procedures, but we are not too far from having to confront this issue. I believe that we do not know what to do with validation of subjective procedures at this point. We are looking for help in this area.

III

TESTING AND THE LAW:
THE ROLE OF THE COURTS

Testing, Public Policy, and the Courts

Michael A. Rebell[1]

Public policy makers dealing with testing issues often assume that test scores measure "innate intelligence" or "competence" in a scientifically objective way, much as thermometers invariably gauge the correct temperature. In fact, however, tests measure only limited domains of knowledge, in certain specific ways; their accuracy and their usefulness depend on the manner in which they are constructed and on how their results are interpreted. This is precisely why issues of test construction and test use often become controversial public policy concerns.

The courts' involvement in testing cases needs to be seen in a similar perspective. Psychometricians and others affected by court decisions often assume that judicial pronouncements represent "black letter" statements of some objective truth. Like tests, however, court decisions are not concrete calibrations against which future issues can easily be assessed. Rather, they are judgmental resolutions of competing legal principles; they cannot be fully understood without a thorough knowledge of the factual and legal contexts in which they arose, and of the particular problems to which they were addressed.

In recent years, courts have had a significant impact on the formulation of public policy issues associated with testing, so much so that it may not be an exaggeration to say that they have become a major public policy forum in this area. Consequently, it is important for lawyers, psychometricians, and the general public to understand the unique attributes, both positive and negative, that courts bring to an enterprise of this sort. One of the major responsibilities of a National Commission on Testing and Public Policy clearly should be to research the influence that courts have had on the development of testing policy in the past and to influence constructively the judicial role in the future. This article is intended to serve as a background paper to initiate a dialogue

[1] B.A., Harvard, 1965; LL.B., Yale, 1970; Partner, Rebell and Katzive, Attorneys at Law, New York, New York; Visiting Lecturer in Law, Yale Law School. The author has represented plaintiffs in a number of testing and special education cases, and he has also served as counsel to the testing company whose products were the subject of the Alabama litigation discussed in §B2 of the article. The author would like to thank the following individuals for their helpful comments and suggestions: Jaclyn Frankfurt, Bernard R. Gifford, William P. Gorth, William Mehrens, Edward Opton, Jr., Daniel J. Reschly, and Rhoda Schneider.

within the commission, and among those with whom it is in contact, on these critical issues.

I. COURTS AS POLICY MAKERS

The extensive judicial oversight that psychometricians have experienced in recent years is merely one manifestation of the more general phenomenon of "judicial activism." Estimates of the number of lawsuits filed in all state and federal courts annually range from five to twelve million, and the rate of expansion in the number of filings is in the range of 80-90% per decade.[2] This quantitative explosion has been accompanied by a substantial qualitative enhancement of the judicial role, especially in major class action cases raising fundamental public policy issues. The Supreme Court's landmark decision outlawing school desegregation in *Brown v. Board of Education*[3] has led to extensive judicial involvement in institutional reform, not only in the implementation of desegregation decrees, but also in a broad range of reform contexts, from the redesign of state prison systems[4] to the treatment of residents of institutions for the mentally retarded.[5]

Numerous explanations have been offered for the litigiousness of American society and the activist role undertaken by the courts in recent years. These include a need for norms and values to bind a heterogeneous culture, the inherent legalistic orientation of a liberal society, and the importance of a rights-oriented counterforce to the large bureaucracies that dominate modern governments.[6] Whatever the cause of the litigation explosion in modern America, and however inconsistent current assertions of judicial authority may be with traditional concepts of the separation of powers among the three

---

[2] J. Liberman, *The Litigious Society* 5 (1981).

[3] 347 U.S. 483. For case study analyses of the role of the federal district courts in desegregation cases, see H. Kalodner and J. Fishman, *Limits of Justice* (1978).

[4] See, for example, *Rhem v. Malcolm*, 371 F.Supp. 594, 377 F.Supp. 995 (S.D. N.Y. 1974), *aff'd and remanded* 507 F.2d 333 (2d Cir. 1974), *aff'd* 527 F.2d 1041 (2d Cir. 1975); *Palmigiano v. Garrahy*, 443 F.Supp. 956 (D. R.I. 1977), *remanded* 599 F.2d 17 (1st Cir. 1979), 639 F.Supp. 244 (D. R.I. 1986); *Rhodes v. Chapman*, 452 U.S. 337 (1981).

[5] See, for example, *Wyatt v. Stickney*, 344 F.Supp. 373 (M.D. Ala. 1972), *aff'd in part sub. nom. Wyatt v. Adenholt*, 503 F.2d 1305 (5th Cir. 1974); *Halderman v. Pennhurst State School and Hosp.*, 451 U.S. 1 (1981), 465 U.S. 89 (1984). See also H. Rothman and S. Rothman, *The Willowbrook Wars* (1984).

[6] See, for example, L. Friedman, *Total Justice* (1985); S. Huntington, *American Politics: The Promise of Disharmony* (1981); Fiss, "Foreward: The Forms of Justice," 93 *Harv. L. Rev.* 1 (1979); M. Rebell, "Judicial Activism and the Courts' New Role," *Social Policy* 24 (Spring 1982).

branches of American government,[7] one point is clear: judicial involvement in social reform issues, including testing, is likely to be a permanent part of the public policy landscape for the foreseeable future. Consequently, it is important to understand both the strengths and the weaknesses of the judicial process as a public policy decision-making mechanism.

In relation to testing, the courts' positive attributes as policy makers would appear to have four major dimensions. First, the courts' orientation is to articulate principled bases for resolving major disputes. In comparison with legislative and administrative decision-making forums, courts do not tend to engage in political compromising and instrumental balancing of competing factors in their deliberations; instead, their institutional orientation is to focus on the ultimate implications of the issues in dispute. In the testing context, this means that courts can be highly effective in detecting and eliminating gross abuses, and in clarifying basic principles and standards. Moreover, since it is the courts' special institutional orientation to protect individual rights, judicial intervention, on the whole, adds significant weight in the broad public policy dialogue on testing to issues of test use and the actual impact of particular practices on affected individuals.

Second, courts are highly efficient fact-finding vehicles. It has been said that cross-examination is "the greatest legal engine ever invented for the discovery of truth."[8] Recent trials of test validation issues well exemplify this assertion. Probably the most exhaustive analyses of psychometric issues undertaken anywhere occur in class action litigations of controversial tests. In a trial context, all questions on the test under consideration, as well as all methodologies utilized in the test construction process, are closely scrutinized by teams of experts working with the attorneys for each side. The detailed information obtained on actual testing practices which emerges from this

---

[7] For discussion of the separation of powers issues raised by judicial activism, as well as comparisons of the functioning of the legislative, administrative, and judicial branches on social policy issues, see M. Rebell and A. Block, *Educational Policy Making and the Courts: An Empirical Study of Judicial Activism* (1982) (hereinafter referred to as EPAC); and M. Rebell and A. Block, *Equality and Education: Federal Civil Rights Enforcement in the New York City School System* (1985). See also D. Horowitz, *The Courts and Social Policy* (1977); Chayes, "The Role of the Judge in Public Law Litigation," 89 *Harv. L. Rev.* 1281 (1976); N. Glazer, "Towards an Imperial Judiciary?," 41 *Publ. Int.* 104 (1975).

[8] 5 Wigmore, Evidence §1367 (Chadbourn rev. 1974). "When interviewed after the trial, Dr. [Gene] Glass [a noted psychometrician] stated that knowing that his testimony as defendants' expert in this case would be dissected by a skillful adversary motivated him to intensify his preparation to such an extent that he put more work into this task than he normally would devote to writing an article, preparing to deliver a paper before his colleagues, or giving a statement before a legislative committee." EPAC, *supra* note 7 at 292, n. 102.

adversary process influences future practices, not only of the parties to the immediate suit, but also of the broader professional public to whom trial results are disseminated.

Third, judicial oversight can be extensive and long lasting. Unlike a legislature or an administrative agency which tends to turn its attention to other concerns after the immediate problems have been resolved in some form, courts retain ongoing jurisdiction over the implementation of a testing program. Such continued jurisdiction constitutes a probing accountability mechanism which promotes improved practice over a sustained period of time. It maximizes the likelihood that effective solutions to the deficiencies that caused the initial problem will be developed and implemented.

Fourth, courts convey an aura of authoritativeness and legitimacy which garners substantial respect. Judicial authoritativeness not only promotes compliance by the parties to the immediate lawsuit, but it also influences the behavior of those in the broader professional community who are engaged in similar practices. Thus, although courts technically rule only on particular issues in individual cases, their opinions tend to hold the entire psychometric profession accountable for their published standards and their actual practice.

The judicial process also exhibits countervailing negative attributes in regard to the formulation of public policy on testing issues. Not surprisingly, these negative attributes of the courts' institutional functioning are, to a large extent, the inverse implications of the same four characteristics which constitute its strengths.

First, the courts' "principled" orientation to dispute resolution may lead them to step back from deciding certain controversies, or aspects of a particular controversy, which do not exhibit judicially-cognizable issues of principle. This orientation tends to produce inconsistencies which can create significant problems from a public policy perspective. For example, because the applicable laws provide for greater scrutiny for claims of test invalidity or test misuse asserted by racial minorities, such allegations brought by blacks will often be upheld while similar claims brought by whites would be denied or ignored.[9] As a result, test users may seek to avoid judicial jurisdiction by focusing on devices that artificially increase the minority pass rates without solving underlying problems of test construction or validation that affect all test takers, including minorities.

Judicial jurisdictional limitations also may create other policy gaps. For example, since tests given directly by public employers are covered by Title VII of the 1964 Civil Rights Act, while many tests given indirectly by state licensing

---

[9] See, for example, *Bigby v. City of Chicago*, 766 F.2d 1053 (7th Cir. 1985) (white police officers denied standing to assert claims against an examination found to be nonvalidated for blacks).

boards are not, some civil service exams (like police hiring tests[10]) will receive intense judicial scrutiny, while other tests (like bar exams[11]) which reflect the same—or worse—validation problems, will be subjected to little judicial oversight.

Second, although the adversary process is highly effective in ferreting out all relevant facts, judges are "generalists," who do not purport to have a scientific background for properly assessing the complex psychometric issues which are brought before them. Accordingly, judges who are called upon to determine social science controversies tend either to rely on their assessment of the "credibility" of the witnesses for one side or the other, or on various legal "avoidance devices" that allow them to decide the controversies on scientific grounds.[12] In other words, there is a danger that although a wealth of relevant evidence may be brought into focus through the judicial process, judges' lack of expertise may cause them to issue rulings that, from a professional perspective, are ill conceived or erroneous.

Third, jurisdictional longevity can disintegrate into monitoring rigidity. During the remedial phase of a litigation, there is sometimes a tendency on the part of all the parties to do what is approved and required, no more and no less. Since courts may maintain jurisdiction over complex class actions for ten years or more, creative new approaches which emerge in the profession can be ignored or delayed in implementation because they are inconsistent with, or are not explicitly required by, the particular court decree. Of course, judicial decrees can be modified or reinterpreted to cover changed circumstances if the issues are brought to the judge's attention, but parties are often disinclined to resubmit themselves to the exhaustive litigation process.

Finally, the aura of judicial authoritativeness can become counterproductive when the general public, or in this case, the professional psychometric community, read language in court decisions (or summaries or reports of them) without an awareness of their intended limitations or qualifications. One problem in this regard is that minor matters of *dicta* in a court decision are sometimes considered major holdings. Another is that idiosyncratic pronouncements of a single judge can be considered binding

---

[10] See, for example, *Guardians Association of New York City v. Civil Service Comm.,* 630 F.2d 79 (2d Cir. 1980); *Williams v. Vukovich,* 720 F.2d 909 (6th Cir. 1983); *Vanguard Justice Society v. Hughes,* 592 F.Supp. 245 (D. Md. 1984).

[11] See, for example, *Woodward v. Virginia Board of Bar Examiners,* 420 F.Supp. 211 (E.D. Va. 1976), *aff'd* 598 F.2d 1345 (5th Cir. 1979); *Tyler v. Victory,* 517 F.2d 1089 (5th Cir. 1972); *Chaney v. California State Bar Examiners,* 386 F.2d 962 (9th Cir. 1967).

[12] Such devices include declaring certain controversial issues irrelevant, basing a decision on burden of proof factors, culling out areas of agreement between the parties, or relying on precedents from other judicial decisions. These are discussed in more detail in EPAC, *supra* note 7, Ch. 4.

precedent throughout the country. Probably the most serious situation from the perspective of long-range policymaking is a tendency within the psychometric community to assume that holdings relevant to a particular context are automatically generalizable to analogous contexts; professional practices are revised accordingly, even before the courts—or the profession— have fully analyzed the implications for the analogous area. A case in point is the recent widespread tendency of developers of teacher competency tests to assume that "instructional validity" concepts formulated by the courts in the student testing context automatically apply in this analogous setting.[13]

In short, then, courts simultaneously offer both institutional advantages and disadvantages when seen as alternative policymaking forums on testing issues. An important responsibility for scholars in this field, and particularly for the National Commission on Testing and Public Policy, is to analyze these institutional strengths and weaknesses and to propose approaches for judicial involvement in testing matters which are most likely to succeed. In order to provide a basis for such thinking, the next section will discuss some particular examples of both positive and negative judicial involvements in testing.

II. THE COURTS' PAST PRACTICES

Positive Interventions

Implementation of Title VII Employment Testing Requirements

Title VII of the Civil Rights Act of 1964 broadly prohibits employers from engaging in discriminatory practices in their hiring procedures.[14] Congress was aware at the time that the use of employment tests was on the rise, and that in some quarters, invalid tests were being used to deprive minority groups of fair employment opportunities.[15] For these reasons, Congress included employment testing within the strictures of the act. However, because of strong feelings raised by a decision of a hearing examiner for the Illinois Fair Employment Commission, which suggested that standardized tests on which

---

[13] This issue is discussed in detail in M. Rebell, "Disparate Impact of Teacher Competency Testing on Minorities: Don't Blame the Test Takers—Or the Tests," 4 *Yale L. and Pol. Rev.* 375, 384-389 (1986).

[14] 42 U.S.C. §2000e-2. Originally, private educational institutions and state and local government agencies were exempt from the act; in 1972, however, most of these exemptions were abolished and employees of state and local governments were covered by the antidiscrimination mandates of the law. 42 U.S.C. §2000e(a).

[15] See Cooper and Sobol, "Seniority and Testing Under Fair Employment Laws: A General Approach to Objective Criteria of Hiring and Promotion," 82 *Harv. L. Rev.* 1598, 1637 (1969); "Special Issue: Testing and Public Policy," 20 *Amer. Psych.* 857 (November 1965).

whites performed better than blacks could never be used,[16] a specific provision was incorporated in Title VII which authorized an employer "to give and to act upon the results of any professionally developed ability test," provided that such test is not "designed, intended or used to discriminate because of race."[17]

Title VII also established the Equal Employment Opportunity Commission (EEOC), and empowered the EEOC to investigate allegations of discriminatory employment practices and to seek conciliation agreements to rectify any discrimination found. In its early attempts to effect compliance with the act, the EEOC apparently determined that conducting ad hoc negotiations with individual companies was not proving fully effective. Consequently, the commission decided to issue broad guidelines promulgating standards that would be used uniformly in its compliance endeavors.[18] Such guidelines, not being formally enacted in accordance with procedures under the Administrative Procedure Act, would not normally be expected to have the binding legal impact of administrative agency regulations. Rather, they would constitute "interpretative material," reflecting the agency's interpretation of the statutory intent, and, as such, would be entitled to no greater weight than "other well-founded testimony by experts in the field."[19]

A review of the major early Title VII cases indicates that the EEOC *Guidelines*, to the extent that their relevance was noted by the courts, were used precisely in this manner. For example, in *United States v. H. K. Porter Co.*,[20] the court upheld the use of general aptitude and mental ability tests which clearly had not been validated in accordance with the EEOC *Guidelines*. It decided to give greater credence to the testimony of defendants' expert witnesses,[21] and accepted the legality of the tests under Title VII on a "common sense" premise that mental ability tests obviously had some relationship to the jobs at issue. In others of the early cases, the courts

---

[16] *Myart v. Motorola, Inc.*, No. 636-27, reprinted in 110 Cong. Rec. 5662 (1964), *modified sub nom. Motorola, Inc. v. FEPC*, 58 L.R.R.M. 2573 (Ill. Cir. Ct. 1965), *rev'd*, 34 I11.2d 266, 215 N.E.2d 286 (1966).

[17] 42 U.S.C. §2000e-2(h).

[18] A. Blumrosen, "Strangers in Paradise: Griggs v. Duke Power Co. and the Concept of Employment Discrimination," 71 *Mich. L. Rev.* 59, 97 (1972).

[19] *Albemarle v. Moody*, 422 U.S. 405, 452 (1975) (Burger, C.J. dissenting in part). See, Note, "Weight of EEOC Guidelines in Evaluation of Employment Selection Procedures," 50 *Tulane L. Rev.* 397 (1976).

[20] 296 F.Supp. 40 (N.D. Ala. 1968).

[21] The court specifically stated in *Porter* that validation by a professional psychologist would not be required where a nonprofessional company personnel director, who appeared to be familiar with the job duties at issue, offered a "credible" opinion of the test's relevance to the job. 296 F.Supp. at 76.

invalidated testing practices under similar general "reasonableness" approaches, without reference to the EEOC *Guidelines*.[22]

It was in this environment that the United States Supreme Court's landmark decision in *Griggs v. Duke Power Company*[23] was decided. Prior to the effective date of the Civil Rights Act of 1964, the Duke Power Company had openly discriminated against black employees and job applicants. In response to the new law, the company abandoned its policy of segregating blacks into the "labor department," but it maintained two requirements for entry into the other, more desirable departments: a high school diploma and successful completion of two professionally-prepared aptitude tests. At the time the case was filed, all but one of the company's fourteen black employees remained in the labor department, largely because of these barriers.

The trial court that first heard the case upheld the legality of these diploma and testing requirements; it explicitly rejected the EEOC's position that Title VII required a showing that the tests or diploma requirements at issue were specifically related to the duties of a particular job.[24] The court reasoned that Title VII merely required that employment tests be "professionally developed," and that the tests at issue (the Wonderlic Personnel Test and the Bennett Mechanical Comprehension Test) were well-known standardized tests which had been developed by competent professionals. In affirming the lower court's decision, the United States Court of Appeals for the Fourth Circuit further indicated that the company had a valid "business purpose" in seeking to upgrade the general level of intelligence of its employees in a manner that would facilitate later internal promotions. The court specifically ruled that the EEOC *Guidelines* were not binding on the court because they were contrary to the legislative history which the court read to approve the use of general intelligence tests such as the Wonderlic.[25]

A central issue in the case when it reached the Supreme Court, then, was whether Title VII should be interpreted, as the lower courts did, to permit the use of general intelligence tests "designed by professionals" or whether, as required in the EEOC *Guidelines*, an employment test would be considered "professionally developed" only if an adequate showing had been made of its relationship to the duties of the specific job at issue. In its *Griggs* decision, the Supreme Court held that ". . . the EEOC's construction of [Title VII] to require

---

[22] See, for example, *Arrington v. Massachusetts Bay Transportation Authority*, 306 F.Supp. 1355 (D. Mass. 1969); *Dobbins v. Local 212, International Brotherhood of Electrical Workers*, 292 F.Supp. 413 (S.D. Ohio 1968).

[23] 401 U.S. 424 (1971).

[24] *Griggs v. Duke Power Company*, 292 F.Supp. 243, 250 (M.D. N.C. 1968).

[25] *Griggs v. Duke Power Company*, 420 F.2d 1225, 1234 (4th Cir. 1970).

that employment tests be job related comports with Congressional intent."[26] In addition, the court in later decisions also applied, and thereby gave authoritative legitimacy to, the specific standards for assessing job-relatedness set forth in the *Guidelines*.[27]

Griggs and the Supreme Court's subsequent Title VII decisions exemplify positive judicial interventions in testing policy under all four of the categories discussed in Part I of this article. First, the court took a strong, principled stand against testing practices that were being used to deny fair opportunities to minority employees. Second, the court's acceptance of the detailed EEOC job-relatedness standards meant that henceforth federal courts would need to consider extensive evidence of all aspects of the test construction and validation process in Title VII cases. Third, the Supreme Court's emphasis on properly validated, job-related exams would lead the federal courts to maintain continuing jurisdiction over employment discrimination cases until such time as acceptable testing vehicles were devised and put into place. Finally, the high court's authoritative support for thoroughgoing validation practices would motivate adherence to high professional standards in this area.

The Supreme Court's strong endorsement of the EEOC *Guidelines* in *Griggs* and the later Title VII cases also tended to mitigate each of the four negative attributes of the judicial process. Emphasis on this uniform set of *Guidelines* avoided the possibility of inconsistent testing standards being adopted or accepted by the lower courts; in fact, the EEOC standards came to be the general industry benchmark for professional practice, whether or not Title VII jurisdiction technically applied to a particular testing context. Second, the *Guidelines* provided a sound, readily available technical basis for the generalist judges to utilize in assessing testimony and in deciding complex

---

[26] 401 U.S. at 436. The other major holding of *Griggs* was that a *prima facie* case of a violation of Title VII could be established by a showing that a test had the *effect* of discriminating against minorities, regardless of whether such adverse impact was intentional.

[27] Since the Duke Power Company admitted that it had not undertaken any meaningful study of job-relatedness, the Court did not have occasion in *Griggs* to spell out in detail the manner in which a "demonstrable relationship to successful performance of the job for which it was used" (*Id.* at 431) should be established. The Court's follow-up 1975 decision in *Albemarle Paper Company v. Moody*, 422 U.S. 405 (1975), however, invoked numerous specific provisions of the *Guidelines* as the benchmarks for determining job-relatedness.

psychometric issues.[28] Third, the potential rigidity of continuing judicial oversight was minimized by direct or indirect incorporation into judicial decrees of the *Guidelines*, and related professional standards, which are subject to ongoing modification in light of changes in professional practices. Finally, the danger of overly-broad interpretation of judicial precedents was minimized because the *Guidelines* provided clear, defined parameters for public perceptions of what standards the courts meant to apply in this field.

In short, a major reason why the courts' involvement in employment testing issues has been largely successful is that *Griggs'* strong endorsement of the EEOC *Guidelines* established a channel for communication between the courts and the psychometric profession that has proved remarkably effective for all concerned. The original 1970 EEOC *Guidelines*, as well as later versions adopted by the EEOC and other federal agencies, have specifically incorporated the professional standards for educational and psychological testing developed by the American Psychological Association and related organizations.[29] In enforcing the *Guidelines*, therefore, the courts were also enforcing the testing profession's fundamental standards. This meant that, on the one hand, the profession was able to aid the courts by providing relevant, technical standards on most of the complex psychometric issues under review; on the other hand, the EEOC and the courts were able to aid the profession by promoting continued attention to the formulation and refinement of the professional standards, and by assuring that they would be assiduously enforced. The numerous court cases that have been decided over the past two

---

[28] One might speculate that the Court took the unusual stance of strongly approving *Guidelines* that normally would be considered mere "interpretive material" because it sensed that it was opening a new field for judicial intervention, one in which judges lacked technical expertise. The availability of the *Guidelines* as a convenient and authoritative source of professional guidance for judges may have been astutely perceived. Whether or not this was the conscious understanding of the justices who adopted this position, such, in fact, has been the result of their holding.

[29] The original version of the EEOC *Guidelines* was largely generated by a group of testing experts brought together for that purpose by the EEOC's Office of Research. Blumrosen, *supra* note 18 at 97. Similarly, the 1978 *Uniform Guidelines* currently still in use, which have been jointly adopted by the EEOC and other federal executive agencies, were enacted only after consideration of voluminous written and oral testimony by individual psychologists and official representatives of the American Psychological Association (APA), the International Personnel Management Association, and more than 200 groups. See *The Uniform Guidelines on Employee Selection Procedures* (1978), 43 Fed. Reg. 38290, 38295 (Aug. 25, 1978) 29 C.F.R. Part 1607. For detailed discussions of the history of the development of the various versions of the APA *Standards* and the EEOC *Guidelines*, see W. Haney, "Testing Reasoning and Reasoning about Testing", 54 *Rev. Ed. Res.* 597 (1984); and M. Novick, "Ability Testing: Federal Guidelines and Professional Standards" in *Ability Testing II* 70, 78 (A. Wigdor and W. Garner, eds., 1982).

decades have also provided the profession with an extensive data base for researching and formulating new standards[30] or for reconsidering old ones.[31]

The results of this positive interrelationship between the courts and the profession[32] are reflected in the impressive improvements which have

---

[30] For example, Standard 8.7 of the 1985 version of the APA *Standards* appears to have adopted the concept of "instructional validation" as developed in *Debra P. v. Turlington*, 644 F.2d 397 (5th Cir. 1981), 730 F.2d 1405 (11th Cir. 1984) and other challenges to student minimum competency testing requirements.

[31] For example, although §1607.5(a) of the 1970 EEOC *Guidelines* specifically required a showing of criterion validation, except where it could be shown that criterion validation "is not feasible," the evidence developed in many cases showed this high degree of preference to be unwarranted or not appropriate in many situations. See *Vulcan Society of the New York City Fire Department Civil Service Commission v. Civil Service Commission*, 490 F.2d 387, 394-5 (2d Cir. 1973). Accordingly, the 1978 *Uniform Guidelines* and the 1985 APA *Standards* have modified the priority emphasis on criterion validation, and followed the actual practice of most courts in accepting content validation as a full equivalent alternative validation approach. See §5(A), *Uniform Guidelines on Employee Selection Procedures* (1978), 29 C.F.R. §1607.5(A); *Standards for Educational and Psychological Testing.* (1985), Part I, Ch. 1. (Known as APA *Standards*.)

[32] Dr. Edward Opton took issue with this article's conclusion on this point in written comments as follows:

> The American Psychological Association, which is the principal author of the so-called "APA Standards," is a democratic association, and so its standards on psychological tests are produced by an internal political process: those who are interested in the subject vie to obtain seats on the committee that produces the standards, and others interested in the subject appear in writing or in person at meetings to argue for revisions in one direction or the other. In response to judicial decisions, there were political struggles within the APA between psychologists employed in the testing industry and psychologists who were concerned about equal opportunity. Since most psychologists interested in psychometric theory and standards are employed in the testing industry, that group prevailed in the democratic process, and the APA *Standards* were revised. In other words, the response to judicial application of the APA *Standards* was that special interest groups lobbied for changes that would be to their advantage and obtained those changes.

Partisan interests undeniably influence professional decision making by the APA, as with all democratic processes. From a comparative perspective, it nevertheless seems clear that the formulation of professional standards in conjunction with ongoing judicial oversight of testing practices has enhanced the public interest content of these standards and certainly of their enforcement. As one commentator has noted: "One beneficial aspect of these cases . . . was the light they shed on actual testing practices and on their discriminatory impact. Until the testing practices of American business were scrutinized under Title VII, it was impossible to calculate their effects on minorities or, indeed, to even know what testing practices were in use." C. Haney, "Employment Tests

occurred in the years since *Griggs*, both in the refinement of technical
standards, and more generally, in the extent to which compliance with
professional standards is accepted as an operational norm by test makers and
test users throughout the country. The "common sense" perception that a
sophisticated-looking test, developed by professionals, could be used even if
there was no specific showing of its relevance to the job in question, which was
accepted by many lower federal courts before *Griggs*, would be dismissed out
of hand by any judge or by any competent professional today. Improvements
in professional practice also appear to be reflected in patterns of court
decisions. Overwhelming proportions of plaintiff victories in the first few years
after *Griggs* have been succeeded by a more balanced breakdown of
plaintiff/defendant verdicts.[33]

The NTE Cases

A second, and more discrete, example of a testing area marked by positive
judicial intervention is the series of cases decided in the early 1970s which
challenged the use of the National Teachers Examination (NTE) as a
certification device in the deep South. The NTE was created by the Educational
Testing Services (ETS) to assess students' knowledge of the typical curricula
taught at teacher training institutions throughout the country. ETS did not
recommend or authorize the use of the NTE as a certification device in any
particular state, since the exam had not been validated for this purpose.
Nevertheless, in the early years of desegregation following the passage of the

---

and Employment Discrimination: A Dissenting Psychological Opinion," 5 *Indus Rel. L. J.* 1, 16 (1982).

[33] A study of all reported Title VII testing cases decided by the federal district courts between 1971 and 1979 indicated that for the period 1971-1976, plaintiffs were victorious in fifty-six cases, defendants in thirteen, and each side partially prevailed in the one remaining case. For cases decided from September 1976 through January 1979, plaintiffs prevailed in eighteen cases, defendants in nineteen, and five involved remands or other situations whose outcomes were as yet undetermined. M. Rebell and A. Block, *Competency Assessment and the Courts: An Overview of the State of the Law* (prepared for the National Institute of Education, Contract NIE-400-78-0028, ERIC No. ED 192-169 1980) at 13, 22.

A more specific illustration of the impact of judicial intervention is provided by the marked improvement over time in testing practices of a municipal employer who was a defendant in two different litigations before the same judge. Compare in this regard the testing practices for selection of municipal policy officers invalidated by Judge Newman in *Bridgeport Guardians v. Members of Bridgeport Civil Service Commission*, 354 F.Supp. 778 (D. Conn. 1973), *aff'd in relevant part*, 482 F.2d 1333 (2d Cir. 1973), with the same judge's decision several years later upholding testing practices of the same defendants, *Bridgeport Guardians v. Bridgeport Police Department*, 431 F.Supp. 931 (D. Conn. 1977).

1964 Civil Rights Act, a number of states and school districts required minimal scores on the NTE as a prerequisite for obtaining or retaining a job. This unvalidated use of the test had the effect of denying continued employment to black teachers in the newly desegregated schools.

In a consistent line of decisions, the federal courts emphatically enjoined the use of the NTE as a certification or job retention requirement.[34] In these cases, the courts' principled "rights" orientation compelled them to stop abuses which substantially affected black teachers, and to set aside definitively the various "common sense" defenses that had been offered for utilizing the exams. The extensive scrutiny of the testing instruments undertaken during some of these trials provided ETS an opportunity to understand how the tests were being misused and to take a stand against such unprofessional practices.

The consistency of the courts' position in these cases, and the authoritativeness of their message, had a direct impact on the state of the art in teacher competency testing. In recent years, those states seeking to implement teacher certification testing requirements—which, since the issuance of the report of the National Commission on Excellence in Education in 1983, has been a majority of the states[35]—have undertaken extensive validation efforts in connection with these programs.[36] Thus, there can be no doubt that the state of the art in teacher competency testing has been notably improved as a result of judicial intervention in this area.[37]

---

[34] See, for example, *Walston v. County School Bd. of Nansemond County,* 492 F.2d 919 (4th Cir. 1974); *Georgia Association of Educators v. Nix,* 407 F.Supp. 1102 (N.D. Ga. 1976); *United States v. North Carolina,* 400 F.Supp. 343 (E.D. N.C. 1975), *vacated,* 425 F.Supp. 789 (E.D.N.C. 1977); *Baker v. Columbus Municipal Separate School Dist.,* 329 F.Supp. 706 (N.D. Miss. 1971), *aff'd,* 462 F.2d 1112 (5th Cir. 1982). See also *Armstead v. Starkville Municipal Separate School Dist.,* 461 F.2d 276 (5th Cir. 1972) (requirement for minimum score on graduate record exam for initial appointment or retention of faculty positions invalidated).

[35] See M. Rebell, *supra* note 13 at 375.

[36] Currently, states tend either to conduct a separate validation of the NTE for use in the particular locale, or they create a "customized" exam which is validated during the test construction process to insure that it reflects the educational priorities and practices of the particular geographic setting. See R. Flippo, "Teacher Certification Testing Across the United States and the Consideration of Some of the Issues" (paper presented at annual meeting, American Education Research Association, Chicago, 1985).

[37] It should be noted, however, that judicial enforcement of validation standards does not appear as consistently rigorous in teacher competency cases as in the employment context. In the leading case in the area, *United States v. South Carolina,* 445 F.Supp. 1094 (D. S.C. 1977), *aff'd* 434 U.S. 1026 (1978), a three-judge panel, affirmed by the U.S. Supreme Court, upheld a validation process which related the content of the NTE to the subject matter taught in teacher training institutions in the particular state, rather than to the skills and knowledge needed for effective performance as a classroom teacher in the schools in that state, as required by the job-relatedness provisions of the EEOC

Negative Interventions

IQ Testing

In a number of recent cases, federal courts have considered the use of IQ tests for the placement of public school students in classes for the educable mentally retarded. The two most well-known such cases are *Larry P. v. Riles*,[38] in which a California federal court banned the use of IQ tests for such purposes, and *PASE v. Hannon*,[39] in which a Chicago federal judge upheld them. Although the results in these two cases differed, they both represent examples of problematic judicial interventions.

In *Larry P. v. Riles*, the court considered the disproportionate number of black children in classes for the educable mentally retarded, first in the San Francisco public schools and later, after the class definition was extended, throughout the state of California. Evidence submitted in the case indicated that approximately 25% of the students in educable mentally retarded (EMR) classes in California were black, although blacks represented only 9% of California's school population.[40] The court focused on the IQ tests as the prime cause of this disproportionate placement pattern, especially since the

---

Guidelines. See, for example, §14(A). Although the efforts to relate the national exam to local conditions was a marked improvement over the test's misuse in the earlier situations, the process upheld by the Court here did not meet rigorous job-relatedness standards. See C. Haney, *supra*, note 32 at 44-46.

The comparative lack of rigor of judicial enforcement of validation standards in the teacher compentency context may reflect the fact that the courts' involvement in this area has been less extensive than with the employment discrimination cases. Defendants in the initial NTE cases tended to drop the contested requirements altogether, rather than submit to ongoing judicial supervision of new testing practices. Moreover, as indicated above, judicial jurisdiction over certification and licensing exams is more limited than with job selection tests. See also G. Madaus, "Measurement Specialists: Testing the Faith, A Reply to Mehrens," 5 *Edu. Measurement*, 11, 14 (1986) (arguing that the adversary legal climate has impeded progress toward development of criterion-related performance measures for tests in this area).

[38] 343 F.Supp. 1306 (N.D. Cal. 1972) (preliminary injunction granted), *aff'd*, 502 F.2d 963 (9th Cir. 1974); 495 F.Supp. 926 (N.D. Cal. 1979), *aff'd in part and rev'd in part*, 793 F.2d 969 (9th Cir. 1984), 1986-87 EHLR Dec. 558:141 (N.D. Cal. 1986) (remedial decree modified).

[39] 506 F.Supp. 831 (N.D. Ill. 1980).

[40] 495 F.Supp. at 942.

legislature had recently enacted a statute that required IQ testing, on an instrument selected from an approved list, to precede every EMR placement.[41]

Judge Peckham proceeded to undertake a detailed analysis of the history of the development of IQ tests, emphasizing that they originated in a social Darwinist age which assumed that the tests measured innate intellectual capacity, and that the original standardization of the IQ test was done on exclusively white populations.[42] This analysis was extensive and perceptive, and served as a refutation of the "Jensenist theories" concerning alleged intellectual inferiority of blacks and other minorities, which were current at the time, and which were very much in the background of the litigation.[43] It is far from clear, however, that this emphasis on the innate/acquired intelligence issue was responsive to the central contemporary issues presented by the lawsuit.

All the parties in *Larry P.* agreed that IQ tests measure certain types of acquired knowledge. Defendants offered socioeconomic and cultural explanations, not innate intellectual inferiority, as the justifications for the disproportionate number of blacks in EMR classes.[44] The judge rejected these defenses in a brief "tentative" discussion,[45] and certainly without the type of

---

[41] 495 F.Supp. at 939. Ironically, passage of this statute in 1970 appeared to have been motivated by legislative concern at the same disproportion in minority representation that was now before the court. For this reason, the law, Educ. Code §6902.06 (now §56505), not only mandated the use of certain approved IQ tests, but it also (a) prohibited placement into an EMR class if a child scored better than two standard deviations below the norm on the test; (b) provided for the testing of children in their primary language; (c) required written parental consent prior to placement; and (d) called upon the Department of Education to prepare an annual report for the legislature on placements into EMR classes. Other statutes enacted about the same time required retesting of all students presently in EMR classes and the filing of annual reports by school superintendents in districts where there was a significant disproportion in the enrollment of minorities in the EMR program. See Cal. Educ. Code §56508.

[42] 495 F.Supp. at 957.

[43] See, for example, A. Jensen, "How Much Can We Boost IQ and Scholastic Achievement?," 39 *Harv. Ed. Rev.* 1 (1969); R. Herrnstein, "IQ," 228 *The Atlantic* 43 (Sept. 1971); Comp. *The New Assault on Equality: IQ and Social Stratification* (A. Gartner, C. Greer and F. Riessman, eds., 1974) (collection of articles critical of Jensen/Herrnstein positions).

[44] Although the state's attorney was said to be personally "sympathetic" to the Jensenist view, it is clear that the defendants, especially Wilson Riles, the superintendent of public instruction, who was himself black, disavowed the genetic explanation and did not base their defense on Jensenist arguments. R. Elliot, *Litigating Intelligence: IQ Tests, Special Education and Social Science in the Courtroom* 45 (1987).

[45] See 495 F.Supp. at 956-959. One commentator summarized the court's approach as follows:

probing analysis he used in discussing the Jensenist issues. Moreover, the court also minimized the rapidly-changing educational context in which these issues were being tried in the late 1970s, as dramatic new breakthroughs concerning educational opportunities for children with handicapping conditions, including mental retardation, were taking place.

Specifically, the trial in *Larry P.* coincided with the era of initial implementation of extensive new state and federal statutes[46] and regulations which, for the first time, acknowledged the basic rights of the handicapped to an equal educational opportunity, and which set forth an elaborate series of specific educational requirements and due process protections to insure that programs appropriate to each child's individual needs were provided in suitable special education classes. Given this climate, the court's failure to recognize the full significance of the new statutory rights, and its conclusory assumption that EMR classes are "dead-end classes" with low turnover rates,[47] was unfortunate.

Indeed, the court noted that California had recently enacted legislation which, consistent with the trends of enlightened thought in the profession, required EMR placements to be made only after a multi-faceted assessment

---

Though the court rested its decision on the finding that the tests were culturally biased, it provided little hard data to support such a conclusion and was tentative in discussing it. In fact, the court's determination that the tests contain questions biased against black children is not uniformly accepted, and there is some data to suggest that whatever discrimination there is in tests, lower scores in blacks are not the result of content bias. The court was correct in criticizing test publishers for not adequately standardizing their instruments on discrete minority populations, but beyond that, its analysis of cultural discrimination is weak and the issue certainly is not as settled as the court appears to think. D. Bersoff, "Regarding Psychologists Testily: Legal Regulation of Psychological Assessment in the Public Schools" 39 *MD L. Rev.* 27, 97 (1979).

[46] See, for example, Cal. Educ. Code §56300, *et seq.*; The Education for all Handicapped Children Act of 1975 (EHA), 20 U.S.C. §§1400-1461 (1982 and Supp. II 1984). For histories and analyses of the EHA, see *Special Education Policies* (J. Chambers and W. Hartman, eds., 1983); Note, "Enforcing the Right to an 'Appropriate' Education: The Education for All Handicapped Children Act of 1975", 92 *Harv. L. Rev.* 1103 (1979); M. Rebell, "Structural Discrimination and the Rights of the Disabled," 74 *Geo. L. Rev.* 1435, 1470-1480 (1986).

[47] 495 F.Supp. at 941-42.

process which utilized a number of criteria in addition to IQ tests.[48] Admittedly, these new procedures had not been widely implemented by local school districts. Instead of acknowledging the broad professional support for use of IQ tests as part of an overall clinical evaluation, and focusing on ways to achieve effective compliance with these requirements, the court rejected the state's movement as "slow and ambiguous,"[49] and proceeded to solve the problem in its own fashion.

The court's solution was, of course, to ban the use throughout the state of California of IQ tests for placement of black children into EMR classes, without prior approval of the court. In order to obtain such approval, a school district would need to show that an IQ test is not racially or culturally discriminatory and has no adverse impact on minorities.[50] In addition, districts with disproportionately high black EMR enrollments (defined in terms of one standard deviation above white EMR enrollment) are required to adopt corrective plans to eliminate such disparities.[51]

Judge Peckham's dramatic solution to the issue of disproportionate placement of black children in EMR classes raises a number of serious problems. First, it prevented the newly-emerging professional answers to the problem of test misuse and educational inadequacies in EMR classes from being implemented in California. To the extent that the California districts had overutilized the IQ test as a sole measure, the proper remedy would have been

---

[48] 495 F.Supp. at 939-40. Specifically, in 1971, a year before the court's first preliminary injunction decision, the California legislature had enacted a requirement that "retarded intellectual development indicated by the individual test scores" be substantiated by "a complete psychological examination by a credentialed school psychologist investigating such factors as developmental history, cultural background, and school achievement." Cal. Educ. Code §56506. The statute also called for studies of "adaptive behavior," the ability to engage in social activities and perform everyday tasks to be undertaken, as well as home visits, with the consent of the parent or guardian.

[49] 495 F.Supp. at 941. The court may have been influenced by Judge Skelly Wright's well-known decision in *Hobson v. Hansen* 269 F.Supp. 401 (D. D.C. 1967), *aff'd sub nom. Smuck v. Hobson*, 408 F.2d 175 (D.C. Cir. 1969) which invalidated tracking practices in the Washington D.C. school district because these represented dead-end tracks for minority students. *Hobson v. Hansen* did not, however, deal with special education programs for handicapped students in the EHA era.

[50] The fact that in the past fifteen years, apparently no IQ tests meeting these standards have been developed, in and of itself, is an indication of the distance between the judge's perceptions and the state of the art in the profession.

[51] 495 F.Supp. at 990. In the 1986 modification of the judgment (based on a stipulation of the parties), the court made clear that the ban on the use of IQ tests is "complete." Such tests could not be used, even with parental consent, as part of any assessment which could lead to special education services, or for any indirect, related purposes. 1986-87 EHLR DEC 558:141, 142.

to require strict adherence to statutory requirements calling for multi-faceted testing and placement procedures.[52] Similarly, to the extent that EMR classes in any particular California school districts were providing "dead-end classes" instead of ". . . specifically designed instruction . . . to meet the unique needs of a handicapped child"[53] as required under the new law, the appropriate approach would have been to compel the provision of such remedies.

Second, the *Larry P.* decision may have resulted in the use of placement practices that are more subjective and less accountable than the IQ tests they replaced. A wide variety of evaluation approaches have been brought into play in California in recent years, none of which have yet been validated, and some of which, such as "teacher judgment," may constitute subjective practices that deny parents clear-cut information concerning the true reasons behind a placement decision—and an opportunity to challenge it.[54] Finally, it is likely that the *Larry P.* decision, while undoubtedly preventing the improper placement into EMR classes of some children who should not have been placed in special education, also has impeded proper placement into EMR classes of some who should be there.[55] The court's implicit assumption that EMR

---

[52] The applicable federal regulation, 34 C.F.R. §300.533, provides that in making placement decisions, a public agency shall:

(1) draw upon information from a variety of sources, including aptitude and achievement tests, teacher recommendations, physical conditions, social or cultural background and adaptive behavior.

Since it had not been shown that placements effectuated in accordance with the statutory requirements would have resulted in disproportionate or discriminatory placement of black students, the legal basis for Judge Peckham's setting aside of the statutory solution is questionable.

[53] 20 U.S.C.A. §§1412(1), 1401(16), (18).

[54] For a discussion of the various alternative assessment approaches being tried in California, see the *Report of the California Association of School Psychologists Task Force on Alternative Assessment* (December 1986). The court's 1986 stipulated modification of the judgment was apparently an attempt to preclude certain indirect, less accountable uses of the IQ tests, such as obtaining scores from other institutions or administering IQ tests for "general purposes" before specifically considering an EMR placement.

[55] See, Shea, "An Educational Perspective of the Legality of Intelligence Testing and Ability Grouping," 6 *J. Law and Ed.* 137, 142 (1977) (importance of IQ test information for educational placement decisions). The fact that placement in EMR classes is not necessarily punitive also raises substantial questions about the validity of Judge Peckham's adverse impact analysis. As the extensive decision of the Eleventh Circuit in *Georgia State Conference v. State of Georgia*, 775 F.2d 1403 (11th Cir. 1985) pointed out, disparate impact analysis becomes difficult, if not impossible, in a situation such as this where the relevant pool (i.e., all misclassified children, and not all children placed in

placements are punitive, and its statistical cap on the proportion of black enrollees, may actually be denying access to EMR classes for members of the plaintiff class for whom such placements would be appropriate.[56]

In essence, the court in *Larry P.* interposed itself into the placement process for mentally retarded students by eliminating one of the major diagnostic tools used by professionals throughout the country, without thoroughly considering alternative remedial approaches or the effect that its ruling would have on future professional practice. Although the diagnostic procedures, the continuum of services, and the due process procedures established by the EHA may not be the ultimate solution to the problems raised by *Larry P.*, they represented an advance in professional practice and in regulatory enforcement, which offered greater potential for progress than the simple prohibitions set forth in Judge Peckham's decree.

If Judge Peckham's handling of the psychometric issues in *Larry P.* revealed some of the shortcomings of the judicial process, Judge Grady's approach to IQ testing in *PASE* exemplified an even more serious lack of appreciation by a generalist judge of professional techniques and standards. Faced with allegations of disproportionate placement of black children in EMR classes similar to those in *Larry P.*,[57] Judge Grady declined to enter into a detailed analysis of the purpose of the tests or how they were actually being used in the Chicago schools. Instead, he rejected the testimony of the witnesses for both sides as "doctrinal commitments to a preconceived idea," and decided to review personally each and every item on the three IQ tests at issue. Thus, the bulk of the district court opinion in *PASE* consists of a reproduction of each item on the WISC-R and Stanford-Binet tests together with Judge Grady's personal analysis of whether the item is culturally biased against blacks.[58]

EMR classes) cannot be easily identified. See also *Larry P. v. Riles*, 793 F.2d 969, 986 (Enright, District J., dissenting in part and concurring in part).

[56] Judge Peckham noted with approval the "mainstreaming" thrust of the EHA (495 F.Supp. at 991-92), but even children with learning problems whose needs can be met by a supportive program in a regular class setting should be assessed through a procedure that can accurately measure their needs. See also Minow, "Learning to Live with the Dilemma of Difference: Bilingual and Special Education," 48 *Law and Cont. Prob.* 157 (1985) (discussing the inherent tension between the educational benefits of self-contained instructional settings and the stigma of segregation).

[57] The disparities actually were somewhat less in Chicago where blacks constituted 62% of the public school student body and 82% of the population of the EMR classes. 506 F.Supp. at 833.

[58] Although Judge Grady ultimately upheld the continued use of the IQ test, the court's extensive breach of test security in listing every item on the tests might well have precluded their further use in Chicago once the decision was published. This problem never arose, however, because the Board of Education decided, as part of a settlement in

The court's approach to psychometric analysis in PASE clearly constituted nothing more than ". . . a single person's subjective and personal judgment cloaked in the apparent authority of judicial robes."[59] It is highly unlikely that Judge Grady had sufficient subject matter competence in all of the fields covered by the examination to support his personal perceptions. Even if he did possess such expertise, the lack of additional input from a representative group of other experts would render his conclusions unacceptably subjective as a validation methodology. The judge's simple, common sense approach also omitted statistical analyses which might have revealed underlying structural biases. Finally, even assuming that the judge's personal scrutiny could somehow properly validate the content of the items in the tests under review, his personalized approach provided no guidance concerning basic test construction methodology; presumably all future modifications of these tests or item substitutions would need to be submitted for continuing judicial approval.

Judge Grady's personal analysis convinced him that only one item on the Stanford-Binet and eight items on the WISC are culturally biased. He then held that these few items did not render the tests unfair.[60] Having reached this conclusion, Judge Grady accepted the defendants' broader arguments, which Judge Peckham had rejected in Larry P., that poverty and socioeconomic factors were the main explanations for the disproportion of minority students in EMR classes; he also noted that, in any event, the IQ test is only part of the placement process.[61]

---

another lawsuit, to suspend IQ testing irrespective of the decision in PASE. Since the use of IQ tests was discontinued in Chicago, Judge Grady's ruling was never appealed. See Prasse and D. Reschly, "Larry P: A Case of Segregation, Testing or Program Efficacy," 52 Exceptional Children 333, 342.

[59] D. Bersoff, "Larry P. and PASE: Judicial Report Cards on the Validity of Individual Intelligence Tests," in Advances in School Psychology 62 (Krotochwill, T., ed., 1982).

[60] The judge's detailed item-by-item analysis did allow him to assess more effectively the credibility of plaintiffs' main witness, who was shown to have given the misleading impression that the few examples of bias he cited were representative of a large number of items on the tests. (Some of the examples apparently did not even come from the tests under review.) In the adversary system, such a detailed analysis of the evidence, which might provide a basis for refuting the credibility of an expert witness, would normally be the responsibility of the opposing attorney, and not of the trial judge.

[61] 506 F.Supp. at 876-78. Rogers Elliot, in an extensive comparative analysis of Larry P. and PASE, indicates that EMR classes in Chicago generally were educationally sound placements and that the Chicago school system's black leadership supported these EMR placements. These factors, as well as the greater competence of the defense counsel in Chicago, and the orientations of the judges, seem to account for the differing results in the two cases. See generally, Elliot, supra, note 44 at 109, 111, 159.

Although differing in their ultimate outcomes, both *Larry P.* and PASE constitute troublesome precedents for judicial review of testing issues. Both cases took a narrow approach to the public policy issues involved, focusing on the immediate impact on certain minority students, rather than on the broader policy implications of the use of these tests on all minority—and majority—populations. In both instances, there also was a failure to utilize the full capacity of the judicial factfinding process to assess the complex psychometric and social science issues. A skeptical attitude toward the expert witnesses also apparently led Judge Peckham to design a rigid remedy, without professional input, that impeded implementation of new models of special-education evaluation and placement.[62] Finally, the authoritative aura of *Larry P.'s* dramatic ban on the use of IQ tests has tended to affect negatively the attitudes toward the use of the test, both inside and outside the State of California,[63] even though the profession continues to find its proper use to be beneficial.[64]

Although their decisions reflected differing levels of sophistication on the psychometric issues involved, Judges Peckham and Grady shared a significant common characteristic, which, to a large extent, explained the ultimately unsatisfying outcomes of these litigations: neither of them entered into an effective dialogue with the psychometric profession on the technical

---

[62] A more fruitful approach in this type of complex remedial litigation might have involved appointing a panel of professionals, representing all parties and interests, to draft a remedial decree and oversee its implementation. See, EPAC, *supra*, note 7 at 210-12.

[63] Note in this regard that the Los Angeles Unified School District recently issued a directive banning the use of IQ tests for all children referred for special education assessment, not only the black children covered by the *Larry P.* decree (Directive of Phillip P. Callison, Assistant Superintendent, December 19, 1986). Chicago's decision to discontinue use of IQ tests, despite their victory in the PASE case (see discussion *supra*, note 58), also undoubtedly was affected by the climate created by *Larry P.*

[64] The trend in recent ligitations appears to be countering the impact of *Larry P.* and approving use of IQ tests as part of a multi-faceted assessment process. See *Georgia State Conference, supra,* note 55 (use of IQ tests and EMR placement procedures upheld), *S-1 v. Turlington,* F.Supp., 1986-87 EHLR DEC. 558:136 (S.D. Fla. 1986) (challenge to EMR placement procedures dismissed on grounds that none of individually-named representatives of the plaintiff class had been misclassified pursuant to state requirements), and *Gregory K. v. Longview School Dist.,* 811 F.2d 1307 (9th Cir. 1987) (school district special education placement based on IQ tests, academic functioning, and adaptive behavior assessments upheld under the EHA). The strong defense mounted by the state defendants in these cases, as well as the more sophisticated understanding of placement practices in the decade since passage of the EHA, distinguish the litigation setting in these cases from that in *Larry P.* See D. Reschly, Kicklighter, and McKee, "Recent Placement Litigation: *Larry P., Marshall* and *S-1* and Implications for Future Practices" (forthcoming). Interestingly, plaintiffs in the Georgia case did not ask that use of IQ tests be prohibited, but rather that state regulations concerning cutoff scores be applied more stringently.

issues involved. In contrast to *Griggs* and the employment discrimination
cases, where the courts saw their prime role as assuring effective
implementation of the EEOC *Guidelines*, Judge Grady explicitly rejected
professional testimony and Judge Peckham largely ignored the emerging
professional standards for proper evaluation and placement of mentally
retarded children. Consequently, *PASE* has had little lasting impact on
psychometric practice, and *Larry P.*, rather than becoming a mechanism for
clarifying and enforcing emerging professional standards which address the
deficiencies the court deplored, actually became an obstruction to their
effective implementation.[65]

Following the Golden Rule

In response to the general pattern of minorities, as a group, scoring lower on
standardized tests,[66] test developers have established a number of bias review

---

[65] The criticism of Judge Peckham as a "generalist judge" should not be overstated.
Larry P. does represent a sophisticated understanding of many technical testing issues.
The point is, however, that public policy formulation on "cutting edge" issues requires
courts to engage fully current professional thinking. Judge Peckham's approach
precluded such interchange. The issue of validation of IQ tests for placement of students
in EMR classes well exemplifies this point.

   Larry P. was the first case to attempt to apply the requirement in the EHA that tests
used for educational placement of handicapped children ". . . have been validated for
the specific purpose for which they are used" (34 C.F.R. §300.532(a)2). Judge Peckham
noted that the educational context presents different validation problems from the
employment context (primarily because a test that predicts future performance justifies
a decision not to hire a potential employee, but no such test can justify a decision to
exclude a potential student from an educational setting). 495 F.Supp. at 969-70.
Nevertheless, the judge proceeded to apply concepts borrowed from the employment
discrimination sector in a wooden and unconvincing manner. The defendants were, in
essence, faulted for not proving that a validation process had been undertaken, even
though there was, as yet, no professional consensus as to what validation means in this
context. (For insightful analyses of the difficulties inherent in validating tests used for
placement purposes where there are no measurable outcomes, see Note, "Test
Validation in the Schools," 58 *Tex L. Rev.* 1123 (1980) and Note, "Intelligence Tests: To
Be or Not to Be Under the Education For All Handicapped Children Act of 1975," 76 *N.
W. L. Rev.* 640 (1981). A creative interrelationship between the court and the profession
could have been undertaken by calling for the establishment of validation panels as part
of the remedial decree in *Larry P.* Judge Peckham's failure to pursue such possibilities
left California students with no IQ tests and no properly validated alternative
assessment devices.

[66] See, for example, *Ability Testing, Part I* 18 (A. Wigdor and W. Garner, eds., 1982)
("certain social groups tend, as groups, to score consistently lower on the average than
more advantaged groups."); R. Samuda, *Psychological Testing of American Minorities:
Issues and Consequences* 1 (1975) (". . . the mean score of blacks is one standard
deviation below that of whites.")

procedures. Generally, these call for a review of the content of each test item, usually with substantial participation by members of minority groups on the review panels, before the item appears in a test. Statistical techniques have also been developed which attempt to identify items on which minorities do comparatively poorly so that these can be subjected to further scrutiny to ensure that there is no bias in their wording or content.[67]

Recently, a variation upon this theme emerged in the context of a litigation against a certification exam for insurance agents. Under this variation, items on which minorities as a group tend to do less well are not merely given special scrutiny for bias, but are set aside to be used only as a last resort, or not at all, on the basis of these statistical propensities alone. The dissemination of this technique through the legal process has expanded its implications well beyond its apparent original intent—so much so, that the prime author of the concept came to repudiate it.

The controversial item bias technique was developed as part of a settlement entered into by the Educational Testing Service in *Golden Rule Insurance Company v. Washburn*.[68] I have discussed the background and implications of this case in more detail elsewhere.[69] Suffice it to say for present purposes that the core of the *Golden Rule* settlement was a requirement that all items used on various administrations of the test be analyzed and classified into two categories, those on which the correct answer rates of black examinees and white examinees differ by no more than 15 percentage points at the .05 level of statistical significance, and those on which there was no such disparity. The agreement then required, generally speaking, that ETS use questions on which blacks as a group tend to perform as well as whites before it uses items on which the performance differential is greater.[70] Under this arrangement, ETS was not compelled to change its current item bank or to scuttle any

---

[67] For discussions of a number of such techniques, see *Handbook of Methods for Detecting Test Bias* (R.A. Berk, ed., 1982); W. Shepard, et al., "Validity of Approximation Techniques for Detecting Item Bias," 22 *J. of Ed. Measurement* (1985).

[68] No. 419-76 (Ill. Cir. Ct. 7th Jud. Cir. Nov. 20, 1984). See also *Golden Rule Insurance Co. v. Mathias*, 86 Ill. App. 3rd, 323 (4th Distr. 1980) (motion to dismiss challenge to certification exam upheld in part and denied in part).

[69] M. Rebell, *supra* note 13 at 391-97.

[70] *Golden Rule Ins. Co. v. Washburn*, Consent Decree of Nov. 20, 1984, *supra* note 68, at ¶6. The formula also takes into account correct answer rates by racial groups and by all examinees in its categorization. Moreover, the settlement also allowed the Illinois Insurance Department flexibility to omit certain items whose use would otherwise be called for by the stated decision rules "for good cause"; explanations of each such election and the reasons therefore were to be submitted to an advisory committee established under the agreement.

particular items. All that was specifically required was that items be drawn from the overall pool in a certain designated order.

The major difference between the *Golden Rule* approach and previous use of statistics to indicate differential performance by racial groups on particular items is that under *Golden Rule* decisions would be made solely on the basis of statistical indicators, without any necessity to identify questionable content in the targeted items. This methodology raises a number of serious concerns. First, there is a danger of distortion of the proportionate weight of subject matter covered by an exam, which is established by the content validation process to reflect "on-the-job" competence requirements. The weighting of the different subjects covered by the exam is known as "the blueprint." If many items necessary for the test blueprint are eliminated or modified, the integrity of this blueprint may be jeopardized.

Second, test content may be further distorted by the preference of the *Golden Rule* approach for "easy" items. Questions that all groups answer correctly will not exhibit high differential statistics. Accordingly, difficult concepts will be measured less often, even if such concepts are an important measure of ability to perform on the job.[71] Finally, the item bias approach may invite negative psychological and political reactions from white candidates who feel the technique is unfair because it eliminates questions on which they do well.[72]

ETS was apparently aware of these problems and attempted to qualify the *Golden Rule* decision rules to avoid or mitigate them.[73] In the months following the settlement, however, widespread publicity within the testing industry created an item bias bandwagon which led to legislative proposals and test development approaches that have picked up on the basic *Golden Rule* technique, while discarding many of the original qualifications. Legislative

---

[71] "When items are in fact unbiased, the application of the *Golden Rule* procedure is more likely to eliminate psychometrically desirable items than psychometrically undesirable items." R. Linn and Drasgow, "Implications of the *Golden Rule* Settlement for Test Construction" 6 *Edu. Measurement* 13, 16 (1987).

[72] Current evidence indicates that the specific items eliminated under statistical item bias techniques do not have any apparent culturally or racially biased wording or content. See, for example, Hoover, "The Reliability of Six Item Bias Indices," 8 *App. Psych. Meas.* 173, 180 (1984). For discussion of a conceptual approach that would avoid the arbitrariness of the *Golden Rule's* rigid decision rules, but would allow some consideration of the adverse impact of a particular item, all other things being equal, see Bond, "The *Golden Rule* Settlement: A Minority Perspective," 6 *Edu. Measurement* 18 (1987).

[73] See note 70, *supra*.

bills to this effect are currently pending in New York, California, and Texas,[74] and a consent decree containing an unqualified version of the *Golden Rule* formula was recently entered in the Alabama teacher certification case.[75]

Under the Alabama settlement, the 15% differential analysis concept used in *Golden Rule* to classify items for order of use was extended to preclude totally the use of any items falling outside the 15% range. The Alabama approach, in essence, bans the use of any items having a substantial adverse impact on minority candidates. Thus, the limited item bias approach of the

---

[74] The National Council on Measurement in Education recently stated in letters opposing legislation that would mandate utilization of *Golden Rule* techniques in New York and California that:

> These bills would result in severe adverse consequences for those individuals and educational institutions that objective tests are designed to serve. We have studied the most recent drafts of these pieces of legislation carefully. They are based on the erroneous assumption that differences in the proportions of students in various groups that answer test items correctly provide evidence that test items are biased against members of these groups...these assumptions are seriously flawed. They do not correspond to measurement specialists' understanding of the meaning of group performance differences and do not lead to acceptable professional practice in test development and use.

Letter from Richard M. Jaeger, President, National Council on Measurement in Education, to New York State Senator Arthur Eve (Apr. 29, 1986), 6 *Edu. Measurement* 21, 21-22 (1987). See also letter from Lauren B. Resnick, President, American Educational Research Association, to William P. Cunningham, Education Advisor to California Governor (Feb. 2, 1987) (*Golden Rule* legislation would "threaten and quite possibly destroy the validity of any educational tests based on them") (on file with the author).

[75] *Allen v. Alabama State Bd. of Educ.*, No. 81-697-N (M.D. Ala. July 12, 1985) (Consent Decree). This decree has had an unusual history. Immediately after counsel for the state education department had agreed to the consent decree, the attorney general objected both to its substance (among other things, it required the state to certify 500 members of the class who had failed the examination and to pay $500,000 in liquidated damages) and to counsel's authority to bind the state to settle. Counsel's consent was based on the position of the state commissioner of education, and on the lack of opposition from members of the state board of education when the proposed settlement had been discussed with them.

After the attorney general publicized his objections, the members of the state board of education formally met and officially voted to reject the consent decree. Although initially ruling that their prior actions constituted an approval which was now binding, *Allen v. Alabama State Bd. of Educ.*, 612 F.Supp. 1046, 1052 (M.D. Ala. 1985), the court, upon rehearing, held that in light of the broad public policy issues involved, it would vacate the settlement order and not impose the controversial consent decree on the now clearly unwilling defendants. *Allen v. Alabama*, 636 F.Supp. 64 (M.D. Ala. 1986). That decision, however, was itself overturned by the appeals court which has now reinstated the consent decree. *Allen v. Alabama*, 816 F.2d 575 (11th Cir. 1987).

Illinois case established a precedent that blossomed into a substantially more radical form in its very next application. Given the political pressures to reduce the adverse impact of teacher certification exams, and the extensive advocacy campaign being mounted to adopt and extend the *Golden Rule* formula, this radical Alabama version, rather than the limited Illinois approach, could well become the predominant model. Such use of the item bias approach could seriously compromise the integrity of teacher certification testing.

The crescendo of criticism of use—or more precisely misuse—of the *Golden Rule* approach became so overwhelming that in January 1987, Gregory Anrig, president of the Educational Testing Service, issued an open letter to the profession in which he stated:

> I now believe that I made a mistake in approving the so-called 'Golden Rule' settlement agreement entered into by Educational Testing Service in 1984. That agreement seemed to make sense at the time in the limited context of the particular testing program involved. However, the settlement has since been used to justify legislative proposals that go far beyond the very limited term of the original agreement. I did not anticipate this result and should have.[76]

Mr. Anrig's error of judgment was, in essence, a failure to appreciate the extent to which the authoritative imprimatur of judicial documents can create an aura of legitimacy for controversial new ideas. This aura of legitimacy allows concepts expressed in legal form to gain influence within the profession, and in legislative and administrative forums, that is far beyond what might be merited by their actual substance or importance.

Ironically, no judge had actually reviewed and approved the substance of the *Golden Rule* approach, either in its initial form or in its Alabama variation. Both formulations were contained in settlement documents negotiated by attorneys, which were then approved in a *pro forma* manner by the courts.[77] Nevertheless, the mystique of judicial authoritativeness is so great that few within the profession seemed to recognize the distinction between a court mandate which has broad precedential significance, and a settlement, which does not. Operating with an excess of caution, many test users began to

---

[76] *APA Monitor*, January 1987, p. 3.

[77] From this perspective, the *Golden Rule* situation exemplifies a negative judicial intervention because of a *lack* of judicial involvement rather than, as in *Larry P.* or *PASE*, because of an excess of such involvement. If the *Golden Rule* proposals in Illinois or Alabama had arisen in the context of a remedial decree after full trial, rather than as a settlement between the parties, the courts would probably have scrutinized them more closely and some of the difficulties described in the text may have been avoided.

insist on inclusion of *Golden Rule* methodologies in new testing programs in order to avoid litigation challenges, despite the almost unanimous critical rejection of this technique by psychometric experts. It remains to be seen whether even Mr. Anrig's dramatic *mea culpa* statement can stem this rising tide.

III. CONCLUSION

The preceding review of *Griggs* and the employment discrimination cases has indicated that "generalist" judges are capable of undertaking sophisticated analyses of complex psychometric issues and of implementing long-lasting, workable compliance mechanisms. The employment cases, as well as the NTE cases, also demonstrate how the courts' "rights orientation" can result in decisive action in clear-cut instances of test misuse. Judicial intervention in these areas has had the effect of upgrading the general level of psychometric practice throughout the industry.

On the other hand, the analysis of the IQ test cases has shown that "generalist" judges can also venture into areas that may be beyond their technical competence, with attendant detrimental results, and that rigid judicial mandates, such as a total ban on the use of IQ tests for EMR placements, can create as many—or more—problems as they may solve. These cases, as well as the *Golden Rule* example, illustrate how the courts' rights-orientation may become too limited, causing them to give insufficient consideration to broader public policy implications of the issues they are addressing. The extent to which both the ban on use of IQ tests for certain specific purposes in *Larry P.*, and the qualified item bias technique agreed upon in *Golden Rule*, took on more extreme forms as they were disseminated, also exemplies the distortion that can occur when solutions to particular testing problems become cloaked in the broad mantle of judicial legitimacy.

In retrospect, it is relatively easy to recount examples of positive and negative policymaking through the judicial process. A much more difficult undertaking would be to understand the factors that correlate with positive and negative judicial involvements and to devise a conceptual framework that could promote successful judicial encounters in future testing litigations. Such a task is obviously beyond the scope of a single article or a single author. Rather, it is an enterprise that requires—and justifies—the attention of a commission of scholars and practitioners who can undertake the comprehensive research and engage in the extensive deliberations that are necessary for such an ambitious task.

The suggestive analysis set forth in this article does, however, indicate an important point of departure for a broader study of these issues. The major theme that has permeated the discussion of the positive examples of judicial intervention is that of an ongoing, mutually productive dialogue between the courts and the psychometric profession. Thus, beginning with *Griggs* and continuing with subsequent employment discrimination cases, courts were highly respectful of the technical standards set forth in the APA *Standards* and the EEOC *Guidelines*; correspondingly, the drafters of the revised versions of these documents took due note of the relevant court decisions and the implementation experiences in the major cases. Similarly, with the early NTE exams, the courts felt confident in striking down their misuse because of the clarity of the professional testimony they received; this judicial stance, in turn, has positively affected the professionalism of the current generation of teacher competency tests.

On the other hand, with both the IQ test cases and the *Golden Rule* dissemination, there was an absence of effective dialogue with the profession. In the former set of cases, this resulted from a skeptical attitude on the part of the judges to technical input from professionals; in the later situation, important psychometric policy decisions were decided by settlements by the parties without the courts actually having had an opportunity to engage in sustained dialogue with the parties or the profession on their implications.

How can effective dialogue between judges and psychometricians be promoted in court cases involving testing issues? Educating courts, lawyers, psychometricians, and the general public on the importance and feasibility of such ongoing communication is one part of the answer. Creating specific judicial mechanisms, and shaping judicial doctrine to promote such dialogue, is another. These are both critical—and extremely difficult—undertakings. They clearly constitute appropriate subjects for further deliberation by the National Commission on Testing and Public Policy.

Testing in Elementary and Secondary Schools: Can Misuse Be Avoided?

Norman J. Chachkin

The use of nationally standardized tests, both norm-referenced and, more recently, criterion-referenced or content-based[1] tests, administered to elementary and secondary pupils in the public schools, has steadily increased over the past generation and has most recently mushroomed in response to legislative and popular demands accompanying the "educational reform" movement. This phenomenon raises a host of serious legal and policy issues because—often despite the good intentions of those individuals and companies which develop the tests—these instruments are widely misused and misinterpreted by school personnel. As a result, the educational opportunities and occupational aspirations of thousands upon thousands of school children are thwarted. This paper is intended to sketch the dimensions of the problem, in order to provide a basis for reflection by the members of the National Commission on Testing and Public Policy on how such abuses can best be curbed. It also reviews the history of legal challenges to test use and assesses the future of litigation in the area.

An Overview of the Problem

No one disputes the need for appropriate measures of student learning and performance across a variety of disciplines. Indeed, recent educational research on "effective schools" concludes that frequent assessment of skills and cognitive learning is an essential element of an effective instructional strategy, because it assists teachers in focusing their efforts on subject matter which students have not successfully grasped on first presentation.[2] This function of testing, which might justifiably be labelled diagnostic, grows out of the historic development of testing instruments.

---

[1] Except where specifically indicated, these terms are used in a relatively colloquial, rather than technical, sense.

[2] See, for example, Ronald Edmonds and John Frederiksen, *Search for Effective Schools: The Identification and Analysis of City Schools That Are Instructionally Effective for Poor Children* (1978); William Purkey and Marshall Smith, "Effective Schools: A Review," *Elementary Sch. J.* 427 (1983), v. 83:4, 427–82.

The first tests were teacher-devised and teacher-administered. They were not, obviously, nationally standardized; but they did have the potential of insuring a close fit between the material surveyed and the material taught in the classroom. Indeed, as most of us probably recall from our childhoods, the most significant issue associated with such tests was the question of grading on a curve.[3] Whatever the system of grading, when the measurement device was an instrument designed and administered by the teacher directly responsible for delivering the instruction, who was also familiar with the learning styles and personal characteristics of his or her students, there was usually room for additional "play in the joints" in the grading process.

Thus, classroom teachers commonly took into account their perception of students' effort. They also were in a position to assess whether an individual pupil was in fact well versed in a subject, even though the pupil's performance on a particular test or quiz was not as high as might have been expected, for whatever reason. When this evaluation system functioned as one might ideally hope, therefore, it could minimize inaccurate assessment of student achievement and the inappropriate curtailment of opportunities based on assumptions that an individual student could not master specific subject matter.

Without question, the system did not always function as one might hope. Indeed, the sole use of teacher-made tests could mask the unrestrained exercise of substantial subjective discretion by individual instructors on bases wholly unrelated to pedagogical goals.[4] Regrettably, these circumstances often

---

[3] Some teachers felt their tests provided an accurate measure of the minimum cognitive attainment which their students should have achieved in order to earn a passing grade. These teachers maintained a rigid raw score floor below which a student would flunk a course. When a substantial number of students failed, controversy often surrounded the teacher.

Other teachers proved more flexible. Whether because they doubted the adequacy of a pencil-and-paper examination of limited duration to capture the intellectual attainments of their students, because they viewed any test which produced a cluster of low scores as an indication that the effectiveness of their own pedagogical techniques should be questioned, or for some other reason, these teachers assigned grades on the curve so that most pupils received passing marks. Occasionally, these teachers could also become enmeshed in disputes, since grading on the curve could, in certain circumstances, limit the chance for individual pupils in an unusually bright and highly motivated class to excel, at least in terms of the grades awarded.

[4] The Pygmalion effect documented by Rosenthal, see Robert Rosenthal and Lenore Jacobson, *Pygmalion in the Classroom* (New York: Holt, Rinehart and Winston, 1968); Caroline Persell, *Education and Inequality*, 123-34 (New York: Free Press, 1977), is just one example of the ways in which conscious or unconscious teacher behaviors could affect student performance and assessment.

permitted ethnic and racial discrimination to operate to the detriment of black and other minority students.[5]

To the extent that standardized (including nationally standardized) measures of cognitive achievement could be developed, they offered a potential tool for policing and avoiding the excesses of a predominantly subjective process.[6] For those teachers who consistently sought to evaluate the entire range of students' behaviors and cognitive attainments, the opportunity to measure themselves and their students against a wider cohort added information which could only be helpful in shaping their curricular and pedagogical choices. The data provided by score reports on standardized tests in such a situation served as a check rather than a substitute for close supervision and evaluation by the classroom teacher; and in these instances, there was little danger that a student would be misclassified, misplaced, or otherwise harmed because of overemphasis on a numerical score representing a narrow band of the student's cognitive abilities and achievement.

The availability of standardized instruments, however, furnishes no guarantee that these problems will not occur. For one thing, not all teachers wish to take the time, and to exert the necessary effort, to make their grading and assessment of pupil performance a balanced, comprehensive process. To an even greater extent, test misuse and misinterpretation which harms students occurs because of imperfections in testing design and theory, and because test consumers at the local level lack the technical grounding to appreciate and act upon the warnings and caveats which test publishers bury in their technical manuals. Instead, beleaguered school administrators and teachers seize upon standardized tests as a panacea to solve problems of classroom management and instructional technique for which they were never intended.

The development and history of standardized testing is deeply disappointing. The initial developers of test instruments had their own agendas, which did not include facilitating improved educational outcomes for all students by giving teachers better diagnostic tools.[7] Testing and mental

---

[5] Discrimination could take many forms, not just giving minority students lower grades or placing them in lower tracks. For instance, for years the Denver school system characterized below average performance on standardized tests at heavily minority schools as acceptable, or as demonstrating good results compared to the low expectations which the system maintained for these schools, thus masking from black and Hispanic parents the failure of its instructional program. See Brief for Petitioners 44-56, *Keyes v. School District No. 1, Denver*, 413 U.S. 189 (1973).

[6] But see *supra* note 5.

[7] Terman and others who pioneered the field made assumptions about the differential performance which they could expect to find across racial and ethnic groups, if not across class or socioeconomic lines, and they shaped their test designs to produce data which appeared to confirm these assumptions. See Leon Kamin, *The Science and*

measurement has been dominated by the effort (largely through pencil-and-paper instruments) to formulate and assess on a single scale the wide variety of skills, aptitudes, knowledge, and behaviors which make up the concept popularly referred to as "intelligence." This is quite the opposite from recognizing written test performance scores as simply one limited measure of cognitive achievement, which must be evaluated together with other indicators to produce a complete picture of a pupil's attainment.[8]

Moreover, since their initial development, standardized tests have been used for purposes of sorting and stratification.[9] In a similar fashion, and particularly as the completion of years of formal education became a larger and larger determinant of an individual's societal wealth and position, tests began to be used within educational systems for the purpose of selecting those students who would have the opportunity to pursue advanced academic studies and those who would be offered lower-level, career preparatory options. Test publishers have become increasingly sophisticated and now report student performance by translating raw scores into a wide variety of metrics, such as percentile rankings, stanines, normal curve equivalents, and so on. In addition, many tests are not only standardized but norm-referenced, and publishers offer a menu of available samples, including national, regional, urban, and rural cohorts.

Politics of IQ 5-30 (New York: J. Wiley and Sons, 1974); James Lawler, *IQ: Heritability and Racism*, 44-51 (New York: International Publications, 1978); Jeannie Oakes, *Keeping Track, How Schools Structure Inequality*, 35-37 (New Haven: Yale Univ. Press, 1985).

[8]   See, for example, Ann Bastian, et al., *Choosing Equality, The Case for Democratic Schooling*, 74-75 (Philadelphia: Temple University Press, 1986); Howard Gardner, "Notes on Some Educational Implications of the Theory of Multiple Intelligences," in *Measures in the College Admission Process*, 130 (New York: College Entrance Examination Board, 1986); Jerry Patterson, et al., "How to Avoid the Dangers of Testing," in Paul Houts, ed., *The Myth of Measurability*, 341-45 (New York: Hart Publishing Co., 1977); Ronald Samuda, *Psychological Testing of American Minorities: Issues and Consequences*, 131-57 (New York: Dodd, Mead and Co., 1975); Daniel Goleman, "Rethinking the Value of Intelligence Tests," *N.Y. Times*, November 9, 1986, §12, p. 23.

[9]   For instance, the Army Alpha Examination was administered to all recruits and draftees in the First World War and became, at least to some degree, the basis for the army's acceptance or rejection of individuals for service and also for their assignment to tasks within the armed forces. See Ralph Tyler, "Introduction: A Perspective on the Issues," in Ralph Tyler and Richard Wolf, eds., *Crucial Issues in Testing*, 4 (Berkeley: McCutchan Publishing Co., 1974). "Educational testing thus began as a means for selecting and sorting pupils, and the principles and practices of testing that have been worked out since 1918 are largely the refining of these functions rather than other educational purposes."

Standardized tests have functioned as the instruments of a variety of bureaucratic behaviors within educational systems.[10] As test use became entrenched, the notion that standardized tests were the best, or even the only, measure of student learning gained currency. A single test score is made to substitute for the comprehensive evaluation process which should occur before a student's educational future is constricted or compromised.

Today, testing plays an ever-increasing role in public education. Most pupils in every grade level take several standardized tests each year, in addition to a number of home-grown competency measures. The education reform movement in state legislatures has produced even more pressure upon school administrators and teachers to demonstrate success in terms of test performance. Indeed, widely publicized instances of students who received high school diplomas but were functionally illiterate,[11] as well as discussion of the social promotion phenomenon, has conditioned the lay public to view teachers' assessments of student performance with skepticism. Instead, it is becoming all too common for school districts and school personnel to use a numerical score on some standardized instrument to make a "yes or no" decision about an individual student, or to place the student in an instructional level or grouping, without adequate understanding or recognition of (a) what the test is actually measuring, (b) the strength of the relationship between the test content and the local instructional program, or (c) the appropriateness of using the test instrument to make that kind of individual decision at all.

To the extent that such questions are raised, they are often disposed of quickly in reliance upon the summaries of validation and reliability studies which are provided in test publishers' technical manuals. If a publisher represents that its tests conform to current professional standards set by the American Psychological Association, that is taken to be the end of the matter. Unfortunately, most teachers and school administrators do not comprehend that the publishers' validation studies may be of little significance if the purposes for which the local school system is using the instrument are not

---

[10] Administrators can use student test scores as a basis for evaluating faculty performance, rather than conducting classroom observations. Those distrustful of the teachers who work for them can emphasize the significance of the scores as "objective" measures of student attainment and exclude teacher judgment from playing any substantial role in student assessment and evaluation. Classroom teachers can focus their lesson planning upon the test content and narrow the range of material which they seek to present; often they can even more directly "teach to the test" in order to satisfy public or administrative demands for successful performance–without regard to whether the test content measures the appropriately broad scope of subject matter which a course was designed to include.

[11] For example, *Donahue v. Copiague Union Free School Dist.*, 47 N.Y.2d 440, 391 N.E.2d 1352, 418 N.Y.S.2d 375 (1979).

congruent with the function which the test was designed to serve.[12] And neither

[12] For example, a Georgia school district adopted a grade-equivalent cutoff score on the California Achievement Tests (CAT) as a diploma requirement rather than utilize locally awarded grades and other information, or even the state's own criterion reference test "because the Board wanted to graduate students who compared favorably to national achievement levels." *Anderson v. Banks*, 520 F. Supp. 472, 485 (S.D. Ga. 1981), *appeal from subsequent order dismissed sub nom. Johnson v. Sikes*, 730 F.2d 644 (llth Cir. 1984). The federal court before which this use of the test was challenged excused the practice. The court noted that the score cutoff requirement grew out of a "concer[n] that some of the schools in Tattnall County were considered substandard by the State of Georgia" and was an attempt to establish "that the diploma, for the first time in years, would meaningfully represent a particular level of achievement." *Id.* at 485 (emphasis supplied). Summarizing its holding, the court said:

> Here the school authorities have redesigned the criteria for graduation stating that a student must perform at least on a level four years below his average counterpart across the nation. The CAT was capable of producing just such a comparison. That a student be able to perform at an average ninth grade level was a legitimate and relevant expectation for the school authorities to hold for their students. This state of affairs is in contrast to the situation in *Armstead v. Starkville Municipal Separate School District*, 461 F.2d 276 (5th Cir. 1972) where a teacher's aptitude for doctoral studies admittedly had no relevance to his ability to teach.
>
> Since the CAT is being used to measure what it was designed to measure, i.e., relative achievement levels in mathematics and reading, the Court is of the opinion that local revalidation was not necessary. Basing the receipt of a diploma on a ninth grade achievement level was not unreasonable. Defendants did not concoct a homemade examination but chose instead to rely on a professionally constructed and well-regarded examination.

Id. at 507. With due regard to the court, the question has been begged. A properly constructed criterion-referenced test is the best indication of what an individual student knows, and such a test was available to this system. The issue is not giving the student's score on a norm-referenced examination as an additional item of information along with the diploma; rather, the issue is whether it is appropriate to base denial of a diploma to a student (who, it must be assumed, passed all of his courses satisfactorily and demonstrated adequate mastery of the material on the state criterion-referenced test) on the grade-equivalent score earned on a norm-referenced test. The practice is especially questionable because the original impetus for employing the instrument was to identify schools which were substandard. For this purpose, mean or median scores (or the size of the standard deviation of scores) for all of the students within a school, as a group, may be useful. But it hardly follows that using an individual score to impose a diploma sanction can be justified.

Equally significant, the 9.0 grade-equivalent score on the CAT is clearly *not* a determination that a twelfth grader is performing at the level of a ninth grader; it is merely a *relative* statement about the extent of deviation of the pupil's raw score from the median of the norming group, expressed in one of the most misleading metrics ever devised. It is particularly unfair to deny diplomas to students who meet local requirements but receive low scores on this norm-referenced test when there is no basis test publishers nor their salesmen police the utilization process to avoid abuse.[13]

The Limitations of Standardized Tests

It is worthwhile to summarize, at this point, some of the major limitations which inhere in the standardized pencil-and-paper tests used at the elementary and secondary school level. While all of us are familiar with the general propositions mentioned below, it is all too easy to lose sight of them as one moves from the academic arena into the field, where harried and overextended school personnel must make quick decisions about school placements and courses of study for students on the basis of limited information.

First, any pencil-and-paper test is necessarily of limited scope and duration. Inherently, therefore, it can only test for a small sample of behaviors (correct responses) in a limited set of formats (multiple choice, fill-in-the-blanks, and so on) within the vast domain of cognitive knowledge and application which a teacher spends a full school year presenting to a class. The inadequacy of making a critical judgment about student performance on the basis of any single test performance is therefore obvious.

To put it in oversimplified, practical terms, however, consider a test designed to evaluate second- or third-grade students' multiplication skills. Suppose there are ten questions on the test, designed to measure students' mastery of the domain which includes the multiplication tables from one to ten. Although there are fifty-five combinations of numbers to be multiplied (ignoring the order in which the numbers are stated), only ten combinations

---

for assuming that pupils in *other* districts in the nation with the same scores (the students' "average counterparts across the nation") will also be denied diplomas.

Finally, the court's reference to one of the National Teacher Examinations (NTE) challenges (*Armstead*) is incoherent in the absence of a meaningful elucidation of what the high school diploma is supposed to signify. I suggest that it would be difficult to persuade Georgia parents or employers that the purpose of awarding the diploma is to indicate whether a student achieved a 9.0 grade-equivalent score on a norm-referenced examination prepared by a commercial publisher–rather than whether the student successfully completed a prescribed course of study or demonstrated mastery of curricular objectives measured by a properly devised criterion-referenced test.

[13] The exception to the statement in text is the position which the Educational Testing Service (ETS) has taken regarding the use of cutoff scores on the National Teachers Examination for the purpose of hiring, retaining, or promoting incumbent faculty. ETS does not recommend this use of the test and when it learns that a state or locality is ignoring that recommendation, it will refuse to report applicants' scores to the jurisdiction. Unfortunately, the same zeal to insure proper test use does not extend to the publishers of most tests used at the elementary and secondary levels. For example, see *infra* pp. 25-16.

can be measured on the examination. A student who misses one question, therefore, has lost 10% of his or her possible raw score on the examination—even though the question represents 1.8% of the domain of knowledge to be tested. Even if the student's incorrect answer to the question was a reliable reflection of the student's knowledge, rather than the result of a momentary distraction occurring in the examination room, the test score, without additional information, is but an imperfect measure of the student's actual knowledge.

Second, as indicated in the preceding example, given the limited number of questions on any written examination, particularly one which is to be computer-scored, an incorrect response on a single item may account for a large raw score or percentile difference. The problem is exacerbated when raw scores are converted to grade-equivalent scores or other metrics; and is especially acute with many norm-referenced tests, since these are designed for the purpose of spreading examinees out along a ranking continuum. When such tests are scored, as one moves away from the median in performance, small item correct-response differences account for larger and larger differences in percentile or other scores. These somewhat technical characteristics of the tests indicate how important it is that test reports be viewed not in isolation, but against the background of teacher judgment and other indicators of student achievement.

Third, as mentioned above, an examinee's actual performance on any given occasion is subject to a wide variety of environmental influences that can have a substantial impact upon scoring. In one sense, the test may, in such circumstances, provide an accurate measure of real-life performance under varying conditions—but that normally is not the purpose for which the examination is administered. We are all familiar with teachers allowing retakes of tests on which a student or a class seemed to score unusually poorly. Unfortunately, because of the way in which standardized tests are purchased and administered, this same opportunity can rarely be made available within elementary and secondary schools.

Fourth, many of the most commonly administered achievement tests in public education are norm-referenced examinations. There are a whole variety of problems which relate to using such tests to make educational decisions about individual students. Perhaps the worst feature of these examinations occurs when results are reported in grade-equivalent format. We currently have the situation in which hundreds of school districts are seeking to raise the median performance of their students above grade level.[14] Obviously, this effort is incapable of succeeding, for by definition half of all students in the country on a properly normed examination will be performing "below grade

---

[14] See *supra* note 12.

level." School systems which adopt this goal may be engaging in a fruitless quest which is doomed to failure when the tests are re-normed (since even if instruction is significantly improved and performance rises across the country, proper re-norming will raise the median number of correct item responses necessary to grade-level performance).

Fifth, exactly what these tests are measuring is not self-apparent. The demands of practicality deeply affect the design of test instruments, especially those prepared for mass scoring by national publishers. What the tests are actually measuring is a surrogate for the trait or skill about which information is desired.[15]

Finally, most standardized tests, especially norm-referenced tests, are designed to be administered in a group setting and to provide distributional and other information about group performance, but all too often they are utilized to make important decisions with long-term effects on the lives of individual children.

---

[15] Again, to give an over-simplistic example: one of the best ways to determine whether or not an individual can read is to hand him or her a book and request an oral reading of several passages. To explore the matter of comprehension, that experiment would be followed by a dialogue between the examiner and the subject, in a non-threatening atmosphere, about the material. If properly conducted, the dialogue will permit the examiner to draw conclusions about the subject's degree of comprehension as well as about his or her articulateness. Unintentional ambiguities in the examiner's questions will be immediately identified and corrected.

What does the standardized test measure? In most instances the subject is presented a short passage, isolated from its context, followed by a series of questions in a multiple choice format. Rather than being able to express his or her own reactions to the material, the subject is asked to select from among a group of prepared responses that formulation which best reflects the principal theme of the passage. Given the notorious imprecision of language, no matter how carefully prepared the examination, the opportunities for ambiguity are rife. But the most significant point to be made is that what the test is measuring is not a skill which we have labelled "comprehension" (which itself is the product of a number of processes, including decoding, contextual placement, vocabulary, and memory) but "comprehension" as mediated by a number of other traits or processes, including the subject's familiarity with the procedures for taking multiple choice tests. It is for this reason that a common response to the administration of these tests has been to stress test-taking skills and that many educators have expressed great concern about the degree to which standardized test administration results in a distortion of the curriculum.

There is nothing original or novel in this brief survey of some of the
limitations of standardized, norm-referenced tests.[16] Testing professionals and

---

[16] Omitted from this discussion has been the matter of accounting for the widespread
racially differential performance on most nationally standardized tests, and the
possibility of cultural or item bias. An adequate treatment of these questions is beyond
the scope of this paper. I wish to make only a few simple points:

(1) Unless one is willing to engage in the assumption that minority students will
characteristically score lower on any standardized instrument for hereditary or genetic
reasons, or the assumption that the socioeconomic status and environmental
influences upon all minority children are identical, the characteristic racially differential
test performance observed today is cause for deep concern and renders the status quo
unacceptable.

(2) Without seeking to determine whether tests or individual questions are
culturally or otherwise biased, there does exist a mechanism by which irrelevant or
apparently false differentials can be eliminated. This method, typified by the settlement
in the "Golden Rule" insurance licensing exam case, is based upon the fact that
standardized tests are constructed by selecting sample questions, within specific areas or
domains to be covered, from among a large number of items written by experts or
consultants. After a detailed item analysis by race of the results of a pilot or field test,
valid sample questions that do not produce skewing along racial lines can be substituted
for those which do, thus reducing or eliminating the chance that bias or irrelevant
factors could affect scoring.

(I emphatically do not accept the thesis that the "Golden Rule" approach is
inconsistent with high standards or proper test construction. See, however, Michael
Rebell, "Disparate Impact of Teacher Competency Testing on Minorities: Don't Blame
the Test-Takers–or the Tests," 4 *Yale Law and Pol'y Rev.* 375, 391-97 (1986).)

As to cultural bias, see *Larry P. v. Riles*, 495 F. Supp. 926, 956-60 (N.D. Cal. 1979), *aff'd*
793 F.2d 969 (9th Cir. 1986); Gerald Bracey, *On the Compelling Need to Go Beyond
Minimum Competency* (Address to Twelfth Annual Conference on Large Scale
Assessment, Boulder, Colorado, June 8, 1982) (emphasis supplied):

> What happens during the course of schooling? Schools teach "reading"
> as a subject but they also teach math literacy as part of math, and science
> literacy as part of science and social studies literacy and poetry literacy and
> so on. The grammar and syntax of these specific literacies vary
> somewhat. In the course of X years of school [it may be] that these
> literacies fuse and maybe even become abstracted in the way that Harry
> Harlow talked about abstracted learning sets 30 years ago or become the
> "g" factor that Thurstone argued for even earlier. *Most children become
> able to read most passages that they encounter more or less well because
> they've encountered so many different kinds of passages, but I would bet
> that if you constructed two tests of equal difficulty as indicated by
> readability, syntax, grammar, item specifications, etc., but varied the
> degree of familiarity that the child had with the subject matter, scores
> would vary in the same direction. Of course, this is never done because
> of the way CRTs are constructed.* Those of you who read the *Scientific
> American*, a magazine for that mythical being, the "educated layman,"
> will immediately intuit this truth. Can you read an article on quantum

many educational administrators are familiar with them; indeed, these individuals often seek to restrict the use of tests to an appropriate role. Unfortunately, there is not the same degree of understanding among policymakers, including those in state education departments and legislatures—to say nothing of the general public. The result has been an almost hydraulic pressure upon school systems to improve educational outcomes *as measured by test scores.*

A Paradigmatic Example

In the early 1980s, I litigated a case against a rural southern school system which, I alleged, was misusing a standardized, norm-referenced examination for the purpose of promoting segregation within its schools, with considerable harm to black students in the district. The case did not establish any new legal principles because it was settled, on terms which the plaintiffs considered favorable, before trial. Nevertheless, it is a useful example of the extent to which standardized testing can be misused and can become a vehicle for creating or perpetuating the very arbitrariness and inequality which standardization was thought to eliminate.[17]

This K-12 district has enrolled a total of between two thousand and three thousand students annually during the past decade and a half. It maintained a dual system of separate schools for blacks and whites prior to 1969, when it was required by federal court order to develop a desegregation plan.

Initially, the school authorities suggested that for the secondary grades, separate academic and vocational high schools should be established, with assignments to each to be based upon students' standardized test scores. Similarly, in the elementary grades, those black students whose scores on standardized tests indicated that they were "ready" would be assigned to the formerly white schools. After the federal court requested information concerning the test score performance of black and white children, it determined that this scheme would result in continued maintenance of segregated facilities and it disapproved the plan.

---

physics with the same speed and comprehension as one on test utilization?

[17] In the discussion which follows, it should be borne in mind that the school authorities' conduct is described as it was alleged in the lawsuit. A common feature of settlements in federal court litigation is that there is no admission of liability, and since there was never a trial, the facts asserted were never formally proved. However, prior to the negotiations which resulted in the settlement, a considerable amount of data concerning test performance and class enrollments was gathered through the court's discovery procedures. In my view, this information amply supports the basic outlines of the plaintiffs' case given here.

Thereafter, the court ordered the school district to adopt a pairing plan of student assignment, pursuant to which all children in the same grade attended a single school. This plan effectively desegregated the schools when it was first implemented. Several years later, however, the school system adopted new promotion and grouping practices. For the announced purpose of raising standards, the district began to retain large numbers of students in grade rather than promote them; in the first year that this policy was implemented, more than a third of the entire student body in the district was retained. A disproportionate share of the retentions were received by black students. In addition to full-year retentions, the system also implemented a practice of partial promotion or partial retention. Students so treated received instruction in the first half year's work for a particular grade during the spring semester and the second half year's work in the fall semester. Nearly all of the children placed in these groupings were black.

The plaintiffs alleged that, once given a partial promotion or partial retention, rarely if ever did a student return to the regular curricular sequence. Instead, they suggested, most of these students remained isolated from their peers and, in the eighth or ninth grade, were counseled to select an alternative, non-diploma-granting vocational course of study at the secondary level.

Although the school system denied it, the plaintiffs alleged that a student's standardized test score was the sole determinant of whether or not the child would be promoted. The school district printed and distributed a document providing teachers with guidelines for promotions and retentions. This document was worded in a way which appeared to establish rigid cutoff scores, expressed in terms of grade equivalents on the Science Research Associates (SRA) Achievement Series (which had previously been used for statewide assessment purposes only), to qualify for promotion.[18] Thus, for example, a student who was retained a half year had to score at grade level for the month in which the test was administered in order to return to his or her normal grade level. Since the tests were administered in the spring, when these children were studying the curriculum for the first semester of that grade level and had not yet been exposed to sixth-through tenth-month material, it would appear to have been virtually impossible for students to move out of the half promotion or half retention track.

The school system maintained that exceptions to these guidelines could always be made based upon teacher judgment. However, the black teachers with whom we spoke indicated their clear understanding that the test score was to be the determinative factor in the decision whether to promote. It should also be noted that, during the period when the SRA Achievement Series was administered only for statewide assessment purposes, this school district

---

[18] Promotion from kindergarten to first grade was dependent upon performance on the Metropolitan Readiness Test.

ordered individual score reports calculated according to the publisher's rural norming sample. However, when the tests began to be used for promotion and grouping, the system switched to national norms, which had the effect of further depressing the reported performance of its own students.

This school district received considerable publicity, including favorable coverage in a national news magazine, for its effort to raise standards. Over a period of several years its mean test score performance in grade levels tested for purposes of statewide assessment did rise. However, this could be explained[19] by the fact that, because of the staggering increase in retentions in grade, the cohort of children taking the examinations was considerably older than its counterparts in the rest of the state. In fact, after several years of protests by superintendents of neighboring districts, the state board of education began to collect and report, along with test scores, the median age of students at each grade level whose performance was being measured.

Test scores were not used in this district solely for promotion. About the same time it implemented its retention policy, the school system established three achievement groupings within each grade level (treating the partial promotion or partial retention classes as separate grade levels): low, medium, and high. This created the potential of having more than thirty allegedly differentiated achievement levels in grades 1-6, within a school system that had less than two thousand children in these grades—virtually all of whom came from extremely impoverished and homogeneous rural backgrounds!

The district used a composite grade-equivalent national norm score for grouping students for the entire school day, rather than, for example, separate verbal and math scores for subject matter grouping. Statistics collected during discovery indicated that blacks made up a disproportionately large share of the lowest groupings, while whites were overrepresented in the high-level classes. Many of the low-achievement grouping classes were all black. Plaintiffs alleged that there was virtually no mobility among grouping levels. And, the plaintiffs alleged, there was no program of remediation whatsoever made available to students in the low-achievement groupings designed to assist them in raising their level of performance.

During the course of investigation prior to filing suit, my co-counsel and I talked with a number of black teachers within the district. We were anxious to determine whether the SRA tests had what might today be termed instructional validity. That is, we asked teachers whether the SRA tests covered material which they had presented to their students. Our interviewees were unable to give us this information. In the name of test security, to prevent too much teaching to the test, the SRA examinations were administered each year by specially hired proctors, and classroom teachers were not permitted to inspect

---

[19] It was not so explained in the media coverage.

the test content. Instead, they (like pupils and their parents) received only a single composite test score report (again, I emphasize, expressed as a grade-equivalent score) for each child. Thus, no one could tell us anything about the subject matter of the examinations as it related to the curriculum of the school system.[20]

Although the test manuals prepared by the publisher cautioned against using individual student test scores as the basis for decision-making, the company declined to take a strong position in the litigation or to curb its customers' misuse of the instrument. Its attorneys did prepare and send to both sides in the case a two-and-one-half-page statement entitled, "The Appropriate Uses of the SRA Achievement Series." In this document, the publisher states that:

> [t]esting materials, including manuals and ancillary publications, should help users interpret test results correctly and should warn against common misuses (APA Standard Bl). The manual should state explicitly the purposes and applications for which the test is recommended (APA Standard Bl). Science Research Associates (SRA) complies with each of these standards. *It is not feasible, however, for a test publisher to monitor or to enforce the uses which customers may make of a test after the test materials have been purchased* [emphasis supplied].[21]

Copies of the APA *Standards*[22] and various SRA User's Guides and Technical Reports were appended to the statement, which in general terms hinted at disapproval of the local school system's practices:

> Exhibits 1, 2, 3 and 9 describe the purposes [of the SRA Series] and emphasize the importance of using test results to help improve student learning through instruction.

---

[20] When we took the sworn testimony of the school superintendent by deposition, he revealed that he had never checked into the match between test content and the subject matter in the local curriculum, before adopting the practices described above!

[21] Although the author's experience in this case was with SRA, I do not mean to suggest that this publisher is exceptional nor to single it out for criticism. The incident is illustrative of a more general problem which the commission should address: encouraging or requiring test publishers to assume more responsibility and to take vigorous action against test misuse.

[22] American Psychological Association, American Educational Research Association, and National Council on Measurement in Education, *Standards for Educational and Psychological Tests* (Washington, DC: American Psychological Association, 1974). The APA *Standards* were revised in 1985.

Importance of considering other information about the student, along with the test results.

Exhibits 4, 5, 6 and 9 deal with this point and emphasize the importance of not considering test results alone in making decisions affecting students.

Exhibits 3 and 4 and particularly Exhibit 9 deal with this point and emphasize the analysis of performance in reading comprehension, math concepts, language arts, and so on—as opposed to concentration on the Composite score.

Weaknesses of the grade-equivalent (GE) score.

This score is often misinterpreted. Exhibits 7 and 8 deal with this point, pointing out that "scoring at grade level should not be regarded as a minimum achievement level for normal progress." A GE is a median score and, by definition, half of the students in the norm group for that grade receive scores below the GE. In addition, the differences between GEs vary greatly across both subtests and grade levels—just as the amount of progress that can be reflected in GEs from one year to the next varies.

This case was settled when the school system involved agreed to:

(a) eliminate the half-year promotion or retention;

(b) adopt a formal board policy committing the system to avoid one-race, or virtually one-race, classroom assignments, and directing the superintendent to review principals' class assignments each year and to take appropriate action to carry out the policy;

(c) adopt a formal board policy articulating parity in retentions and promotions for both black and white students as a goal, and directing the provision of remediation to students retained in grade;

(d) cease entirely the practice of using an individual grade-equivalent (composite or subtest) score on the SRA Series, the ITED, or the Metropolitan Readiness Test as a factor in deciding either (i) whether to promote or retain a student, or (ii) to what achievement level class grouping a student should be assigned;

(e) make all promotion and classroom assignments *prior* to distribution to principals or teachers of individual student score reports from any standardized tests given in the spring; and

(f) eliminate grouping across subject matter areas in grades 6-12.[23]

The example of this school district may appear to be an extreme one. But the substantial misuse of standardized tests in American educational practice is hardly an isolated phenomenon. Let me provide a few additional examples:

1. A South Carolina school district was recently held by a federal administrative law judge to have violated Title VI of the 1964 Civil Rights Act[24] by using composite (total battery) scores to group students across all subject matter areas, leading to substantial numbers of racially identifiable classes, which could have been reduced if achievement grouping were performed separately for verbal and mathematical subjects, and heterogeneous grouping used in other classes.[25]

2. A federal court found that California utilized standardized IQ tests as a "determinative or pervasive [factor] in the placement" of students in special education classes, with resulting unjustifiable disproportionate placement of black children in classes for the retarded. See *Larry P. v. Riles*, 495 F. Supp. 926, 949-50 (N.D. Cal. 1979), *aff'd* 793 F.2d 969 (9th Cir. 1986).[26] The court noted that the IQ tests were normed on white middle-class sample groups and had never been validated for use with black children.[27]

3. The public schools in Peoria, Illinois, were held by a federal court to have deprived handicapped children of fair notice and due process when the school district denied them high school diplomas for failure to pass a minimum competency test. The court found that the students and their parents never had been afforded the opportunity to have included within their Individualized Education Plans (IEPs) the curricular objectives measured by the tests.[28]

---

[23] Statistical reports submitted by the school system in the years since this agreement was approved by the court indicate fewer one-race classes and substantially less racial disproportion in retentions and promotions.

[24] Title VI bars discrimination by a recipient of federal funds in the program or activity supported by federal funds.

[25] *In re Dillon County School District No. 1*, Docket #84-VI16 (U.S. Department of Education, July 25, 1986).

[26] Earlier proceedings in this case are reported at 343 F. Supp. 1306 (N.D. Cal. 1972), *aff'd* 502 F.2d 963 (9th Cir. 1974).

[27] 495 F. Supp. at 970-71, 973. Indeed, one study cited by the court concluded that the tests had "little or no validity" for use with minority children. *Id.* at 972.

[28] *Brookhart v. Illinois State Board of Education*, 697 F.2d 179 (7th Cir. 1983).

4. The public schools in Tattnall County, Georgia, adopted an inappropriate grade-equivalent score as an absolute prerequisite to receiving a high school diploma, in spite of the availability of alternatives such as the state's own criterion-referenced examination.[29]

These are but a few examples. They do not encompass the more mundane misuse of tests which takes place daily in our schools: the use of standardized test performance as a significant or controlling factor for entry into special programs or optional courses, the misinterpretation of percentile or grade-equivalent scores by teachers and guidance counselors, or the criticism of school performance by public officials if less than a majority of the students are performing above grade level. Add to this listing the much-hailed turnaround in public education, which was diagnosed in the late 1970s and early 1980s, as scores on standardized tests began to rise because most publishers had re-normed their instruments on more contemporaneously representative samples. It is evident that, spurred in part by the profit motive of test publishers, writers, and academic consultants, the testing craze is out of hand. We must ask ourselves: with all that is known about the limitations and problems with standardized testing, why is its use continuing to grow?

The Reasons for Testing in Education

If one is unwilling, as I am, to presume that most school personnel wish deliberately to use inaccurate or irrelevant information in making decisions about the future of their students, it is important to seek to understand the needs, perceptions, and forces which are responsible for the continuing and expanding heavy reliance upon testing in our schools. Only in this way can we hope to fashion a program of publicity, education, and advocacy which offers test users realistic alternatives to current practices. Among the many influences which contribute to today's testing mania are the following:

1. The increasing complexity of the world and of human knowledge, as well as the increasing degree to which specialized training is necessary to perform today's high-technology jobs, has produced great concern about the content of a basic elementary and secondary education. Business leaders and others have called for the establishment of minimum curriculum and graduation standards. However, these proposals run counter to the strong tradition of state and local control of education in the United States, so that the most logical way of achieving the desired result—creation and implementation of a national curriculum—is simply not feasible politically. Instead, schools and legislatures have turned to standardized output testing to demonstrate indirectly that the goal is being achieved.

---

[29] See *supra* note 12.

Unfortunately, there continues to be vast differentiation in the curriculum and course content offered by public school systems throughout the country. For this reason, there may in fact be relatively little commonality of experience and subject matter among students who are enrolled in the same grade in different school systems around the country.[30] Given the manner in which most standardized tests are constructed, students' reported scores may well be more sensitive to this differentiation than to meaningful differences in knowledge.

2. Americans are a blaming population who desire to pin responsibility for difficulties and disappointments on someone, who can then be ostracized. Complex phenomena are often reduced to simpler formulae (for example, "who lost China?"). A rapidly changing economic structure, within which individuals can no longer be expected to find employment when they are equipped only with the limted intellectual skills that elementary and secondary schools commonly developed in the past, causes dislocation—as do lifestyle and social changes that have eliminated stable cohorts of meek, respectful children who report to school each day.

Today's buzzword is "accountability," and standardized tests are an integral part of most accountability systems proposed in education. The illusion that we can make constructive progress toward solving our society's problems if we identify and blame individual students, teachers, or administrators for poor performance on standardized tests—by denying them diplomas (thus further stigmatizing them), suspending, or firing them—may be illogical, but it nonetheless appears to be quite comforting to politicians and civic leaders. Even the positive news from the public schools today is often presented in over-simplified, critical terms.[31]

---

[30] The simplistic example concerns mathematics study. Suppose most ninth graders take algebra but one district or one state presents geometry in ninth grade and then algebra in the tenth grade. If a test includes algebraic problems and is normed on a sample of students who have all taken algebra, the scores of ninth graders from the odd county or state are likely to be depressed. Perhaps the score is an accurate measure of achievement, defined broadly, but for the most part such scores are understood to be measures of students' personal achievement rather than of curricular offerings.

[31] For example, the "effective schools" research indicates that any number of schools and school personnel have been successful in improving the educational climate in their institutions, with consequent improvement in the traditional measures of academic success, including test scores. Ronald Edmonds pioneered the effort to learn more about these schools and to develop replicable models that could be utilized elsewhere. (Replicability is not yet fully established.) While Edmonds summarized the variables under five main headings, he recognized that establishing an effective school required a process of experimentation and change. See Ronald Edmonds and John Frederiksen, *Search for Effective Schools: The Identification and Analysis of City Schools That Are Instructionally Effective for Poor Children.*

3. There is a considerable amount of support for standardized testing among teachers, because it facilitates their use of grouping and tracking within schools, especially secondary schools. Despite considerable debate over the educational soundness of these practices,[32] most classroom teachers are sincerely concerned that heterogeneous grouping will make their jobs much more difficult or even impossible to perform because of wide variations in ability or attainment among their pupils. Teachers have learned, however, that grouping or tracking children based solely on their own subjective assessments of pupil progress often leads to complaints from parents and to controversy. The "objectivity" of standardized test scores is thus an important factor legitimizing tracking in this country.

Since 85-90% of the average school system's annual operating budget is used for direct personnel costs, most districts have little or no in-service or other supportive programs for their faculty that might help popularize new teaching techniques[33] that are particularly well adapted to heterogeneous classes. Most teachers remain unaware, for instance, that even with homogeneous class assignments based on some composite measure, the variability in achievement remains very substantial.[34] A great deal of educational work, and changes in school building management (to increase planning time for teachers, and so on) will be required before most will accept an end to testing and grouping.

More recently, however, it has been suggested that courts should order schools to "adopt" the five "attributes" of effective schools research, see Gershon Ratner, "A New Legal Duty for Urban Public Schools: Effective Education in Basic Skills," 63 *Tex. L. Rev.* 777 (1985), as if, for example, "high expectations" could be legislated with the snap of a judicial finger and improved outcomes would necessarily follow. See John Elson, "Suing to Make Schools Effective, or How to Make a Bad Situation Worse: A Response to Ratner," 63 *Tex. L. Rev.* 889 (1985). Ratner's implicit message—that some schools in urban districts have become "effective" and that only bureaucratic inertia or spite prevents similar enhancement of all other facilitiess—is simply not a credible one.

[32] See, for example, Jeannie Oakes, *Keeping Track, How Schools Structure Inequality.*

[33] See, for example, Gene Glass, *The Effectiveness of Four Educational Interventions*, Project Report No. 84-A-19, Institute for Research on Educational Finance and Governance (Palo Alto: Stanford University, August, 1984); Jeannie Oakes, *Keeping Track, How Schools Structure Inequality*, 208-11; Robert Slavin, *Cooperative Learning* (New York: Longman, 1983).

[34] See, for example, Ralph Tyler, "Using Tests in Grouping Students for Instruction," in Ralph Tyler and Richard Wolf, eds., *Crucial Issues in Testing*, 66-67 (Berkeley: McCutchan Publishing Co., 1974).

Legal Challenges to Educational Testing

Over the past two decades, there have been a substantial number of legal challenges to the use of standardized testing in education. Some of these cases have already been adverted to. We can anticipate that these kinds of challenges will increase in the future, stimulated both by the limited degree of success which has thus far been achieved and also by the advocacy work of groups such as FairTest.

It should be understood from the outset that court suits rarely involve the broad range of educational policy issues surrounding the proper use of standardized tests which will be considered by the commission, and which should be the focus of consideration by decisionmakers at the local, state, and federal levels. Generally, courts do not have a roving warrant to second-guess the pedagogical or curricular determinations of educators.[35] Under the federal Constitution, for example, education is not classified as a fundamental right which receives special protection.[36] For this reason, federal court lawsuits involving the use of tests have been successful only where there was a claim that testing resulted in a violation of some other independent federal right, for instance, the right to be free from racial discrimination or the right to due process of law.[37] In state courts, too, judges traditionally have shown considerable deference to local school district decision-making.[38]

---

[35] Thus, for instance, one court in a non-race case declined to overturn a test score cutoff for admission to special gifted programs, finding that it was not "arbitrary." *Doe v. Commonwealth of Pennsylvania*, 593 F. Supp. 54 (E.D. Pa. 1984).

[36] *San Antonio Independent School District v. Rodriguez*, 411 U.S. 1 (1973).

[37] The reference here is to procedural due process, that is, the right to fair notice of a governmental body's intentions before a sanction is imposed. Thus, in the Brookhart case, *supra* note 27, the court concluded that handicapped students had been denied due process because they were never properly notified of the curricular objectives which they would have to master in order to receive a high school diploma.

There was a time in our jurisprudential history when the federal courts developed and administered a body of law which has come to be known as substantive due process. This doctrine permitted the courts to invalidate governmental policies or practices which they considered to be too illogical or irrational. Its main application was in the economic arena, where it was used by the Supreme Court during the first several decades of this century to strike down state protective legislation such as that regulating women's work, or children's working hours, or establishing minimum wages. See, for example, *Lochner v. New York*, 198 U.S. 45 (1905).

[38] This is consistent with the country's tradition of "local control." Even in those states with strong centralization of authority over education, such as New York, Massachusetts, and New Jersey, the primary substantive review of local policies takes place within the executive branch; the court's authority is limited to an "abuse of discretion" or similar standard. See, for example, *James v. Board of Educ.*, 42 N.Y.2d 357,

One of the earliest lines of cases involving testing[39] was decided in the late 1960s and early 1970s, as school districts in the major southern states began thoroughgoing desegregation. A number of systems proposed to institute grouping or tracking within newly desegregated schools; most planned to make class assignments based on testing, and in most instances the result was significant racial separation within otherwise desegregated schools. Without examining the technical questions of validity or reliability, and in general without exploring the merits of grouping or testing very deeply, most federal courts quickly barred such programs so long as they caused resegregation within the schools,[40] ultimately announcing the principle that school districts could institute them only once their schools became unitary— once they had eliminated the vestiges of prior segregation—and once they could show that minority children who would be assigned to lower tracks were

---

366 N.E.2d 1291, 397 N.Y.S.2d 934 (1977); *Board of Educ. v. Board of Educ.*, 80 A.D. 564, 435 N.Y.S.2d 759 (2d Dept. 1981).

On the other hand, judges are interested in what policymakers, researchers, and expert witnesses have to say. Once a credible claim has been made that some protected right has been violated, a court's perception of policy soundness is often the underlying force driving its judgment on the legal controversy before it (whether the court admits it or not). This is just as well; as the explosion in mandated testing in elementary and secondary schooling of the past decade indicates, policymakers with power are rarely moved by dispassionate analysis (even assuming that that is what they see, rather than slanted, distorted, incomplete, and polemical representations). Policymakers and legislators often operate at the level of symbolism. In doing so, they are remarkably insensitive to the individual injustices which can result from implementing symbolically satisfying policies. That is why there is an important role for courts, which have traditionally focused on rectifying individual injustices.

[39] In one earlier, and unique, decision, *Hobson v. Hansen*, 269 F. Supp. 401, 473-92 (D.D.C. 1967), *aff'd and remanded sub nom. Smuck v. Hobson*, 408 F.2d 175 (D.C. Cir. 1969), the court found that the standardized tests used to place pupils in highly inflexible tracks within the District of Columbia public school system were inappropriate for use with disadvantaged and minority children. The ruling's effect was largely limited to the specific and complex system which it analyzed.

[40] For example, *Morgan v. Kerrigan*, 530 F.2d 401, 422-25 (1st Cir. 1976), *cert. denied*, 426 U.S. 935 (1976); *Lemon v. Bossier Parish School Board*, 444 F.2d 1400 (5th Cir. 1971); *United States v. Sunflower County School District*, 430 F.2d 839 (5th Cir. 1970); *United States v. Tunica County School District*, 421 F.2d 1236 (5th Cir. 1970), *cert. denied*, 398 U.S. 951 (1970); *Singleton v. Jackson Municipal Separate School District*, 419 F.2d 1211, 1219 (5th Cir. 1969), *rev'd in part on other grounds sub nom. Carter v. West Feliciana Parish School Board*, 396 U.S. 290 (1970); *Reed v. Rhodes*, 455 F.Supp. 569, 598 (N.D. Ohio 1978); *Moses v. Washington Parish School Board*, 330 F. Supp. 1340 (E.D. La. 1971), *aff'd* 456 F.2d 1285 (5th Cir. 1972); *cf. Monroe v. Board of Commissioners of Jackson*, 427 F.2d 1005, 1008 (6th Cir. 1970).

no longer affected by the inequalities which pervaded the racially dual system.[41]

Since minority students in this country, for whatever reason, have tended to obtain lower scores on standardized instruments than white pupils, in most cases school systems' use of tests will produce racial disproportions, either in assignment of pupils to classes or in the distribution of some benefit or opportunity for which a certain test performance is a prerequisite. The task of courts is to determine whether such disproportions reflect discrimination. The general approach which they have taken to this inquiry is adapted from employment discrimination law,[42] which presumes tests or selection devices which have a racially differential impact to be discriminatory unless they can be justified as necessary to the conduct of an employer's trade and they meet professional validation standards. See *Larry P. v. Riles*, 495 F. Supp. at 968-73, *aff'd in relevant part*, 793 F.2d at 979-83 (Title VI and Rehabilitation Act claims); *Copeland v. School Board of Portsmouth*, 464 F.2d 932, 934 (4th Cir. 1972):

> [I]t is essential that the record establish that the tests and examinations used in making assignments [to special education classes] are relevant, reliable and free of discrimination. *Griggs v. Duke Power Company* (4th Cir. 1970) 420 F.2d 1225, 1233. . . . If they are, then it is of no moment that, as a result of the use of such fair and nondiscriminatory tests, more blacks than whites proportionately are assigned to these schools. On the other hand, if the assignments are made on the basis of irrelevant or unreliable tests, then it is the duty of the Court to take appropriate corrective action.

Although there has not been complete unanimity among the courts with respect to the application of this standard,[43] it is likely to persist in some form as the governing legal principle in most future testing challenges. As the

---

[41] *McNeal v. Tate County School District*, 508 F.2d 1017 (5th Cir. 1975).

[42] The approach has been widely used in cases challenging the use of tests for teacher certification, hiring, or retention. For example, *Morgan v. Kerrigan*, 509 F.2d 580 (1st cir. 1974), *cert. denied*, 421 U.S. 963 (1975); *Walston v. County School Board of Nansemond County*, 492 F.2d 919 (4th Cir. 1974); *Armstead v. Starkville Municipal Separate School District*, 461 F.2d 276 (5th Cir. 1972); *Georgia Association of Educators v. Nix*, 407 F. Supp. 1102 (N.D. Ga. 1976); *Baker v. Columbus Municipal Separate School District*, 329 F. Supp. 706 (N.D. Miss. 1971), *aff'd* 462 F.2d 1112 (5th Cir. 1972); *contra, United States v. South Carolina*, 445 F. Supp. 1094 (D.S.C. 1977), *aff'd mem.*, 434 U.S. 1026 (1978); *United States v. North Carolina*, 425 F. Supp. 789 (E.D. N.C. 1977), vacating 400 F. Supp. 343 (E.D. N.C. 1975).

[43] Compare, for example, *Morales v. Shannon*, 516 F.2d 411 (5th Cir. 1975); *Anderson v. Banks*, 520 F. Supp. 472, 500-08 (S.D. Ga. 1981), *subsequent order aff'd sub nom. Johnson v. Sikes*, 730 F.2d 644 (11th Cir. 1984).

excerpt quoted above indicates, application of the standard to testing emphasizes relevancy (validity) and reliability. Thus, in a recent decision concerning the Texas Pre-Professional Skills Test (PPST) (required for entry into teacher training programs), a preliminary injunction against the test (which produces vastly disproportionate results along racial lines) was reversed by the appellate court because the trial court did not make findings that the instrument lacked validity for its intended use. See *United States v. LULAC*, 793 F.2d 636 (5th Cir. 1986), *rev'g* 628 F. Supp. 304 (E.D. Tex. 1985).

An important exception to this line of authority involves minimum competency and other exit tests, and even extends, as in the PPST situation, to some entry barriers. The outstanding example is *Debra P. v. Turlington*, 730 F.2d 1405 (llth Cir. 1984),[44] the Florida statewide challenge to the competency examination required for high school graduation which had a significant racially differential effect. Although initially the courts enjoined the use of the test until all students to whom it would be applied were pupils who had not attended segregated public schools, once that line of demarcation had been crossed the courts refused to make a searching inquiry into the validity of the examination and the significance of the Florida high school diploma. Instead, they accepted a version of face validity which they called instructional validity—taking an opinion survey of practicing teachers and administrators as evidence that Florida school systems presented to their students most of the material contained in the testing instruments.

The difficulty which courts have had with minimum competency and other supposed criterion-referenced instruments exists because of the lack of a general agreement on the criteria which should be satisfied by any particular level of education. Thus, for example, it is easy enough to articulate the proposition that mastery of basic skills at the ninth-grade level is a perfectly reasonable prerequisite to the award of a diploma, but it far more difficult to determine what skills one is talking about. Quite naturally, the courts have insisted that, at a minimum, the skills be those which students have actually been taught—even though they have not applied very sophisticated techniques for investigating whether or not this demand has been satisfied. Generally, courts have not yet conducted item analyses to see for themselves whether or not the knowledge measured by test instruments represents a sensible assessment of school attainment. I would suggest that there will be closer scrutiny of test content in the future and that more tests are likely to be questioned.

---

[44] This decision affirmed a district court ruling, 564 F. Supp. 177 (M.D. Fla. 1983); earlier rulings in the case are reported at 474 F. Supp. 244 (M.D. Fla. 1979) (enjoining denial of diplomas based on test until all students who began public schooling before period of desegregation had graduated), *aff'd and remanded*, 644 F.2d 397 (5th Cir. 1981).

Two other significant legal approaches deserve mention. First, the Rehabilitation Act of 1973 bars discrimination against handicapped individuals by recipients of federal assistance. In the educational arena, the act has been interpreted to protect against misclassification as retarded, learning disabled, and so on, and in at least one instance the act has been applied to strike down the use of IQ tests for EMR placement. *Larry P. v. Riles*, 495 F. Supp. at 968-70. Second, the "Golden Rule" principle[45] can and should be applied to the construction of educational instruments so as to eliminate irrelevant racial differences in scores to the extent possible.

My own experience in the testing and tracking litigation described above suggests that the most difficult part of such litigation is the process of factual investigation to determine exactly what use is being made of what tests in a particular district. As we accumulate more knowledge about both test construction and test misuse in educational settings, it will become easier for attorneys to gather these facts and litigation will continue and expand. For this reason, policymakers, legislators, and educational administrators are well advised to conduct their own reviews for the purpose of restricting test use to appropriate functions within their institutions and systems.

Policy Issues

This paper has suggested, based on the author's own experience and some reference to research and literature in the area, that standardized educational testing has become a growth industry which is not only inadequately regulated but which must be reformed in order to eliminate, insofar as possible, the real abuses which are harming individual pupils across the United States every day. These abuses reflect some inadequacies in test preparation and construction, but to an even greater extent they grow out of the quick fix attitude of our society which causes many instruments to be utilized for purposes for which they are totally unsuited. The current level of protection against test misuse is extremely low, consisting only of warnings in publishers' manuals which are not followed and, in one or two states, of legislation allowing public scrutiny of test instruments and scoring practices.[46] Only the largest public school systems have research or testing departments of sufficient size and staffed by persons of appropriate professional backgrounds to be aware of the proper role of standardized examinations. For most districts, there is overwhelming public and legislative pressure to participate in extensive testing of students but little support enabling them to make proper, cautious interpretation of the data which are produced.

---

[45] See *supra* note 16.

[46] For example, N.Y. Educ. Law §§ 340 *et seq*. (Consol. 1985).

For policymakers, therefore, the challenge is to put the testing movement back on an appropriate course: to curb abuses and encourage the sound application of testing theory and practice in local schools in order to improve educational attainment for all pupils. This will require extensive public education and, in particular, training of state legislators and public officials. It will require bold leadership that is willing to eschew catchy phrases (such as the "rising tide of mediocrity") in favor of reasoned elaboration and persuasion. If we fail to undertake the effort, however, we are condemning the next generation of our youth to suffer a series of arbitrary, irrational, and sometimes discriminatory abuses which we would not impose upon ourselves[47]—a moral default which no professional can justify.

---

[47] For example, college professors do not receive tenure based on a test score; lawyers are admitted to the profession based on their ability to regurgitate on an examination details for which, once in practice, they would never rely upon their memories, see, for example, *Tyler v. Vickery*, 517 F.2d 1089 (5th Cir. 1975), *cert. denied*, 426 U.S. 940 (1976); and I suspect that most of the participants in the work of the commission would not want their contributions to be evaluated by taking a two- or three-hour multiple choice examination!

IV

TESTING IN THE WORKPLACE:
THEORETICAL AND PRACTICAL PERSPECTIVES

Economic Models of Discrimination, Testing, and Public Policy

Robert F. Adams

Research into the economics of discrimination has led to the development of a considerable body of literature in the past two decades (Marshall 1974). As we might expect, the economists do not come to any conclusive answers; however, the work does propose a framework of analysis for contemporary policy issues.

The work plan of this paper is to consider the economics of discrimination, and from this vantage point to evaluate the policy implications of Title VII of the Civil Rights Act of 1964 on testing, affirmative action, and the Equal Employment Opportunity Commission's regulatory procedures. Such an economic perspective is essential to the setting of intelligent research priorities on testing and job discrimination.

I. DISCRIMINATION IN THE LABOR MARKET

Labor Market and Pre-Labor Market Discrimination

Economists usually define discrimination in the labor marketplace as valuation of personal characteristics of the individual worker that are unrelated to productivity (Arrow 1972). To be clear, labor market discrimination occurs when personal characteristics unrelated to or not affecting productivity become part of the value of an individual in the labor market. Such personal characteristics typically include race, ethnicity, religion, gender, and sexual preference.

Market discrimination, by this definition, is measured by differences in wages or job placement when productivity characteristics are the same. In circumstances where productivity characteristics can be held constant, identifying labor market discrimination is relatively easy. However, it is a considerably more complex problem to identify discrimination if the only available information is observed differences in wages or job placement among groups of workers having different personal characteristics. Absent labor market discrimination, it is still possible for wages to vary by personal characteristics across the economy. Differences in wages or jobs placement may reflect not only direct labor market discrimination, but also what economists have come to call pre-labor market discrimination. Adam Smith saw this possibility in one of his most eloquent and insightful passages in *The Wealth of Nations*.

> The differences of natural talents in different men is, in reality, much less than we are aware of; and the very genius which appears to distinguish men of different professions, when grown up to maturity, is not upon many occasions so much the cause, as the effect of the division of labor. The difference between the most dissimilar characters, between the philosopher and a common street porter for example, seems to arise not so much from nature, as from custom, habit, and education.

Smith rejected the argument (traceable to Aristotle) that work in the economic society should be allocated by natural abilities identified at birth or in one's youth. It is not that the porter and the philosopher were so different in childhood. Rather "custom, habits, and education" were more important determinants of their different values in the marketplace. Perhaps Smith, but surely J. S. Mill, would have argued further that when, on the basis of personal or family characteristics, two individuals are not permitted an equal range of choices as they move through their lives, the result will be differences in productivity which vary by personal characteristics, and thus differences in wages and job placement. The observation that the wages of black male workers are lower than those of white male workers reflects not only labor market discrimination—black workers with the same productivity characteristics as white workers are paid less than white workers—but also pre-market conditions of education, family income, and environment that lead a higher proportion of black workers than white workers to have lower productivity and to be so evaluated by the marketplace (Orazem 1987).

Further, because market information is used by individuals to make pre-market decisions in regard to years and type of education to pursue, market discrimination is reinforced by pre-market decisions. A black youth whose expected return to higher education is considerably lower than that of a white because of discrimination in the marketplace will choose, in what he perceives to be his best interest, not to pursue higher education.

Considerable effort has been made to establish the relative importance of pre-market versus market discrimination. As one might expect, these studies suggest that the importance of labor market discrimination as an explanation of earnings differentials varies significantly by group. For example, it is estimated that between 20 and 50 per cent of the earnings differential between blacks and whites comes from market discrimination. On the other hand, market discrimination appears to play a considerably less important role in explaining earnings differentials between Hispanics and non-Hispanics, or between whites and those of Chinese or Japanese ancestry. Studies of the earnings differential between males and females suggest that two-thirds of the differential can be explained by market discrimination. Although these studies are inconclusive, they do provide some indication of the relative significance of pre-market and market types of economic discrimination to different subpopulation groups.

For the purposes of this volume, I have limited this paper to labor market discrimination and testing, but obviously pre-market discrimination is also of major significance If the *cycle* of discrimination is to be broken, pre-market discrimination and the role of testing in pre-market discrimination need to be high research priorities.

II. MODELS OF LABOR MARKET DISCRIMINATION

In order to reduce labor market discrimination one needs to understand both the cause of discrimination and the mechanism by which it operates. Economists have approached this problem from a variety of directions. Let us consider these models individually.

Neoclassical Models

The standard neoclassical approach is to assume competitive consumer and resource markets and then to evaluate the way prejudice on the part of employers, employees, and customers works (Becker 1971; Arrow 1972). In these models prejudice is defined as unwillingness to associate with individuals from a particular group, or favoring members of one's own group, even though no differences in productivity exist. This approach does not explain why discrimination exists, but rather demonstrates that in a world where markets work, individual utility maximization by consumers and workers, and profit seeking by firms all play an important role in disciplining economic agents who discriminate. All agents have full information. Let me review the neoclassical approach to discrimination as it applies to employers, employees, and consumers.

In the case of employer prejudice, the employer is seen to undervalue the productivity of a minority group. In fact this model assumes that the employer has a "taste" for discrimination. This is the unadulterated case of prejudice; it is not a mistake or lack of information. The employer knows that the discrimination will cost; that it will have an impact. Minority workers are forced to offer their employment at lower wages in order to compete. The discriminating employers will use fewer minority workers than their actual productivity would dictate and will do so at the cost of lower profits. This kind of discrimination cannot last, for nondiscriminating employers will be able to produce at lower cost and make higher profits. Eventually competition will lead to the decline of market discrimination as prejudiced employers are driven out of the market.

Let us now turn to the situation in which majority workers carry prejudices about working with or for minorities and women. Now nonminority workers have a taste for discrimination, and employers will have to offer them higher pay to induce them to work with minorities, or attempt to keep costs down by only hiring women and minorities for "traditional" lower-status jobs wherever possible.

Finally, there is the situation in which customers carry prejudices and prefer not to be served by a minority employee or insist upon doing business with a white male employee. Firms will demand white male workers and wage differentials will appear as minority or women employees will have to offer to work for lower wages or not at all. Substantial occupational segregation may also result. Where such segregation occurs in jobs of high responsibility and pay, minorities and women are further disadvantaged.

A number of economists are troubled by the standard approach. The criticisms are aimed at different levels. Some find the model too confining. In a recent paper, Lang argued that he could not be satisfied with a model where people are assumed to have a "taste" for discrimination. In such a model, if one wishes to explain the persistence of labor market discrimination one is left the choice of "denying the existence of perfect competition or deciding that we are all bigots" (Lang 1986). Others have also been troubled by the long-run persistence of discrimination and job segmentation and the inability of the model to explain this result. With market discipline and the possibility of higher profits, one would expect nondiscriminatory employers to be at an advantage and those who discriminate to be driven out by competition. Why does discrimination persist?

It should be of no surprise that there are those who argue that the persistence of evidence of labor market discrimination, measured in terms of both wage differentials and occupational segregation, is dependent upon noncompetitive elements in the labor market that create a circumstance that makes discrimination possible. The loosening of competitive forces gives the prejudiced employer more leeway to discriminate. The taste for discrimination still imposes a cost, but the discrimination will not disappear automatically as the competitive model suggests.

Before leaving the treatment of discrimination in traditional microeconomic theory, we should also consider the possibilities of discrimination in two important situations: (1) unions which can control the labor supply, and (2) the public sector.

The Role of Unions

Turning to employee discrimination first, it is plausible to argue that union control of the supply of labor, particularly the means of job entry, presents an opportunity for labor market discrimination. Those economists who have taken this approach have argued that union discrimination is more likely to be successful in craft unions than in industrial unions, which do not control job entry (Ashenfelter 1973). Employees' taste for discrimination seems to be the causal factor. It is clear that unions may raise their wages by controlling the supply of labor, but it is not obvious why they might choose to discriminate against minorities or women. Others have argued that the whole question of unionization and discrimination is a complex issue for which there is no simple model and have simply tried to look at the evidence. Recent research on the effect of unions upon job opportunities for minorities and women in the past two decades suggests that these opportunities have not been diminished by unions (Leonard 1985).

In passing, we should note the difficulty that has arisen between seniority clauses in collective bargaining agreements—last in first out—and federal antidiscrimination and affirmative action policies. The issue here is that by setting seniority rights and units as part of the collective bargaining process, unions may have undone progress in the hiring of women and minorities. Do seniority systems freeze out those who have been discriminated against in the past? The Supreme Court, in the cases of *Teamsters v. United States*, 431 U.S. 324 (1977) and *Firefighters Local 1784 v. Stotts*, 104 S. Ct 2576 (1984), has supported seniority units that have been created and administered in a nondiscriminatory fashion and supported seniority clauses over affirmative action. Of course, as minorities and women establish parity in seniority, this becomes a moot issue.

Discrimination in the Public Sector

Curiously, very little research has attempted to develop a model of discrimination in the public sector. One approach has argued that discrimination in the public sector is caused by prejudice on the part of the taxpayer/consumer and that the discrimination is, in essence, "consumer" discrimination. Such an approach tries to fit public discrimination into a model better suited to competitive private markets. A more efficacious approach is to assume that the public sector is a bureau that is trying to maximize its budget, which it can then direct toward perquisites or output (Niskanan 1976). In such a model the bureau may discriminate because the employees, the customers, and/or the "management" are prejudiced. From the management point of view, discrimination can be seen as one of the perquisites. And, in fact, the lack of attention to productivity as a reason for hiring that results from a lack of competition is precisely one reason that legislation regarding public sector personnel policies has specified hiring procedures that appear to minimize the personal discretion which may lead to cronyism. I shall return to these policies when I consider the question of testing.

The procedures that are introduced in order to remove any arbitrary and personal elements from the hiring process in the public sector may also reduce the opportunity for discrimination on the basis of race, religion, and gender. Hence, one would expect to find less discrimination in the public sector in those bureaus where modern personnel practices are standard. Indeed, several recent studies (Smith 1976; Asher and Popkin 1984; Perloff and

Wachter 1984) found less discrimination in the federal service than in the private sector.

Not all bureaus in the public sector are organized to produce outputs. Some are designed to regulate and control markets. In particular, state and local governments often oversee the licensing and credentialing of individuals in private organizations. Over eight hundred occupations require licensing, and about five hundred use tests for this purpose. To the extent that such licensing controls job entry and the licensing process is not impervious to the influence of private, self-interested organizations, it is vulnerable to discrimination. In this regard, the public sector is not dissimilar to a craft union. But, as is the case with unions, an opportunity to discriminate is only an opportunity, and a model of discrimination needs a motive force. Very little study has been done on the possibilities of discrimination in the licensing and credentialing process, but we can argue that such discrimination can be thought of as either income maximizing or based in prejudice. In either case the possibility of long-run and persistent discrimination exists.

Institutional Models

The above considerations are only analytical elaborations around a partial microeconomic model in which individuals are assumed to be prejudiced. Others have taken a broader, more general, systemic approach to discrimination which focuses upon monopoly power (Piore 1970). Some have argued that lower wages and occupational segregation occur because the workers who are discriminated against are "crowded" into lower level productive work where there is a plentiful supply of workers forcing wages down. In a variant of this model there exists a dual labor market, a primary market made up of skilled workers who earn good wages and who are often protected by union and corporate work rules, and a secondary market of unskilled jobs for which the market is very competitive. The competition comes from ease of entry and the lack of need for job training. Those who are in the low-paying, less desirable jobs are identified as unskilled workers with poor work histories. Once one is so identified it becomes very difficult to move into the other market of better, high-paying jobs. Hence, once women or minorities become so identified there is no reason for firms to seek them out in the primary market. This dual labor market approach allows for long-run persistence of discrimination, without assuming fully competitive markets and a taste for discrimination, by introducing a structural element that reflects job training and skills requirements. Pre-market discrimination is carried forward.

Finally, the neo-Marxist view argues that prejudice and discrimination are an inherent activity of a capitalistic society because, for whatever reason discrimination arises, it is perpetuated by the capitalists who wish to create conflict among workers and draw attention away from the workers' real problem: the capitalists' efforts to increase surplus value by worsening work conditions for all.

Informational Models

As much as each of the above models may have compelling aspects and strong advocates, they provide little room for explaining discrimination that persists and flows from the everyday decisions made by well-meaning individuals. Understanding the basis of economic discrimination from this perspective may not be as dramatic and the motivation may not appear to be as evil, but such understanding may prove much more useful because it leads to policy conclusions that go beyond finding evidence of the intent to discriminate, and provides a useful backdrop for understanding the relationship between discrimination and testing.

In these models of the labor market, discrimination is not embedded in the personal prejudice of the economic agents or in the structure of the economy, but is inherent in the lack of full information on the part of employers. Because such discrimination in the labor market does not depend on personal prejudice, it has been labeled "statistical" discrimination. A number of economists have argued that statistical discrimination arises because firms often have difficulty obtaining full information about the actual productivity of a worker (Phelps 1972; Arrow 1972). How can a firm really know that one worker will be more productive than another? First, it can supplement the information it has by considering some group statistic inherent to the worker, such as race, gender, or religion. Some authors define such stereotyping to be discriminatory in itself (Blau and Jusenius 1976), even when the employer's perception of differences in average group productivity are correct.

Insight into discrimination can also be developed by considering the *signaling* approach to the problem of incomplete information developed by Spence and Arrow (Spence 1973; Arrow 1974). In this model, individuals are perceived to differ in their abilities. The market estimate of their productivity is based upon acquired "signals" of ability, particularly amount and kind of education. Since the cost of acquiring signals is lower for individuals with higher abilities, firms find that the signals of higher abilities are consistent with productivity. Acquired signals are like estimates based upon group averages. The signaling model closely fits notions of "statistical discrimination." The signaling approach also raises fundamental questions about the usefulness of schooling, and is contrary to the model of productivity differences based upon accumulation of "human capital"—skills acquired through education.

If the signaling approach is correct, attempts at dealing with problems of pre-market discrimination through school policies should not be oriented toward retention, but rather quite the opposite. Dropping out becomes one of the output measures of schooling. According to the signaling model, Adam

Smith was only half correct. The difference between the philosopher and the porter really occurs during the schooling period through the signal process. However, the basic cause of the difference is not schooling, but an inherent natural difference in abilities. So, although I only include reference to the signaling literature in this discussion of market discrimination, any analysis of pre-market discrimination must deal with this fundamental question of signaling and schooling.

Other economists have taken a narrower position with regard to statistical discrimination. In the view of Aigner and Cain (1977), discrimination in the labor market exists only when the average wage for the group is not proportional to its average productivity. They argue that within-group discrimination is inevitable in a world of limited information. In models such as this one, discrimination by employers is fueled, not by prejudice, but by lack of perfect information, and a concomitant aversion to risk. The employer, operating in a world of imperfect information, seeks to find the most productive workers, but must rely on indirect indicators of productivity potential, such as standardized tests. Individual information about the worker available to the employer will never exactly predict productivity.

Aigner and Cain have identified at least two circumstances that could be narrowly defined as "statistical" discrimination and which raise questions about testing. They hypothesize that test scores may not be equally informative for all groups. If groups differ in the degree to which test scores provide reliable information about individual aptitude and productivity, then employers who are aware of this will tend to select their employees from the groups whose test scores are the most reliable. This lowers the risk that they will hire an individual whose productivity does not reach the level one would expect, given his test score.

In the first case Aigner and Cain discuss, the employer tries to hire workers so that expected productivity is maximized, given a fixed level of labor input. The employer's problem is to select between two groups. If one of the groups has a lower test reliability than the other, employers will pay the group with the lower reliability less, even though the actual productivity for both groups is equal. The difference in pay arises from the risk costs to the employers, stemming either from variance in the output within similar jobs or from mistakes in assigning workers to dissimilar jobs. The interesting conclusion for us is that discrimination of this type can be reduced by introducing test instruments which more carefully account for those differences between groups which affect the reliability of tests which are used to predict performance.

In their second case, Aigner and Cain suggest a variation of this model which depends upon differences in test reliability, but in which there is assumed to exist a threshold test score below which no worker is hired. Above the threshold, productivity and test scores are assumed to be positively related.

Given transaction costs of hiring and the risk of hiring error, the employer will select workers with the higher test scores from the group with higher test reliability. Those with low test scores and low test reliability are not hired because they fall below the threshold.

Although these two cases demonstrate the possibility of labor market discrimination in a world where the discrimination does not result from prejudice but from group differences in the reliability of tests as predictors in a world of imperfect information, no evidence or study exists that shows the importance of these possibilities in the real world.

I have not presented these various models of discrimination to make a choice, but rather to provide a context to evaluate policy toward discrimination and testing. However, some generalizations can be made. First, discrimination may occur because of the decision-making environment of the firm and the lack of full information. One need not assume a "taste" to discriminate. Second, discipline in market competition and the free movement of resources reduce the possibilities of discrimination. Third, the marketplace will invariably validate the needs of pre-market discrimination.

III. TITLE VII OF THE CIVIL RIGHTS ACT

Before turning to the question of testing, let me make some comments about Title VII of the 1964 Civil Rights Act. Our brief survey of the economics of discrimination should leave one with a sense of the complexity and diversity of the causes and propagation of economic discrimination throughout the economic system. It is evident that policies directed toward the elimination of market discrimination need to go beyond looking for evidence of the intent to discriminate. Without a doubt, the Civil Rights Act of 1964 took a major step against discrimination in the labor market by making it unlawful for an employer to "refuse to hire or discharge any individual, or otherwise to discriminate against an individual with respect to his compensation, terms, conditions or privileges of employment because of such." Recognizing the possibility of discriminatory union practices, Title VII also made it unlawful for labor organizations to discriminate with regard to membership, employment, referral, apprenticeships, or other union programs. The inclusiveness of Title VII, focusing not only on firm behavior but also on union behavior, has been further enhanced by Supreme Court interpretations.

The court has applied two standards: disparate treatment and disparate impact. Under disparate treatment, discriminatory practices are unlawful when it can be shown that there was an intent to discriminate. From our previous discussion, such an interpretation would be consistent with the concept of discrimination based upon prejudice. Of course, such intent is not easily shown; it should be no surprise that the court has applied disparate impact more often. In this case, the judgment of discrimination is not based on intent, but rather on result. If a hiring practice results in an adverse impact on a particular group, even though it appears to be neutral in the abstract, it must be abandoned unless it can be directly related to job performance. The evidence for the suspicion of discrimination is a disparity between the groups selected for employment or promotion and the pool of available applicants. In moving in the direction of disparate impact the court has broadened the policy against discrimination to include the possibilities of statistical discrimination defined in the broadest terms. Nondiscrimination is not only an issue of individuals of equal productivity being treated equally but also of individuals from different groups being treated the same.

There can be little doubt that Title VII has far-reaching impact and that most of the empirical studies of wage and job discrimination conclude that Title VII has had a positive and valuable result. Employers are held accountable for auditable procedures that allow for public oversight for reliability and validity. Individuals and groups have a forum of informal and judicial review of possible discriminatory behavior. However, Title VII leaves some issues unresolved. It does not deal with pre-market discrimination, which affects the applicant pool. It does not deal with the incidence of unemployment in general. It has left somewhat unresolved the issue of the seniority system and incidence of layoffs. Finally, it avoids the important issue of possible discrimination of licensing and credentialing agencies, either in intent or in impact.

IV. TESTING AND THE FIRM'S INFORMATIONAL NEEDS

Having established that labor market discrimination in various forms may result from attempts of firms to cope with imperfect information, including unreliable tests, let me turn to the role of tests in the labor market. Testing is part of the firm's investment in the hiring process. The firm needs to assess the future productivity of an applicant. Other things being equal, the firm will want to hire the best possible workforce at minimum cost. There exists a variety of methods for the firm to obtain this information. It may choose to investigate each applicant with great care. Such an investigation could include tests to establish potential productivity. A firm may also choose to forego testing and close scrutiny and use signaled information as noted in Section II above. Such use of signals may lead to the hiring of a "lemon," or less productive employee, but the overall result may still be more cost effective than carefully checking out each employee. As a third alternative, a firm may find that close scrutiny and testing may be better than using signals, but that neither is as effective as making an on the job assessment of the individual's skills. This approach to the hiring process follows a pattern of hiring individuals into the lowest job categories and observing their productivity. The productive employees become eligible to move into higher job classifications and the not-so-productive employees are screened out. Most of the non-entry level jobs are filled by employees of the firm and jobs are allocated through an "internal labor market" (Kerr 1954; Williamson, Wachter, and Harris 1975). A firm will use one or more of these three methods in its hiring process.

It has been observed that internal labor markets are used extensively in steel, petroleum, chemical, and other industeries which utilize highly automated, complicated production technologies. On the other hand, testing is more often found in firms that hire large numbers of low-level, white collar workers such as banks (Wigdor and Garner 1982).

How do firms decide which hiring methods to use? Given levels of information, alternative methods of obtaining information, and the relative costs of different information methods, the firm will seek the least-cost method of obtaining this information. For example, Figures 1.1, 1.2, and 1.3 represent different combinations of signaling and testing for given levels of information. Given the costs of each method per unit and the budget the firm is able to appropriate for information seeking (as represented by constraint AA), a cost-minimizing firm will pick point E, which is its least-cost combination of testing and signaling.

FIGURE 1.1

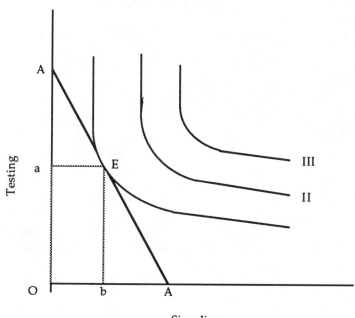

Signaling

FIGURE 1.2

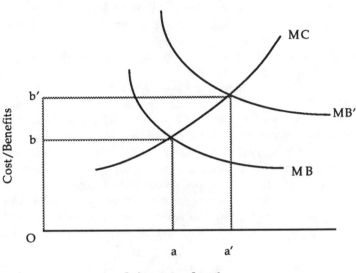

Information Level

How does a firm decide what level of information to seek? A firm will choose its combination of hiring methods by maximizing net hiring benefits; it will buy a level of information for which the marginal cost is equal to the marginal benefit of increased productivity. The optimal level will differ by occupation and firm. In Figure 1.2, marginal cost, MC, of seeking hiring information is seen to increase as the firm attempts to gain additional information about its applicants. On the other hand, the marginal benefit, MB, of this additional information declines as the additional information adds less and less to the knowledge of the expected productivity of the workers. In this case, the firm will seek information to the level Oa. If, on the other hand, being correct about the expected productivity of a group of workers is very important in terms of the productivity of the firm, then it will be willing to invest more in information seeking. For example, in this case the marginal benefit from information seeking would be MB, and the level of information seeking would be Oa'.

In our example, the firm may choose to do its own information seeking, it can purchase tests, or it can contract out to an employment agency. The firm may choose to hire applicants on temporary contracts and then promote them if the productivity is there. As economists, we need to ask if there is anything about this investment in the hiring process that cannot be left to the private market system. The level of information seeking is determined by the marginal cost of this effort and the benefits in productivity to the firm. However, let me take the position that society also benefits from the careful selection of employees, over and above the productivity of the firm. The social benefits arise from the assurance that, in most specific terms, hiring is done on a nondiscriminatory basis. In this case, discrimination is not merely an equity or moral issue, it detracts from the efficient use of resources. For example, a newspaper may do only a casual review of applicants in hiring people to deliver the paper. Such a job does not warrant much time spent screening applicants. But if the traditional method of screening leads predominantly to the hiring of boys, although a number of equally- or better-qualified girls applied, there will exist an efficiency loss to society.

Let us assume that the possible discrimination is an inverse function of the amount of effort put into the information seeking. Then, as shown in Figure 1.3, MSB represents the marginal social benefit to information seeking about applicants. In this simple case the firm will, from a societal point of view, underinvest in the hiring process. The optimal level of information seeking is Oa'. Public policy needs to be directed to encourage information seeking in the selection process.

FIGURE 1.3

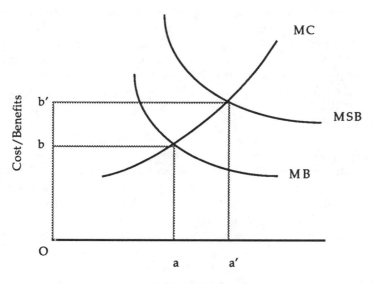

Information Level

Since testing is one of three methods of obtaining information about an employee's expected future performance, it becomes clear that the reliability or the validity of a test must be evaluated relative to the possible vulnerability to discrimination of the other two methods of hiring and promoting. Where there is reason to believe that testing may have inherent reliability problems, hiring and screening may be seen to be preferable from a societal point of view. The problem is that these alternative methods must be evaluated in the context of different circumstances. The same kinds of issues of reliability and validity can be raised with respect to hiring processes that are not test-based. It is understandable that testing, with its aura of objectivity and its "scientific" base, would draw the attention of both supporters and opponents. Testing deserves close scrutiny. All hiring processes require close surveillance.

All methods of hiring are unreliable in a world of incomplete information. Testing is only one aspect of the hiring process from which discrimination can arise without conscious, overt prejudice. A focus on testing will only encourage those firms that test to reduce testing programs. That is, these firms will incur added costs in demonstrating the reliability and validity of their tests, making tests more expensive. The firm may choose to substitute other forms of hiring that may be no less unreliable from the point of view of society. For example, one interpretation of the internal labor market is that pay structures and job assignments may result from custom, tradition, and other institutional factors that may not be dictated by productivity and human capital differences. These customs and traditions may in themselves have adverse impact upon individuals or groups.

In my home institution, typing tests are disallowed as part of the hiring process for secretaries because the institution chose not to incur the added costs of validation. The "applicant's declared typing speed" is used. My suspicion is that the lack of test information directs more attention to other application or interview information that may be less useful in estimating productivity, for example, physical appearance and/or the use of application information as test information without the applicant's knowledge, that is, a typing or spelling error.

A recent study of publications in economics journals provides another example of the need to undertake further research that deals with non-test promotion procedures (Ferber and Teiman 1980). In this study, the authors compare the rate of acceptance of articles by author gender, with and without a double-blind refereeing system. The preliminary result is that the rate of acceptance for articles by women is almost twice as high in the blind system. Such a difference in acceptance has a marked impact upon the promotion possibilities for women economists in a publish-or-perish world. This kind of adverse impact is not covered by Title VII. Universities show no interest in investigating or setting standards for professional journals, the journals may not have any interest in changing their procedures for reasons that may appear quite reasonable to them, and the profession may not care to involve itself.

V. TESTING IN THE PUBLIC SECTOR

Earlier in this paper, I made some tentative remarks about the economics of discrimination in the public sector. Let us turn to the possibility of discrimination resulting from imperfect information and the reliance upon hiring practices that are imperfect in their application in the public sector. The evidence is that selection and placement by testing is pervasive throughout federal, state, and local governments. Why is the search for information by testing so much greater in a sector where the discipline of the profit motive and competition is so limited? Part of the answer to this question lies precisely in the absence of the market discipline. Testing is part of a mechanism to limit and constrain graft, corruption, and cronyism that would otherwise flower in a world with limited constraint. Testing, and the merit system of which it is a part, is designed to take arbitrary and personal elements out of public service hiring.

Furthermore, testing in the public sector in many cases is a licensing or credential procedure that has been internalized into the public sector. The purpose of this certification is to limit entry to those who fulfill the requirement of any job for which technical competency is of great concern. For example, given modern military technology, the armed services need to know that those who have access to weapons also have the credentials to use them. This credentialing role explains much of the extensive use of tests for promotion in the military services.

In the public sector, as in the private sector, we must consider testing as one of several alternative ways of estimating an applicant's future productivity. Even though, in the absence of a market discipline, the extensive use of tests and other formal hiring rules may not be cost effective to the bureau, it presumably carries out information seeking to a level that is socially acceptable, that is, nondiscriminatory. Not only will the additional information seeking reduce the opportunity for hiring a politician's friend, but it also should reduce the possibility of discrimination on the basis of race or gender.

What, then, is the problem with testing and discrimination in public sector hiring? First, it is still possible that test use results in a disparate impact on one group or another. Although there is sensitivity to this issue in the public sector itself, continued research and development of good test materials is necessary. Second, the rules and regulations for public sector hiring are not uniform among levels or sectors of the public sector. The amount of research and development effort also varies. Although the setting of standards is an important public function that surely reduces discrimination, these standards need to be set appropriately at all levels of government.

Sometimes testing is part of a certification or licensing process that is either internalized in the public sector or is shared with a private board of governors. In these cases, we need to be clear about the purposes of the testing. The testing is not part of a process designed to hire the most productive future employee. It is rather part of a process of establishing minimum standards of performance in a particular profession—law, medicine, teaching, and so on. Test results and the applicant's educational background are used to provide information to the consumer about the abilities of the individual. In this context, testing is the best way of obtaining this information. Certainly, some have argued that tests to enter an occupation do not serve to give much information or assurance to the public and leave open the opportunity for control of the supply of labor and enrichment of those already in the profession. In this chapter, I only wish to note what the issue is: the most efficient way for the consumer to get information about professional competence. However, the use of testing—valid or not—does raise some further issues. First, examinations of this type are often put together by professionals in their respective fields without the advice and counsel of experts on the reliability or validity of the tests. In this regard, it is unfortunate that Title VII procedures on testing are not applied. Given the large number of tests of this type, it would be cost-effective to establish a research and development program focused upon testing for licensing and credentialing.

VI. POLICY TOWARD TESTING

It is quite clear from the federal *Uniform Guidelines on Employee Selection Procedures* that the intent of public policy is to focus on more than testing as part of hiring and promotion procedures. The *Guidelines* impose the same standards of validation for non-test-based selection techniques as are required for tests. This focus upon the validity and reliability of all hiring and selection techniques makes much sense in a world where tests play a significant but limited role. Certainly, the *Guidelines* have caused employers to be more careful to insure that hiring techniques such as an unscored interview employ valid questions, and that these questions are asked uniformly of all job candidates. When validation is not possible and procedures are suggestive of discrimination, the employer has the option to adjust procedures. I am certainly not arguing against scrutiny of tests, but rather for extending scrutiny to all hiring practices.

My suspicion is that, as with testing, the application of standards to nontest procedures is not uniform across employers, industries, or employment categories. Higher education presents some interesting issues in the application of Title VII. When a university department hires a new professor, it does not use a test. Universities use a hiring process, developed over many years, that depends upon confidential letters, peer review, and an elaborate, more often than not mystifying, bureaucratic process. Although it is understandable that procedural standards are difficult to apply in academic situations, it is also clear that the present process is very vulnerable to arbitrary and discriminatory behavior. Universities do collect the required Title VII data on ethnicity and gender of the applicants and hiring rates by department. It is probably not in the interest of any one university to do more because it does not want to impose standards alone that might put it at a competitive disadvantage. On the other hand, I suspect that a review of nontest procedures on the nonacademic, or administrative side, of higher education would show that considerable improvement towards the spirit of the *Guidelines* has occurred in nontest selection procedures. I also suspect that, in other segments of the economy, the experience is similar to that in higher education. There exists considerable room for improvement.

Broadening of concern to nontest selection procedures is also important because there is some evidence that the *Uniform Guidelines* have brought about a reduction in the use of tests. From the analysis above, this behavior should be of no surprise. The *Guidelines* have also caused a more critical use of tests (Wigdor and Garner 1982).

VII. SUMMARY

Testing in the labor market should be seen as part of investment in the hiring process. This approach means that (1) testing should not be singled out from other hiring processes and given special attention, and (2) government should support investment in research and development in all hiring practices, including testing. Moreover, efforts should be made to achieve further uniformity in the application of the *Uniform Guidelines*, including in those areas and levels of the labor market that have traditionally operated with more subjective selection processes. A comprehensive review of regulatory policy in the licensing and credentialing process should also be undertaken. Such a review should consider alternatives to the present forms of credentialing and licensing, and result in a policy with regard to the reliability and validity of such processes, including testing.

Finally, let me return to an earlier point by noting that economic decisions about hiring and promotion focus upon the productive skills of the individual workers. In a world of less than full information, firms will rely on selection processes that may be less than perfect. The introduction of public policies such as Title VII, as well as further research, have improved and will continue to improve the way in which workers are allocated to jobs. All of society gains.

This improvement in the allocation process will not increase the opportunities of those who come to the marketplace already disadvantaged, as the result of prejudice before they face the harsh validation of the marketplace. To the extent that differences in job access and pay reflect this pre-market difference in opportunity because "custom, habit, and education" were flawed by prejudice, we will have made little progress for those upon whom the weight of this bias has the greatest impact. Instead of reducing discrimination, testing and other employee selection techniques at the job entry point will corroborate the effects of pre-market discrimination. Profit-maximizing employers will avoid hiring the victims of pre-market discrimination and market discipline will support their decisions. Markets, competition, and profit-seeking leave little room for prejudice, while custom and habit are persistent and pervasive. From this economist's point of view, pre-market discrimination is the major problem which must be eliminated. The attention of conscientious educational research should be focused in that direction.

REFERENCES

Aigner, Dennis J. and Glen Cain. 1977. "Statistical Theories of Discrimination in Labor Markets." *Industrial and Labor Relations Review* XXX:175–87.

Arrow, Kenneth J. 1972. "Models of Job Discrimination." In *Racial Discrimination in Economic Life*, ed. A. H. Pascal. Lexington, Ma.: D. C. Heath.

Arrow, Kenneth J. 1972. "Some Models of Race in the Labor Market." In *Racial Discrimination in Economic Life*, ed. A. H. Pascal. Lexington, Ma.: D. C. Heath.

Arrow, Kenneth J. 1974. "The Theory of Discrimination." In *Discrimination in Labor Markets*, ed. O. Ashenfelter and A. Rees. Princeton, N.J.: Princeton University Press.

Ashenfelter, Orley. 1973. "Discrimination and Trade Unions." In *Discrimination in Labor Markets*, ed. O. Ashenfelter and A. Rees, 88–112. Princeton, N.J.: Princeton University Press.

Ashenfelter, Orley. 1978. "Union Relative Wage Effects: New Evidence and a Survey of Their Implications for Wage Inflation." In *Econometric Contributions to Public Policy*, ed. Richard Stone and William Peterson. London: MacMillan Co.

Asher, Martin and Joel Popkin. 1984. "The Effect of Gender and Race Differentials on Public-Private Wage Comparisons: A Study of Postal Workers." *Industrial and Labor Relations Review* 38 (1).

Becker, Gary S. 1971. *The Economics of Discrimination*, Chicago: University of Chicago Press.

Blau, Francine B. and Carol L. Jusenius. 1976. "Economists' Approaches to Sex Segregation in the Labor Market: An Appraisal." In *Women and the Workplace*, ed. Martha Blaxall and Barbara Reagan, 181–99. Chicago: University of Chicago Press.

Ferber, Marianne A. and Michelle Teiman. 1980. "Are Women Economists at a Disadvantage in Publishing Journal Articles?" *Eastern Economic Journal* 6 (3–4): 189–93.

Freeman, Richard B. and James Medoff. 1984. *What Do Unions Do?*, New York: Basic Books.

Hale, Matthew. 1982. "History of Employment Testing." In *Ability Testing: Uses, Consequences, and Controversies, Part II*, ed. Alexandra K. Wigdor and Wendell R. Garner, 3–38. Washington, DC: National Academy Press.

Kerr, Clark. 1954. "Balkanization of the Labor Market." In *Labor Mobility and Economic Opportunity* , ed. E. Wight Bakke et al., 22–110. Cambridge: MIT Press.

Lang, Kevin. 1986. "A Language Theory of Discrimination." *Quarterly Journal of Economics* 2 (May): 363–81.

Marshall, Ray. 1974. "The Economics of Racial Discrimination: A Survey." *Journal of Economic Literature* 12(3): 849–71.

Niskanen, William. 1971. *Bureaucracy and Representative Government.* Hawthorne, NY: Academic Publishing.

Oaxaca, Ronald. 1973. "Male-Female Wage Differentials in Urban Labor Markets." *International Economic Review* 14 (3): 693–709.

Orazem, Peter F. 1987. "Black-White Differences in Schooling Investment and Human Capital Production in Segregated Schools." *American Economic Review* 77 (4): 714–23.

Perloff, Jeffrey M. and Michael L. Wachter. 1984. "Wage Comparability in the U.S. Postal Service." *Industrial and Labor Relations Review* 38 (1): 26–35.

Phelps, Edmund S. 1972. "The Statistical Theory of Racism and Sexism." *American Economic Review* LXII:659–61.

Piore, Michael J. 1970. "Jobs and Training." In *The State and the Poor,* eds. Samuel H. Beer and Richard E. Barringer, 53–63. Cambridge, Mass.: Winthrop Press,

Reimers, Cordelia W. 1983. "Labor Market Discrimination Against Hispanic and Black Men." *Review of Economics and Statistics* 65 (November): 570–79.

Smith, Sharon P. 1976. "Pay Differentials Between Federal Government and Private Sector Workers." *Industrial and Labor Relations Review* 29 (2): 179–97.

Smith, Sharon P. 1976. "Are Postal Workers Over- or Underpaid?" *Industrial Relations* 15 (2): 168–76.

Smith, Sharon P. 1976. "Government Wage Differentials by Sex." *Journal of Human Resources* 11 (2): 185–99.

Smith, Sharon P. 1977. "Government Wage Differentials." *Journal of Urban Economics* 4 (3): 248–71.

Spence, A. Michael. 1973. "Job Market Signaling." *Quarterly Journal of Economics* 87 (3): 355–74.

Spence, A. Michael. 1974. *Market Signaling,* Cambridge, Mass.: Harvard University Press.

Wigdor, Alexandra K. and Wendell R. Garner. 1982. In *Ability Testing: Uses, Consequences, and Controversies, Part I,* ed. Alexandra K. Wigdor and Wendell R. Garner. Washington, DC: National Academy Press.

Williamson O., Wachter and Harris. 1975. "Understanding the Employment Relation: The Analysis of Idiosyncratic Exchange." *Bell Journal of Economics* 6 (1): 250–78.

Ability Testing for Job Selection: Are the Economic Claims Justified?

Henry M. Levin

I. INTRODUCTION

As recently as 1973, the evidence on the ability of personnel tests to predict job performance was considered to be modest, at best (Ghiselli 1966, 1973). Thus, it is rather astounding to find that by the early 1980s published research was arguing that the use of general ability tests to select workers could increase U.S. productivity by almost $90 billion (Hunter and Schmidt 1982, 268). A report prepared for the U.S. Employment Service estimated that if tests were given optimal use, the federal government could save about $16 billion each year and employers who hire through the U.S. Employment Service could save almost $80 billion each year (Hunter 1983a).

These claims were quickly picked up by the U.S. Employment Service and by private employers as a basis for using general ability testing for employee placement in jobs. For example, the Job Service of the State of Missouri distributes a pamphlet to employers that states "Recent studies by the U.S. Department of Labor show that test-selected workers produce an average of about $5,500 more per year than those selected using typical hiring procedures" (Mueser and Maloney 1987, 32).

Before the mid-1970s, such claims would have been unthinkable, because validity coefficients obtained by correlating results of standardized aptitude tests with performance in the workplace varied widely across jobs. Thus, the generalization of test validity across different jobs and different work sites seemed not to be practicable. Frank L. Schmidt, John E. Hunter, and their associates, however, introduced evidence that the variability of validity coefficients may have been due to small sample size, criterion unreliability, and restriction of range in employee samples (Anastasi 1982, 143). Their sophisticated statistical reinterpretation of the results on test validity generalization made plausible the widespread use of general ability tests, those testing a core of cognitive skills, as predictors of performance on a wide array of job types.

In 1987 the public employment service systems of thirty-seven states were using ability tests based upon the validity generalization approach of Schmidt and Hunter (1977) to evaluate and refer job applicants to employers. This approach (described in detail in Section II) essentially allows employers to avoid the step of doing criterion-related validity studies of ability tests in every job category. Instead, results from a small number of such studies are generalized to all job categories that share features with the few closely studied categories.

In addition to the thirty-seven states already using the validity generalization approach to employment testing, three more states were planning to use the approach. Nationally, some ninety local public employment service offices have made validity generalization procedures an integral part of their operational procedures for assessing job applicants and referring them to employers' job openings.[1] In many cases the employment services were responding to the requests of private sector employers that this approach be used.

Clearly a major reason for the widespread revival and expansion of ability testing for employee selection is the claim that it has been "scientifically" shown to increase significantly the economic value of work output and productivity. Its leading advocates have asserted:

> In the past, the value of selection procedures had usually been estimated using statistics that did not directly convey economic value. These statistics included the validity coefficient, the increase in the percentage of "successful" workers, expectancy tables, and regression of job performance measures on test scores. In general, organizational decision makers were less able to evaluate these statistics than statements made in terms of dollars. (Schmidt, Hunter, Outerbridge, and Trattner 1986)

That is, Schmidt, Hunter, and their associates have suggested that a major policy breakthrough has been the purported capability of expressing the advantages of ability testing in terms of dollar benefits to employers and the economy. In this way, the value of test-based selection procedures can be made more persuasive to decision makers.

The purpose of this paper is to examine whether the evidence justifies these economic claims. Placement of a dollar value on gains in productivity associated with the use of ability tests for personnel selection requires (1) that general ability test performance of workers is superior to alternative selection procedures in predicting worker output; and (2) the additional work output associated with their use has been properly converted into monetary values. A systematic evaluation of the evidence suggests that neither tenet is supported.

The next section will provide background for the economic claims by briefly describing the use of ability testing for personnel selection and its extension to the validity generalization framework. Section III will discuss the basis for claims that link ability test scores of prospective workers to their productivity, and Section IV will examine the procedures that have been used

---

[1] For a discussion of the current status of ability testing by the U.S. Employment Service, see Wigdor and Hartigan (1988).

to connect alleged increases in worker productivity to economic measures of increased output. The final section of the paper will provide a summary.

II. ABILITY TESTING FOR PERSONNEL SELECTION

The use of tests for personnel selection has a relatively long history (Cronbach and Gleser 1965; Ghiselli 1966). The present claims of relatively high validity, however, are based upon a body of test research that began largely in the late 1970s. This research has attempted to ascertain the validity of general ability tests in predicting work output and the extension of findings to a wide range of jobs in the economy.[2] The research has also estimated the economic value of the gains in productivity associated with more and better use of general ability testing.

There are two major aspects of this body of work: validity generalization and the economic valuation of benefits. As stated in the *Standards for Educational and Psychological Testing*, issued jointly by the American Educational Research Association, the American Psychological Association, and the National Council on Measurement in Education, in general, validity generalization refers to "applying validity evidence obtained in one or more simultaneous estimation, meta-analysis, or synthetic validation arguments" (APA 1985, 94–95).

In the specific context of employee selection, validity generalization entails doing intensive validation on the relation between personnel tests and work performance in a few occupations and generalizing the outcomes to a large number of other occupations. This is accomplished by taking a small set of occupations and analyzing them according to their tasks and duties. Ability tests are given to a group of workers in these occupations to ascertain the relation between the tests and measures of work performance, so-called *criterion-related validity*.

However, criterion-related validity studies are difficult and costly to carry out for a wide variety of apparently disparate occupations. Since all or most occupations share various categories of work duties, it is claimed that the predictive ability of the tests can be extended to other occupations without doing "local" criterion-related validity studies. Rather, the results for the few jobs on which criterion-related studies have been done are *generalized* to other occupations by "reweighting" the scores according to the different distributions of duties in the other occupations, hence the name "validity generalization."

---

[2] A good elementary review of validation approaches for personnel selection in the present context is U.S. General Accounting Office (1979, Chap. 3). See also Cascio (1982, Chap. 7) and Cronbach and Gleser (1965).

In order to do this a different category of validity is used, *construct validity*. Construct validity is established through four steps: (1) analysis of occupations to ascertain which duties are performed; (2) analysis of duties to ascertain which abilities are needed for performing those duties; (3) selection of specific sub-tests which measure these abilities; (4) and development of a system of weighting the various sub-tests to match occupational requirements.

Based upon such construct and criterion validation procedures, a single test, the Professional and Administrative Career Examination (PACE), was used until recently by the U.S. Civil Service Commission to select workers for over one hundred occupations.[3] This test attempts to measure (1) *deduction* or the ability to reason from principles; (2) *induction* or the ability to examine specific facts to arrive at an understanding of their relations; (3) *judgment* or the solving of a problem under conditions of imperfect information; (4) *memory* or the ability to retain a large quantity of information; (5) *number* or the ability to manipulate numbers; and (6) *verbal comprehension* or the effective command of the English language (McKillip et al. 1977). Although PACE was used to select workers for 120 different federal jobs, its construct validation was based upon only twenty-seven occupations and its criterion validation was based upon studies of only three occupations.

Statistical support for validity generalization is found in reviews of research on the General Aptitude Test Battery (GATB) (Hunter 1983b) and meta-analyses of validation studies (Hunter, Schmidt, and Jackson 1982). Meta-analysis refers to a family of statistical methods for summarizing the results of many different studies of a specific phenomenon (Glass, McGaw, and Smith 1981; Hedges and Olkin 1985). Hunter (1983b) has claimed that meta-analysis of 515 research studies using the GATB over forty-five years has shown the generalized validity of that test battery for selecting employees for twelve thousand jobs.

Although the validity generalization approach has had great influence in shaping the personnel selection policies of the federal and state governments, the U.S. Employment Service, and some private employers, it has been far more controversial among researchers. For example, other meta-analyses have not found ability testing to show higher validity than alternative selection devices such as biographical data and peer/supervisor ratings (Schmitt et al. 1984; Reilly and Chao 1982). Mueser and Maloney (1987) demonstrate convincingly that the concurrent validity studies that are used as a basis for validity generalization understate seriously the validity coefficients for education relative to ability tests. Linn and Dunbar (1986) have raised

---

[3] PACE is no longer used for personnel selection by the U.S. Civil Service Commission under the terms of a consent decree. The consent decree settled a lawsuit brought against the U.S. Civil Service Commission by minorities who charged that the use of PACE resulted in employment discrimination.

issues regarding predictive biases from validity generalization. Many other questions have also been raised, as acknowledged by Schmidt et al. (1985), and commented on by Sackett et al. (1985), who express particular concern for the penchant of validity generalization advocates Schmidt and Hunter to exaggerate the magnitude, certitude, and policy consequences of modest findings.

In what follows, I will not address the validity generalization issue directly. I will address, however, the three criterion-related validity studies that the federal government used as a basis for the validity generalization approach to the use of PACE. Much of the criterion-based evidence for validity generalization and for the economic claims associated with the use of ability testing for worker selection is attributable to these three studies (Schmidt et al. 1986). Accordingly, if the three studies are not supported by the claims, extensions of the studies' results to other occupations are also suspect.

III. VALIDITY CLAIMS AND PRODUCTIVE WORKERS

Using general ability test scores for personnel selection appeals to employers because they assume that such a simple device will lead to selection of more productive workers than alternative selection devices, and that the benefits of additional worker output will exceed the additional cost of testing. Since the marginal costs of testing job candidates is low, this element is typically discounted. Thus the appeal rests primarily upon the assumption that general ability testing will provide workers who are more productive than those selected by alternative devices. In this section, I will examine the way in which worker productivity has been measured for assessing the validity of general ability testing.

Economists have devoted considerable thought and empirical work to conceptualizing and measuring worker productivity. In general, it is agreed that worker productivity is not easy to measure (Kendrick 1984). Much work is done in teams where the output is a result of an interactive process in which it is difficult or impossible to separate the contributions of individual workers (Alchian and Demsetz 1972). The result is that studies of labor productivity usually use a production function approach in which the output of firms is explained statistically by inputs of different kinds of workers, capital, and other productive resources (Kendrick and Vaccara 1980). The contribution of each input (including different groups of workers) to output is considered to be a measure of the productivity of that input.[4]

The productivity of a worker will depend upon the capital investment of a firm in plant and equipment and the technology or vintage of that investment, the organization of the firm, and the number and characteristics of

---

[4] See Tsang (1987) for an example of an empirical study.

its workers. In explaining differences in worker productivity in a given job in a given firm (that is, with other things held constant), two factors are pertinent: worker capacity and worker effort.

Worker capacity refers to the capability of the worker to be productive with respect to the job requirements. A huge literature explores the various dimensions of worker skills considered to be important for worker performance (Dunnette 1983; Fleishman and Quaintance 1984; McCormick 1979; U.S. Employment Service 1965, App. A and B). These include cognitive dimensions such as verbal, mathematical, and thinking ability, categories that are reflected in general ability tests. They also include physical attributes such as perceptual and psychomotor skills, strength, and coordination, characteristics that are at least partially measured by the General Aptitude Test Battery (GATB). Finally, they include social/affective dimensions such as interpersonal skills and dimensions related to temperament. The social/affective skills are particularly relevant to the four-fifths of the labor force who work in service occupations. Yet, of the more than fifty specific cognitive, physical, and social dimensions of abilities reviewed in the industrial psychology literature, only a small portion are covered by the GATB, and none of these are in the social domain.

Even when workers have the capacity to provide a high level of work performance, their actual performance will depend upon the exertion of energy or work effort in applying these skills to the objectives of the workplace. The effort of a worker is thought to be related to his or her personality as well as the supervision, organization, and incentives present in the workplace (Stiglitz 1975; Pencavel 1977). In most workplaces it is not uncommon to find diligent workers with modest skills who appear to be more productive than others with superior skills. These differences may be systematically related to the match or mismatch between job requirements and worker characteristics, where those workers who are most closely matched provide greater effort than those who are not (Tsang and Levin 1985).

The literature on worker productivity suggests that to be productive workers need both skills or human capital (Becker 1964) and a conscientious application of those skills. In addition to the many dimensions of general ability that may be pertinent to a job, there are likely to be specific cognitive abilities, physical attributes, and socio-affective characteristics that are necessary for particular types of work. Finally, the mere existence of these capacities does not produce work output. Somehow, these skills must be transformed into work output through the application of worker effort—a matter of particular concern to work organizations (Vroom 1964).

Given this brief background on the relation between worker characteristics and worker productivity, I will proceed to review the literature that ties general ability testing to worker performance. I will focus on a recent article by Schmidt, Hunter, Outerbridge, and Trattner (1986), which relies on cumulative findings and summarizes the latest thinking on ability testing for job selection:

> This study examines . . . productivity gains for most white-collar jobs in the federal government. In the present study, these job performance differences were determined empirically, based on direct multi-method measurement of the job performance of employees who had been selected years earlier, either (a) using cognitive ability tests or (b) using other methods (mostly evaluations of education and experience). . . . Results from three different studies show that the job performance of test-selected employees averages approximately one-half a standard deviation higher than that of non-test-selected employees. Results also indicate that use of measures of cognitive skills in place of less valid selection methods for selection of a one-year cohort in the federal government would lead to increases in output worth almost $600 million per year for every year the new hires remain on the job.(Schmidt et al. 1986, 25–26)

It is important to review the specific way in which employee job performance is measured in light of the discussion set out above. The authors premise their findings on three studies that were done for the U.S. Civil Service Commission in 1977. Although Schmidt et al. (1986) refer to these studies as measuring "job performance of employees" (p. 25) or even "increases in output" (p. 1), none of the studies measured actual job performance or productivity. Rather, the studies validated the selection tests on various indicators that are *presumed* to be related to productivity.

Each of the three studies used Test 500 of the federal government's Professional and Administrative Career Examination (PACE) to predict "job performance." The three occupations that were covered by the studies included: Internal Revenue Service (IRS) revenue officers (O'Leary and Trattner 1977), customs inspectors (Corts, Muldrow, and Outerbridge 1977), and social insurance claims examiners (Trattner et al. 1977). Let us examine briefly how "job performance" was measured for each occupation.

Indicators Linked to Job Performance and Productivity

For the 305 IRS revenue officers in the sample, job performance was measured using a job information test, a work sample, and supervisory ratings. The fifty-nine job information items were constructed in a multiple-choice format that addressed the twelve major job duties. The work sample asked the respondents to determine what actions should be taken to collect delinquent taxes in five separate cases. Respondents were given the case files and asked to select the appropriate actions. The supervisory ratings were based upon behavioral scales for each of the twelve major job duties.

For the sample of 190 customs inspectors, the criteria included a job information test, a work sample, and supervisory ratings and rankings. The job information test was composed of fifty multiple-choice questions based upon the major job duties. The work sample was not actually a sample of the work of the respondents, but an evaluation by the respondents of a videotaped work sample of another customs inspector. Respondents were given a booklet in which they were asked to record errors in procedures and ways that performance could be improved. The supervisory ratings were based upon the use of a ten-point graphic scale to rate thirty-three dimensions of performance over twelve major duties. Supervisory rankings were also based upon rank ordering of the respondents' proficiencies according to each of the duty statements.

TABLE 1

Validity Coefficients of Test 500 Total Scores for Three Occupations with Three Indicators of Job Performance[a]

	Job Information Test	Work Sample	Supervisory Rating
Customs Inspector[b]	.56	.52	not significant
Internal Revenue Officer[c]	.55	.51	.25
Soc. Ins. Claims Examiner[d]	.59	.39	.28

[a] All validity coefficients are based on the method of obtaining multiple correlation with optimally weighted raw subscores. The patterns are similar when other methods are used. The coefficients are also corrected for bias according to the Burket (1964) procedure.

[b] Corts et al. (1977, 49).

[c] O'Leary and Trattner (1977, 22).

[d] Trattner et al. (1977, 29).

For the sample of 252 social insurance claims examiners, the criteria included a job information test, a work sample, and supervisory ratings. The job information test comprised forty-two multiple-choice questions. The work sample was a standardized claim that had to be adjudicated by the respondent. First-line supervisors were asked to rate respondents according to their performance on eight job duties as well as to rank-order the respondents.

Table 1 shows the validity coefficients for the indicators of job performance for each of the three occupations.[5]

Job Information Test. Coefficients for the job information test range from about .56 to .59. In interpreting these relatively high coefficients, however, we must keep in mind that (1) a test of job information is not a direct assessment of job performance, but only a measure of job knowledge; and (2) that the specific method of measuring job information is a multiple-choice test with a format similar to the predictor, Test 500.

The first stipulation means that we must not equate a multiple-choice test of job information with an actual assessment of job performance, regardless of the casual interchangeability among those terms in Schmidt et al. (1986). A test of job information is not a direct measure of job performance, but only one of many potential indicators or determinants of job performance. It tells us nothing about worker effort or the many interpersonal skills that are important in production and organizational life.

The second stipulation means that the validity coefficient is likely to be overstated to the extent that it reflects overlapping method variance, that is, the degree to which respondents who do well on multiple-choice tests will have higher scores on both Test 500 and the job information test, exclusive of their true ability and knowledge levels. Persons with good test-taking skills on multiple-choice items will tend to do better on both types of tests than equally able persons with poorer test-taking skills.

The advocates of validity generalization do not attempt to correct validity coefficients for methods variance. Rather they argue that the existence of such a problem is negated because the general ability tests correlate equally highly with job sample measures:

> Job sample measures are not written tests and would not be expected to share methods variance with ability tests. The fact that ability tests correlate about equally with job sample measures and with training performance measures indicates that what is important are the ability, knowledge, and skills measured, not the methods used to measure them. (Schmidt et al. 1985, 733)

And, as table 1 shows, this assertion appears to be supported by the relatively high and comparable validity coefficients for the work samples. However, a closer inspection of the work samples shows that far from being

---

[5] The validity coefficient is generally defined as the correlation of test score with the outcome or criterion score. For classic discussions of validity coefficients and employee selection, see Brogden (1949) and Cronbach and Gleser (1965). For the derivation of multiple correlations with optimally weighted raw subscores, see the details in the three studies cited in table 1.

samples of job performance in an actual workplace, they are at best simulations of work tests that depend heavily on test-taking skills.

Work Samples. As the name implies, *work samples* are representative samples of work activity used as a basis for validity. But in the case of customs inspectors, no work sample was administered to the respondents on whom the ability tests were being evaluated. Rather, they were asked to view a videotaped sample of the work of some other customs inspector (selected especially for the videotaping) to identify errors in procedures and to indicate ways in which procedures could be improved. A special booklet was provided to write down answers in a test format. This criterion is certainly not an evaluation of a work sample of the customs inspectors who were the basis of the validity study, even though it is referred to as a work sample. Rather, it appears to be relevant only as a different form of a job information test. For the internal revenue officers and the social insurance claims examiners, the work samples were "simulated" rather than actual samples of work evaluated in real work settings. The internal revenue officers were given five taxpayer delinquent accounts for which they had to make collection decisions based upon the information contained therein. Their goal was to determine the course of action to take to resolve the case in the best interests of the government. The work sample for the social insurance claims examiners was a single case that had to be adjudicated on the basis of the information submitted in support of the claim. Each was scored on the appropriateness of the actions taken.

But, even in these cases, the simulated samples were reduced to paper-and-pencil tests that were abstracted from the real work setting. For example, in setting out the work duties of the internal revenue officer, the duty on which the officer spends the largest amount of time was ignored in both the job information and work sample tests. "This duty, Locating and Contacting Taxpayers, mainly involves social contact with taxpayers and did not lend itself to measurement in either of these two criteria. Performance on this duty was, however, measured on the supervisory rating form" (O'Leary and Trattner 1977, 12).

An inquiry to the Internal Revenue Service indicated that an evaluation of worker performance in delinquent tax cases cannot be made without seeing how the officer uses information and discussions in these contacts to resolve issues. For example, first, there is the problem of finding the taxpayer. Some officers are better at this than others. Second, there is the issue of negotiating a settlement that maximizes the government's interest, taking into account feasibility of the agreement from the taxpayer's perspective and avoiding expensive collection procedures and legal action on the part of the government. Third, there is the search for leverage on the situation, such as obtaining information about the employer in order to pose the threat of wage garnishment or locating other financial interests and assets of the taxpayer that could be attached to pay the debt. All of these acts require detective work, intuition, and important social skills in determining how to proceed, and none can be carried out without contacting the delinquent taxpayer and other persons with whom he is linked.

In the case of the simulated work sample for the social insurance claims examiner, there are also serious flaws relative to the real work setting. Only a single case was used as a basis for evaluation. No provision was made for investigation or communication with others to obtain more information, even though many claims are incomplete and require more documentation or assistance from specialists. No study was made of actual productivity in terms of the number of cases examiners handled within a given work period.

In summary, one of the work samples was not a sample of work of the subjects who were being evaluated, and the other two work samples were far removed from the real work setting and reflected only limited dimensions of the jobs. These evaluations could be better described as assessments of simulated task performances using a pencil-and-paper format under testing conditions rather than evaluations of actual work performance. They were limited to exercises that did not allow for the wider range of behavior that is necessary to performing competently in the workplace, and they were carried out within testing time constraints. The result is that they too are likely to share methods variance in the calculation of validities.

Supervisory ratings are the one criterion likely to take all of the characteristics of the job into account. First-line supervisors are able to assess actual productivity of workers or at least to observe the proficiencies of workers in performing work tasks as well as productive work effort. Both the job information tests and the simulated work samples tend to focus on much narrower dimensions of the job and ignore such matters as effort or cooperation and communication with colleagues, behaviors that are important to organizational productivity. Indeed, in the case of the internal revenue examiners, it was claimed that the most time-consuming aspect of the job could only be validated by the supervisory ratings.

Supervisory Ratings. Supervisory ratings for the three occupations are shown in the third column of table 1. The most noticeable pattern is that the validity coefficients for the supervisory ratings are considerably lower than those for the testing situations reflected in the job information tests and work samples. In the case of the customs inspectors, there is no statistically significant relation between supervisory ratings and Test 500 scores. In the other cases, the validity coefficients are in the range reported for many selection criteria and are hardly impressive. Indeed, they are less than half of those calculated from the job information test.

In terms of specific validity coefficients, those for customs inspectors and for internal revenue officers are worthy of further comment. The researchers explained the insignificant validity coefficient for the customs inspectors by asserting that the job environment and nature of supervisory duties do not permit adequate direct observation of inspectors performing individual duties (Corts, Muldrow, and Outerbridge 1977, 43).

> It is also recognized that the ratings and rankings obtained may be based upon general impressions of the inspectors' work, and therefore could contain a large component of cooperativeness, speediness, "knowing the ropes," acceptability within the group, maturity, and other similar characteristics. . . . The conclusion is that these data contain components of error and other variance with which Test 500 could not be expected to correlate. (Corts, Muldrow, and Outerbridge 1977, 43)

There are two important features of this explanation. The first is that the explanation is *ex post facto*. That is, after ascertaining that the validity coefficient was insignificant, there is a concerted effort to show that the supervisory ratings are not appropriate measures of validity for this occupation. It is instructive to note that this concern did not emerge in the very extensive design phase of the study with its close attention to detailed analysis of the occupation and its supervision.

The second aspect is the emphasis on individual performance as the exclusive focus of productivity differences. Productivity analyses in economics (Spence 1974; Williamson 1975) and industrial organization (Pasmore and Sherwood 1978) have emphasized an organizational approach in which activities among workers are considered to be interdependent. As such, they require analysis of productivity by work group rather than limiting assessments to individual performance for narrowly specified duties. That is, interpersonal skills, communication with clients and co-workers, and group problem-solving skills are often as important as the work skills for individual work performance. Although supervisors can evaluate this entire range of skills and work performance, the authors of the customs inspectors study view such components of work performance as "error" rather than as central to an understanding of work output and productivity.

Given that supervisors can observe work performance directly both in its individual dimensions and in those that affect organizational productivity, supervisory ratings are likely to be more valid than measures derived from paper-and-pencil tests in nonwork settings. This conclusion is reinforced by the fact that for internal revenue officers the most important duty in terms of time allocation is "social contact with taxpayers," which could only be evaluated by supervisors.

On the basis of this information, it is reasonable to hypothesize that the supervisory ratings are more nearly valid indicators of work performance than the test data for job knowledge and work samples. The coefficients for supervisory ratings are well within the boundaries of validity coefficients associated with a wide variety of selection devices (Reilly and Chao 1982; Schmitt et al. 1984).

Although the validity coefficients for the two other validity criteria have higher coefficients, they are only indirect indicators of work performance. If we assume a relatively high correlation of .50 between these indicators and actual work performance, there would still be an overall validity coefficient of less than .30 between Test 500 and the true score for work performance. Using either this coefficient or those associated with supervisory ratings, less than 10 percent of the variance in work output is explained by Test 500. This result is about the same as for other selection criteria, and it is hardly a basis for arguing that general ability tests are a *powerful* predictor of worker productivity.

IV. ECONOMIC VALUE OF ESTIMATED GAINS
IN WORKER PERFORMANCE

Schmidt et al. (1986) stress the usefulness of converting the value of selection methods into dollar terms. Such terms suggest to decision makers the concrete and calculable economic gains to be made from using various methods of worker selection. Schmidt et al. argue that on the basis of the validity coefficients set out in table 1, they can estimate the economic gains from using general ability tests to select white-collar workers in the government. This requires the conversion of the putative gains in worker performance into dollar values. Specifically, they find that on the basis of these validity coefficients, the use of Test 500 for selecting a one-year cohort of such workers would increase government output by up to $600 million a year or increase output by almost 10 percent.

Although economists have had considerable experience in estimating the value of worker productivity (Chinloy 1981; Denison 1985; Kendrick 1984), Schmidt et al. do not refer to any economic literature. Moreover, they reject a cost-accounting approach without reference to that literature. Rather, they rely on Cronbach's disparaging comments (Cronbach and Gleser 1965) about Roche's doctoral dissertation in psychology done in 1961 at Southern Illinois University that used a cost-accounting approach (Hunter and Schmidt 1982, 248). Cronbach stated that:

> This study relies heavily on the discipline—or art—of accounting, and Roche, a psychologist, was necessarily dependent on the advice of the accountants. It is not entirely certain that the accountants perceived the program clearly, and it may well be that in future studies a more thoroughly interdisciplinary attack will produce better solutions to the accounting problems. (Cronbach and Gleser 1965, 266)

Nevertheless, a summary of Roche's psychology dissertation (not even the original document) from almost three decades ago is used as the basis for rejecting a cost-accounting approach.

Schmidt et al. then use their own approach to estimate the economic value of the putative increases in worker productivity by asking supervisors to estimate the dollar value to the organization of the products and services produced by the average employee, by one at the 85th percentile, and by one at the 15th percentile (Hunter and Schmidt 1982, 248–51). Since the 15th and 85th percentiles are one standard deviation above and below the mean respectively, they estimate the standard deviation of worker performance in terms of dollars. Estimated increases in worker performance from using general ability tests for selection are converted into standard deviation units and translated into dollar values. Such values are set out into ratios of the standard deviation of productivity in dollars relative to the arithmetic mean of productivity in dollars.

Schmidt and Hunter (1983) argue that the standard deviation of worker output ranges between 20 percent and 40 percent of the mean output of workers. These assumptions are used to estimate gains in national productivity from worker selection based upon general ability testing (Hunter and Schmidt 1982) as well as to estimate such gains for all white-collar workers in government (Schmidt et al. 1986) and for specific occupations such as computer programmers (Schmidt et al. 1979).

This procedure is fundamentally flawed for at least two reasons. First, the method for obtaining the economic value of additional productivity is highly dubious. Basically, the procedure entails a survey of supervisors that asks their *opinions* about the value of output of workers on different parts of the productivity distribution. There are internal contradictions in this procedure that emanate from the very studies on which Hunter and Schmidt build their argument.

When supervisors are asked to rate worker performance, something directly observable by them and within their domain of experience, the validity coefficients tend to be low or even insignificant, as in the case of customs inspectors (see table 1). The authors of the validity generalization literature explain these weak results by stating that supervisory ratings of workers are highly prone to error, even though they reflect a central duty to which supervisors are regularly assigned (Corts, Muldrow, and Outerbridge 1977). But, if supervisors do such a poor job of performing a function at which they are presumably skilled and knowledgeable and which is directly observable, how can we assume that they can estimate the economic value of a standard deviation of worker performance—something for which they lack experience, information, and a basis for calculation? If cost-accounting approaches as interpreted by a doctoral student in psychology are considered to be problematic, opinion sampling approaches without cost-accounting information are likely to be even more unreliable.

Second, even if the economic values were appropriate, the straightforward application of the validity coefficients in table 1 will vastly overstate differences in productivity due to differences in worker selection criteria. This procedure equates a z-score, or a standard deviation increase in the indicators of work performance as measured by tests of job knowledge, "simulated" work samples, and supervisory ratings, with a similar increase in worker productivity. As I argued in the previous section, the validity of general ability tests to predict actual worker productivity is likely to be less than .30, explaining less than 10 percent of the variance.

Schmidt et al. (1986) use the much higher validity coefficients generated by the *indicators* of worker performance, not the actual worker performance. This means that any estimated improvement in worker performance on the validity criteria associated with general ability tests will represent a much smaller increase in *actual* worker productivity or work output. Such unmeasured dimensions as worker effort, interpersonal abilities, and a variety of other determinants of worker performance not reflected in the criteria validation studies will explain the rest of the variance in worker performance.

In light of this, it is striking that the technique of placing dollar values on standard deviations of worker performance attributes *all* of the difference in worker performance to differences in estimated productivity created by ability selection. This is far from the true case, since the validity criteria are never based upon actual work performance but only upon potential indicators of that performance. That is, a one standard deviation improvement in the indicators of worker performance as measured in the validity studies is likely to yield a much smaller increase in actual worker productivity than one standard deviation. The result is a substantial overstatement of the dollar value of probable productivity gains attributable to ability testing.

V. SUMMARY

The work of the validity generalization theorists is rich in heuristic value, and its attempt to extend the value of test-based employee selection to a large set of occupations and decision criteria is of both theoretical and applied interest. This should not, however, detract from the fact that it is a literature of vast overstatement that often appears to be drafted more for its persuasive power than for its scientific validity.

The utility of any selection procedure depends upon (1) its ability to predict worker performance better than alternatives; (2) the selection ratio of employee openings to applicants; and (3) the economic value of the better employee selection relative to the costs of the selection. On the first of these, the evidence is not convincing that general ability tests are superior to other selection devices in predicting the various indicators of worker performance. Mueser and Maloney (1987) have shown that validities of general ability tests will be systematically overstated relative to education in concurrent validity studies where the subjects of the study have already been selected on education (Mueser and Maloney 1987). Meta-analyses of selection devices by other researchers find that biographical data and peer/supervisor evaluations show equal or even higher validities than general ability tests (Schmitt et al. 1984; Reilly and Chao 1982).

Second, the advocates of validity generalization assume that selection ratios are low, where the selection ratio is defined as the number of persons accepted for employment relative to the number of applicants. This means that it is possible to choose from among a large number of job candidates. The larger the choice, the greater the potential benefits of the most preferred selection criterion. In contrast, if the applicant pool does not exceed the number of persons hired, no selection is possible and no selection benefits are forthcoming. The research of validity generalization advocates suggests that professional and technical jobs represent the occupations for which general ability testing is likely to yield the largest selection benefits (Hunter 1983b). However, these are the occupations in which there is rarely a surplus of candidates relative to positions. In fact, there are often shortages of candidates. By assuming low selection ratios, validity generalization advocates overstate substantially the benefits of any improvement in selection.

For example, in a study of computer programmers, Schmidt et al. (1979) assume a selection ratio of .20 (only 20 percent of the applicants will be hired). Using this assumption, they calculate the benefits of using a programmer aptitude test over previous selection procedures. They conclude that the test would produce a benefit to the employer of almost $65,000 for each programmer hired, or a total gain in productivity for the American economy of $11 billion. Such a claim is not grounded in reality. As Cronbach (1984) summarizes:

> This projection is a fairy tale. The economy utilizes most of the persons who are trained as programmers, and only the most prestigious firm can reject 80 percent of those who apply. If 90 percent of the programmers are hired somewhere, the tests merely give a competitive advantage to those firms that test (when other firms do not test).

Third, there are other sources of overstatement of the economic consequences of general ability testing. For example, the literature makes claims about how the use of general ability tests can increase worker productivity, worker output, and the output of industries and the economy, but the measures of worker performance are either highly incomplete or artificial measures of workplace behavior. Further, the setting of economic values on putative gains in worker performance is vastly overstated by the rather simplistic estimation technique that is used. Finally, in some attempts to extend findings from a few occupations to entire industries, there is a tendency to ignore the compositional fallacy in which gains in worker abilities for some employers will mean losses to other employers (Schmidt et al. 1986). Even when this is recognized (Hunter and Schmidt 1982), it is not clear how a highly decentralized economy in which employment decisions are made at micro-levels would result in an optimal redistribution of talent along the lines that are recommended (Rothschild 1979).

The effects of these biases and overstatements are likely to be substantial. Rothschild (1979) has tried to analyze some of them in a formal model of the worker selection and production process and suggests that they are multiplicative rather than additive. He concludes that:

> Hunter and Schmidt's estimates should be scaled down by a factor of 8. Thus, the range of possible improvements in productivity due to a more systematic use of ability tests is .40% to 1.75% instead of 3.2% to 14%. Similar gains in productivity would be observed if everyone worked from 9.6 to 42 minutes longer in a forty-hour week. (Rothschild 1979, 25)

Even this assessment does not exhaustively account for the full range of sources of overstatement. In short, the economic claims in support of the use of general ability tests are vastly exaggerated, and the research and findings are not adequate to support such claims.

Future Research

Although there are many problems with the approach taken by the validity generalization advocates, a substantial number of them seem to be attributable to an inadequate understanding of labor markets and the measurement of worker productivity. These are domains in which economists have worked for over a century. It would seem that a major endeavor to improve the estimates of the effects of different worker selection criteria on productivity must be a multidisciplinary effort—one in which economists and industrial psychologists work together. Such a collaboration should also take account of the incentives to employers and potential employees of selection criteria (Mueser and Maloney 1987) as well as the relative costs and benefits of different selection approaches. The fact that so much of the validity generalization literature on the economic gains from general ability testing has made virtually *no* reference to the pertinent economic literature is a very telling sign.

This concern is especially sharpened by the potential to measure worker productivity directly for the three occupations that were discussed in this paper and that have represented the base of so much of the validity generalization work. The productivity of internal revenue officers could be measured by randomly assigning delinquent taxpayer cases to a sample of such officers over a two- or three-year period. Productivity would be measured by the yields in additional payments that they were able to obtain for the U.S.

government, taking account of any differential costs imposed on the government (for example, through collection procedures or litigation).

Customs inspectors could be evaluated by initiating a secondary search of randomly selected persons who had been initially screened by the customs inspectors in the study. Estimates could be made of their productivity by valuing their services in terms of the average number of persons they serve in a given period and the accuracy of their assessments. Such assessments could be converted into monetary terms by evaluating the recovery of customs duties and the avoidance of social costs associated with illegal contraband, such as drugs or banned agricultural products, as well as savings. Benefits would also include the resource savings when additional persons are served by an inspector in a given period. A similar approach could be used to evaluate the performance of social insurance examiners by randomly assigning cases and assessing the number of cases that are processed as well as the costs of errors to the agency and to taxpayers (for example, the cost of appeals and reevaluations of cases).

These measures of output would take account of the ability of workers to use their interpersonal skills and to obtain information from others in a collaborative setting. In addition, they would permit a better benefit-cost analysis of alternatives than the validity generalization method allows by taking account both of the costs of selection and workplace costs associated with productivity for each worker. For example, internal revenue officers who are able to obtain collections from delinquent taxpayers with minimal dependence on the courts, collection agencies, and other personnel in the bureaucracy impose a lower cost on their employer than ones who obtain settlements that rely heavily on these other resources. Differences in institutional costs associated with performance will not be picked up in job information tests or the synthetic work samples that depend on individual behavior under test conditions and that do not consider differences in organizational consequences among workers.

In the long term, it is best to view the choice of employee selection methods in the context of benefit-cost decisions (Levin 1983, 1987; Mishan 1976). An attempt should be made to consider all of the benefits and costs of the alternatives. Benefits and costs for the employer should be calculated for the organization as a whole rather than for individual workers in the absence of organizational consequences. In addition, estimates of impacts on the economy as a whole must be far more sophisticated than ones that assume that a result obtained for a few workers or firms can be generalized to the entire economy without taking account of compositional fallacies and interdependence among decentralized decisions.

REFERENCES

Alchian, A., and H. Demsetz. 1972, December. Production, information costs, and economic organization. *American Economic Review* 62:777–95.

American Educational Research Association, American Psychological Association, and National Council on Measurement in Education. 1985. *Standards for educational and psychological testing*. Washington, DC: American Psychological Association. (Known as APA *Standards.*)

Anastasi, A. 1982. *Psychological testing*. 5th ed. New York: MacMillan Co.

Becker, G. S. 1964. *Human capital*. New York: Columbia Univ. Press.

Brogden, H. E. 1949. A new coefficient: Application to biserial correlation and to estimation of selective efficiency. *Psychometrika* 14:169–82.

Burket, G. R. 1964. A study of reduced rank models for multiple prediction. *Psychometric Monographs* 12:1–66.

Cascio, W. F. 1982. *Costing human resources: The financial impact of behavior in organizations*. Boston: Kent Publishing Co.

Chinloy, P. 1981. *Labor productivity*. Cambridge, MA: Abt Books.

Corts, D. B., T. W. Muldrow, and A. M. Outerbridge. 1977, December. *Research base for the written test portion of the Professional and Administrative Career Examination (PACE): Prediction of job performance for customs inspectors*, PS-77-4. Washington, DC: U.S. Civil Service Commission, Personnel Research and Development Center.

Cronbach, L. J. 1984. *Essentials of psychological testing*. 4th ed. New York: Harper and Row.

Cronbach, L. J., and G. C. Gleser. 1965. *Psychological tests and personnel decisions*. Chicago: Illinois Books.

Denison, E. F. 1985. *Trends in American economic growth, 1929–1982*. Washington, DC: Brookings Institution.

Dunnette, M. D. 1983. Aptitudes, abilities, and skills. In *Handbook of industrial and organizational psychology*, ed. M. D. Dunnette, 473–520. New York: John Wiley and Sons.

Fleishman, E., and M. Quaintance. 1984. *Taxonomies of human performance*. New York: Academic Press.

Ghiselli, E. 1966. *The validity of occupational aptitude tests*. New York: John Wiley and Sons.

Ghiselli, E. 1973. The validity of aptitude tests in personnel selection. *Personnel Psychology* 26:461–77.

Glass, G. V., B. McGaw, and M. L. Smith. 1981. *Meta-analysis in social research*. Beverly Hills, CA: Sage Publications.

Hedges, L. V., and I. Olkin. 1985. *Statistical methods for meta-analysis*. Orlando, FL: Academic Press.

Hunter, J. E. 1983a. *The economic benefits of personnel selection using ability tests: A state of the art review including a detailed analysis of the dollar benefit of U.S. employment service placements and a critique of the low-cutoff method of test use.* USES Test Research Report no. 47. Washington, DC: Employment and Training Administration, U.S. Department of Labor.

Hunter, J. E. 1983b. *Test validation for 12,000 jobs: An application of job classification and validity generalization analysis to the General Aptitude Test Battery.* USES Test Research Report no. 45. Washington, DC: Employment and Training Administration, U.S. Department of Labor.

Hunter, J. E., and F. L. Schmidt. 1982. In *Human performance and productivity,* 233–84. Vol. 1 of *Human capability assessment,* ed. E. A. Fleishman and M. D. Dunnette, Hillsdale, NJ: Erlbaum.

Hunter, J. E., and F. L. Schmidt. 1983, April. Quantifying the effects of psychological interventions on employee job performance and workforce productivity. *American Psychologist* 38: 473–78.

Hunter, J. E., F. L. Schmidt, and G. Jackson. 1982. *Meta-analysis: Cumulating research findings across studies.* Beverly Hills, CA: Sage Publications.

Kendrick, J. W. 1984. *Improving company productivity.* Baltimore: Johns Hopkins Press.

Kendrick, J. W., and B. N. Vaccara, eds. 1980. *New developments in productivity measurement and analysis.* Studies in Income and Wealth, vol. 44. Chicago: University of Chicago Press.

Levin, H. M. 1983. *Cost-effectiveness: A primer.* Beverly Hills, CA: Sage Publications.

Levin, H. M. 1987, Summer. Cost-benefit and cost-effectiveness analyses. In *Evaluation practice in review—New directions for program evaluation,* no. 34, ed. D. S. Cordray, H. S. Bloom, and R. J. Light, 83–99. San Francisco: Jossey-Bass.

Linn, R. L., and S. B. Dunbar. 1986. Validity generalization and predictive bias. In *Performance assessment: Methods and application,* ed. R. A. Berk. Baltimore: Johns Hopkins Press.

McCormick, E. 1979. *Job analysis: Methods and applications.* New York: AMACOM.

McKillup, R. H., M. H. Trattner, D. B. Corts, and H. Wing. 1977, April. *The Professional and Administrative Career Examination: Research and development,* PRR-77-1. Washington, DC: U.S. Civil Service Commission, Personnel Research and Development Center.

Mishan, E. J. 1976. *Cost-benefit analysis.* New York: Praeger Publishers.

Mueser, P., and T. Maloney. 1987, June. Cognitive ability, human capital and employer screening: Reconciling labor market behavior with studies of employee productivity. Unpublished paper available from Peter Mueser, Department of Economics, University of Missouri, Columbia.

O'Leary, B. S. 1977, August. *Research base for the written test portion of the Professional and Administrative Career Examination (PACE): Prediction of training success for social insurance claims examiner*, TS 77-5. Washington, DC: U.S. Civil Service Commission, Personnel Research and Development Center.

O'Leary, B., and M. H. Trattner. 1977, August. *Research base for the written test portion of the Professional and Administrative Career Examination (PACE): Prediction of job performance for internal revenue officers*, TS 77-6. Washington, DC: U.S. Civil Service Commission, Personnel Research and Development Center.

Pasmore, W. A., and J. J. Sherwood. 1978. *Sociotechnical systems: A sourcebook*. San Diego, CA: University Associates.

Pencavel, J. H. 1977. Work effort, on-the-job screening, and alternative methods of remuneration. In *Research in labor economics*, Vol. 1, ed. R. G. Ehrenberg, 225–59. Greenwich, CT: JAI Press.

Reilly, R. R., and G. T. Chao. 1982. Validity and fairness of some alternative employment selection procedures. *Personnel Psychology* 35:1–62.

Rothschild, M. 1979, June. Social effects of ability testing. Unpublished paper available from author at Department of Economics, University of California, La Jolla.

Sackett, P. R., N. Schmitt, M. L. Tenopyr, J. Kehoe, and S. Zedeck. 1985. Commentary on forty questions about validity generalization and meta-analysis. *Personnel Psychology* 38:697–798.

Schmidt, F. L., and J. E. Hunter. 1977. Development of a general solution to the problem of validity generalization. *Journal of Applied Psychology* 62:529–40.

Schmidt, F. L., J. E. Hunter, R. C. McKenzie, and T. W. Muldrow. 1979. Impact of valid selection procedures on work-force productivity. *Journal of Applied Psychology* 64:609–26.

Schmidt, F. L., J. E. Hunter, A. N. Outerbridge, and M. H. Trattner. 1986. The economic impact of job selection methods on size, productivity, and payroll costs of the federal work force: An empirically based demonstration. *Personnel Psychology* 39:1–29.

Schmidt, F. L., J. E. Hunter, K. Pearlman, and H. R. Hirsh. 1985. Forty questions about validity generalization and meta-analysis. *Personnel Psychology* 38: 697–798.

Schmitt, N., R. Z. Gooding, R. A. Noe, and M. Kirsch. 1984. Meta-analyses of validity studies, published between 1964 and 1982 and the investigation of study characteristics. *Personnel Psychology* 37:407–22.

Spence, A. M. 1974. *Market signaling: Informational transfer in hiring and related screening processes*. Cambridge: Harvard Univ. Press.

Stiglitz, J. 1975, Autumn. Incentives, risk and information: Notes toward a theory of hierarchy. *Bell Journal of Economics* 6:552–79.

Trattner, M. H., D. B. Corts, P. P. van Rijn, and A. M. Outerbridge. 1977, September. *Research base for the written test portion of the Professional and Administrative Career Examination (PACE): Prediction of job performance for claims authorizers in the social insurance claims examining operation*, TS 77-3. Washington, DC: U.S. Civil Service Commission, Personnel Research and Development Center.

Tsang, M. C. 1987. The impact of underutilization of education on productivity: A case study of the U.S. Bell Companies. *Economics of Education Review* 6:239–52.

Tsang, M. C., and H. M. Levin. 1985. The economics of overeducation. *Economics of Education Review* 4:93–104.

U.S. Employment Service. 1965. *Dictionary of occupational titles*. 3d ed. Washington, DC: U.S. Government Printing Office.

U.S. General Accounting Office. 1979, May 15. *Federal employment examinations: Do they achieve equal opportunity and merit principle goals?* Washington, DC: Comptroller General of the United States.

Vroom, V. H. 1964. *Work and motivation*. New York: John Wiley and Sons.

Wigdor, A. K., and J. A. Hartigan, eds. 1988. *Interim report, within-group scoring of the General Aptitude Test Battery*. Washington, DC: National Academy Press.

Williamson, O. E. 1975. *Markets and hierarchies*. New York: Free Press.

Examples of Testing Programs in the Insurance Industry and a Discussion of Employment Testing Policy Issues

Andrew G. Neiner and William D. Love

I. INTRODUCTION

This paper presents issues related to the use of standardized employment tests in business and industry. First, it suggests that business organizations, like all formal groups, need rules to govern membership, and that standardized tests can be used to empower membership rules. Second, it demonstrates by example how standardized tests are developed and used to improve the quality of hiring decisions in two insurance industry employment testing programs. And third, it outlines policy issues related to the use of standardized tests in employee selection.

Rules to Govern Membership

At the most basic level business organizations can be viewed as simply groups, social units consisting of individuals with defined role relationships and a set of values or norms that regulate group-related behavior. As groups become more formal, rules are adopted—either explicit or implicit—which control group membership; the more formal a group is, the more explicit the membership rules tend to be.

Membership rules serve to maintain the integrity of groups by limiting participation in group activities to those who are able and willing to support group objectives. Business organizations almost always have established rules, more traditionally called employee selection policies, for choosing members. The primary function of employee selection policies is to permit membership to those who are most likely to contribute to an organization's success, while denying entry to those who are less promising. If employee selection policies are effective, a membership (work force) characterized by individuals who promote and support organizational objectives will be achieved.

The principal way employees support organizational objectives is to successfully perform the jobs to which they are assigned. Employee selection policies foster successful job performance by assigning the right people to the right jobs. Because jobs differ in requirements and individuals differ in skills, abilities, and other job-related characteristics, matching people with appropriate jobs is a challenge inherent to employee selection.

The notion of pairing personal characteristics with compatible job demands is not new (although the technology for doing so is). For example, Plato believed that within each individual's soul some parts were more pronounced than others and that these differences influenced success in three major occupational groups. Plato reasoned that for government workers (rulers) the seat of intellect (logistikon) is most pronounced. Military personnel (guardians) need a pronounced themes, the part of the soul responsible for courage and will. For merchants, the appetitive part of the soul, the source of pleasure and greed, is most important. While it is hoped that today's business leaders engage in some form of soul-searching, more scientific and modern methods are available for selecting employees.

Standardized tests play an important role in employee selection. They are commonly used to transform employee selection policies from abstract philosophical statements (We only hire the best people) to concrete operations (Secretaries must type sixty words per minute with fewer than three errors). Test results, and the decision rules which accompany them, serve as mechanisms to block, redirect, or expedite entry into an organization.

Brief History of Employment Tests

The purpose of this paper is not to provide a history of employment tests. Excellent reviews of this topic are available elsewhere (Hale 1982; von Haller Gilmer 1981). Some background is helpful, however, to add perspective to the idea of using standardized tests as an employee selection tool.

The use of standardized, objective, and validated employment tests is a relatively new phenomenon in the history of work. One of the first organizations to use standardized employee selection tests was the United States government. In 1883, the Civil Service Commission was established to replace the "spoils system" approach to filling government positions; by 1911, 105,000 applicants for government work were administered open competitive examinations.

The military was also an early user of standardized tests. With the sudden entry of the United States into World War I, the military needed to rapidly classify 1.5 million recruits. Army Alpha and Army Beta, two easily administered and scored mental-ability tests, were used to screen out the mentally unfit, classify recruits according to intellectual ability, and identify officer potential. The military also tested recruits during World War II. By the end of the war, the Army General Classification Test had been administered to 9 million recruits to assess their trainability.

Following the lead of the military, the private business sector soon adopted testing as a valuable selection tool. In 1954, the National Industrial Conference Board found that 37 percent of businesses surveyed used employment tests; by 1964, the percentage had risen to 80 percent (NICB 1964). In a survey conducted by Prentice-Hall and the American Society for Personnel Administration (1975), 60 percent of responding companies with more than twenty-five thousand employees used employment tests, while test use was reported by 39 percent of employers with fewer than one hundred employees. Today, it is safe to assume that the majority of business organizations currently use some form of standardized testing in employee selection.

II. TWO EXAMPLES OF LARGE-SCALE EMPLOYMENT TESTING

To demonstrate how standardized tests are developed and used in business and industry, two large-scale employment testing programs in the insurance industry are reviewed. Both testing programs are managed by insurance industry associations: Life Office Management Association (LOMA) and Life Insurance Marketing and Research Association (LIMRA). LOMA's testing program uses cognitive ability tests to help select entry-level employees to work in the home office. LIMRA's program uses a biographical information approach to estimate an individual's chances for success as an insurance sales agent.

Life Office Management Association (LOMA)

LOMA is an international association founded in 1924. Through education, training, research, and information sharing, LOMA is dedicated to promoting management excellence in leading life and health insurance companies and other financial institutions. LOMA currently has eight hundred member companies in thirty-three countries.

LOMA is organized into four operating divisions: Financial Planning and Control, Human Resources, Life Management Institute, and Operations and Systems. Areas that support these divisions include accounting, administration, editorial/graphics, information resources, marketing, meetings, and personnel. LOMA employs 130 individuals, most of whom are technical/professional.

LOMA staff, often working with consultants or staff from other industry associations, conduct research projects of importance to the industry and issue the results in widely read reports. In addition, LOMA publishes a bimonthly magazine, a quarterly journal, and several divisional newsletters.

The development of the Job Effectiveness Prediction System (JEPS), a battery of standardized employment tests, is an example of a major LOMA research project undertaken to fill an industry need. The next section covers why this project was necessary, reviews the research and development, and discusses how the tests are used today.

Job Effectiveness Prediction System

In the early 1970s, corporate America was reeling from the effects of well-publicized employee discrimination lawsuits challenging the fairness of employment tests. The Civil Rights Act of 1964, and the interpretation of that act by the courts and the Equal Employment Opportunity Commission (EEOC), made employment testing a public issue (Hale 1982). Federal regulations governing the use of employment tests, namely, the *Uniform Guidelines on Employee Selection Procedures*, require that in cases where protected groups are adversely impacted by the use of tests—typically shown by relatively lower hiring rates (percent of applicants hired) among minority groups—the use of the tests must be shown to be job-related. Unfortunately, the steps necessary to demonstrate job-relatedness can be expensive, time-consuming, and in some cases, technically infeasible.

Insurance companies, like other organizations at the time, were caught between the proverbial rock and a hard place. Inability to defend the use of tests when it appeared that protected groups (minorities) were adversely affected by their use often resulted in expensive settlements against employers. On the other hand, abandoning tests meant using less objective and less accurate (thus, less fair) techniques to help make hiring decisions.

One answer to this dilemma for the insurance industry was to develop employment tests that were not only effective for screening job applicants, but also capable of meeting federal and state requirements regarding fair employment practices. JEPS was seen as a possible solution. JEPS helps insurance companies screen internal and external applicants for home office entry-level jobs. To do this, cognitive ability tests are used to estimate an applicant's chances for success on a job. The system is based on the scientifically supported finding that differences in cognitive ability are related to differences in performance for most jobs (Hunter 1980; Schmidt, Hunter, and Pearlman 1981).

In addition to aiding in employee selection of external job candidates, JEPS can in some instances be used to help make promotional decisions. When more than one internal candidate is being considered for a higher-level job, JEPS scores can be used to make a relative assessment of the candidates' job-related cognitive skills. JEPS is not used to assist in noncompetitive (only one candidate) promotion decisions.

Some examples of the jobs for which JEPS is appropriate are filing clerk, secretary, claims approver, underwriter trainee, claims examiner trainee, and annuity analyst. These kinds of jobs typically have a clerical and administrative orientation. Relevant tasks and duties may include processing paperwork (for example, reports, files, forms, applications) and information (for example, rates, prices, schedules). Important skills required may include reading comprehension, spelling, coding, transcribing, mathematical computations, and checking.

JEPS—Research and Development

LOMA established the Personnel Research Committee to allow insurance company personnel researchers to exchange information, form professional contacts, and advise LOMA of research needs within the industry. The committee meets biannually and comprises fifteen members representing many of the largest insurance companies in the United States and Canada. Upon the committee's advice, LOMA embarked upon a major research effort in 1970 to develop and validate employee selection tests for entry-level home office employees. LOMA accepted responsibility for generating funds for the study, soliciting research participation from LOMA members, contracting with technical experts to conduct the study, and administering the testing program once completed.

Requests for proposals to conduct the research were sent to private consulting firms, universities, and other organizations specializing in test development and validation. In nearly all cases, those who responded to the call had a strong background in industrial/organizational psychology. The contract was awarded to a Minneapolis-based firm, Personnel Decisions Research Institute, Inc.

Research Design

The research was conducted in five general phases: development of a sampling plan, job analysis, test development, job performance evaluation, and validity analysis. The sampling plan was used to determine which jobs and which insurance companies were to be included in the research. The job analysis phase provided the researchers with information about the job tasks and duties, and the skills and abilities needed to perform them. In the next phase, tests were developed to measure these requisite skills and abilities, and the tests were administered to employees. Following this, a performance evaluation system was developed and performance data collected on the same employees who had been tested. Finally, test data and job performance data were examined to assess the relationship between the two. The research phases are summarized separately below.

Phase 1: Sampling Plan. The study was designed to cover all nonexempt ("time card") entry-level (no prior job experience is necessary) home office jobs. Exceptions included supervisory jobs, highly technical or specialized jobs (for example, computer programmer, printer), and building or grounds maintenance jobs. Because there were an estimated seventy thousand target jobs in more than one thousand life and property/casualty insurance companies in the United States and Canada at the time of the study, it was not practical to collect data from all possible sources.

Since all jobs and all companies could not be included in the research, it was important that representative samples be obtained. To do this, job and company sampling plans were developed. The job sampling plan called for jobs in each of thirteen broad categories to be included and, within each job category, jobs from each of three salary levels. The company sampling plan called for representatives in each of five geographic regions and three home-office size categories to be included in the research.

Phase 2: Job Analysis. This research phase was designed to give the researchers better insight into the activities performed by incumbents in the targeted jobs. To do this, four sources of information were used:

Current job descriptions—Information related to the general purpose of the jobs, job duties, job requirements (education, special skills, and so on), and special working conditions was provided by insurance company personnel offices.

Literature review—Relevant studies published in the educational and professional research literatures were reviewed.

Supervisor workshops—Information was collected from experienced supervisors during workshops held in New York, Chicago, Dallas, and Toronto. Included were such issues as behaviors; type of supervision received; and knowledge, skills, and abilities needed to perform the jobs. Also collected were critical incidents—examples of particularly effective or ineffective job performance.

Site visits—Visits to insurance companies were made to observe and interview supervisors and incumbents in the jobs being studied.

These four sources of information were used to generate a comprehensive list of 186 job activities believed to cover all targeted jobs. This list served as the basis for the Job Activities Questionnaire, which was administered to incumbents and supervisors. To complete the questionnaire, each activity was rated according to three scales: (1) is the activity part of your job (or the job you supervise); if yes, then, (2) how much time is spent performing the activity; and (3) how important is the activity to overall job performance? Questionnaires were completed by more than eight thousand incumbent-supervisor pairs in 108 insurance companies.

Through statistical data reduction and simplification techniques, the 186 job activities were combined into forty-six general job performance areas (see Appendix A for performance area examples). While it was unlikely that all forty-six areas would be included in any single job, nearly all entry-level nonexempt insurance company jobs were composed of one or more of them.

Phase 3: Test Development. The next phase of the research was to identify the abilities needed to perform the jobs and to develop standardized tests to reliably measure them. A review of the research literature and a close examination of the job analysis data suggested that the following abilities were important for successful performance on the jobs being studied: numerical reasoning, verbal comprehension/vocabulary, filing, reading comprehension, language usage/grammar/spelling, coding, general reasoning ability, and perceptual speed. To measure these abilities, eleven standardized mental ability tests were developed. To supplement these tests, a battery of noncognitive measures was also prepared, which included personality scales, biographical items, and vocational interest measures. Both sets of tests were pre-tested among a sample of 1,390 applicants applying for nonexempt entry-level jobs in ninety-seven insurance companies. The pre-test was conducted to determine time limits, to compare results with other published test results, and to assess psychometric properties such as level of difficulty. Except for the noncognitive battery, the tests were speeded (had strict time limits). Job applicants were paid to take the tests, and test results did not affect hiring decisions.

Following the pre-test, revisions were made, and the tests were administered to ninety-five hundred entry-level nonexempt employees in 105 insurance companies. Employees were administered the tests during their first two weeks of employment. Test scores were kept confidential and used for research purposes only. Appendix B lists the test names and time limits.

Phase 4: Performance Evaluation. To measure the ability of the tests to predict job performance, reliable job performance measures were needed. The Job Activity and Performance Description Questionnaire (JAPDQ) was developed. The JAPDQ allows supervisors to rate their subordinates' job performance on a variety of job-related dimensions. The JAPDQ lists the same forty-six performance areas identified in the job analysis research phase. For each performance area, a description of the area and seven-point job performance rating scale with behavioral anchors was provided. To complete the JAPDQ, a supervisor first indicated for each performance area whether the area was part of the subordinate's job. If it was, the supervisor rated the area on (a) how much time the subordinate spends performing the job activities described in the area, (b) how important the activities are to overall job performance, and (c) how effectively the subordinate performs the activities.

In addition to individual performance area ratings, an overall job performance measure was attained for each employee. This was done by first assigning a criticality weight to each performance area; areas in which a lot of time was spent and which were deemed important were assigned high criticality weights. Then, the performance ratings for each area were weighted accordingly and combined to yield a composite score representing overall job performance.

Supervisors were trained to complete the JAPDQ and asked to rate the performance of those subordinates who had previously taken the JEPS tests. Job performance measures were collected approximately six months following testing.

Once test scores and job performance measures were collected for each employee, researchers had the essential ingredients necessary to conduct the next research phase, validity analysis.

Phase 5: Validity Analysis. When discussing employment tests, validity refers to the relationship between test performance and job performance. While there are a variety of methods used to assess the validity of employment tests (Guion 1980) and many technical aspects to consider, it can generally be said that a test is considered valid if test scores improve the accuracy of hiring decisions. For a test to be a useful employment tool, it is essential to show that job applicants who yield good test scores tend to be successful on the job while those who yield poor test scores do not.

Traditionally, test development and validation studies have been conducted one job at a time. For each position, job analyses are performed, tests are developed and administered, performance measures developed and collected, and validity analyses conducted. This approach can be expensive, time-consuming, and often technically infeasible when large numbers of jobs and/or jobs with few incumbents are involved.

Because the JEPS project included thousands of different jobs, and some jobs had few incumbents, conducting separate validity studies for each job was impractical. Instead of the traditional approach, a test validation model termed *synthetic validity* (Lawshe 1952; Mossholder and Arvey 1984) was used. In this model, the relationship between test scores and overall job performance is not measured directly. Instead, it is inferred (or synthesized) from information on the relationship between test scores and performance on individual job tasks and duties (called job elements).

The relationship between test scores and job elements was examined for approximately five thousand individuals who had completed the JEPS battery and who were subsequently rated on forty-six job elements with the JAPDQ. Pearson product moment correlation coefficients (McNemar 1969) were calculated for each test–job element combination and coefficients representing nonchance positive relationships (increases in test scores associated with increases in job element performance) were noted.

In the synthetic validity model, once validity coefficients have been derived for each job element, the validity of a test(s) to predict overall job performance can be estimated for any job within a job family (Hamilton 1981). The synthetic validity paradigm is based on the following principles:

1. A job is a composite of various identifiable tasks and duties called elements: any job can be decomposed into a list of

elements. (Phase 2 of the research identified forty-six job elements for the jobs being studied.)

2. Overall job performance is a combination of performance on each job element. (Phase 4 of the research derived a measure of overall job performance by a mathematical combination of performance on each relevant job performance area or element.)

3. Jobs can be grouped into job families: a group of jobs which are in some manner interrelated (Pearlman 1980). For a given job family, a finite set of elements can be defined, and each job within the family is a composite of one or more elements from that set. (All jobs included in the study are members of the same family [nonexempt entry-level insurance jobs], and each could be decomposed into one or more of the forty-six job elements that comprised the element set for this job family.)

4. The relationship between test performance and performance on each element in a given job family set can be established (discussed in Phase 5).

5. The validity of a test to predict overall job performance on any job within a job family can be estimated by (a) identifying which elements from the set of job family elements constitute the job; (b) identifying the validity coefficients of the test(s) to predict performance for each of those job elements; and (c) combining those validity coefficients to estimate the validity of the test(s) to predict overall job performance.

Figure 1 is a schematic model of how the synthetic validity approach can be used to identify which JEPS tests should be used for two hypothetical jobs, X and Y, and how the validity of the tests for predicting overall job performance can be estimated.

In this example, the lines between Tests and Job Elements represent the validity of tests A through K to predict performance for each of the forty-six job elements. The lines between Job Elements and Overall Job Performance indicate for each job which elements constitute the job.

Since job X comprises elements 1, 2, and 3, and tests A, B, and C are valid predictors for those job elements, then a test battery that includes tests A, B, and C is appropriate for job X. The validity of this test battery for job X is calculated by a mathematical combination of the individual validities for the relevant tests and job elements. Following the same reasoning, a test battery for job Y would consist of tests C and D since these tests are valid predictors of performance on elements 3, 4, and 5.

FIGURE 1

Synthetic Validity Model

| Tests | Job Elements | Overall Job Performance |

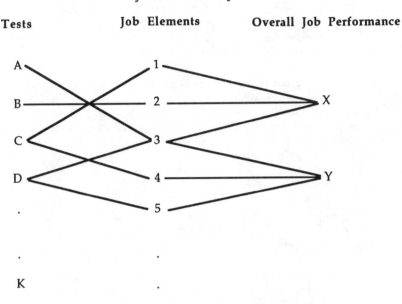

Research Findings

The noncognitive test battery, which included personality scales, vocational interest, and biographical information, was not found to be a useful predictor of job performance. However, each of the eleven mental ability tests was found to be positively associated with job performance measures. Validity coefficients, the empirical correlations between individual tests and job performance ratings, range between .15 and .27 (corrected for criterion unreliability) for the eleven tests. The estimated validity coefficient for any given test battery (a combination of two or more tests) is .31.

Because most jobs consist of several different performance areas, overall job performance is better predicted by a battery of tests than by any single test. Once the important performance areas are identified for a job, the tests that best predict those performance areas can be combined into a test battery. Using the synthetic model (figure 1), a test battery can be created for any job within the job family, and its validity to predict overall job performance can be estimated.

Research showed that scores on customized test batteries were related to performance on the job and that the scores could be used to estimate an individual's chances to succeed on a given job.

JEPS Usage

Companies using JEPS must first conduct job analyses on the jobs in which tests will be used. This is done with an easily administered survey, the Job Description Questionnaire, designed to identify which of forty-six performance areas are important for a job. Job analysis results are sent to LOMA for processing. Using research data on the relationship between the selection tests and the forty-six job performance areas, a customized test battery is prescribed for each job. A typical test battery will include two to four tests.

For each job, the company receives a summary sheet showing which performance areas are important for the job, which tests should be used for employee selection, and how the individual test scores should be combined to derive an overall score. Using interpretative charts, an overall test score can be translated into a probability of success for the applicant. This information, in conjunction with information from other sources (interviews, reference checks, and work history,) is used to make hiring decisions.

Today, more than 180 insurance companies in the United States and Canada use JEPS. Since the completion of the research in 1981, more than one million tests have been sold.

Life Insurance Marketing and Research Association (LIMRA)

LIMRA is a not-for-profit research, educational, and consulting organization serving approximately 320 member companies in the United States and Canada, and approximately 270 international member companies throughout the rest of the world. LIMRA's purpose is to generate and disseminate information to promote the welfare and interest of the public through sound and progressive marketing of insurance and other financial products and services. A substantial proportion of LIMRA's operating budget comes from dues from its member companies.

One of LIMRA's major areas of research, education, and consultation is in the selection of insurance and financial services sales representatives. LIMRA provides several tools, educational materials, and schools on this topic. The Career Profile system is the major selection tool produced by LIMRA.

The best selection tests are usually generated where there exists a large amount of data as well as expert professionals who know how to use that data to produce fair and valid selection tests. LIMRA provides an opportunity for the insurance industry to perform cooperative research leading to quality employee selection tests. A review of this organization and its selection test for insurance sales representatives illustrates the value of such tests both to the employer and the employee.

The Career Profile System

The Career Profile system is a paper-and-pencil questionnaire filled out by candidates interested in the position of sales representative. The questionnaire covers background information, such as previous work history, education, vocational, income, and social activities. (See Appendix C for examples of Career Profile questions.) Answer sheets are sent to LIMRA for computer scoring. A rating on a nineteen-point scale is returned to the employer along with information to be used in the rest of the selection process. The rating is based on predictive validity research by LIMRA.

In general, the rating indicates the probability of on-the-job success for the candidate based on an analysis of the success of similar candidates who have become sales representatives. In this way, the Career Profile system is designed to answer the candidate's question, "How successful have individuals like me been when they became sales representatives?" The rating gives the candidate an idea of whether his or her chances of success are above average, average, or below average. If the rating from the Career Profile system is low, it is probably advisable for the candidate to redirect his or her career search.

For the employer, the Career Profile rating indicates whether a candidate has sufficient potential to continue in the selection process. If the rating is low, the employer might want to terminate the selection process. On the other hand, if the rating is high, the employer may wish to take a closer look at the candidate and let the candidate take a closer look at the career. The Career Profile system provides a report to help in this selection process.

For the applicants, the Career Profile rating indicates whether this career is worth a closer review as a possible future career. Again, a low rating indicates to applicants that others similar to them have had problems with the career; a career search in other fields would be recommended. On the other hand, a high rating indicates that others similar to them did find some success in the career and thus a closer look is indicated.

Job applicants have few opportunities to gain such information. Rarely are applicants able to preview what normally happens to individuals like themselves in a career before they make what can be a very costly career decision. Without the Career Profile questionnaire, many of the lower-rated applicants would go into the career only to suffer financial and emotional loss from failure that could have been predicted before entering the career.

Further, without the Career Profile questionnaire, many higher-rated applicants would not look seriously at a career that could provide them the financial and emotional rewards of a successful career. Employee selection testing results in fewer hiring errors, and thus, more individuals are directed into careers where they will find success.

A Brief History of the Career Profile System

The research that led to the first version of the Career Profile system (previously known as the Aptitude Index (AI) and the Aptitude Index Battery (AIB) was begun in 1919 at Phoenix Mutual Life Insurance Company. In 1932, Albert K. Kurtz of the Life Insurance Sales Bureau (now LIMRA) used this and other individual company research to plan an industrywide study. Arthur W. Kornhauser of the University of Chicago worked on a variety of personality tests for the effort; Kurtz pursued research on the biographical items. This led to the first edition of the LIMRA selection tool in 1933.

In developing this first edition, many research procedures were followed that were quite new then, but are commonly regarded as good practices today: for example, the use of multiple-regression techniques for adding items to the scoring system, cross-validation of the scoring system, testing the validity across a variety of companies in both the United States and Canada, use of a predictive validity model, and insistence on a continuing research program to ensure that the questionnaire continued to work.

An early example of the continuing research is reported in a 1941 research report entitled *How Well Does the Aptitude Index Work?* (reprinted in LIMRA 1980a). In this report, the validity of the questionnaire was looked at using various criteria—age group, country (Canada and United States), company size, company usage, and region of the country. This report even took an early look at women candidates.

One of the major improvements in the research effort was derived from the centralized processing of the questionnaire by computer, which began in 1961. With this processing came the possibility of more complex, accurate, and fair scoring systems; the availability of data on all candidates; and the ability to make changes in the scoring system quickly, to monitor the proper usage of the questionnaire, and to keep a candidate's responses confidential (LIMRA 1980b). Thayer (1977) summarizes the impact of this research and its meaning for selection research.

The Predictive Validity and Value of the Career Profile System

The predictive validity of the Career Profile system is established through its relationship to on-the-job performance. The scoring systems have been developed using multiple-regression techniques with modification for the use of moderator variables. These scoring procedures were then cross-validated or cross-checked on a sample of candidates who were not used in the development of the systems.

Extensive research has been conducted to assess the validity of the Career Profile for identifying potentially successful insurance sales representatives. Researchers administered the Career Profile to 9,849 representatives at the time of their job application. One year later, researchers identified those who were successful on the job and those who were not.

A sales representative is defined as successful if, during the first twelve months of employment, that individual earned commissions or income from all lines of business that were in the top 20 percent as compared with other first-year sales representatives in the company. Because individuals who terminate would not normally have had production in the top 20 percent, this definition of success classifies as failures both terminating sales representatives and surviving, but less productive, sales representatives.

Table 1 shows for each possible Career Profile rating the percent of sales representatives who were successful. For example, only 8 percent who received a rating of six became successful, compared to 30.7 percent who received a rating of nineteen.

One way to make these percentages more meaningful is to express them as the number of representatives who would have to be hired (or contracted) in order to yield one successful representative. For example, at a rating of sixteen, four representatives are needed to expect one success; at a rating of eight, ten are needed.

TABLE 1
Success Rate at Each Career Profile Rating

Career Profile Rating	Percent Successful
19	30.7
18	28.8
17	26.9
16	25.0
15	23.1
14	21.1
13	19.2
12	17.3
11	15.4
10	13.5
9	11.6
8	10.4
7	9.2
6	8.0
5	6.8
4	5.6
3	4.4
2	3.2
1	2.0

TABLE 2

The Value of the Career Profile System: Calculation of the Relative Reduction in Total Costs to Obtain One Successful Sales Representative at Various Cutoff Ratings

Career Profile cutoff rating	% Success rate at and above cutoff	No. hired	No. tested	% Reduction in total cost for one successful representative
19	30.7	3.26	273	29
18	29.8	3.36	158	39
17	29.1	3.44	108	43
16	28.1	3.56	88	43
15	27.1	3.69	73	43
14	25.9	3.86	65	41
13	24.6	4.07	59	39
12	23.4	4.27	54	37
11	22.4	4.46	48	35
10	21.3	4.69	44	32
9	20.2	4.95	41	29
8	19.3	5.18	39	26
7	18.1	5.52	38	21
6	17.0	5.88	38	17
5	16.5	6.06	37	14
4	15.9	6.29	36	11
3	15.2	6.58	36	7
2	14.5	6.90	36	3
1	14.0	7.14	36	0

Value of the Career Profile

The value of this predictive validity can be expressed in the savings gained from the use of the Career Profile system, given the various cutoff ratings. Table 2 summarizes the value of using the Career Profile system by outlining the cumulative success rate at each Career Profile cutoff (column 2), the number of persons that would have to be hired in order to get one successful sales representative at each cutoff (column 3), and the number of candidates that would have to be tested in order to obtain the number of people that need to be hired (column 4).

When the Career Profile questionnaire is not used, it is estimated that approximately seven persons would have to be hired in order to obtain one successful representative. Thirty-six persons would have to be tested in order to hire these seven individuals.

LIMRA has investigated the cost of identifying and processing candidates as well as the early costs of such factors as compensation, training, supervision, housing. The total cost for one successful representative when not using the Career Profile questionnaire would be $165,357.

The percent reduction in total cost using the Career Profile questionnaire at the various cutoff ratings can be estimated and is given in column 5 of table 2. As the table indicates, a maximum of 43 percent reduction in total costs might be realized at a cutoff rating of fifteen. Other reasonable cost estimates produce estimated maximum reductions in total cost from 37 percent to 46 percent at cutoff ratings of fifteen or sixteen.

Tying the use of the selection tests directly to the total reduction in cost per successful sales representative puts the value of the test in terms that are important to business managers who must control costs, increase profits, and enhance the return on the investment in new employees. They find the illustration that costs can be reduced by 43 percent quite convincing.

For practical reasons, LIMRA does not normally recommend a specific cutoff rating. Individual companies using the Career Profile system should choose the appropriate cutoff rating based on an assessment of their needs and abilities in the recruiting and selection of sales representatives. LIMRA provides technical guidance to individual companies based on the validity research that it conducts.

The Value of the Career Profile Rating for the Applicant

The validity and value of the Career Profile rating for the applicant are illustrated in table 1. As the data indicate, applicants with low rating have little chance of success in the career. For example, an applicant with a rating of four has approximately one chance in eighteen of being successful. Normally, such a high risk would indicate to an applicant that a job search in other careers is in order.

On the other hand, applicants with the higher ratings have a low enough risk that a closer look at the career is indicated. For example, an applicant with a rating of sixteen has about one chance in four of finding success in the career. A careful review of the career requirements might help the applicant determine whether he or she is the one in four who will succeed. This risk level may be appropriate for the applicant.

Without the information from the Career Profile questionnaire, applicants who are high risks might enter the career only to fail. Applicants with lower risks might never seriously consider the career and thus miss the opportunity to embark on a successful career.

The Generalizability of the Validity of the Career Profile Rating

The generalizability of the Career Profile rating has been established over time, over different types of candidates, and over different types of environmental conditions.

Brown (1978) has shown that the 1933 scoring procedure for the original selection questionnaire worked as well with candidates hired in the early 1970s, despite major changes in the environment, from a depression era to a high employment era, and major changes in the characteristics of the job.

The generalizability of the validity of the Career Profile system over different types of candidates has been shown for minority groups, for women, and for different age groups. The use of the questionnaire for these groups shows no adverse impact. That is, at the various possible cutoffs there is little difference in the percentage "passing" for each of these groups.

The Career Profile rating has also been shown to have validity for students, recent students, retired military personnel, candidates from different occupations (sales, executive, and so on), candidates with different educational backgrounds, candidates with different income needs, candidates with different amounts of life insurance ownership, candidates with different lengths of residence in the community, and candidates who have previously sold life insurance.

The Career Profile rating has been validated for companies selling different types of insurance products, such as health insurance companies and multiple-line insurance companies (auto, homeowners, life, and so on) as well as for life insurance companies. In addition, the Career Profile rating has been validated for different methods of distributing insurance, such as combination (debit, industrial) and ordinary.

The Career Profile rating has also been validated for various environmental situations (see LIMRA 1980a for research report reprints): different types of compensation plans, such as commissions versus salary plus commissions; different regions of the country; different quality of local management; the United States, English-speaking Canada, French-speaking Canada, and the British Isles; different usages of the rating, such as for a rejection tool versus a selection tool as well; different methods of contacting candidates, such as newspaper advertisements, employment agencies, personal contact by the agency manager or the agency staff; and different methods of using the rating, such as early in the selection process versus later in the process.

III. POLICY ISSUES RELATED TO STANDARDIZED EMPLOYEE SELECTION TESTS

Because the results of employee selection tests are used to make important decisions affecting the vocational livelihoods of individuals and the survival of organizations, employment test usage is a public concern. When employment tests are professionally developed and properly used, both individuals and businesses benefit and there need be no public concern. As with any technology, however, abuse and error can never be completely removed and the consequences of this should be evaluated.

Several policy issues often draw the public's attention to employee selection tests. The following is a discussion of the most prominent of these issues.

Tests and Privacy Rights

A commonly held belief among personnel specialists is that the ability to make good hiring decisions increases proportionally with the amount of information known. Given that the purpose of all tests is to collect information, the current popularity of employment tests was inevitable. The perceived need among personnel specialists to collect information and the availability of standardized tests for doing so begs the question: Do employment tests represent an invasion of individual privacy?

Privacy rights and employee selection debates usually center on two major issues, the type of information sought by personnel specialists and the manner in which it is collected. Regarding data collection methods, standardized paper-and-pencil tests do not appear to be problematic. Compared to other forms of employee information gathering techniques, paper-and-pencil employment tests are less coercive and invasive. Unlike reference checks and background searches, a paper-and-pencil test makes the applicant the sole source of information, and the success of the test requires his or her full cooperation. Privacy issues are more likely to arise when information is obtained without the job applicant's knowledge or consent.

Regarding the type of information collected, traditional standardized paper-and-pencil employment tests are rarely associated with privacy rights issues. The information tapped by most commonly used employment tests (for example, typing speed, spelling ability, mathematical skills) is not typically considered sensitive, personal, or offensive by job applicants and, therefore, does not require protection. The same cannot be said of some new types of employment tests, such as polygraph examinations and drug tests, which are gaining popularity.

Regardless of the manner in which it is collected, certain information is generally considered private and not relevant when making personnel decisions. For example, gender and race can be unobtrusively noted (in fact, they are hard to ignore), but in only very specific circumstances can they be used legally to make personnel decisions (ironically, by their nature, affirmative action programs require that such information be recorded). Less easily accessible information, such as attitudes, opinions, and interests, which are often measured with paper-and-pencil inventories, may be viewed by some job applicants as being too private to divulge. Given that job applicant information is essential for making good hiring decisions, that it is in the best interests of both the applicant and the employer to avoid hiring mistakes, and that standardized paper-and-pencil tests are efficient, reliable ways to collect data, should there be limits on the type of information covered by employment tests?

There are no simple answers to these questions. While the Fourth Amendment guarantees the protection of privacy, it is purposely ambiguous regarding the circumstances that constitute a violation. While it is the role of the judicial system to interpret the law and to render judgment for specific cases, the variety of employment tests currently in use and the proliferation of new, experimental tests (for example, genetic screening), make the establishment of legal precedent difficult. As a result, employers and applicants often feel that they have little guidance about, or understanding of, the limits to which employment tests may go before infringing upon the right to privacy.

Possibly the most effective protection against the invasion of privacy by employee selection tests is public relations. Basically, employers need employees; employers who can attract the most skilled workers have an advantage over those who cannot. To the extent that an employer offends job applicants by seeking information deemed too private, that employer will lose job candidates to competitors more sensitive to privacy issues.

Effects of Testing on Minority Employment

Employment tests in the 1960s were viewed by many as a barrier to employment for minorities. This was largely a result of the consistent finding that average test scores for minority groups, primarily blacks, were significantly lower than for whites. Thus, if hiring decisions were based on test scores alone, and those hired were chosen from the top of test-score distributions, nonwhites would have fewer employment opportunities than whites.

At first it was thought that test-score differences between whites and minorities were the result of racially biased test items. Most test experts, however, began to doubt that test differences could be accounted for by item content when researchers continued to find differences on carefully developed "culture or race free" tests. Today, most test experts and the courts are not surprised by white and minority test differences, particularly with cognitive ability tests, and tend to attribute them to true differences in ability.

The issue then turned toward differential prediction. It was also thought by some that tests were more accurate predictors of job performance for white than nonwhite applicants. This would be true if test-score differences were not paralleled by job performance differences and the same prediction rule was applied to both whites and nonwhites. However, no compelling evidence exists to suggest that differential prediction is real. Research has consistently found that the same tests are valid for all groups, and inferior test performance on a valid test is accompanied by inferior job performance (Tenopyr 1985).

The Career Profile is one example where selection tests have increased employment opportunities for a minority group. In the early 1970s, there was no selection test that was deemed appropriate for women applying to be insurance agents, although a test did exist for male applicants. Because field managers had no valid method to predict which women would make successful agents, the temptation was not to hire women. In the early 1970s, only 4 percent of all new insurance agents were women.

In 1975, the predecessor of the Career Profile (the Aptitude Index Battery) was validated for women applicants. Managers now had a selection test that could tell them which women applicants had potential for success. The percentage of new women agents jumped to 26 percent. Studies have shown that given the desirability of the insurance agent's career for women, one would expect between 20 and 30 percent of all new agents to be women. Thus, rather than limiting its opportunities, the selection test actually increased a protected group's opportunity for employment.

The major issue is not, however, the use of employment tests, but how to ensure that they are used fairly. Psychologists have defined in technical terms the properties of an unbiased test, but an unbiased test may not be a fair test. The properties of a fair test have not been defined by psychologists. Indeed, such a definition is the society's responsibility. Both the federal and state governments have attempted definitions, and courts have tried to provide interpretations of these definitions for use in real-life situations. Yet neither governmental agencies nor the courts have resolved some major conflicts, such as between the rights to equal treatment and affirmative action programs. Employment tests can be an instrument of either.

The Validity, Value, and Utility of Employee Selection Tests

The *validity* of a selection test is its relation to what the test is intended to measure. The *value* of a test is the value of having a measure of what the test is purported to measure. The *utility* of a test is its value minus the cost of obtaining the measure. Thus the validity of an intelligence test is how well the test actually measures intelligence. In an employment situation, the value of an intelligence test is how much the test's measurement of intelligence has to do with on-the-job success. The utility is the gain in the amount of success (perhaps measured in amount of production) minus the cost of using the test.

Tests do not perfectly measure what they are intended to measure and what they do measure might not be totally relevant to job success. Thus, some people who would have succeeded will be turned away from the job, while others who will fail at the job will be hired.

Individuals who stand high on those traits measured by the test are more likely to "get the job" than those individuals who stand high on traits not measured by the test. Thus, the use of the selection test may doom certain individuals to rejection, not because they are any worse than other applicants, but because the areas where they are good are not being used in the selection process.

Since tests are not perfect predictors, how much weight should be given to them in the overall hiring decision? The issue can be viewed as a balancing between two types of errors. One type of error is hiring someone who fails, while the other is passing up someone who would have succeeded. If an organization wants to minimize the failure rate of those hired, it should require relatively high test scores for hiring. This will ensure that those hired have the highest success rates. Yet many individuals turned away with this heavy emphasis on the test would have succeeded had they been hired. If an organization is more concerned with minimizing the error of rejecting potentially successful individuals, then it should reject only individuals with the lowest ratings.

Utility

The cost to the company is lowest if few failing individuals are hired. Thus, heavy reliance is placed on the test. Passing up individuals who would have succeeded usually is of little loss to the company. On the other hand, being passed over for a career in which the individual would have succeeded is very costly for that individual. Some individuals, because their talents are not normally measured by tests, will be passed up more often.

Substantial research shows that employment tests, even those with only moderate levels of validity, can have a surprising impact on an organization's productivity and profitability (Hunter, Schmidt, and Rauschenberger 1984). Utility models state that a dollar value can be assigned to job performance and that levels of performance vary among employees. Part (if not all) of the variation in job performance can be attributed to differences among workers' skills and abilities or other constructs measurable by employment tests. When employment tests are used to raise the skill level of those hired, comparable increases in job performance will result, and dollar savings will occur.

For example, Hunter (1979) estimated that using a general-ability test to select police officers in the Philadelphia Police Department would result in a $180 million savings over a ten-year period. Even though great benefits can be achieved through the use of valid employment tests, Tenopyr (1985) comments that they are being underutilized:

We have available a technology, that is, testing, which can greatly help in solving the productivity problems of many of our American businesses. However, we have a technology which is not being used. This is the only field I know of in the country where there is a well developed research-based technology which is not being used.

Does the Education System Prepare Students for the Workplace?

It is the naive student who believes that the end of formal education also means the end of taking tests. In fact, some of the most important tests that await today's students will be administered not in a classroom, but in a personnel office. Here the competition will be for jobs, not grades.

For example, it is common for entry-level job applicants in an insurance company to be administered a battery of standardized written tests. While the tests are designed to measure aptitude to perform job-related tasks, the content of the questions and the constructs being measured are not necessarily insurance specific. In fact, most of the tests measure general skills supposedly learned in grammar and high school. For example, the JEPS testing program (discussed earlier) includes tests measuring skills such as spelling, mathematics, and reading comprehension.

Why do employers feel that it is necessary to test job applicants for knowledge, skills, and abilities taught in school? First, professionally conducted validation studies consistently demonstrate that general mental-ability test scores are positively associated with job performance. Second, individual differences exist among job applicants on all mental-ability tests. Third, a high school diploma is not a guarantee that basic mental skills and abilities have been mastered. The first and second reasons represent benign scientific findings and are not cause for public concern; however, the third reason is a public policy issue.

The quality of education in America and the curricula around which degrees are granted are social and political issues, not scientific ones. If the quality of education needs enhancing or the curricula need to be altered, the impetus to do so must come from strong public support. Are such changes necessary? To the extent that formal education is intended to prepare individuals to be productive society members, and that maintaining employment is a primary means for being productive, then the education system is not succeeding for all its recipients. Standardized mental-ability tests indicate that an alarming number of job applicants holding high school diplomas do not meet minimum standards for employment.

It is time for two of the largest testing communities—education and business—to join forces. With the business community setting hiring standards for new employees, and the education community setting standards for graduation, and both using tests to define their standards, an opportunity exists for cooperation and convergence.

At the least, students should be aware of the types of tests they are likely to face when seeking employment. One effective way to do this is to have them take some or all of the tests required for employment by one of the local businesses, and to compare their scores against the company's standards for employment. The types of employment tests in popular use today are strong indicators of the knowledge, skills, and abilities necessary to succeed (or at least get hired) in the workplace.

Validity Generalization Versus Situation-Specificity

Validity generalization refers to the degree to which inferences from scores on tests can be transported across different situations (Burke 1984). Validity generalization was not a major testing issue prior to the 1970s, when it was a commonly held belief that a test valid for a job in one organization or setting may be invalid for the same job in another organization or setting. Also, a test valid for one job may not be valid for other jobs, even when the jobs comprise similar tasks and responsibilities. This belief that test validity cannot be generalized across organizations or jobs is referred to as the *situation-specificity* theory.

Proponents of the situation-specificity theory argue that separate validity studies are required for each test, each job, and each organization. This is based on the belief that job and organizational variables exist that modify a test's validity across settings. On the other hand, validity generalization advocates have applied sophisticated statistical models to large data bases to demonstrate that most of the observed variance in validity coefficients across settings is not due to job or organizational variables, but is a statistical artifact. Schmidt and Hunter (1981), relying on numerous validity studies incorporating a variety of paper-and-pencil mental-ability tests in multiorganizational settings, boldly stated that "professionally developed cognitive ability tests are valid predictors of performance on the job and in training in all settings."

The validity generalization versus situation-specific controversy is more than an academic debate. It has very practical implications for test users and test developers. Large-scale acceptance of validity generalization principles would likely result in greater employment test usage and reduced costs. Many of the deterrents to employment tests, such as lack of validity evidence and the expense of conducting numerous validity studies, would be removed or made less onerous. As with the JEPS research, the cost of testing can be reduced to material and administrative expenses after an initial investment in consortium research (costs spread across the participating companies) to identify tests that are valid within broad job families.

Situation-specificity theorists warn that increased acceptance of the validity generalization doctrine will promote an "off-the-shelf" approach to employment test usage. They fear it will lead to indiscriminate use of general intelligence and personality tests, and dangerously relaxed attitudes toward test validity in general.

As test users, organizations are caught in the middle of this controversy. They rely on the advice of industrial psychologists and other personnel specialists to design efficient and accurate employee selection systems, and the guidance of government officials and lawyers to comply with fair employment practices and laws. Often, the messages they receive are conflicting. For example, the *Uniform Guidelines on Employee Selection Procedures* (1978), jointly adopted by the EEOC, Departments of Labor and Justice, and the Civil Service Commission, requires that in cases where adverse impact exists, employment tests must be validated. While three validation strategies are suggested (content, criterion, construct), validity generalization is not discussed. Consequently, the federal government's position regarding validity generalization is not clear. On the other hand, the current trend among industrial psychologists is toward favoring validity generalization principles. The *Principles for the Validation and Use of Personnel Selection Procedures* (Society for Industrial and Organizational Psychology 1987) states: "It now seems well established from both validity generalization studies and cooperative validation efforts that validities generalize far more than once supposed" (p. 26). To the extent that validity generalization evidence is available, researchers may rely on it to support the use of selection instruments (p. 27).

While the controversy is still strong, a definite trend is emerging. As more scientific data supporting validity generalization accumulates, the greater is its acceptance. Judges are becoming more sophisticated in handling test-related cases and federal agencies are reevaluating their own guidelines. The gap in understanding between the industrial psychology and legal communities is slowly lessening. It is hoped that all this will lead to more efficient and appropriate test usage and less confusion for employers.

The Use of a Strict Cutoff and Ranking

When a strict cutoff score is applied, no one below that cutoff can be hired. Thus an applicant who is low on the traits measured by the test will not be hired.

A strict cutoff score is a convenient and practical procedure for companies to use. Without the strict cutoff score, a company would have to determine what other information could be used to overrule a low score on the test. Normally such data simply do not exist.

A related issue is the use of the test results to rank order applicants. A given company may wish to hire only a certain number of individuals. The test is used to rank the available applicants and then only the top-scoring individuals are hired. For these individuals, performance on the test has become the sole reason they were hired.

Test Manipulation and Test-Wise Applicants

In our view, individuals who manipulate tests in order to obtain an artificially high score present a major problem. These individuals may use their abilities to "second guess" the test, or they might have actually obtained information about how the test is scored.

Manipulation of the test's results has an impact both on the employer and the applicants. Test manipulation means that individuals who are not likely to succeed receive higher scores and thus are more likely to be hired. The employer suffers a loss by hiring individuals who are not likely to be productive.

The manipulation of test results also affects the hiring opportunities of applicants who do not manipulate the results. Normally, companies hire only those individuals with the highest scores. Individuals who have obtained a high score through manipulation will eliminate from consideration honest applicants who receive a slightly lower score.

To control for test manipulation, companies must keep their scoring process secret. This secrecy eliminates, however, the possibility of applicants knowing "why they failed." Thus applicants do not obtain any career guidance in such situations. The issue is the balance between the employer's right to an accurate assessment of an applicant's potential and the applicant's desire for career guidance.

APPENDIX A

Examples of Performance Areas

1. Keeps and maintains records of work, or work production, or work quality, or of pending applications, claims, requests for information, etc.

2. Reads and reviews legal briefs, medical reports, police reports, contracts, journal articles, and/or new legislation or rulings which require technical knowledge; informs others of relevant changes.

3. Performs or checks complex calculations or a series of complex calculations and/or determines the appropriate mathematical formulae or statistical analyses to use.

4. Performs or checks simple calculations (add, subtract, multiply, or divide), for example, calculating premium rates, refunds, loss amounts, valuations, depreciation and/or replacement costs, etc.; operates adding machine or simple calculators.

5. Reads and follows work procedures instructions as described in procedures manuals.

6. Obtains authorizations, approvals, signatures, and other information required by various forms from appropriate persons (e.g., applicants, policyholders, police officers, medical personnel, etc.)

APPENDIX B

Test Names and Time Limits

Test Name	Time Limit (in minutes)
Numerical Ability - 1	8
Numerical Ability - 2	15
Mathematical Skill	20
Spelling	7
Language Usage	12
Reading Comprehension - 1	30
Reading Comprehension - 2	30
Verbal Comprehension	6
Filing	5
Coding and Converting	8
Comparing and Checking	7
Critical Thinking Appraisal	50
Self-Description and Opinion Inventory (non-cognitive battery)	untimed

APPENDIX C

Examples of Career Profile Questions

How much experience have you had selling insurance?
A. I have never sold insurance.
B. I have sold insurance on a part-time occasional basis only.

I have sold insurance on a full-time basis for:
C. less than 6 months
D. 6 months but less than 1 year
E. 1 year but less than 18 months
F. 18 months but less than 2 years
G. 2 years but less than 3
H. 3 years but less than 4
I. 4 years but less than 5
J. 5 years or more

In how many different church, business, political, fraternal, social, professional, and military groups are you an active member?
A. None
B. 1
C. 2
D. 3
E. 4 or more

For how long have you held a sales position where at least part of your income came from commissions? If you have held more than one such position, add the total amount of time.
A. I have never held a commissioned sales position
B. For less than 6 months
C. For 6 months but less than 1 year
D. For 1 year but less than 2
E. For 2 years or more

Over the last five years, for how many employers have you worked on a full-time basis? Do not count going to school as being employed.
A. I was a student, a homemaker, a retired person, self-employed, etc., during the last five years.
B. 1
C. 2
D. 3
E. 4 or more

During the typical week, how many Monday through Thursday evenings do you spend outside of your home in social or recreational activities?

A. None
B. 1 evening a week
C. 2
D. 3
E. 4

When you are trying to convince someone, with which method are you most effective?

A. Written communication
B. Telephone
C. Face-to-face with no one else present
D. Face-to-face with others present
E. Some other method

REFERENCES

Brown, A. 1985. Employment tests: Issues without clear answers. *Personnel Administrator* (September): 43–56.

Brown, S. H. 1978. Long-term validity of a personal history item scoring procedure. *Journal of Applied Psychology* 63:673–76.

Burke, M. J. 1984. Validity generalization: A review and critique of the correlational model. *Personnel Psychology* 37:93–115.

Equal Employment Opportunity Commission, Civil Service Commission, Department of Labor, Department of Justice. 1978 Uniform guidelines on employee selection procedures.. *Federal Register* 43(166): 38290–309.

Guion, R. M. 1980. On trinitarian doctrines of validity. *Professional Psychology* 11(3): 385–98.

Hale, M. 1982. History of employment testing. In *Ability testing: Uses, consequences, and controversies–Part 2*, 3–38. Washington DC: National Academy Press.

von Haller Gilmer, B. 1981. The early development of industrial-organizational psychology. In *Virginia Tech symposium on applied behavioral science*, ed. J. A. Sgro, 3–16. Toronto: D.C. Heath and Co.

Hamilton, J. W. 1981. Options for small sample sizes in validation: A case for the J-coefficient. *Personnel Psychology* 34:805–16.

Hunter, J. E. 1979. *An analysis of validity, differential validity, test fairness, and utility for the Philadelphia police officers selection examination prepared by the Educational Testing Service.* Report to the Philadelphia Federal District Court, *Alverez v. City of Philadelphia*.

————. 1980. *Validity generalization for 12,000 jobs: An application of synthetic validity and validity generalization to the General Aptitude Test Battery (GATB).* Washington, DC: U.S. Employment Service, U.S. Department of Labor.

Hunter, J. E., F. L. Schmidt, and J. Rauschenberger. 1984. Methodological, statistical, and ethical issues in the study of bias in psychological tests. In *Perspectives on bias in mental testing*, ed. C. R. Reynolds and R. T. Brown. New York: Plenum.

Lawshe, C. H. 1952. Employee selection. *Personnel Psychology* 5:31–34.

Life Insurance Marketing and Research Association. 1980a. How well does the Aptitude Index work? In *Agent selection questionnaire research: Selected literature.* I/R Code 86.16. Hartford, CT: LIMRA.

————. 1980b. Six-month validity of the U.S. Aptitude Index? In *Agent selection questionnaire research: Selected literature.* I/R Code 86.10. Hartford, CT: LIMRA.

McNemar, O. 1969. *Psychological statistics.* New York: John Wiley and Sons.

Mossholder, K. W., and R. D. Arvey. 1984. Synthetic validity: A conceptual and comparative review. *Journal of Applied Psychology* 69:322–33.

National Industrial Conference Board. 1964. *Personnel practices in factory and office.* Studies in Personnel Policy No. 145. New York: National Industrial Conference Board.

Pearlman, K. 1979. Job families: A review and discussion of their implications for personnel selection. *Psychological Bulletin* 87:1–27.

Prentice-Hall and American Society of Personnel Administration. 1975. PS/ASPA survey probes employee testing and selection procedures. In *Personnel management policies and practices report.* Englewood Cliffs, NJ: Prentice-Hall.

Schmidt, F. L., and J. E. Hunter. 1981. Employment testing: Old theories and new research findings. *American Psychologist* 36:1128–37.

Schmidt, F. L., J. E. Hunter, and K. Pearlman. 1981. Task differences and validity of aptitude tests in selection: A red herring. *Journal of Applied Psychology* 66:166–85.

Society for Industrial and Organizational Psychology, Inc. 1987. *Principles for the validation and use of personnel selection procedures.* 3d ed. College Park, MD.: Author.

Tenopyr, M. 1985. *Test and testify: Can we put an end to it?* Invited address to the Society for Industrial and Organizational Psychology, Professional Practice Award Winner, Los Angeles, August.

Thayer, P. W. 1977. Somethings old, somethings new. *Personnel Psychology* 30: 513–24.

Test Scores and Evaluation: The Military as Data

John Sibley Butler

The purpose of this paper is to examine the use of test scores for evaluation within the military. The intellectual roots of such an analysis are grounded in two theoretical traditions: one is the development of bureaucracy and the emergence of rational evaluative criteria; the other is the creation of testing to evaluate individuals working within bureaucracies. Although these two intellectual traditions have been viewed as overlapping, they stand apart and have unique histories.

This paper begins by briefly considering theoretical ideas about the emergence of bureaucracies and testing. As will be seen, the development of testing must be viewed in conjunction with the importance of race and ethnicity in America. I then present examples of testing and evaluation within the military. The first two examples are taken from the experiences of servicemen at military schools, and do not allow us to examine race effects on testing and evaluation. The third example explores the relationship between testing and promotions, perhaps the most important topic for military personnel. This example does allow us to examine the effect of race and testing on evaluations. The paper concludes by drawing the findings together and discussing policy implications.

I. THEORETICAL CONSIDERATIONS

One of the underlying assumptions of sociological analysis is that the social organization of societies has a great impact on the relationships between people. This fundamental assumption led Ferdinand Tonnies (1940) to posit two extreme "idea types" of societies which could guide the study of the relationship between social organizations and human relations. At one end of the continuum was the traditional communal society, or what Tonnies referred to as the *Gemeinschaft*. In these societies (1) the population is small; (2) role specialization or division of labor is limited; (3) social relationships are primary, or personal and emotional; (4) custom and tradition determine the patterns of behavior, and expectations are well defined; (5) the family is the major institution, carrying out duties such as religious training and education; and (6) there is a great deal of homogeneity.

Found at the other end of Tonnies's continuum is the *Gesellschaft* or modern industrial society. This kind of society is characterized by (1) large population; (2) a complex system of division of labor; (3) secondary or transient, impersonal, and unemotional social relationships; (4) the replacement of the family as the primary unit with social institutions (for example, political, educational); (5) the regulation of patterns of behavior by formal and informal laws, even while behavioral expectations are unclear and ill-defined; and (6) diminished unity because the society is heterogeneous and multi-group (Tonnies 1940). In the Gemeinschaft type of society, evaluations are usually based on kinship and other ascriptive criteria. In the Gesellschaft, there is a movement toward the development of "universalistic" criteria, so that kinship ties, or other ascriptive criteria, become less important. Differential knowledge of a given subject matter is considered more important than kinship ties when evaluations are made.

Although we can make the case that modern societies are an interesting mix of Gemeinschaft and Gesellschaft societies, a reading of the scholarly social-science literature reveals that Gesellschaft characteristics are stressed more than those of the Gemeinschaft. This is especially true of the relationship between the evaluative criteria and the distribution of rewards. The goal of bureaucracy is rational efficiency, or the use of the best and shortest method to reach an objective. According to Weber, an ideal bureaucracy has the following traits:

1. *A division of labor.* Activities are assigned to individuals based on expertise. These individuals are held responsible for their work by superiors and are expected to perform at a high level.

2. *A chain of command or hierarchy of authority.* The range of each individual's responsibility and authority is well defined. Each official is responsible to the one above him/her, and each, in turn, is responsible for his/her subordinates.

3. *A body of rules.* There are abstract rules applying not to a specific person but rather to the office itself. The rules specify the relationships between the positions within a bureaucracy. Thus human relations are dictated not by personality but by rules.

4. *Impersonality.* Functions within a bureaucracy must be performed impartially—the equal treatment of all is seen as contributing to efficiency.

5. *Selection based on merit and job tenure.* Selection or promotions to positions are based strictly on the employee's merit. This procedure ensures the competence of workers and the maximization of talent, which affects the selected goal of the bureaucracy. Performance is evaluated by superiors using a number of indicators, and a person may expect to be upwardly mobile as he/she continues a career.

Thus, bureaucratic organizations emphasize evaluating persons according to merit or universalistic standards. But in the world of power struggles and competition between groups, this has often been difficult to accomplish. The central characteristics of Weber's ideal type of bureaucracy have served to guide the development of instruments that would allow evaluations based on merit. Paper-and-pencil testing has emerged as the controversial but established form of evaluation.

It is very difficult to live in our society without taking a test of some kind. Whether utilized as a measure of IQ or a predictor of job performance, the standardized test is imbedded in organizational life. A comprehensive industry has developed around testing. Progression from grade school to professional school is monitored by a series of tests seen as being predictive of some form of excellence. Individuals who score exceptionally well on tests have even established their own organization, MENSA, whose only criterion for membership is IQ score (Eckberg 1979). As I tell my students, grades and testing do not mean anything; they simply have a great impact on determining one's future.

The origin of testing, however, cannot be traced solely to the need to evaluate individuals for promotions within organizations. Instead, it can be traced to a concern with showing that certain groups of people are biologically inferior. Scholars have labeled this literature "scientific racism" (Chase 1977). This "scholarship" bears this name because it sought to show that outcomes associated with certain groups (for example, poverty, social disorganization, unequal treatment) can be traced to the biological traits of individuals in those groups. Of course, throughout the history of humankind, groups have made distinctions between themselves. But it has been argued that most of these distinctions were based on culture rather than biology. For example, the ancient Greeks made a distinction between Greeks and Barbarians. Once an individual possessed the Greek culture, however, distinctions were dropped despite racial background. But scientific racism, which has manifested itself in Europe as well as in the United States, makes the distinctions between groups immutable: if inequality is fixed at birth, then no amount of training or education can change that fact. Scientific racism has an interesting international history, which is not the concern of this paper. For matters of exposition, we are interested in the theoretical issues that surrounded the development of IQ testing in the United States.

Military organizations have stood at the center of social change and policy in America. Taylor (1911) tested his ideas of "scientific management" within military institutions; the groundwork for *Brown v. Board of Education* was laid by the experiences of blacks and whites in the military, as reported by Stouffer and his colleagues (1949). Their contact hypothesis simply showed that under certain conditions, the attitudes of black and white soldiers toward each other improved as they experienced quality contact with each other. Thus perhaps it is not surprising that for more than a half century after intelligence tests were given to 1,726,966 recruits in World War I, educational policies were based on those test results. The results, when viewed from a "scientific" point of view, were shocking. They indicated that "about 75 percent of the [American] population has not sufficient innate [hereditary] capacity for intellectual development to enable it to complete the usual high school course" (Chase 1977, 226).

As the data for the army tests became available to the public, it became obvious that the test was not measuring what psychologists were beginning to call IQ. Overall, those tests showed that (1) there was a positive relationship between education and test scores; (2) regardless of race (black or white), soldiers from states that spent the least amount per capita on education scored the lowest; (3) the longer a foreign-born soldier had lived in the United States, the higher was his IQ test score; and (4) because the tests were written and administered in English, immigrants from England, Scotland, and other English-speaking countries did better than soldiers who had learned English as adults (Chase 1977, 227). Given these conclusions, one would think that the developing issue of innate intelligence would be laid to rest. As Chase notes:

> In short, what the Army intelligence tests—like the civilian IQ tests written by precisely the same psychologists—measured were not genetic mental levels, but, rather, the degrees to which the genotypic intellectual potentialities of 1,726,966 individual draftees developed in continuing interaction with the entire spectrum of widely varying psychological, nutritional, hygienic, emotional, cultural, climatic, socioeconomic, and thousands of other factors that make up the total environment in which every individual fetus and child grows and develops. Whatever else it proves to be, intelligence, or whatever is actually measured by the IQ tests, is not a genotype—like species or eye color—but a phenotype, like height, weight, or health. (p. 227)

The data from the army tests should have resolved the issue of racial differences in IQ due to testing. As shown by table 1, blacks from the North clearly had higher IQ's than whites from the South.

TABLE 1
Scores on Army IQ Tests of Southern Whites and Northern Blacks (by State)

Whites		Blacks	
State	Median Score	State	Median Score
Mississippi	41.25	Pennsylvania	42.00
Kentucky	41.50	New York	45.02
Arkansas	41.55	Illinois	47.35
Georgia	42.12	Ohio	49.50

Source: Chase (1977).

But the results of the army tests did not put the IQ issue to rest. For nested within the "scientific measurement" of IQ was also the issue of which racial and ethnic groups were suitable to occupy America or receive the rewards of its massive frontiers. Buried deep within European thought was the idea that Northern Europeans were superior to all other groups. Herbert Spencer, among others, argued that Northern Europeans were biologically superior to Southern Europeans. Sir Francis Galton had argued similarly. But it was Alfred Binet who coined the term "intelligence quotient." In 1912 William Stern suggested that when the mental age (MA) was divided by the chronological age (CA) of the person tested, and multiplied by 100, the result could be considered the IQ. Intelligence could now be presented in mathematical terms, and society had a very scientific-looking formula that purported to represent accurately the innate intellectual capacity of human beings (Chase 1977, 232).

The very scientific formula was applied to the study of race and ethnicity in America. In 1917, Henry Goddard, studying immigrants on Ellis Island, brought "scientific" backing to the idea that Northern Europeans were superior to Southern Europeans. Goddard found that 83 percent of all Jews are feebleminded and 79 percent of all Italians are morons.

In 1923 Carl Brigham, a psychologist from Princeton who would later help develop college entrance tests, completed an analysis on the intellectual inferiority of immigrant groups. His analysis concluded that the average scores for foreign-born draftees ranged from highs of 14.87 for Scottish draftees, to an overall average of 13.77 for white draftees, to lows of 10.74 for Polish draftees and 11.01 for Italian draftees (Feagin 1979, 113).

As European groups became assimilated into American society and had the same cultural experiences, the biological explanations popular during the early part of the century became less important. The debate would emerge again in the 1960s, when blacks began to argue for full participation in American society. It is sufficient to say that while the groups involved in the analysis changed, the arguments remained the same. Arthur Jensen's well-known article, "How Much Can We Boost IQ and Scholastic Achievement?" (1969), became the central work in the reemergence of issues involving race and IQ.

Although testing has become a universalistic standard for the measurement of personnel in organizations, its origins lay in the field of ethnicity and race. Put another way, the "scientific" measures designed to show the biological inequality of groups have become the measures of excellence for present-day America. Although the examinations themselves are standardized, the American experience continues to vary by economic background, region, race, and ethnicity. But the reality of testing must be confronted; how do tests help to evaluate personnel in organizations? At this time we turn to examples from the military experience.

II. TESTING AND EVALUATIONS WITHIN MILITARY ORGANIZATIONS: THE LITERATURE AS DATA

The literature on testing within military organizations stems from two sources. The military itself conducts hundreds of "in-house" studies, which serve as valuable tools for the evaluation of personnel. Since these studies are done within the establishment, they are less likely to circulate among practicing scholars of military organizations. The other source of literature is researchers who publish in academic journals. In this paper we have chosen significant studies from both these sources.

Mental Qualifications for Participation

Since World War II, the military services have established minimum passing scores on psychological tests to qualify for service. This procedure stems from the fact that a rapid method of mass screening is necessary to evaluate individuals' usefulness within the military. Since 1950, the standard method of testing has been the Armed Forces Qualification Test (AFQT). This test is composed of one hundred questions divided equally among four areas: (1) vocabulary, (2) mathematics, (3) spatial relations, and (4) mechanical ability. As on most standardized tests, the scores on the AFQT are normally expressed as percentiles. As established originally by the World War II testing experience, a percentile score of 10 represents the score that would be attained or exceeded by 90 percent of the standard population. Although categories have changed over the years, for purposes of qualitative allocation of new entrants, broad mental group categories were established in 1951 as follows:

Mental Group	Percentile Score
I	93–100
II	65–92
III	31–44
IV	10–30
V	9 and below

Mental groups I and II contain individuals who are considered above average; groups IV and V, below average; and group III, average (Department of Defense 1972).

The military services have also used a set of battery tests during initial selection and occupational classification of personnel. Especially before the All-Volunteer force, these tests were important because they were used to predict the success of individuals in various occupational areas. The battery tests were also used during this period as a supplementary device to screen draftees who received marginal passing scores on the AFQT, such as those in mental group IV.

Over the years, Congress has changed the standards for entrance into military service. For example, in the late 1950s and early 1960s, the raising of mental test standards was justified on the grounds that the services were becoming more technical. It was also noted that individuals in mental group IV accounted for a disproportionate share of disciplinary problems. But raising standards became problematic. Consider the following analysis:

> These relatively high qualification standards were, however, subject to criticism for several reasons. They were inevitably accompanied by a sharp increase in rejection rates from an estimated overall rejection rate of about 25 percent, during the Korean war period, to 35 percent in 1963. . . . In turn, the high rejection rates were subject to intermittent criticism on the grounds that they were incompatible with the principle that the military service obligation should be shared as widely as possible among youth of military age. (Department of Defense 1972, 42)

The important point is that during the years following World War II, although testing was used, the procedure developed a history of criticism. In addition to the concern cited above, that individuals in certain age groups would not serve their country, there were also criticisms about what the tests were measuring. Again, consider the following comments:

> The fact that the psychological tests are written tests, whose results depend substantially upon verbal skills and acquired knowledge, led some critics to question the inherent validity of these tests when applied to youth from deprived backgrounds. The tests, it was alleged, were geared primarily to measuring success in a formal classroom situation rather than to measuring other qualities, such as motivation, courage, manual dexterity and innate practical intelligence—qualities which are, perhaps, even more important in actual performance of enlisted personnel, particularly in combat and other non-technical duties. The contention that low test scores were necessarily predictive of high disciplinary problems was also found to be questionable as a result of more recent research which indicated—for example— that the fact of high school graduation was a much more reliable predictor of future adjustment to military life than mental test scores, as such. (Department of Defense 1972, 44)

Based on these considerations, the military began to consider other standards for acceptance. The most celebrated program was "Project One Hundred Thousand," which was initiated in August 1966. Under this program, Secretary of Defense McNamara announced a plan, which would begin in

October 1966, to accept in a twelve-month period forty thousand men and women who would not previously have qualified for service. In each succeeding year, one hundred thousand such registrants would be accepted. To accomplish this, the supplementary aptitude-test standards were waived for draft registrants in mental group IV who were high school graduates, as well as for those who were not high school graduates, but had AFQT scores of 21 or higher. The effect of these revised standards was to lower the overall rejection rate for draft-age men from an estimated 35 percent in 1964 to about 28 percent in 1967—the lowest since the mid-1950s (Department of Defense 1972, 44).

One can see that although the military services began to rely on testing to evaluate personnel, the rules have been renegotiated several times. The important point is that realities of manpower shortages can take precedence over the evaluative powers of testing. It is also important to note that studies were beginning to show that other factors, especially a high school diploma, were better predictors of success within military organizations than the results of tests themselves. But standardized testing remained a practical, quick way for the military to evaluate the quality of personnel.

Today the quality of the All-Volunteer force is judged exclusively by test results. As noted by Nelson (1986), the term "quality" has come to mean the attributes the individual brings into military service rather than performance measures while in military service. The research on quality in the All-Volunteer force shows that mental levels are being filled and that by all other measures (for example, attrition, reenlistment, and so on), the All-Volunteer force is measuring up. While quality is an interesting question in itself, we move to our major concern, the relationship between measurements of quality and performance.

Testing and Performance: A Case Study from the Air Force

One of the most interesting studies done within the military research system examined the relationship between Air Force Officer Qualifying Test scores (AFOQT) and success in air weapons controller training (Finegold and Rogers 1985). The primary purpose of the study was to develop a selection strategy based on the AFQT for the air weapons controller Air Force Specialty career field. Nested within this primary objective were the following secondary concerns:

1. To investigate relationships between AFQT composites and various measures of training success.

2. To determine training performance differences attributable to background and bio-demographic factors.

3. To document current aptitude levels of personnel assigned to this career field (Finegold and Rogers 1985, 1).

This research was done because of concern over the attrition rates at the five air weapons controller training schools for the years 1980 to 1982. Finegold and Rogers found that these rates differ for each school and range from a low of 0 percent to a high of 41 percent. It is interesting to note, however, that the rates increased for the three-year period covered, especially for what the air force considers important courses.

Of course, attrition also means additional costs. Finegold and Rogers estimated that attrition cost the air force between $2.3 and $4.6 million in wasted training. With these data, it was necessary to develop a procedure to ensure that the attrition rate decreased significantly.

To perform their research, Finegold and Rogers examined questionnaire data on 1,465 students, or about 79 percent of all students trained during the period of data collection. The questionnaire contained data on the students' course completion; from the AFOQT data base the authors selected percentile scores on the students' Academic Aptitude, Verbal, and Quantitative composites. Out of the original sample of 1,465 questionnaires received, Finegold and Rogers used a total of 968 (66 percent) in their analysis.

The authors first checked to see if AFOQT scores correlated with student performance in the five air weapons controller training organizations. As can be seen from table 2, the authors found a significant correlation between AFOQT composite scores and student performance. All five of the areas examined (pilot, technical, aptitude, verbal, and quantitative) were positively correlated with the performance criteria at the .01 level of significance. Thus all of the AFOQT composites were successful in predicting student performance.

Finegold and Rogers also showed the relationship between AFOQT and success or failure in training: "Students who failed to complete their training had lower scores on the AFOQT Academic Aptitude composite than those who completed their training. . . . Below the 35th percentile, there were more attritions than completions, while above the 60th percentile the reverse is true" (1986, 5).

Based on their data, the authors recommended that a minimum selection criterion, using the AFOQT Academic Aptitude composite, be implemented. This research shows that testing was successful in predicting performance within military organizations. In this research there were no race effects; to the extent that blacks were in the sample, there were no significant differences between their test scores and those of whites.

TABLE 2

Correlation of AFOQT Scores with AFSC 1741 Training
Performance Data—Total Group Input

Criteria	Pilot	Navigator-Technical	Academic Aptitude	Verbal	Quanti-tative	Mean	SD	N
Academic Grade	.228[b]	.284[b]	.352[b]	.280[b]	.329[b]	93.90	4.82	1,186
Success[a]	.191[b]	.230[b]	.263[b]	.214[b]	.256[b]	.9154	.289	1,453
Student Class Rank	.280[b]	.392[b]	.384[b]	.311[b]	.378[b]	.5097	.291	941

Source: Finegold and Rogers (1986).
Note: Average training costs per student were reported by Headquarters Air Training Command and Headquarters Tactical Air Command. For estimation purposes, it was assumed that attritions averaged completion of half the training program. Therefore, the estimated FY82 attrition cost per student is one-half the training costs. The minimum estimated course attrition cost is the student cost multiplied by the number of attritions for the course. The maximum estimated course attrition cost includes the full cost of previous training and assumes the student was trained for a manual system (E30BP-1741-A003) and transitioned to an automatic system (1741B00).

[a] Success was coded 0=FAIL, 1=PASS

[b] Significant at .01 level.

Testing and Target Shooting: Tankers as Data

It is quite easy to assess the relationship between standardized test taking and completing a training block. It is much more difficult, however, to measure the effects of testing on everyday activities of soldiers, such as target shooting, the ability to stick with a problem, and creativity in the field. In an innovative project, Scribner, Smith, Baldwin, and Phillips (1986) designed a model that attempted to look at the relationship between the AFQT and military productivity. Productivity was measured by the ability of tankers to hit a target. As in the AFOQT example, race effects were not considered.

The authors obtained their data from tank-crew firing exercises at the Seventh Army Training Center in Germany. There were 1,131 crews equipped with M-60 series and M-1 tanks. What is referred to as the "tank table" had a total of thirteen engagements, seven during the day and six at night.

Each engagement, equally valued at 100 raw points, included the two targets (except for the last daytime engagement) that consisted of different combinations of main gun and machine gun targets. Some were engaged while the tank was on the move; additionally, several were moving targets. Distance to and location of the targets on the tank range varied between engagements. Mechanical devices raised and lowered the targets so that the tank crew was not aware when and where each target was exposed before each engagement actually began. The targets were scored by Corps evaluation teams (trained by the training center), sensing tanks, audio recordings, TOW sights, and a computer scoring unit. Data were collected on individual crew members so that their firing data could be matched to the enlisted master file, which contained their biographic and demographic information. (Scribner et al. 1986, 195)

The authors were aware of the importance of variables like experience and role playing. Considering these variables, they boldly stated their expectations:

We may hypothesize several potentially important factors that will determine the score a tank crew obtains. Quite plausibly, military experience and time in position in the tank crew could play important roles. We expect that the more experience a tanker has, the better he or she can do the job. Similarly, we expect that tankers who have been in the same crew position on the same tank for an extended period would perform better than those with less crew assignment stability. Additionally, the claim is made that crew quality, as defined by AFQT score or civilian education level, could influence crew performance, with higher mental category individuals outperforming their lower mental category counterparts. The theoretical justification for including this variable is that smarter individuals, on average, are better able to cope with the pressures associated with operating a complex weapon system under severe time constraints. (Scribner et al. 1986, 195)

These authors found that there is a relationship between AFQT and "tank kills" (see table 3). Category I soldiers did significantly better than soldiers in other categories.

TABLE 3

Percentage of Increase in Tank Equivalent Kills By Mental Category

Type of Tank	Gunner and Tank Crew Mental Category				
	I	II	IIIA	IIIB	IV
M-60	75.17%	62.84%	45.9%	27.9%	BASE
M-1	18.9%	16.3%	12.4%	8.0%	CASE

Source: Scribner, Smith, Baldwin, and Phillips (1986).

The two examples above are interesting in that they show a relationship between testing and performance based on education and experience within the military. Within this area in the military, there has traditionally been little conflict in terms of race and evaluation. It is in the area of promotions, the backbone of the military career, where the importance of race effects have been noticed. We now turn to an examination of the relationship between testing and promotions.

Testing and Promotion Time: Evidence from the Army Enlisted Ranks

Perhaps the most important relationship in this area of study is the impact of testing on promotions. In all organizations, whether military or civilian, members look forward to upward mobility. Within the military, because higher rank is associated with increased power, prestige, pay, and better housing, the process is perhaps more important. Although this is true, only one study has examined the relationship between testing and promotions (Butler 1976) within military institutions. This section will systematically examine this study for three reasons. First, the study allows comparisons within and between races of the relationships between testing and promotions. Second, the study contains controls for significant variables such as education and occupational type. Third, the Department of Defense initiated the replication of the study in 1986. Although the study has not been officially released, I feel free to comment on how its findings deviate from or converge with my original work. The discussion below follows the presentation of the data that appeared in the *American Sociological Review* (Butler 1976).

Data in my study were generated from the Enlisted Master Tape Record (EMTR) in order to meet the requirements of Army Contract number DAHC19-73-C-0037. The research was funded by the U.S. Army Research Institute for the Behavioral and Social Sciences. The EMTR, which is located at the Pentagon, is a personnel data base file for army enlisted personnel on active duty,[1] except for those on active duty for training. The data used reflect

---

[1] The EMTR consists of three subsystems:
 1. Weekly Edit: checks the validity of field and Department of the Army level input. Notification of errors are forwarded to the field for evaluation.
 2. Weekly Update: posts the input data that has passed the edit to the master file and provides notices and errors to the field.
 3. Monthly Report Tapes: update organizational data from the Deputy Chief of Staff for Military Operations Organizational Master File and prepare output report tapes tailored to the requirements of the personnel and manpower-management information systems.
Input for the system is generated from several sources:
 1. Transactions from the field are submitted in accordance with Army Regulation 680-200. Most of these transactions originate from the unit morning reports

the entire population of the enlisted force for the year 1973; thus there were no sampling considerations.[2]

The procedure used in the paper is simple cross tabulation.[3] The dependent variable is "months in service to make current grade". This variable is defined as the time that it took an individual to be promoted to his present grade from the time of entrance into the army. This variable was created from the EMTR code book by subtracting the variable "basic active service (the date of service entry)" from the variable "date of grade (the date that a person made his last grade)." The data were converted to Julian dates.

The control variables used are civilian education, AFQT, and military occupational specialty (MOS). Civilian education is trichotomized as follows: low

---

or personnel data change report. A copy of these reports is forwarded to the Department of the Army for coding, keypunching, and processing.

2. Tape input is provided from the Trainee Control System.

3. Official changes of name and social security account number are furnished by U.S. Army Personnel Services Support Center, Fort Benjamin Harrison, Indiana.

4. Promotions of Senior Enlisted Personnel generated from the Department of the Army Centralized Promotion system.

The Enlisted Master Tape Record is scheduled to run once a week. This is to look for edit errors, which are divided into three classes:

1. Essential errors on control fields which indicate the transactions may not be the files' input.

2. Essential errors on missing or invalid data, without which the transaction cannot be updated, are checked.

3. Nonessential errors on miscellaneous data items, which do not stop processing of the transaction, are also checked.

This tape system is scheduled to be updated each Friday. Each update is approximately nine days behind the calendar day of the transactions, that is, the update of the ninth work day would process transactions through the last day of the previous month. Thus the month-end status of the entire enlisted population of the army is available for personnel and manpower management reports approximately ten working days following the receipt of month-end traffic (that is, approximately the middle of the following month).

The data thus reflect the attributes of personnel on active duty. When personnel depart from the army, their records are pulled from the active file. Thus if a person entered the army in 1971 and was released in 1974, his or her records are not on active file.

[2]   The total number of records processed (for enlisted men in grades E4 through E9) was 433,845; for blacks N = 76,643, and for whites N = 357,202.

[3]   The raw data were not made available. The entire question of blacks' inequality in the military is a somewhat touchy subject. To fulfill the contract, a "dummy" cross-tabulation table was presented to army personnel at the Pentagon.

education (less than twelve years of formal education); medium education (high school graduation); and high education (some college or a college degree plus). As discussed earlier, the AFQT is a universalistic criteria examination used by the army to measure or assess the mental capacities of incoming personnel, who score a percentile rank on the examination. In the EMTR code book, scores of individuals are broken down by mental groups and appear as follows: mental group I, AFQT = 93–100; mental group II, AFQT = 65–92; mental group III, AFQT = 31–64; mental group IV, AFQT = 10–30; and mental group V, AFQT = 01–09.

For the purpose of the larger project, because of cost-related factors, the major interest was to dichotomize mental groups into high and low. Therefore appointments were made with personnel at the Pentagon who knew about the AFQT's impact on the careers of service personnel. It was learned that those personnel who score in mental groups I and II were thought more likely to have a successful army career. From these series of meetings, data on the AFQT were recoded as high AFQT = 65–100 and low AFQT = 01–64. There were some personnel who entered the service before the AFQT was used (those would be in the E9 category). These personnel were placed in the high AFQT category. MOS, following army tradition, is dichotomized as technical and nontechnical.[4] The enlisted MOS classification guide (AR 611-201) was used.

The entire analysis is concerned with the difference between the mean (X) number of months in service that it took blacks and whites to make a certain grade. Usually when the researcher deals with the difference between means, a summary statistic is used for significance purposes, that is, student's "t" or some form of analysis of variance. This paper does not report levels of significance since the entire population is used. Thus we are not interested in estimating parameters; the N's are very large. To engage in reporting tests of significance would be merely academic.

The analysis also groups certain grades together. Thus we will be looking at the average time that it took blacks and whites to reach grades E5 and E6. Some may argue that this grouping of ranks may serve to distort the findings. To a certain extent this is true. But the research has already shown, as noted earlier, that blacks are disproportionately represented in lower grades. It is also true that promotion time between grades is shorter at the lower ranks (that is, it takes individuals less time to move from E4 to E5 than it takes them to move from E7 to E8). Since this is true, it follows that the grouping together of ranks, or the aggregate effect, would actually hide inequality vis-à-vis blacks. That is, if there are any distortions in the data, they would actually bring blacks and

---

[4] Technical occupations are defined as those requiring extensive training that cannot be acquired on the job. Examples are X-ray technicians and computer programmers. Nontechnical occupations are those that do not require extensive training and can be learned on the job. Examples are cooks and water-supply specialists.

whites closer together, when considering months in service to make current grade, rather than pulling them farther apart.

The data are presented in serial fashion, one grade at a time. First the effect of each control variable will be assessed vis-à-vis the dependent variable; then the combined effect of the control variables will be considered. The analysis will begin with the time it took blacks and whites to make E4. This is the starting point of the analysis because, at the time of data collection, personnel entered the service at E1, for the most part, were awarded E2 upon completion of basic training, and were awarded E3 upon completion of advanced individual training. Thus at the time of data collection, the ranks E1 through E3 were somewhat "automatic," awarded upon entry and after completion of training periods that prepare soldiers for permanent duty in the army.

Findings

We begin the analysis by looking at the mean number of months in service it took blacks and whites to make their current grades, irrespective of their background characteristics (table 4). The data reveal that blacks took nineteen months in service to make E4 and whites took fifteen months to make the same grade. Likewise, the mean number of months to make E5 to E6 was sixty-eight for blacks, and fifty-nine for whites. This pattern remains unchanged for months in service to make E7 to E9.

TABLE 4

Mean (X) Months in Service to Make Grades E4, E5-E6, E7-E9 Without Controls by Race*

Grade(s)	Blacks		Whites	
E4	19	(18,673)	15	(107,949)
E5-E6	68	(30,046)	59	(112,212)
E7-E9	173	(11,152)	169	(47,179)

*N presented in parentheses; months rounded to nearest whole.
Source: Butler (1976).

Table 5 presents the effect of the first control variable to be considered, AFQT. One would expect that blacks and whites who scored in mental groups I and II (the two highest groups) would move faster through the ranks than those who scored in the lower mental groups. Furthermore, no matter what the mental group, one would expect that, based on the universalistic standard argument, blacks and whites matched on those mental groups would move at the same pace. But when we concentrate on grade E4 (table 5), it took blacks who scored in the low AFQT mental category eighteen months to make that grade. On the other hand, it took whites sixteen months to make E4. Blacks who scored high in the high AFQT mental category took twenty-three months to make E4, compared to fourteen months for whites in the same category. Especially noteworthy is that when we compare within race, blacks who scored in the AFQT low mental group took less time (eighteen months) to make E4 than blacks who scored in the high mental group (twenty-three months). But this does not hold true for whites at the E4 grade. Whites who scored in the high AFQT mental group took fourteen months to make E4; whites in the low AFQT mental group took sixteen months to make E4. Put another way, "smart" whites (as measured by the AFQT) moved faster than "dumb" whites; but "dumb" blacks moved faster than "smart" blacks. And even more interesting, "dumb" whites moved faster than "smart" blacks to achieve the E4 grade.

TABLE 5
Mean (X) Months in Service to Make Grades E4, E5-E6, E7-E9, Controlling for AFQT Mental Groups by Race*

	Blacks		Whites	
Grades	AFQT Low	AFQT High	AFQT Low	AFQT High
E4	18 (17,016)	23 (1,657)	16 (63,581)	14 (44,368)
E5-E6	60 (22,950)	93 (7,096)	57 (60,048)	62 (52,164)
E7-E9	165 (5,841)	181 (5,311)	161 (16,731)	173 (30,448)

*N presented in parentheses; months rounded to nearest whole.
Source: Butler (1976).

When one looks at the effect of AFQT on attaining grades E5 to E6 and E7 to E9, a similar pattern emerges. When blacks and whites are matched on AFQT category, whites took less time to make those grades. But it is interesting to note that in some cases "smart" blacks and whites took more time to make their grades than "dumb" blacks and whites, an anomaly to which we will return later. But the overall matching of blacks and whites on AFQT category never rendered zero difference.

When controlling for different educational levels, blacks overall took more time to make their present grade(s) (table 6). For example, blacks with low education took twenty-one months to make E4 and whites with low education took seventeen months. In the E4 and E5 to E6 grades, blacks with high education took more time to make grade than their white counterparts. But whites with medium education took the same amount of time to make E4 as blacks with high education. A welcome finding (if I might add) develops when E7 to E9 is considered. Although whites took less time to make rank in the low and medium education categories, blacks and whites took the same average amount of time to make E7 to E9 in the high education category. Put another way, blacks and whites with the same educational level moved through the ranks in an equivalent way. Thus the variable of high education renders no difference between blacks and whites at the E7 to E9 grade.

TABLE 6

Mean (X) Months in Service to Make Grade(s) E4, E5-E6, E7-E9, Controlling for Education by Race*

| | Blacks | | | Whites | | |
| | Level of Education | | | Level of Education | | |
Grade(s)	Low	Medium	High	Low	Medium	High
E4	21 (4,848)	18 (11,626)	15 (2,199)	17 (29,668)	15 (59,586)	12 (18,695)
E5-E6	66 (7,971)	70 (19,333)	56 (2,742)	56 (30,222)	65 (66,921)	41 (15,069)
E7-E9	168 (1,334)	173 (8,341)	173 (1,477)	163 (5,112)	169 (35,947)	173 (6,120)

*N presented in parentheses; months rounded to nearest whole.
Source: Butler (1976).

The final control variable to be considered is military occupational type. Proceeding with our logic presented thus far, one would expect that personnel in technical occupations would move faster than personnel in nontechnical occupations. And, of course, for all categories blacks and whites should move at the same pace when matched.

Table 7 reveals that to make E4, blacks in technical occupations took seventeen months, while whites in the same occupations took fourteen months. The same pattern holds for grades E5 to E6. But in the E7 to E9 category, blacks and whites in technical occupations took the same amount of time. Thus we have two variables, high education and technical occupation, which render no difference between blacks and whites in months of service to make grade.

TABLE 7

Mean (X) Months in Service to Make Grade(s) E4, E5-E6, E7-E9, Controlling for Occupational Type by Race*

	Blacks		Whites	
	Technical Occupation	Nontechnical Occupation	Technical Occupation	Nontechnical Occupation
E4	17 (5,388)	19 (113,285)	14 (36,047)	16 (71,004)
E5-E6	66 (9,735)	68 (20,311)	56 (45,946)	62 (66,266)
E7-E9	165 (4,033)	177 (7,119)	165 (18,756)	172 (28,423)

* N presented in parentheses; months rounded to nearest whole.
Source: Butler (1976).

At this time we will look at the combined effects of our control variable on "months in service to make current grade." Our major concern remains the same: Are there systematic differences between blacks and whites? In order to answer this, we will use simple cross tabulation.

Tables 8-A and 8-B concern blacks and whites in nontechnical and technical military occupations respectively, concentrating on months in service to make E4. The figures show the combined effect on promotion of occupational type, AFQT, and education. Table 8-A shows that within AFQT level, when comparisons are made within race, a similar pattern emerges for both blacks and whites: the higher the civilian education level, the less time it took to make E4. For example, blacks with a low AFQT score and a medium education level took eighteen months to make E4. Blacks with a low AFQT score and a high education level took fifteen months to make that grade. For blacks in the high AFQT category, those with a low education level took twenty-eight months to make E4, and those with a high education level took seventeen months to make E4.

When one makes comparisons within educational levels (table 8-A), an interesting phenomenon emerges. Within educational levels, blacks took longer to make E4 if they had high AFQT scores. For example, blacks in the low education and AFQT categories took twenty-one months to make E4. Blacks in the low education category, who were also in the high AFQT category, took twenty-eight months to make E4; for blacks this pattern is consistent. But for whites, within educational levels, AFQT makes no difference in months to make grade. For example, whites with medium education and low AFQT scores took sixteen months to make E4. Whites with medium education and high AFQT scores also took sixteen months to make E4.

TABLE 8-A

Mean (X) Months in Service to Make E4, Controlling for Nontechnical Occupational Type, AFQT, Education, and Race*

	Blacks Level of Education			Whites Level of Education		
	Low	Medium	High	Low	Medium	High
AFQT Low	21 (3,437)	18 (7,712)	15 (1,137)	18 (17,377)	16 (24,585)	13 (3,561)
AFQT High	28 (208)	26 (598)	17 (193)	17 (4,404)	16 (14,363)	13 (6,714)

*N presented in parentheses; months rounded to nearest whole.
Source: Butler (1976).

The important comparisons the reader should notice in table 8-A are those between races. Whenever blacks and whites matched on the same variables, blacks took more time to make E4. Blacks in nontechnical occupations who scored in the low AFQT category and had a low level of education took twenty-one months to make E4. Whites with the same attributes took eighteen months to make E4. Likewise, blacks in nontechnical occupations who scored in the high AFQT category and had a high level of education took seventeen months to make E4. Whites with the same attributes took thirteen months to make E4. This pattern remains consistent throughout table 8-A.

Another interesting comparison in table 8-A is between blacks who are "high" on AFQT and education, and whites who are "low" on AFQT and education. Blacks in nontechnical occupations who are in the high AFQT category and have a high level of education took seventeen months to make E4. Whites in nontechnical occupations who are in the low AFQT category and have a low level of education took eighteen months to make E4. This is almost the same amount of time that it took blacks with high AFQT and education to make E4. But blacks in nontechnical occupations with low AFQT and education took 21 months to make E4; whites, however, with high AFQT and education took 13 months to make E4.

Table 8-B, as noted above, presents blacks and whites in technical occupations who made E4. The same general patterns seen in table 8-A emerge in this table. Within AFQT levels, when comparisons are made within race, the higher the educational level, the less time it took blacks and whites to make E4. Also, as before, with educational levels (when comparisons are made within race), AFQT level seems to make a difference for blacks, when months in service to make E4 is of concern, but not for whites. Blacks with a low education and high AFQT took twenty-eight months to make E4. But whites with low education and low AFQT took sixteen months to make E4; whites with a low education and high AFQT took fifteen months to make E4. This is a difference of only one month. But the important comparison in table 8-B is that when blacks and whites are matched on the same variables, blacks in technical occupations always took more time to make E4 than whites in technical occupations.

TABLE 8-B

Mean (X) Months in Service to Make E4, Controlling for Technical Occupational Type, AFQT, Education, and Race*

	Blacks Level of Education			Whites Level of Education		
	Low	Medium	High	Low	Medium	High
AFQT Low	18 (1,115)	17 (2,934)	15 (681)	16 (5,765)	15 (10,342)	13 (1,951)
AFQT High	28 (88)	20 (328)	15 (188)	15 (2,122)	14 (12,296)	12 (6,469)

*N presented in parentheses; months rounded to nearest whole.
Source: Butler (1976).

Tables 9-A and 9-B concentrate on the combined effects of the control variables on months in service to make E5 and E6 for black and white enlisted men. Table 9-A, which represents data for those personnel in nontechnical occupations, shows that the overall pattern shown above still exists. Although these overall patterns exist, it is interesting to note the "medium education-AFQT low" cell for blacks and whites. Readers may recall that the data revealed that within AFQT levels (when comparisons are made within race), the higher the education level, the less time it took both blacks and whites to make grade. Table 9-A shows that in terms of this type of pattern, "medium education" is "out of line." For those blacks and whites with a medium level of education, more time was taken to make E5 and E6 than those with a low level of education. But again, over all, when comparisons are made between blacks and whites within the same cells (for both tables 9-A and 9-B), blacks took more time to make E5 and E6.

TABLE 9-A

Mean (X) Months in Service to Make E5 and E6, Controlling for Nontechnical Occupational Type, AFQT, Education, and Race*

	Blacks			Whites		
	Level of Education			Level of Education		
	Low	Medium	High	Low	Medium	High
AFQT	59	62	50	54	64	46
Low	(4,652)	(9,921)	(1,195)	(15,680)	(21,417)	(2,244)
AFQT	94	99	82	68	72	42
High	(1,258)	(2,933)	(352)	(5,546)	(17,007)	(4,372)

*N presented in parentheses; months rounded to nearest whole.
Source: Butler (1976).

TABLE 9-B

Mean (X) Months in Service to Make E5 and E6, Controlling for Technical Occupational Type, AFQT, Education, and Race*

	Blacks			Whites		
	Level of Education			Level of Education		
	Low	Medium	High	Low	Medium	High
AFQT	60	60	49	50	59	42
Low	(1,594)	(4,749)	(893)	(5,784)	(12,911)	(2,012)
AFQT	87	91	68	60	64	38
High	(467)	(1,730)	(356)	(3,212)	(15,586)	(6,441)

*N presented in parentheses; months rounded to nearest whole.
Source: Butler (1976).

Tables 10-A and 10-B present data for months in service to make E7 through E9. As before, table 10-A concentrates on those in nontechnical occupations and table 10-B on those in technical occupations. Both tables reveal that the patterns of inequality still persist. For example, blacks in nontechnical occupations who scored in the high AFQT category and had a medium education (table 10-A) took 187 months to make E7 through E9. Whites with the same attributes took 177 months. Blacks in technical occupations (table 10-B) who scored in the low AFQT category and had a medium education took 160 months to make E7 through E9. Whites with the same attributes took 157 months. There is, however, an exception to the case in table 10-B: blacks who scored in the low AFQT category and had a high education level took less time to make E7 through E9 than whites with the same attributes. Respectively, blacks took 153 months to make those grades while whites took 159 months. But the overall pattern of inequality remains consistent.

TABLE 10-A

Mean (X) Months in Service to Make E7 Through E9, Controlling for Nontechnical Occupational Type, AFQT, Education, and Race*

| | Blacks | | | Whites | | |
| | Level of Education | | | Level of Education | | |
	Low	Medium	High	Low	Medium	High
AFQT	160	170	168	157	165	165
Low	(486)	(2,884)	(405)	(1,432)	(8,992)	(695)
AFQT	177	187	190	171	177	180
High	(417)	(2,510)	(417)	(1,852	(13,027)	(2,425)

*N presented in parentheses; months rounded to nearest whole.
Source: Butler (1976).

TABLE 10-B

Mean (X) Months in Service to Make E7 through E9, Controlling for Technical Occupational Type, AFQT, Education, and Race*

| | Blacks | | | Whites | | |
| | Level of Education | | | Level of Education | | |
	Low	Medium	High	Low	Medium	High
AFQT	154	160	153	153	157	159
Low	(226)	(11,548)	(292)	(645)	(4,422)	(545)
AFQT	173	171	174	165	168	170
High	(205)	(1,399)	(363)	(1,183)	(9,506)	(2,455)

*N presented in parentheses; months rounded to nearest whole.
Source: Butler (1976).

We began this analysis by considering "months in service to make current grade," without the introduction of control variables. This procedure revealed that there were systematic differences between blacks and whites in time to make grade(s). We then introduced control variables, one at a time, to see if they could explain away the differences that were found to exist. This analysis also revealed that blacks consistently took more months in service to make grade(s). When the combined effect of the control variables were considered, the same overall pattern emerged. Thus, we conclude that the introduction of control variables does not alter the pattern of inequality revealed when the analysis did not consider the effect of control variables.

Although blacks consistently took more months in service to make grade(s), some interesting patterns are seen in the data that are anomalous with what would be expected when certain variables were examined. For example, when AFQT was used as a control variable, although blacks were systematically behind whites when comparisons were made between races, blacks who scored in the low AFQT category moved faster than blacks who scored in the high AFQT category. This held true for all ranks and also for whites. Common sense would lead one to expect that personnel in the high AFQT category would move faster than those in the low AFQT category. But this expectation was not realized. One interpretation is that people who scored in the high AFQT category are less likely to conform to army expectations and norms. If this conjecture is accurate, it may also be that within AFQT and educational levels, blacks compared to whites are less susceptible to subservient (or from the army's viewpoint, accommodative) behavior toward superiors. In any event, whether looking at the slower promoted high AFQT categories, or the faster promoted low AFQT categories, black promotion rates consistently lagged behind those of whites.

A second anomaly occurred when the dependent variable of "months in service to make current grade" was explained in terms of the combined effect of all the control variables. One such analysis revealed that within AFQT levels, the higher the educational level, the less time it took both blacks and whites to make their current grades. Although common sense predicts such a linear pattern, this pattern was not realized for the "medium education" cell (high school graduates). When comparisons are made by race within AFQT levels, personnel with a "high education" (some college or more) were promoted faster than those with a "low education" (less than high school), but those with medium education took more time to make their grades than those with a low education. The pattern became curvilinear because of the deviation of the medium education cell.

Because this "deviant" pattern exists, one could ask: What is it about those personnel who have medium education that would explain why they took more time to make grades than those with low education? My interpretation is that personnel who have medium education are not necessarily looking for careers in the army, that is, becoming career soldiers. The fact that these personnel have a high school diploma means that they have other career options. There are jobs in the civilian sector which may be interesting to them. On the other hand, personnel who have not finished high school may feel that they do not have many career options open to them in the civilian sector. Therefore they invest more time in being good soldiers, knowing that the army may be their best career opportunity. Because they invest more time in "soldiering," they are rewarded faster than those with medium education, who, because of alternative career options, do not invest as much time in "soldiering." Given this explanation, one could easily ask: Why is it that personnel with high education progress faster than personnel with low education? It would surely follow that high education personnel have more career opportunities than either low or medium education personnel, and should not work very hard at "soldiering." It is my view that personnel with high education do not work very hard at "soldiering," but rather the army rewards them because it wants to keep them in the army, both because it is easier to train them and because the army wants to attract personnel with college backgrounds.

Another unexpected finding, which is related to the above discussion, is that education appears to be a better predictor of upward mobility in the army than the AFQT. This is interesting because in theory the AFQT is very important in determining not only what type of occupation a person will be assigned, but how successful that person will be during his or her army career. Anyone who has been in the army can recall the words of the sergeant at the Army Entrance Station: "It is very important that you do as well as possible on this (AFQT) test because it will determine your army career." But despite the sergeant's words, and despite the partial deviation of the "medium education" cell, the data reveal that personnel with high education take fewer months in service to make current grades than personnel with high AFQT scores. Indeed it has been shown that both blacks and whites in the high AFQT category generally take more time in service to make grades than those personnel in the low AFQT category. As noted above, those personnel in the high education category take less time to make grade(s) than those in either the low or medium education categories. It is therefore plausible to say that the AFQT is not a good predictor of how well a person will do in the army.

Summary

Using the literature as data, our first two examples looked at the relationship between AFQT scores and performance in school. We saw that there was a relationship between testing and attrition and testing and tank marksmanship. As we consider policy implications based on this type of research, which is growing rapidly within the military, we must keep in mind that it is difficult to measure the "group effect" or what sociologists call "social facts." Put another way, although individuals within the military are evaluated by test, they operate in groups. Let us elaborate on this point.

When we evaluate individuals by testing within the military, the individual is the unit of analysis. We assume that individual attributes, whether psychological or physical, create the outcomes which are observed on evaluative criteria. But it is important to recognize that individuals do things in groups. We cannot assume that individuals who test at a certain level, when placed together, will perform well. Put differently, just as we cannot draw conclusions about individuals based on aggregate data, neither can we draw conclusions about the performance of groups based on individual data. Although the tank study showed a relationship between AFQT scores and the ability to hit a target, we must be aware of the many factors that converge in group dynamics. Although what some refer to as group "chemistry" is difficult to measure, it must be a constant concern for researchers. Let us never forget that the tenet of military service, before the All-Volunteer force, was to take all individuals and mold them into effective participants. This tenet, which was based on the importance of leadership, dictated the training of military personnel for centuries. Perhaps the declining emphasis on leadership and the new importance of management accounts for the fact that testing and evaluation has become such an integral part of contemporary military organizations. Although the convenience of testing will remain a part of the military, scholars should consider carefully those subtle and difficult to measure group factors that have always been important in the military.

This study of the relationship between AFQT and promotions points out that universalistic standards cannot explain the difference within or across race. In 1986 the Department of Defense replicated the results reported in this paper; and the same data patterns emerged. Although this means a convergence with the data presented in 1976, models are being created that examine the conditions under which one would *not* expect differences between black and white promotion time. At this point, the study is still under way. But one can conclude that race should continue to have a significant effect on promotion time to grade, even if new models are created that predict conditions under which equality would exist.

What this means is that we must pay attention to variables that are difficult to measure during the promotion process. When trying to understand performance within military institutions, we must continue to think about means of evaluation to complement testing.

III. DISCUSSION AND CONCLUSION

The purpose of this paper has been to examine the use of test scores for evaluation within the military. We began with a discussion of the movement of societies from a Gemeinschaft to a Gesellschaft. The former is characterized by custom, tradition, and homogeneity. In such a society, evaluations and rewards are based on particularistic characteristics such as family and clan affiliation. The Gesellschaft, or modern society, is characterized by universalistic standards. The complexity of such a society leads to evaluations based on universalistic standards—everyone, regardless of variables such as family, race, or creed, is allowed to compete for a given reward. When this "rational" approach is transferred to organizations, as in Weber's notion of a bureaucracy, the universalistic standards are realized as standardized testing.

In America this rational approach has been used to keep rewards from certain racial and ethnic minorities. In the history of testing, especially when certain groups have been defined as mentally inferior, there has been reliance on the concept of IQ as a reason to deny privileges to certain groups in American society. This was true for immigrants from Southern Europe and for blacks. A tension exists between this aspect of the history of testing, and the fact that standardized tests are one of the fastest and most systematic ways to evaluate individuals.

This paper examined three examples of testing within military organizations. The first two examples, performance in school and performance on a simulated battlefield, showed the ability of testing to predict certain kinds of behavior. These studies contained no race effects. The third example shows the relationship between promotions, testing, and other universalistic standards (for example, education, occupational type) while controlling for race. When race was introduced, it was apparent that universalistic standards, as realized in the test, were not important in predicting promotions. As a matter of fact, in such instances the opposite of what would be expected under a rational organization was realized. For example, blacks who scored high on tests were promoted slower than those who scored low.

Based on the studies presented here, several conclusions can be reached. First, under certain conditions within the military, test scores do predict performance. This is in the rational tradition. Second, when race enters the analysis, then the irrational particularistic model becomes evident. It is important to point out that in the promotion data, the question is not whether blacks are able to make a certain score on a test. Because of the large sample, the data allowed examination of blacks and whites who scored both high and low on tests. One of the traditional questions of testing is the percentage of blacks who are able to score well on a specific test. The preceding analysis went a step further: given that there are blacks who score well on a specific test, how are they evaluated within an organization? It is apparent that in spite of excellent test scores, race enters into the process of evaluation. If organizations are supposed to be rational, policymakers and evaluators should concentrate on making decisions on the basis of universalistic standards rather than on particularistic criteria. In the research on testing, the problem was not so much the test as it was the irrational use of the test, based on race.

REFERENCES

Butler, J. S. 1976. Inequality in the military: An examination of promotion time for black and white enlisted men. *American Sociological Review* 41 (October): 807–818.

Chase, A. 1977. *The legacy of Malthus.* New York: Alfred A. Knopf.

Eckberg, D. L. 1979. *Intelligence and race.* New York: Praeger.

Feagin, J. R. 1979. *Race and ethnic relations.* Englewood Cliffs, N.J.: Prentice-Hall.

Finegold, L., and D. Rogers. 1985. *Relationship between Air Force Officer Qualifying Test scores and success in air weapons controller training.* Brooks Air Force Base, Tx.: Air Force Systems Command.

Jensen, A. How much can we boost IQ and scholastic achievement? *Harvard Educational Review* 39:1–123.

Nelson, G. R. 1986. The supply and quality of first-term enlistees under the all-volunteer force. In *The all-volunteer force after a decade,* ed. W. Bowman, R. Little, and G. T. Sicilia. Elmsford, N.Y.: Pergamon Brassey's International Defence Pubs.

Scribner, B., D. Smith, R. Baldwin, and R. L. Phillips. 1986. Are smart tankers better? AFQT and military productivity. *Armed Forces and Society* 12.2:195–204.

Stouffer, S. A., E. A. Suchman, L. C. Devinney, S. Star, and R. Williams, Jr. 1949. *The American soldier: Adjustment during army life.* Princeton, N.J.: Princeton Univ. Press.

Taylor, F. 1911. *The principles of scientific management.* New York: Harper and Brothers.

Tonnies, F. 1940. *Fundamental concepts of sociology.* New York: American Book Company.

U.S. Department of Defense. 1972. *Report of the Task Force on the Administration of Military Justice.*

Weber, M. 1968. *Economy and society.* New York: Bedminster Press.

Los Angeles Testing Policies

CONFERENCE REMARKS

Raymond C. Fisher

In my remarks, I will describe the City of Los Angeles personnel selection system, not analyze it. By way of background, I was appointed to the Civil Service Commission in 1984 by Mayor Tom Bradley. I was a political science major at the University of California at Santa Barbara and am now a practicing lawyer; I have never done a regression analysis in my life. Nonetheless, it might be useful to you to hear through my lay observations what I have come to appreciate about the civil service and the constraints under which we operate in the Los Angeles city government.

Before I continue, I would like to mention an experience I had the year after I graduated from Stanford Law School while clerking for Judge J. Skelly Wright in the District of Columbia Circuit Court of Appeals. Judge Wright was deciding a discrimination suit, *Hobson v. Hanson*, which challenged the school tracking system in Washington, D.C. You will be delighted to know that we invalidated Carl Hanson's tracking system based largely on our reading of his book. We had no scientific or technical educational training, but we were able to understand Hanson's educational and testing theories, evaluate how they were actually applied in practice, and reach a nonscientific but binding legal conclusion that ability testing and ability grouping in the District of Columbia public schools were an unconstitutional denial of equal protection. You may shudder that laypersons—including a fresh-out-of-law-school lawyer—can make such decisions affecting education testing, but that is the reality of the situation. I thought it was the right decision at the time; I still do. The testing process they used in the District of Columbia tracking system was really a testing process gone wrong. With that as my background, I will now describe the selection system used by the city of Los Angeles.

Los Angeles operates under two major constraints—the Civil Service Commission regulations implementing our city charter and the practical reality of lawsuits. The charter was revised in 1925 and is in effect our constitution. It confers authority and responsibility and limits what we are able to do. The charter has always required job-related examinations. In fact, the language of the charter states that, "Such examination(s) shall be practical in their character and shall relate to those matters which will fairly test the relative capacity of the person(s) examined to discharge the duties of the position to which they seek to be appointed." Somewhat general language, but over the years the civil-service selection system has developed in accordance with this concept.

Although the charter has existed for over eighty years, in the 1930s the city's mayor and personnel director corrupted the personnel system. To remedy the situation, the next mayor appointed new members to the Civil Service Commission, which in turn reformed the personnel-selection process, making it more accountable and more objective. Today we have a highly professional personnel department, which spends a substantial amount of time developing in-house tests.

The other constraint under which we operate is a reality for many employers, both public and private, that is, have you ever been sued, and if so, did you win? Or if you lost, why did you lose? Los Angeles was the defendant in *Contreras v. The City of Los Angeles* and won. The city's validation methodology was challenged, and after the Ninth Circuit Federal Court of Appeals held in our favor, we have adhered to what the court considers to be a valid methodology. This illustrates how court rulings have shaped the personnel policies of many agencies, whose administrators obviously want to avoid lawsuits. Such a perspective is both a constraint and a positive factor for those of us who have to carry out the mandates to engage in proper job selection, affirmative action, and the like.

The City of Los Angeles has approximately fifty thousand employees, including almost ten thousand police and fire personnel and approximately eleven thousand Department of Water and Power employees. The balance of the employees work in our thirty-two other departments. There are eleven hundred classes that cut across the variety of city jobs. On an annual basis, we give over fifty thousand written tests, sixteen thousand interviews, twenty-one hundred performance tests, and twenty-two hundred physical-abilities tests. The candidate pools that we are testing range from ten in the specialized high-level positions to several thousand in the entry-level maintenance or clerical positions.

While we have many entry-level classes, we primarily test for promotions, which again results from charter provisions essentially mandating that we promote from within city service. As a result, the tests developed by the personnel department tend to be content-oriented, specific to the jobs for which we are testing. This is one reason we do not generally use tests created elsewhere. Our test development process, and I refer back to the Ninth Circuit decision that approved this process, involves personnel from operating departments meeting with our job analysts to identify the tasks performed by the incumbents in a particular class, to identify the skills, knowledge, and abilities needed to perform the tasks, and to define the various selection criteria that the personnel department ought to test for in an examination.

Each examination consists of one or more tests, usually a written test and an interview. The written test may be a ranking portion of the examination or a qualifying (pass/fail) test. In both cases the written test is a screening device, requiring candidates to achieve a minimum score in order to be scheduled for the interview. When the examination is completed, each candidate is given an earned score and placed on an eligible list in score order. From this list the personnel department certifies names, according to our "three whole scores" rules, to departments to fill their vacancies.

The "three whole scores" certification system stems from a recent study of the personnel system in the city, and reflects the city's commitment to affirmative action. The process requires each candidate's final score to be rounded to the nearest whole score. This practice results in several names in each score rank. When certifying names to the departments, the personnel department provides the names of all persons within the top three whole scores. Additional whole scores are provided if necessary to reach a minimum of six names. This system has greatly expanded the pool of persons available for appointment, including an increase in the numbers of minorities and women.

The city primarily uses multiple-choice written tests, although for higher level classes we often have essay tests. For example, clerk typist candidates are given a straightforward multiple-choice test covering proofreading, English grammar, and a filing exercise, as well as a performance test of typing ability. As another example, the following question is a sample of the type of questions on our written test for plumbers:

> Horizontal drains must be provided with a clean-out at their
> upper terminals. In addition, each run which is more than 100 feet
> in total length must be provided with a clean-out for each ___ feet
> or fraction thereof. The blank is best filled by:
>
> A. 10
> B. 25
> C. 50
> D. 100

I assume from this question that (1) it presumes knowledge on the part of the test taker; and (2) it focuses on some fundamental plumbing concepts and certainly those specific to Los Angeles.

As for tests at higher levels, the following essay question is a sample from our Senior Recreation Director written test:

Background

> As a Senior Recreation Director, assume you are responsible for a
> large complex recreation center. This center is located in a low
> income area. Historically, the surrounding community has not
> utilized the recreation facilities. The community has been in a
> state of transition and the ethnic composition has substantially
> changed in the last five years. The community is now made up of
> several different and distinct groups, including Asians, Latinos
> and Blacks. Your center has been targeted for special attention.

Your supervisor has made it very clear that the center should become an integral part of the community and that increases are expected in the participation from all groups and the number of recreation programs and center fundraising activities.

Requirements

Prepare a written memorandum to your supervisor outlining your goals for the center. Include in your memo various techniques you would utilize to improve community participation. Also make reference to how you plan to get the community involved in spite of the many language obstacles. Your center does not have a large budget or staff. Outline the types of programs you will offer and how they will be conducted and implemented. Secondly, prepare a news release for the local community newspaper about your first fundraising event.

As this question demonstrates, it takes experience in the field to answer and pass this type of written test. Of course, the written test is not the entire selection process. Prior to taking this test a candidate needs to meet the minimum requirements for the job, which may include experience and/or education. After passing the written test, candidates are evaluated by an interview panel composed of subject-matter experts.

We give examinations for the majority of city positions, including most department heads such as the fire and police chiefs. In fact, in the past we examined for the position of chief of police on a promotional basis only using an essay test and interview. Most recently, however, the examination for chief of police was given on both an open and promotional basis and included an in-basket exercise, an essay test, and a general qualifications interview.

My exposure to the testing process in the city has convinced me that our written tests do seem to fairly identify people with needed job skills. Whether or not they have the effect of screening out qualified applicants who do not read or write well, I do not know. That is something that possibly one could examine. Obviously in all of our experience, the ability to read and communicate is a very effective barrier, in some cases, to passing this kind of test. These same abilities, however, have repeatedly been shown to relate to successful performance in most jobs.

I have indicated that we use multiple-choice and essay questions. We also use management exercises, problem solving, and in-basket tests. These tend to be used at the highest levels such as for chief of police. In addition, we use problem exercises in drafting and engineering examinations. We also give physical-ability tests for those classes that have substantial physical demands, particularly fire, police, and paramedic classes. But again, in each of those categories we are still using written tests and interviews as part of the screening and certification process.

Another critical issue for us is examination security. As I previously discussed, we primarily use content-based tests. Since we rely on the technique of sampling the content areas, it is critical that the actual questions in the test remain unknown until the test is administered. We announce to the entire candidate group which subjects will be examined, but we are very careful to ensure that no candidate has access to the test. Although we use subject-matter experts to assist us in test development, the final test is not reviewed by the experts until after it is administered to the candidates. We have adopted this two-step process to avoid breaches in examination security.

Other speakers at this planning conference have raised questions about privacy, about how far employers should go. The one example I am familiar with is the police department. Not only do we have written tests, orals, and physical and medical tests, but we also conduct background checks. In Los Angeles one of the issues we are dealing with is drug use. Although this issue may be beyond this commission's interest, we view it as a part of the selection process.

I have mentioned the affirmative action considerations that entered into our revision of the certification system to allow for "three whole scores." Affirmative action is also considered in our recruitment efforts to ensure that a sufficient number of minorities and women are in the candidate pool, and that the minimum requirements for the examination are not screening out qualified candidates. In addition, we have made a concerted effort to ensure that our test questions are job related and not culturally biased.

In closing, I would like to mention our efforts to assist disabled candidates so that they can be competitive in the selection process. Blind candidates are given the test on tape or in braille; deaf candidates are provided with sign language interpreters. When appropriate, candidates with motor disabilities often have individual proctors assist them in completing the answer form or taping their answers. In addition, where appropriate, written tests have been modified to eliminate those areas in which a candidate would not be required to work; for example, a blind typist would not be required to proofread.

All of this is what we encounter when trying to take the problems of test construction and administration to the level of actually implementing them. It is an interesting process. The City of Los Angeles would be happy to work with the National Commission on Testing and Public Policy as it pursues its inquiries. We may be a microcosm, or we may be so unique that we are irrelevant; but in any event, we will be happy to assist you.

INDEX